Saintly Influence

John D. Caputo, *series editor*

PERSPECTIVES IN
CONTINENTAL
PHILOSOPHY

Edited by ERIC BOYNTON
and MARTIN KAVKA

Saintly Influence

Edith Wyschogrod
and the Possibilities
of Philosophy of Religion

FORDHAM UNIVERSITY PRESS
New York ▪ 2009

Library of Congress Cataloging-in-Publication Data

Saintly influence : Edith Wyschogrod and the possibilities of philosophy of religion / edited by Eric Boynton and Martin Kavka.—1st ed.
    p.   cm.— (Perspectives in Continental philosophy)
    Includes bibliographical references and index.
    ISBN 978-0-8232-3087-7 (cloth : alk. paper)—
    ISBN 978-0-8232-3088-4 (pbk. : alk. paper)
    1. Religion—Philosophy.   2. Continental philosophy.   3. Wyschogrod, Edith.
I. Wyschogrod, Edith.   II. Boynton, Eric.   III. Kavka, Martin.
BL51.S3493   2009
191—dc22
                                                            2009009040

Printed in the United States of America
11 10 09   5 4 3 2 1
First edition

In memory of
Edith Wyschogrod (1936–2009)
and
Iris Marion Young (1949–2006)

Contents

Preface

When we began to prepare this volume, we decided to dedicate it to the memory of Iris Marion Young, a scholar who began her studies as an undergraduate student of Edith Wyschogrod's at Queens College. Their work shares many of the same concerns, particularly with reference to the emancipatory political possibilities that can open up as a result of thinking about issues of embodiment. In her 2000 book, *Inclusion and Democracy* (Oxford: Oxford University Press), Young adapted Levinas's category of *le dire*, "the saying," to argue for an explicit discourse of greeting in democratic societies. According to Young, this greeting could instantiate discursive equality and achieve, on the part of representatives of political institutions, explicit recognition of those who are less privileged and customarily excluded from political discourse. She writes, "In the moment of communication I call greeting, a speaker announces her presence as ready to listen and take responsibility for her relationship to her interlocutors, at the same time that it announces her distance from the others, their irreducible particularity" (59). Greeting, an act that alters the polis through inviting the redistribution of power, is an apt figure for that which both responds to and performs saintly influence.

As the volume took shape, we incurred some substantial debts. Foremost among our creditors are Helen Tartar of Fordham University Press and Jack Caputo, editor of the Perspectives in Continental Philosophy series, for their perseverance in support of this volume. We also recognize Stephen L. Hood for his help in the early stages of planning this volume,

Miriam Exum and Eric Newman at Fordham University Press for their editorial assistance, and Kira Dault for her indexing. And we are grateful to all the contributors to the volume for their enthusiasm and patience.

While this volume was in press, we heard the sad and sudden news of Edith Wyschogrod's passing. In our shock, we have quickly amended the memorial dedication, but have failed to muster the will to change any of the verb tenses in our Introduction or in the contributors' essays. All we can do is proudly express our sincere gratitude to the one who "steadeth," and wish this volume could be a more adequate testament to her power. We will remain, without a doubt, under her influence.

Saintly Influence

Introduction

Eric Boynton and Martin Kavka

Any volume that intends to honor a scholar whose work has shaped a field of inquiry is always about influence. This tribute to the work of Edith Wyschogrod is no exception. As a testament to the significance and extent of that influence, this volume brings together preeminent scholars in Continental philosophy of religion, as well as in Christian and Jewish theology, pragmatism, phenomenology, textual studies, and religious ethics. Many of these contributors have been Wyschogrod's conversation partners throughout her years of scholarship. The volume includes essays that explicitly consider the salient issues in Wyschogrod's work, as well as essays that might be better described as motivated by her work. This diversity produces a volume that fosters and extends conversations in Continental philosophy of religion that owe their particular vibrancy to Wyschogrod's work—conversations about the desire of and for God, the nature of transcendence, the dilemmas of ethical existence, the obligations of historians, and possibilities in and for the future, as well as the nature of philosophical inquiry itself as it investigates that which requires its reorientation.

These contributions, each bearing witness to the importance and relevance of Wyschogrod's work, are linked thematically by writing from and about the site of influence, a category that embodies a singularly Wyschogrodian concern. By way of honoring the influence *of* her work, contributions to the volume deepen the concerns about influence *in* her work. Organizing the volume around this theme binds the essays together even as it frees contributors, who write from a variety of disciplinary commitments and orientations, to acknowledge her multiple authorial personae—a point that Wyschogrod herself addresses in her response to her interlocutors included at the end of the volume. The force of the site of being influenced and influencing is taken up by all the essays, which investigate issues of where influence lies, whence it arises, its historical operation, and the ways in which the self comes to acknowledge its structures and its possibilities. The contributions to this volume, then, "are not moorings, but passageways,"[1] or "lessons in upbuilding," as Wyschogrod argues in her response.

Wyschogrod's work has always been about influence, from her early essay on sport and the elemental (dating from the late 1960s)[2] up through her recent work using Levinas and Plotinus to consider a novel approach to the philosophy of biology. Indeed, the title of this collection of essays takes its name from one of the chapters in her seminal 1990 book, *Saints and Postmodernism*.[3] Simply put, Wyschogrod's work has sought, and continues to seek, to cultivate an awareness of how the self is situated and influenced, as well as the way that the self can influence others. The self's inability to ascend to ultimate knowledge leaves open a possibility for a singular exterior voice to authorize a mode of action that seeks to transform the world radically. The possibility of influencing arises in, and because of, the ambiguities of life that mark the self as influenced. The site of influence is thus best described as a "being between."

In Wyschogrod's most recent work, *Crossover Queries*, she admits that when troping "crossing over," she pays homage to Nietzsche's insight that "[man] is a bridge and not an end," exposing, for her, the human predicament in an era of death without reversal. Yet crossing over is also deployed to describe a movement from "inside" the cataclysm as a movement involving a "hope *per impossible*," where the ambiguous event of crossing over describes a complex of ropes that "connect efforts to overcome manifestations of the negative [and] claims about its irrevocability."[4]

One possibility for introducing a volume of essays responding to the influence of Edith Wyschogrod is to consider a somewhat autobiographical essay in which she locates those "passageways" of certain "childhood negations" that stand at the beginning of her life and work—testifying to her "life and work as continuous, as exhibiting . . . methodical dilemmas, at once troubling because certainty is precluded and exhilarating because the chain of meanings in both life and work continues to expand."[5] In that essay, published in the late 1990s, Wyschogrod describes the "bewildering ambiguity upon my conception of the transcendent" effected upon her as a child by the tension between her parents' anthropocentrism and her maternal grandparents' piety, both of which were responses to similar events of mass death.[6] Such an opening might appear to be an act of reducing her essays and books to a set of primal scenes or natural causes that led to results according to certain psychological or social laws. If that were what we wanted to accomplish, it could indeed be easily dismissed: after all, not every bewildered child becomes an esteemed philosopher of religion whose writings cross multiple religious traditions (Jewish, Christian, Buddhist) and multiple philosophical families (both analytic and Continental).

What we find interesting, however, in Wyschogrod's narration of her past is the way in which she refuses to narrate the death of the factuality of the transcendent as a historical fact that had already been decided once and for all. Instead, what Wyschogrod has performed in her scholarship has been an explanation of how the ambiguous tensions created by the possibility of the death of God, instead of closing off any hope for meaning, can be understood in ways that create new possibilities for communal belonging, for attending to others in their desire to persevere in life. In other words, Wyschogrod has exposed her readers to the possibility of influencing history and society not for the sake of amassing power but for the sake of letting more life flow into the world, and this at a time when such influence is seen as a pie-in-the-sky utopian dream. Wyschogrod's work, as well as her e-mail handle, "stedith," leads us to associate this work with that of saints and other holy men and women of history. But to hear her give voice to this e-mail address, which she consistently pronounces as "steadeth," should make one reluctant to place her work within an entirely theological sphere. Articulating the possibilities of ambiguity becomes a service rendered to readers, who find themselves in positions of influence from which multiple possibilities can be realized, in accordance with early modern uses of the verb *stead* as meaning to succor, help, serve, or minister.[7]

As Wyschogrod's work demonstrates again and again, influence is possible only if novelty is possible, if an individual can intervene in the historical process or in a system of received meanings. This in turn is possible only if the path of history and the nature of things are not known in advance. Wyschogrod's characteristic analyses of an abiding ambiguity of existence, begun in her early phenomenological work on the body, constitute an effort to hold open such possibility. In an important yet infrequently cited essay, "Sport, Death, and the Elemental," Wyschogrod turned to what some journalists now describe as "extreme sports" to show that the intention of the athlete to domesticate the natural world of elements eventually undoes itself. The training of the professional runner in the pursuit of conquering the limits of bodily endurance gives way to the reduction of the body to exhaustion and bare life; the race car driver in the pursuit of absolute speed ends up flirting with death and on occasion embraces it. Pleasure is concomitant with risk: the mountain climber's goal is impossible to achieve without risking death from freezing temperatures and the deprivation of oxygen, while the surfer's search for the biggest waves is accompanied by the hazard of coral reefs. In all of these pursuits, the drive to conquer the limitations of the body as a longing for enhanced power, to act as if the body were not fragile at all, only brings its fragility closer to the analytical surface: "The attempt to become one with the elemental may doom the organism to death in primordial encounters with the elemental, to pain, suffering, and the risk of death in sport."[8] In addition, because the success of extreme athletic endeavors is associated with an "overflow of sensation,"[9] the grasp of the elements that the athlete seeks never comes to fruition. The elements are not appropriated in the athlete's hedonic drive; instead, the athlete is expropriated by them, so that the elemental is no longer desirable in the language of an ego-center that could possess the sensation of pleasure.

Wyschogrod's close examination of modern sport discloses a facet of the contemporary world other than that portrayed by calculative or procedural rationality. Existence is marked by potentiality, and furthermore by a potentiality that is uniquely plastic, because it cannot be actualized in a movement of appropriation. This inability to attain a broadly Cartesian position in which the ego is master of its matter discloses that the systems of laws and ideas by which we represent the world hook into that world only in a jagged fashion. Systems are fictions expressing our desire to connect the space of causes with a universally valid space of reasons.

Wyschogrod's critique of representationalism is most apparent in her analyses of the work of Emmanuel Levinas, beginning with her early presentation of his work in the 1974 volume *Emmanuel Levinas: The Problem of Ethical Metaphysics* (reprinted in 2000). In that work, Wyschogrod contends along with Levinas that the subject who thinks representationally elides the exteriority of the object being represented, an exteriority that rises to the phenomenological surface in Levinas's talk of the face.

The practical stakes, however, of this critique of representation become most apparent in her contribution to the 1980 volume *Textes pour Emmanuel Levinas*, "Doing Before Hearing: On the Primacy of Touch." There she moved, again with Levinas, beyond the framework of Levinas's *Totality and Infinity* that governed most of her 1974 book, in which the ground of obligation was identified as the encounter with the expressive face of the other person. (*Emmanuel Levinas: The Problem of Ethical Metaphysics* was in press before Levinas's second magnum opus, *Otherwise than Being*, was published, yet after some of the essays that were revised for incorporation into that book had appeared.) She expresses the problem with *Totality and Infinity*—both hers and Levinas's—with economy: "once Levinas concludes that representation can never be detached from *theoria*, it becomes plain that no visual form whatever can lead to the ethical; thus, Levinas increasingly deflects his attention from the Face as bearer of the trace to language."[10]

Nevertheless, in Wyschogrod's 1980 essay "Doing Before Hearing: On the Primacy of Touch," she moved beyond Levinas by succeeding in linking the critique of representation to the texture of lived existence. It was the phenomenology of touch that served to connect mind and world, restoring the normative weight of Levinasian ethics and avoiding what she saw as the risk of following the trail of thought in *Otherwise than Being*, namely that it condemned humans to being users of language detached from the world of objectivity. Her transcendental clue was Aristotle's account in *De Anima* in which the vagueness that he assigns to touch is grounded in its immediacy: "it is as though a man were struck through his shield where the shock is not first given to the shield and passed onto the man, but the concussion to both is simultaneous" (43b). Wyschogrod understood this to mean that "flesh is lived as vulnerability as every tactile encounter,"[11] countering Aristotle's disdain for touch as the lowest of senses.

While the claim that vulnerability is more basic to human existence than rational activity might seem to justify a determinist or even fatalist outlook on the world, Wyschogrod argued that this opened up the possibility for a different account of practice from one that would center on "acts which have a utilitarian or hedonic character or in which the doing is a mode of learning."[12] Ethical action, justified by accounts of what is basic to human existence, expresses a passivity that existential phenomenology has uncovered to be prior to self-knowledge. Insofar as such action does not know the contours of its telos, and does not know whether the state of affairs in which it results has any resemblance to the present state of affairs, ethical action is best described as radically messianic. This kind of ethics is possible because its structure is actual in embodied existence.

Wyschogrod's ethics enacts itself in the form of influence, understood in a quite literal sense as the self's flowing into the world to which it relates. The monadic spontaneous self that sees its death as absolute nonbeing has actualized itself in the various events of mass death over the past century. Without seeing itself as vulnerable to death, the monadic individual envisions no reason to care about those whose political and social lack of power leads to their being killed. In her 1985 *Spirit in Ashes: Hegel, Heidegger, and Man-made Mass Death*, Wyschogrod offered a phenomenological argument for the priority of relation to selfhood in the context of the real possibility of mass death (not only in the context of localized conflicts, but also of global threats such as nuclear war). An unbounded human community, she argued, can successfully persevere only if its members appropriate their relatedness to one another in their acts, by seeing another's language discourse as a call to relatedness.

Yet in spite of the apparent optimism of this argument, Wyschogrod's writing never gives a detailed portrait of what this ethics might achieve in history. She refuses to describe this ethics as an easy recipe that an individual or a culture could simply put into practice, for example, by instituting a curriculum of other-centered virtues. Even when one has moved past a philosophy that sees representation as adequate—or past an ethics which is content with the adequacy of normative theories addressing the contingencies of life—the possibility of influencing history in a direction away from its genocidal past is still a life "lived within the tensions created by" the demand that sociality imposes upon the self.[13] So stands the claim in the last sentence of *Spirit in Ashes*. The greatest tension seems to be that our knowledge of human psychology might tempt us to become Hobbesians in an effort to preserve existence in the face of the death event, although the possibility of such perseverance has its ground in a radically altered intersubjective space. And so Wyschogrod's work from the late 1980s onward has focused on ethical influence exercising itself narratologically, as she has restlessly, even manically, placed before her readers the possibility of altruistic behavior.

We would say that at this point in her career, Wyschogrod came to see that the eros for the future that enacts itself in an ethic of influence requires stories. This urgency for narrative is apparent in the popular Hasidic tale claiming that, as a community's practices of averting misfortune become lost over time, narrative might have redemptive power: "[Rabbi Israel of Rizhyn] spoke to God, 'I am unable to light the fire and I do not know the prayer; I cannot even find the place in the forest. All I can do is to tell the story, and this must be sufficient.' And it was sufficient." Commenting on this narrative and its situation as the epigraph to Elie Wiesel's 1966 novel, *The Gates of the Forest*,[14] Wyschogrod focused more on Rabbi Israel's statement to God than on the Hasidic narrator's insistence that narrative could indeed avert misfortune.

The narrative impulse is embedded in the belief that to retell is to relive, and to relive is to believe that the primal event can, in some way, be repeated. For Wiesel the tale exhibits a new narrative logic: to retell is to remember, and to remember is to relive a story that is not about a disaster averted but about an ingathering of the dead, a tale of the untellable. Such a reliving is caught up in the psychic dissonance of a remembrance that is both desired and feared.[15]

In this last sentence, Wyschogrod attests to the nihilating possibility of remembrance. The constant and obligatory repetition of trauma—as a community's narratives come face to face with the inability to represent the experiences of mass death in narrative form—risks a cultural obsession with death. But the postmodern trope of negation that is used to describe disastrous occurrences as nonevents contains its own resources for the research and development of vaccines against nothingness, because these nonevents cannot be appropriated by a subject for his or her own project of self-making, in accordance with Heidegger's logic of *Ereignis*.

In *Saints and Postmodernism*, Wyschogrod draws on narratives from a variety of religious traditions, as well as from more secular literature—she presents Henry James's *The Wings of the Dove* as a motor of altruism. For Wyschogrod, these narrative forms become particularly significant because of the inability of moral theory to generate moral action within a historical horizon characterized by the death event. In the wake of the death of moral theory, ethics has nothing in which to ground itself. Wyschogrod converts this into a possibility for ethics: the possibility of grounding ethics in nothingness is the possibility of grounding ethics in the narratives of those who renounce themselves for the sake of others.

In the chapter of *Saints and Postmodernism* that gives its name to this volume, Wyschogrod argues that the saintly act is best described in the language of the nonevent. The self-renunciation of the saint means that there is a nonbeing—the saintly self as nullity—that precedes the edification and moral change of the saint's audience. Yet nullities have no force to effect change, and so one cannot describe self-renunciation as a cause of historical transformation. The situation that arises in saintly narratives and saintly moral action therefore involves a "double 'coding.'" What a community takes to be the mark of the saint, self-emptying, can only be assigned a causative role through a retrospective narrative that has the qualities of fiction. The saintly act is magically endowed with power by those in the saint's audience; this magic is verified by the saint's altruistic acts. Saintly influence is actuated in a community by saintly moral action, now causally described.[16] One cannot say that the saint moves either herself or her community from possibility to actuality, from nonbeing to being. Instead, the logic of the saint's influence is one that most closely resembles anti-idealistic understandings of *creatio ex nihilo*[17]; the saint in her self-sacrifice creates possibilities that her audience can appropriate in the service of self-transformation. Saintly acts thus have no predictive power, unlike, for example, Kant's correlation between virtue and happiness, between the universalizable norms that obey the categorical imperative and the kingdom of ends. Saintly power only becomes apparent, if saints become apparent at all, in retrospect.

For this reason, the efficacy of saintly influence depends upon the story of the past that is narrated. So, while Wyschogrod's 1998 book, *An Ethics of Remembering*, might be understood as an imperative for historians to understand themselves as "heterological historians," possessed by an "eros for the past" and bound to the others about whom they write, we wonder whether there might be more productive readings of this book than those that focus on a normative argument for a certain approach to historiography. We see *An Ethics of Remembering* as, at bottom, an argument that a certain approach to the past, acknowledging the openness of the future as a real possibility, is not taken on in vain. In other words, Wyschogrod defends the position of the heterological historian against arguments about the apparent madness and fruitlessness of that position.

Wyschogrod opens *An Ethics of Remembering* with the claim that "To be a historian is to accept the destiny of the spurned lover—to write, photograph, film, televise, archive and simulate the past not merely as its memory bank but as binding oneself by a promise to the dead to tell the truth about the past."[18] Yet she immediately goes on to ask, "Is the historian as the lover who is spurned a faithless lover, who seduces with a promise that cannot be fulfilled?"[19] This provocation structures the entire book; in chapter after chapter, the possibility of the heterological historian's faith is defended, especially in an age when network culture places reference and truth into question. Against the position of Hayden White that cataclysmic events of mass death can appear discursively as an inspiring sublime, Wyschogrod notes the similarity of this position to fascist modernism and argues that the heterological historian can justify her historiography by interpreting cataclysmic events along the lines of the Levinasian *il y a*, formless and purposeless being which "renders the self receptive to alterity."[20]

Against the threat of simulation embedded in the rise of visual culture and its manipulability in Photoshop, Wyschogrod points to the possibility of catachrestic strategies in film for attending to what the heterological historian understands to be the demands of the dead. Against progressivist-absolutist historiographies, she turns to virtual reality and Heidegger's appropriation on Hegelian skepticism to show the impossibility of gain-saying the *il y a*. Against the threat of materialist-scientific approaches to meaning that threaten any attempt to pin ethical stakes on historiography, she invokes Roger Penrose's work suggesting that the workings of human consciousness escape the attempts of mathematical physics to find formu-las for them. In all of these arguments, the cataclysms of the past retain their possibility to shape future communities that can orient themselves around aiding those who persevere to live. In this way, the hope of the heterological historian (and of those who agree with the historiographical assumptions underlying her approach) becomes justified.

Ambiguity strengthens these arguments for an ethics of influence. For Wyschogrod in *An Ethics of Remembering*, the culture of simulacra is both disturbing in its ignorance of the real and useful in its ability to engender skepticism of absolutist narratives of history. Indeed, if Wyschogrod has a general hermeneutical style that can be said to characterize her work, it is to read for ambiguity in culture. For example, in her recent essays on sociobiology and altruism, she has shown how Richard Dawkins's claims about the selfishness of the gene can pose "a challenge to the identity of the individual as phenotype and, as such, to the *genos* or *ethnos* to which she or he belongs."[21] A discourse that in contemporary culture is com-monly seen as reductive, and therefore antithetical to classical humanism and its ethical thrust, is reinterpreted by Wyschogrod as ethically salutary because of its antihumanism, since humanism has for far too long been nothing but an ideology used to support the hegemony of various *ethnoi*. Moreover, she imagines the apparent secularism of dominant approaches in sociobiology as having more in common with the history of religious ideas than one might expect at first blush, especially with the calculative models of the soul that were characteristic of Neoplatonism. The myster-ies (or the mystification) of the gene and its reasons is the contemporary analog of the ancient mystification of number itself. Both of these ac-knowledgments of mystery have ethical consequences: "Plotinus's narra-tive of the relation of the soul's desire for the good is re/disfigured as gene activity that allows for the replication of a particular good, so that this good is not lost."[22] When a child, Wyschogrod saw ambiguity as located strictly in the transcendent; her scholarly work has expanded the reach of ambiguity so that the distinction between the transcendent and the mate-rial falls apart. In the process, history becomes a possible site for that which transcends—and us—to exercise influence.

We have divided the contributors' attestations to Wyschogrod's influence upon them and her influence on ethical and historical thinking into three sections: "The Ethical and Transcendence," "Practices of Influence," and "Channeling History." These three sections broadly consider the structure of influence and whether is it an ethical or a religious category, the ground of influence and the mechanics by which that ground influences, and lastly how influence is conducted into the world through the persona of the heterological historian. Mark C. Taylor's "The Uncertainty Principle" serves as an excellent introduction to the issues that animate Wyschogrod's writings as a whole. Taylor, in this introductory essay, charges Wyschogrod, in effect, with developing an account of "saintly influence" that is unable to influence much of anything at all. Wyschogrod's Levinasian desire to protect the alterity of the other person leads her to argue that the other person not be conceptually grasped in normative structures. Yet while this maximization of difference may have been an appropriate and needed riposte to twentieth-century realities and technologies, in Taylor's view, the information culture that has grown by leaps and bounds in this century requires an "ethic of relation" that allows different agents to network together, and influence both each other and the network as a whole.

The essays in the first section, which deals with the nature and realizability of influence, do not, like Taylor, charge Wyschogrod with not attending to the realities of contemporary secular culture. Rather, they are concerned that Wyschogrod has not sufficiently attended to theological categories. Thomas J. J. Altizer's "The Impossible Possibility of Ethics" argues that the challenges to entrenched systems of authority implicit in Wyschogrod's calls to other-centered ethics become really possible only when the source of the challenge (the reality of the nihilistic death-world) is interpreted in light of the death of God. For Altizer, such an interpretation of nihilism as primordial and theological uniquely allows our ethical actions to be supported by a reading of historical time as an apocalyptic advent waiting to be recognized as such by cultures. In "The Empty Suitcase as Rainbow," Merold Westphal analyzes the acts and motives of the Protestant villagers of Le Chambon sur Lignon in south-central France. For Westphal, a consideration of these descendants of Huguenots who during World War II hid (and thereby saved) approximately five thousand Jews becomes a strategy for showing a desecularized analogue to Wyschogrod's notion of saintliness in *Saints and Postmodernism*. Wyschogrod's hagiographic ethic in that book is not necessarily a religious one, and indeed the chapter in that book entitled "Saintly Influence" takes ecstatic forms of Christian mysticism to task for their sublation of alterity.[23]

Graham Ward also takes up the question of whether Christian theology can acknowledge alterity without becoming less theological. Rhetorically oscillating between the concrete and the spiritual, Ward argues in "Hosting the Stranger and the Pilgrim: A Christian Theological Reflection" that a Levinasian hospitality can succeed only on the basis of a theological reality and not on the basis of a certain economic reality—"no face can be approached with empty hands," as Levinas writes.[24] Inviting another into one's dwelling, for Ward, has dwelling with God as its necessary condition. The section closes with an essay by Adriaan T. Peperzak, " 'God,' Gods, God," that strikes a middle position between the secular analysis of Taylor and the theological analyses of the other contributors in this section. Insisting that language must mediate, Peperzak argues that both secular and theological approaches to ethics are flawed because they are thematizations of that which cannot be articulated in itself in language (God, the neighbor, history, etc.). Yet instead of authorizing cultural pessimism, this leads only to critique, whether or not this critique has difference or relation as a target in its sights.

The contributors to the second section of this volume take up various practices of influence and investigate how those practices do or do not open up possible futures. For Robert Gibbs in "The Name of God in Levinas's Philosophy," the practice that ensures the open and irruptible nature of the future is that of philosophy. Through a treatment of the oscillation between identifying and effacing the Tetragrammaton, both in sacred Jewish texts and various essays by Emmanuel Levinas, Gibbs shows how the name of God, something both ordinary and extraordinary, makes it impossible for the (Jewish) religious life to be one that is lived in devotion to God and to God alone. The vertical dimension of the religious life is ineluctably bound up with the horizontal dimension of community and family, just as the Levinasian saying is bound up with the said; to act for the other is at the same time to act for God.

Elliot R. Wolfson engages in a patient reconstruction of the philosophy of time by turning to a text by the medieval kabbalist Abraham Abulafia that explicitly treats the influence of the divine overflow. In Abulafia's mystical system, based primarily on associating an ontological equality between Hebrew words and phrases that have the identical numerical value, the kabbalist in meditational practice receives an intellectual influx from the Tetragrammaton, which allows the mystic to intuit that opposites are indeed one. Yet despite the rhetoric of union that is omnipresent in Abulafia's work, Wolfson shows that this is not a quasi-Hegelian totalizing move in which all opposites are dissolved in the unity of the divine. Instead, the unity of opposites must include the unity of the static and the dynamic; for Abulafia, the divine is always temporalized. History is the divine life: there is no static nature to the divine being, but only historical becoming. The influx that the mystic receives thereby maintains the contingency of history and produces influence in Wyschogrod's sense. In this way, through his deep and sustained treatment of a text by Abraham Abulafia in "Kenotic Overflow and Temporal Transcendence: Angelic Embodiment and the Alterity of Time in Abraham Abulafia," Wolfson shows that the category of influence allows scholars to uncover the intimacy of the postmodern and the classical.

In the final chapter in this section, Amy Hollywood raises the concern that some of the practices we think perform saintly influence may be repressive. Her essay has important implications for the very genre of the tribute in which we are here engaged. In "Tribute to Derrida," thinking through the intersection of Jacques Derrida's, Yosef Yerushalmi's, and Anna Freud's remarks on the Jewishness of psychoanalysis, Hollywood notes that Yerushalmi and even Derrida—despite his best intentions—are so invested in interpreting Freud along a certain line that Anna Freud becomes only a cipher for her father. Derrida's agreement with Freud that history is structured according to the Oedipus complex (and the fratricidal myth of the primal horde) continues to silence the voices of women. For Hollywood, this risks the conclusion that it is impossible to throw a wrench into the gears of patriarchy, and that the future is less undetermined than we might hope.

The contributors to the final section, following Wyschogrod's suggestions in *An Ethics of Remembering*, take up the specific practice of historiography as a way of loosening the past's apparent stranglehold in the future. In response to a critical review of Wyschogrod's work by the intellectual historian Allan Megill, John D. Caputo's "Hearing the Voices of the Dead: Wyschogrod, Megill, and the Heterological Historian" stages an *Auseinandersetzung* between the historian and the phenomenologist, akin to the altercation announced in the title of Van Harvey's *The Historian and the Believer*[25] in 1966. It is the existential phenomenologist who shows the historian that descriptions of history are always already situated by a stance towards the world (or in more Husserlian language, that the so-called "natural attitude" is not properly basic to consciousness, but indeed already framed by consciousness's meaning-giving acts). This stance is framed by the passions and concerns that the subject brings to the description; memory is the transcendental condition for the possibility of history. This is not an excuse for tendentious history; rather, it is an explanation for how we have come to value neutrality in historiography, a value that Caputo accuses Megill of improperly naturalizing, thus ignoring the passageway of history to a different future.

In a fitting tribute to Wyschogrod's work, Werner H. Kelber, a scholar of Biblical hermeneutics and Christian origins, sketches in "Memory and Violence, or Genealogies of Remembering" an approach to Christian passion narratives that considers them as ethically ambiguous products of remembering. Extending the sense of history as irretrievable loss and future expectancy expressed in Wyschogrod's *An Ethics of Remembering*, Kelber seeks to emulate her capacity for bringing widely differing genres into a productive tension, generating an understated novelty that Kelber calls a "prolonged hesitancy." In this case, Kelber employs a Wyschogrodian sensibility to generate a reading of foundational texts caught in a "duplicitous mnemohistory." Kelber pries open a violent logic working in these foundational texts that memorializes in order to facilitate a pure remembering that nonetheless remains in the service of a certain present and future, even as it covers over the indeterminacy of the remembered past key to the logic itself.

Whereas Kelber translates Wyschogrod's *An Ethics of Remembering* into the field of biblical studies and generates a novel reading of the influence of foundational texts, Bettina Bergo moves in the other direction and engages in a detailed exposition of Wyschogrod's text to enrich the theme of influence. In "The Historian and the Messianic 'Now': Reading Edith Wyschogrod's *An Ethics of Remembering*," Bergo considers what Benjamin called the "secret appointment" between lost generations, which in Wyschogrod's work calls the historian to a remembrance in the midst of the cataclysm, in order to highlight a fragile hope for the future by interruption. Bergo conducts a careful reading of Wyschogrod's text, specifically her analysis of the Kantian sublime and its Levinasian complement, to give expression to a "principle of hope" that funds her ethics of remembering in terms of a weak messianic force.

In the volume's final tribute, "Saints and the Heterological Historian," Peter Ochs explores "the chain of identities" that link author, reader, teacher, and student in Wyschogrod's work as a "saintly pedagogy" for imagining the proximity of One to the Other. For Ochs, the fact that Wyschogrod says precious little about how one learns from the heterological historian or how one becomes saintly reflects a careful consideration of the way influence must be conducted. Indeed, Ochs' reading of Wyschogrod is motivated by the discomfort felt by the reader of *An Ethics of Remembering*, the discomfort of being lead into a significant insight that cannot be harnessed. Considering together *Saints and Postmodernism* and *An Ethics of Remembering*, Ochs locates a veiled "double-codedness" inhering in the act of reading Wyschogrod's work that becomes a training or practice that is transformative for the reader. Learning to be the heterological historian involves participation in a long chain of teacher-sages whose influence Wyschogrod's work conducts yet simultaneously interrupts in a performative attending to the other's voice. The production of multiple relational identities that generates a plurivocity in Wyschogrod's work is the engine of influence.

In the culminating chapter of the volume, Edith Wyschogrod's own response to her commentators extends this theme proposed by Ochs. In that essay, Wyschogrod highlights the production in this volume of multiple authorial personae. Her use of the language of multiple personae hearkens back to her description of the heterological historian in *An Ethics of Remembering* as "alternating disguises, a multiplicity of conceptual personae in something like Deleuze's sense of the term."[26] When Deleuze and Guattari discuss conceptual personae in *What Is Philosophy?* they use it as support for their argument that there are no rules to predict the future of philosophy.

This is because concepts need philosophers as their friends, and have no meaning outside of these bonds of friendship, in which a conceptual persona serves as an "intermediary, intercessor" between the problems of the philosophy and the concepts that are claimed to be their solutions: "A concept like knowledge has meaning only in relation to an image of thought to which it refers and to a conceptual persona that it needs; a different image and a different persona call for other concepts."[27] Yet Wyschogrod assumes that the conceptual personae that she dons and doffs in the course of her response are not simply intercessors for philosophical problems; they are also intercessors for philosophical problems that are raised *by others*. And so, if donning and doffing conceptual personae is a strategy taken on to release history from the risk of the stranglehold of determinism, then this cannot be accomplished without acknowledging those who have called the personae forth. These are concepts' other friends, and insofar as they call out for Wyschogrod to take on various personae as her own possibilities, they are both narratives of creation and of ruins.

Insofar as they are narratives of creation, they are for Wyschogrod, following Kierkegaard, upbuilding discourses; they "construct something from the ground up into the heights. This *up* certainly points to the heights, but only when the heights also mean the opposite—depth—do we say 'build up'!"[28] The calling out of other personae is a reduction of the hearer to her ground, and the imposition of other personae which the hearer can doff and don as new foundations for self-making. Nevertheless, insofar as the calling out of conceptual personae by others is a reduction of the hearer to her ground, these are narratives of ruins.

And so we find it highly suggestive that Wyschogrod chooses to end her response to these essays with a response to Bettina Bergo, who links Wyschogrod's account of historiography with Walter Benjamin's philosophy of history and the possibilities embedded in the ruins of history. For Wyschogrod, ruins serve as sites where humans can exercise their "ability to distinguish their immediate existence from their future usefulness in attesting to that which was." But this is also true of the ruin that is the self while all conceptual personae are doffed. If upbuilding is self-denial on the part of the upbuilder, as M. Jamie Ferreira as suggested is true for Kierkegaard,[29] then Wyschogrod points out that letting oneself be built up also includes a mode of self-denial, although the invocation of Deleuze makes clear that upbuilding certainly does not stop there. To respond to tributes by linking together Kierkegaard and Deleuze—both the philosopher who sees "upbuilding as a repetition of the divine creative act"[30] and the philosopher who sees the donning and doffing of conceptual personae as human acts on the plane of immanence[31]—is to blur the distinction between God and the human, each being the silent ground of the other. This is the bewildering ambiguity that Wyschogrod has felt and lived since childhood, and has influenced—and will continue to influence—in others through her own thinking.

The Uncertainty Principle

MARK C. TAYLOR

> Responsibility goes beyond being. In sincerity, in frankness, in the veracity
> of this saying, in the uncoveredness of suffering, being is altered.
> —**Emmanuel Levinas**[1]

Impossibility

Edith Wyschogrod is first and foremost an ethical thinker. That is not to
say she is an ethicist in the usual sense of the term; to the contrary, it is
precisely because her work exceeds the bounds of ethics as traditionally
defined that it is relevant today. All too often ethical reflection remains
focused on specific problems and does not rise to a consideration of the
broader social and cultural contexts in which it is situated. Furthermore,
there is almost never any serious exploration of the question of the possibility of ethics as such: Ethicists simply presuppose the possibility of ethics
and then proceed to argue about appropriate principles, maxims and
norms. Wyschogrod, by contrast, develops a sophisticated analysis of the
modern and postmodern conditions in which she examines the interrela-
tion between the Western philosophical and theological tradition and science and technology. In today's world, ethical reflection, she insists, is
both imperative and impossible. By drawing on a broad range of philosophical, theological, literary, artistic and scientific sources, Wyschogrod
develops what might be labeled an ethics of uncertainty, which provides
helpful resources for the critical assessment of the conflicting absolutisms
that threaten the world today.

Wyschogrod's most interesting work emerges at the intersection of techno-logic and bio-logic. Though ranging across a rich array of disciplines, her writing has from the outset elaborated a remarkably consistent diagnosis of the cultural crisis of the twentieth and twenty-first centuries. She begins *Saints and Postmodernism: Revisioning Moral Philosophy* by asking: "Why a postmodern ethic now?"

> The twentieth century is witness to the deaths of millions within ever more compressed time frames: death through nuclear, chemical, and biological warfare, through death camps, through concentration and slave labor camps, and by means of conventional weapons. Newly emerging biological and chemical instruments for mass destruction are in the process of development. Conflicts that have thus far remained local offer no guarantee of containment but, instead, may constitute potential flash points for global war.[2]

In an earlier book, *Spirit in Ashes: Hegel, Heidegger and Man-Made Mass Death*, Wyschogrod describes this new condition as the "death event." While the Holocaust is never far from her mind, it is important to stress that the death event is not limited to a single historical occurrence but characterizes many twentieth-century tragedies. Wyschogrod actually goes so far as to argue that genocidal killing is "endemic to the world of postmodernity."[3]

Though calling for careful analysis, the death event is the cataclysm, which cannot be named. Echoing Blanchot's *The Writing of the Disaster*[4] and Derrida's account of apophasis, Wyschogrod explains that the cataclysm is "the obverse of the sacred, a negative epiphany that can only be approached through the strategies of negative theology."[5] Always exceeding thought, which it nonetheless provokes, the cataclysm is the event that cannot, yet must be thought. In the wake of catastrophe, no thinking is more impossible and more imperative than ethical reflection.

Wyschogrod freely admits that a postmodern ethics seems to be a contradiction in terms.

> If postmodernism is a critical expression describing the subversion of philosophical language, a "mutant of Western humanism," then how can one hope for an ethics when the conditions for the meaning are themselves under attack? But is not this paradox—the paradox of a postmodern ethic—just what is required if an ethic is to be postmodern? Does not the term *postmodern* so qualify the term *ethics* that the ideas of ethics, the stipulation of what is to count as lawful conduct, is subverted? And is a postmodern ethics then not an ethics

of the subversion of ethics so that ethics turns into its opposite, a nihilism that is unconstrained by rules?[6]

The question, of course, is what constitutes nihilism. For its critics, postmodernism is nihilistic because it denies the possibility of theoretical and practical certainty and the security they bring. Morality, they assume, presupposes either universal norms or foundational principles, which can be clearly ascertained and confidently apprehended. As Wyschogrod points out:

> Critics of postmodernism argue that in unburdening itself of nomo-logical structure it has thrown away morality, that in shedding the past it has created a historical vacuum upon which totalitarianism can supervene, and that in attacking the self or subject it has opened the possibility of an abuse of the Other because there is in *sensu strictu* no Other and no self to be held responsible. Is postmodernism not an expression of moral decadence rather than a solution to the problem of decline?[7]

But what if Nietzsche is right? What if it is moralism that is nihilistic? What if the claim of moral certitude rather than its denial leads to totalitarianism? What if today's absolutisms are precursors of unimaginable future cataclysms? Perhaps we do not need more fundamental norms and basic values but precisely what Wyschogrod prescribes: a "non-nomological" ethic. Such an ethic might make it possible to subvert the logic of the death event.

Techno-Logic

During the twentieth century, the logic of warfare changes. "What is unprecedented in the new phenomenon," Wyschogrod argues, "is that the *means* of annihilation are the result of systematic rational calculation and the scale is reckoned in terms of the compression of time in which destruction is delivered." The death event extends beyond particular acts of destruction to create new disciplinary regimes instituted to secure the power of those in positions of authority.

> I shall define the scope of the event to include three characteristic expressions: recent wars which deploy weapons in the interest of maximum destruction of persons; annihilation of persons, through techniques designed for the purpose (for example famine, scorched earth, deportation), *after* the aims of war have been achieved or without to reference to war; and the creation of death-worlds, a new

unique form of social existence in which vast populations are subjected to conditions of life simulating imagined conditions of death, conferring upon their inhabitants the status of the living dead.[8]

While the logic of the death event is inseparable from new technologies of destruction, its roots lie buried in the Western philosophical and religious tradition. Wyschogrod follows Heidegger's highly influential analysis in which he argues that modern science and technology are inseparable for modern philosophy, which begins with Descartes' collapse of truth into certainty and reaches closure with Nietzsche's transformation of the will to mastery into the will to power. According to Heidegger, the two defining characteristics of scientific reason are that it is instrumental and calculative. This argument depends upon Hegel's interpretation of utility in *Phenomenology of Spirit*. "The useful," Hegel argues, "is the object insofar as self-consciousness penetrates it and has in it the *certainty* of its *individual self*, its enjoyment (its *being-for-self*); self-consciousness sees right into the object, and this insight contains the *true* essence of the object (which is to be something that is penetrated [by consciousness], or to be *for an other*)."[9] That which is useful, then, does not exist in and of itself but has its "essential" being in another. Through the exercise of instrumental reason, the subject becomes certain of itself by appropriating the object. Over a century before Benjamin's analysis of the work of art in the age of mechanical reproduction, Hegel identified the fatal implications of machinic logic.

> Calculative thinking (*Rechnen*) is an operation so external and consequently mechanical, one has been able to invent *machines* (*Machinen*) which perform arithmetical operations the most perfect fashion. To judge from the nature of calculative thinking starting from this sole fact one would know enough to decide the worth of making calculative thinking the principal means for forming the mind and putting it to the torture in order that it perfect itself to the point of becoming a machine.[10]

Following the logic of *Verstand* (understanding) rather than *Vernunft* (reason), machines operate according to three basic principles:

The externality of parts.
The replaceability of parts.
The iterability of operation.

Derrida concludes his essay "The Pit and the Pyramid: An Introduction to Hegel's Semiology" by pointing out that Hegel's account of the machine anticipates Heidegger's interpretation of technology. To make his point, he quotes revealing lines from Heidegger's *Identity and Difference*[11]: "The time of thinking . . . is different from the time of calculation (*Rechnens*) that pulls our thinking in all directions. Today the computer (*Denkmaskine*) calculates thousands of relationships in one second. Despite their technical uses, they are inessential (*wesenlos*)."[12] We will return to the question of whether the logics of industrial and electronic modes of production and reproduction are the same; for the moment the point to underscore is the similarity between Hegel and Heidegger's accounts of instrumental or calculative reason.

In "The Question Concerning Technology," Heidegger argues that "the essence of modern technology shows itself in what we call Enframing." Enframing, he proceeds to explain, "is the way in which the real reveals itself as standing-reserve." Heidegger's infamously difficult language often obscures relatively straightforward points. His notion of standing-reserve is simply an extension of Hegel's account of utility. In a utilitarian relationship, we have discovered, something or someone exists *for the sake of* something or someone else. Being, which is being-for-an-other, is a standing-reserve awaiting exploitation. While Heidegger offers several helpful examples from the natural world, his most devastating analysis focuses on human relations. When techno-logic is fully deployed, human beings become a standing-reserve for those with the power to master or destroy them.

> Yet when destining reigns in the mode of Enframing, it is the supreme danger. This danger attests itself to us in two ways. As soon as what is unconcealed no longer concerns man even as object, but does so, rather, exclusively as standing-reserve, and man in the mist of objectlessness is nothing but the orderer of the standing-reserve, then he comes to the very brink of a precipitous fall; that is, he comes to the point where he himself will have to be taken as standing-reserve. Meanwhile man, precisely as the one so threatened, exalts himself to the posture of the lord of the earth. In this way the impression comes to prevail that everything man encounters exists only insofar as it is his construct. This illusion gives rise in turn to one final delusion: It seems as though man everywhere and always encounters only himself.[13]

Heidegger appropriates Hegel's account of the master-slave relationship without the dialectical reversal that eventually leads to a reconciling mutuality. When the will to power is unconstrained by effective resistance it issues in the fury of destruction. Human beings become the raw material for the ruthless machinations of those in power.

Wyschogrod extends the analyses of Hegel and Heidegger to develop an incisive interpretation of the logic of the death event, which, far from having ended with the closing of the camps, continues to rend the world from India and Pakistan to Rwanda and Sudan. The death event follows the mechanistic logic of industrialism, which, in turn, is the concrete application of the logic of scientific inquiry.

> The objects of science are spatiotemporal nodes lending themselves to mathematical formulation, abstracted from the qualitative properties of the life-world and then given quantitative expression. These ideal entities represent propertied objects. We can manipulate them conceptually: what they mean is now expressed by homogeneous units which can be exchanged for one another in a system of unlimited conceptual transposability. The advantage of this exchange is that entities of this sort can have unlimited relations with other entities of the same sort.[14]

The first condition for the death event is homogeneous parts, which, as such, are interchangeable. The second condition is an infinite supply of such parts. To make her point, Wyschogrod establishes a relation between ancient philosophy and modern and postmodern atrocities that is as startling as it is persuasive.

> The idea of infinite divisibility which lies behind Zeno's paradoxes presupposes an infinite supply of parts. When this formal structure is unconsciously applied to human societies, they too can be imagined to contain infinite numbers. This logic expresses the bizarre deformations of the death event. When combined with the myths of totalitarian societies, which themselves are born from the ashes of technological society, this mode of reason provides a principle in terms of which those segregated for death can be eliminated. These mythical structures compatible with Zeno's paradox can be found both in post-Biblical apocalyptic thought, and in contemporary remythologizations which retain the essential features of apocalyptic thinking: a metaphysic of impurity.[15]

The metaphysic of impurity forms the basis of taxonomic schemata, which are used to exclude and eliminate others deemed disruptive to the mechanism of society. Though ostensibly antithetical, structure and other are actually codependent.

In a recent essay entitled "The Warring Logics of Genocide," Wyschogrod reformulates the foundational principles of techno-logic in a way that leads to an unexpected conclusion. First, she points to the logic of replicability: "when it is applied to groups of peoples, they are seen as potentially capable of multiplying endlessly. What is more, in targeted groups individuals are viewed as indistinguishable from one another." The second foundational principle, arising from the first, is the logic of indiscernibles: "identical and seemingly isolated monads meld into an undifferentiated sameness."[16] The former she associates with Hegel's bad infinite, the latter with Levinas's notion of the *il y a*. Based upon the nondialectical principles of *Verstand*, the bad infinite involves the production of an endless series of atomistic units. Although these separate entities appear to be distinct, they are in fact homogeneous and hence indistinguishable. The logic of replicability, therefore, passes over into the logic of indiscernibles. Wyschogrod makes this important point first by relating Hegel's bad infinite to Leibniz's principle of the identity of indiscernibles, and then explaining the implications of the collapse of the opposition between warring principles of genocide in terms of Levinas's *il y a*.

> Is there a genocidal logic other than that of unstoppable proliferation to be found in the context of mass extermination? I have maintained that the vast numbers of those targeted are no longer seen as individuals but, in accordance with the logic of replication, as identical units. In conformity with Leibniz's principle of the identity of indiscernibles, if *a* has the properties of *b* and only those of *b* and *b* has only the properties of *a*, then *a* and *b* are identical. Thus in contrast to genocide's innumerable individual victims, this non-difference can also be viewed as the converging of these individuals to constitute a vast formless mass, a mass that is simply there.[17]

Wyschogrod reads Levinas's notion of the *il y a* as evoking the formlessness in which individual subjectivity is lost.[18] Through a reversal that can only be described as dialectical, the radical pluralization of homogeneous units collapses into the radical unity of undifferentiated being. She approaches Levinas's reading of the *il y a* through Kant's account of the sublime, which has been so influential for postmodern theorists: "The Kantian sublime is recast in contemporary philosophy in Emmanuel Levinas's account of the *il y a*, there is, the indeterminateness of Being that would ensue if all beings could be imagined to disappear, an anonymous residue, the Being that wells up when there is nothing."[19] Though her arguments are abstract, their implications are frightfully concrete. As aesthetic theory is translated into political practice, formless being is figured in piles of faceless skulls hidden in grottoes beneath the killing fields as well as in smoke rising from crematoria.

In her early work, Wyschogrod's arguments presuppose the mechanical technologies of industrialism, but in more recent writings, she extends her analysis to include information technologies. Her understanding of media and digital technology is indebted to Debord's account of spectacle and especially Baudrillard's interpretation of media. Though the technologies change, Wyschogrod's argument remains the same: digital technologies extend the logic of replicability and the logic of indiscernibles through what Baudrillard labels "the terrorism of the code." According to Baudrillard, the distinctive feature of today's media culture is the "liquidation of referentials" in an ungrounded play of signs. If everything is mediated, the real disappears in signs that are always signs of other signs.[20] When staged in the media, the liquidation of referentials figures the past and prefigures the future liquidation of real people.

In his provocative essay "The Evil Demon of Images," Baudrillard argues: "the image has taken over and imposed its own immanent, ephemeral logic; an immoral logic without depth, beyond good and evil, beyond truth and falsity; a logic of the extermination of its own referent, a logic of the implosion of meaning in which the message disappears on the horizon of the medium."[21] To explain what he means by the image's "extermination of its own referent," Baudrillard considers the controversial made-for-television movies *Holocaust* and *The Day After*. The former is about life in the camps during World War II, and the latter depicts conditions after a worldwide nuclear disaster. When these programs first appeared, they were widely criticized for their graphic violence and "realism." Baudrillard's interpretation of their significance is the exact opposite—not at all realistic, these TV shows elide the reality of the events they purport to represent. Drawing on Marshall McLuhan's interpretation of TV as a "cool medium," he argues:

What everyone fails to understand is that *Holocaust* is above all (and exclusively) a *televised* event or rather object . . . That is to say, it is an attempt to reheat a *cold* historical event—tragic but cold, the first great event of cold systems, those cooling systems of dissuasion and extermination which were subsequently deployed in other forms (including the Cold War, etc.) and in relation to the cold masses (the Jews no longer even concerned by their own death, eventually self-managing it, no longer even masses in revolt; dissuaded unto death, dissuaded even of their own death). To reheat this cold event via a cold medium, television for the masses who are themselves cold, chill and a posthumous emotion, a dissuasive shiver, which sends them into oblivion with a kind of aesthetic good faith.

Through an unintended reversal, images designed as mnemonic devices to recall past horrors actually function as strategies of forgetting that erase historical events. This insight leads to Baudrillard's most provocative conclusion: "Thus, properly speaking it is *Holocaust* the television film which constitutes the definitive holocaust event. Likewise, with *The Day After* it is not the atomic conflict depicted in the film but the film itself which is the catastrophic event."[22] The TV program *Holocaust*, in other words, extends the historical Holocaust by incinerating the event in the image. The act of forgetting, paradoxically fostered by the proliferation, is the final extermination.

Though Wyschogrod does not cite this particular text by Baudrillard, her argument in *An Ethics of Remembering: History, Heterology, and the Nameless Others* presupposes his analysis of the relation between image and reality. Extending the genocidal logic of mechanical reproduction, "the culture of reproduction" created by digital technologies destroys "singularity" and thereby "exterminates the real."

> The regimentation of images by concepts or by the stipulation of rules governing their production has given way in contemporary culture to an uncontrolled proliferation of images. This sea change is not the result of new technologies; rather technological developments have supervened upon a radical ontological shift. The real as materiality heretofore construed either as what is tangible or as its sign . . . is now envisioned as image, so that the distinction between reality and ideality dissolves.[23]

The dissolution of the relationship between image and reality is the erasure of history in which the death event reaches its terrifying conclusion. These developments demand an ethical response.

Other

In the face of pandemic hyper-reality, Wyschogrod calls for a return to the real in an "ethics of otherness." This return to the real solicits the return of the repressed by an act of historical imagination that recovers the Other in its radical difference. In a manner reminiscent of Michel de Certeau, Wyschogrod argues that the "heterological historian" cannot escape the realm of images and, therefore, must return to the real in and through the symbolic order, which, impossibly, includes the very alterity it is supposed to exclude.

> The dilemma for the historian is not merely to acquire a more nuanced view of images, however, but to see whether it is possible to

reclaim the image for ethics. Can the image, like the sublime, be so dis-figured that it might intrude into the non-space of ethics? For the heterological historian, the demand of alterity issues from the dead others, the multiple wounded and suffering bodies that form a society of bodies and, taken together, repudiate egoity. This past can never be recovered in face-to-face encounter but only as image. To be sure, the visual image disincarnates beings, becomes their reflection, but in so doing, the image opens a space beyond beings, unsays them (as the sublime transformed into the *il y a* was seen to unsay being), and thus allows for the emergence of an ethical space of disclosure.[24]

The space beyond beings opened by the disfiguring of images is not yet the space of ethics.[25] As we have seen, the *il y a* evokes the formless being into which homogeneous subjects dissolve. This ushers in the collapse of singularity into undifferentiated being, which is the negation of the very alterity ethics presupposes. Once again drawing on Levinas, Wyschogrod distinguishes two dimensions of otherness: the alterity of the Infinite and the alterity of other subjects. She defines the Infinite by contrasting it with the *il y a*.

> Consider first that the *il y a* itself is not an insuperable obstacle to ethics in that it undermines an egoity that hampers self-giving. What is more, the *il y a* in its conceptual inapprehensibility and ego-destroying character can be read as the obverse of the infinite, the transcendent locus of Good and, as such, is locked into a structural pairing, as it were. For Levinas, thought must be penetrated by an infinite transcendence that shatters the thought that thinks it. Like the *il y a*, the infinite is excessive in that it exceeds any idea we can have of it. The infinite is not merely unimaginable magnitude but the object of a desire for a Good beyond being. God who remains transcendent is beyond conceptual grasp yet enters existence by way of the Other. The obligation to the Other is itself infinitized so that one becomes one-for-the-other. In so doing, one does not use signs to communicate this self-abandonment. Instead, one makes oneself into a sign, a process Levinas calls sincerity. The referent of this sincerity is termed glory, the glory of the infinite.[26]

While the *il y a* collapses differences in formless being, the infinite reinscribes the singularity of the subject. Through its proximity to an Other that can be neither comprehended nor represented, the subject is decentered or, in Wyschogrod's terms, "denucleated." The transcendent beyond of God is (dis)figured in the transcendent beyond of the Other. The relation or non-relation to the Other interrupts the circuit of self-reflexivity and opens the space of referentiality without positing an identifiable referent. This opening, Wyschogrod contends, is the space of ethics *sensu strictissimo*. Ethics is always an ethic of otherness.

> The other person opens the venue of ethics, the place where ethical existence occurs. To answer the question about whether postmodernism requires some *point d'appui*, this Other, the touchstone of moral existence, is not a conceptual anchorage but a living force. The Other is different from oneself; her/his existence will be shown to carry compelling moral weight. In the context of a postmodern ethics, the Other functions as a critical solvent in much the same way as the notion of difference functions in postmodern metaphysics.[27]

By decentering the subject, the relation to the Other subverts all egoity and creates the conditions for a radical generosity, which ushers in what Wyschogrod describes as "saintly generosity." The actions of the saint involve, in Bataille's terms, an "expenditure without return." The saint's deeds are gifts to the Other who always remains in some sense a stranger. Generosity breaks the hold of instrumental and utilitarian calculation and in this way points beyond the genocidal logic of the death event. The ethics of otherness responds to the other the death event is designed to eliminate.

The imbrication of altruism and alterity transforms the conditions of ethical activity. In contrast to traditional morality, which rests upon general if not universal principles or norms that can be apprehended with certitude, the ethics of otherness presupposes the uncertainty principle. In the relation to the Other, epistemic insecurity is inescapable and, therefore, uncertainty is unavoidable. This relation is not mediated by a universal law but is the concrete relation of a singular to a singular. As "the sphere of the transaction between 'self' and 'Other,'" Wyschogrod argues, ethics must be "construed non-nomologically."[28] The singularity of the Other eludes every normative structure and yet imposes obligation. As the call of the Other issues in norms that are non-norms, the principle of uncertainty is a principle that is a non-principle. Neither a basic truth nor a fixed rule, the uncertainty principle is the trace of the opening where incalculable acts of generosity can emerge.

Relation

Is the ethic of otherness adequate in the twenty-first century, or is it addressed more to the past than the future? Regimes bent on the repression and even elimination of others deemed dangerous are not, of course, going to disappear. Indeed, ethnic cleansing continues to be an alarming fact of life. But the most pressing problems we face no longer conform to the logic of the death event as Wyschogrod has described it. One of the strengths of her argument, I have stressed, is her recognition of the role of technology in creating ethical dilemmas: the logic of the death event is a function of mechanical modes of reproduction characteristic of the modern military-industrial complex. The logic of the death event is the logic of the assembly line that turns out an endless supply of homogeneous units. While Wyschogrod realizes that things have changed in our postindustrial information and media society, she extends the logic of mechanical reproduction to digital systems. It is admittedly tempting to read the iteration of digital code in information processing as an extension of the hegemonic logic in which differences can be reduced to the sameness of an identical fixed structure. But this line of analysis is misleading; a more nuanced interpretation of the contemporary information-entertainment complex is required. Upon closer inspection, it becomes clear that information systems are governed by a different operational logic, which has different implications for ethical theory.

In this context, I can only point in the direction of an alternative line of analysis by focusing on two inseparable issues: difference and relation. We have discovered that for Wyschogrod, techno-logic entails two basic principles: the logic of replicability and the logic of indiscernibles, which, when combined, collapse differences into formless being. In this way, techno-logic totalizes by repressing or eliminating alterity. The problem, then, is to recover the singularity of the Other. But this logic does not necessarily apply to the way digital systems work. Though digital systems presuppose a "genetic" code, the operation of this code creates rather than negates differences. Distributed networks are not necessarily pre-programmed but create the conditions for random connections that issue in aleatory events between and among different agents. Biological, social, economic, and cultural systems demonstrate this process. In a society increasingly governed by productive information systems, the problem is not so much the reduction of differences to sameness in homogeneous units that are indistinguishable, but rather the proliferation of differences whose relations are at best tenuous. Instead of an ethic of otherness, what is needed is an ethic of relation.[29]

The revolutionary changes of the last half of the twentieth century were brought about not merely by the advent of information-processing machines, but by the connection of those machines in networks that quickly became global, yielding a world in which *to be is to be connected*. As network culture emerged, the understanding of information changed. No longer perceived to circulate only in computers and in the media, information is now understood to be distributed throughout physical, biological social, political and economic systems. When connectivity within and among these systems grows, differences increase, so the preoccupation with otherness can actually exacerbate rather than resolve conflicts in network culture. In this setting, the question becomes not so much how to secure differences by recovering the otherness of the Other, but how to find commonalities among people and cultures whose differences continue to become ever more profound. The community we must seek can no longer be "the unavowable community" of "those who have nothing in common," but must be a community whose commonalities sustain it in the face of an uncertain future.[30]

PART I

The Ethical and Transcendence

The Impossible Possibility of Ethics

THOMAS J. J. ALTIZER

Edith Wyschogrod is perhaps our deepest and most serious contemporary ethical thinker, the one who has most comprehensively explored our ethical crisis today, and explored it with such decisive finality as to foreclose seemingly all possibility of a real and actual ethics for us. Although most deeply inspired by Levinas, she nevertheless has not succumbed to his absolute and absolutely primordial or pre-primordial ethics; she could not so succumb, if only because she will not abandon the actuality of our world. That actuality is most powerful for her in a uniquely contemporary "death-world," a death-world ending everything that we have known as ethics. This ending ends history itself, thereby realizing a unique apocalypse, one finally promising life as well as death. This is the supreme challenge which Wyschogrod has chosen, calling forth life out of the depths of death, a life inseparable from the ultimacy and finality of death, but likewise inseparable from a uniquely contemporary *nihil*, a *nihil* exposed by mass extermination, a void that cannot be named but which constitutes a unique moment: the entry of the *nihil* into time. Never before has such a *nihil* been actually manifest, and never previously has nihilism been so pervasive. Nihilism is most apparent in postmodernism, a primary arena of Wyschogrod's critical investigation, and one inseparable from a uniquely modern history and consciousness. It is in this investigation that she most conclusively demonstrates the impossibility of ethics for us—but that is the impossibility that she has chosen as possibility, a possibility which theologically can only be named as an absolutely free and an absolutely unconditioned grace.

Wyschogrod is perhaps our most ecumenical or most comprehensive thinker, as demonstrated by her ethical investigations, which are not only phenomenological and analytic at once, but occur within a truly universal perspective, one comprehending Judaism, Christianity, Buddhism, and a uniquely modern atheism. While Wyschogrod's own theological identity is veiled in her ethical investigations, it is nevertheless a genuine theological identity, one perhaps offering a decisive clue to her deepest quest. One arena that she never explicitly enters is theological ethics, perhaps because she knows how banal and shallow theological ethics has become in our time, but perhaps more deeply because at bottom she is tacitly creating a theological ethics, one unnameable as such in terms of our established categories: an ethics which she can trace our great saints, where holiness is inseparable from a total self-giving, a self-giving that is a model for her of an ethical life. Her book *Saints and Postmodernism: Revisioning Moral Philosophy*[1] investigates saints in the very context of our nihilism, thereby bringing a unique illumination to each of these opposites. Provocatively, perhaps holiness is possible for us only by way of a reversal of nihilism, just as a nihilistic realization of absolute emptiness or absolute nothingness could be a parallel to an absolute self-emptying, thus offering the possibility of an ultimate *coincidentia oppositorum*.

Even though Wyschogrod is a genuine theological thinker, nothing is more absent from her discourse than the word *God*, except insofar as she speaks forcefully of the death of God, a death which she understands theologically, an understanding made manifest in her critical investigations of Hegel. Nor does she divorce the death of God from her own quest for a new ethics, and it is here that she differs most deeply from Levinas. While she has absorbed Levinas's discovery of the *il y a*, an *il y a* that Levinas defines as Being in the absence of beings, Wyschogrod can apprehend an ethical role of the *il y a*, which is to denucleate the self as a complex of mental acts and render the self receptive to alterity. Alterity seemingly vanishes in postmodernity, and this is a fundamental ground of our ethical crisis, but this is an emptying which is the very opposite of self-emptying, and one inseparable from the modern realization of the death of God. Now if this is a realization which Levinas totally refuses, Wyschogrod herself refuses such a refusal. She does so to open herself to our deepest contemporary actuality, and while this is indeed a nihilistic actuality, it is nevertheless essential to a contemporary as opposed to a primordial or pre-primordial ethics. While Wyschogrod retains a primordial ground in her ethics, one preceding all historical judgment, she balances it by accepting an apocalyptic ground as well, thereby not only differing from Levinas, but opening herself to our new apocalyptic actuality.

While apocalypse has become a pervasive category in contemporary literary theory, just as it is in Heidegger and Derrida, it has been refused by our theological orthodoxies, and nowhere are Jewish, Christian, and Islamic orthodoxies more united than they are on this fundamental point. Yet already in *Spirit in Ashes: Hegel, Heidegger, and Man-made Mass Death*,[2] Wyschogrod can know that the religious roots of the death-world lie in Jewish and Christian apocalypticism, and just as the philosophers whom she focuses upon in that book, Hegel and Heidegger, are apocalyptic philosophers, it is precisely apocalyptic thinking which most deeply unveils the death-world. Of course, an apocalyptic imagination goes beyond all such thinking, especially a uniquely modern apocalyptic imagination, as decisively manifest not only by Blake or Joyce, but even more purely by Kafka or Beckett. While Wyschogrod's focus is more philosophical than imaginative, she follows Hegel, Nietzsche, and Heidegger in incorporating the imagination into thinking, thereby not only decisively differing from her ethical compeers, but from the whole world of analytic thinking, and her continual critique of that thinking is sustained by an imaginative ground. While that ground for Wyschogrod cannot be separated from the death-world, our uniquely modern imagination, from Dante through Joyce and beyond, is grounded in the ultimacy of death, an ultimacy inseparable from everything that can be envisioned as life itself, and even inseparable from the ultimacy of eternal life.

This ultimate conjunction, this *coincidentia oppositorum* of eternal life and eternal death, could be a paradigm directing Wyschogrod's quest, on which only an eternal death makes possible an apocalyptic eternal life, or only the deepest darkness makes possible the deepest light. Hence only an ultimate crisis of our ethics could make possible a truly new ethics, and an ethics that could be real in our nihilistic world. If the bulk of Wyschogrod's ethical investigations are a fundamentally negative critique, that is essential to her project, for light can come forth only out of the shadows of our darkness. A primary challenge is calling forth a genuine ethical possibility in Wyschogrod's work out of our darkness. Such a possibility is inseparable from what Levinas knows as the Infinite, an infinite that is the radical, the absolutely other, one that cannot be contained in thought, and which disempowers all selfhood. This is that infinite which is the ultimate ground of alterity, an alterity veiled in our world, if only as a consequence of the death of God, with the result that there is no longer a primordial ground of alterity or otherness, and no longer an absolute "before" at all. True, that absolute "before" may be only veiled, not absent, may be only eclipsed or silent in our abyss, but its eclipse is a primal if not the primal source of the crisis of ethics, a crisis in which no actual ethics appears to be possible for us.

Now it is not insignificant that Levinas, among the greatest ethical thinkers of the twentieth century, should have called forth a primordial or pre-primordial ethics that ends every possible ethics, nor insignificant that the thinking of Levinas is so deeply Neoplatonic, initiating a new and deeply Neoplatonic philosophical movement in France. While Wyschogrod is drawn to Plotinus, she nevertheless resists Neoplatonism, and therein inevitably resists Levinas as well, perhaps most clearly in opening herself to a genuinely apocalyptic horizon. It is not commonly realized that the ultimate struggle in early Christianity was between the absolutely primordial and the absolutely apocalyptic, for Christianity was born with an absolute apocalypse, but it almost immediately gave birth to Gnosticism, the most absolutely primordial of all ultimate ways. We can see a war between the primordial and the apocalyptic most clearly in Paul, that Paul who was the creator of Christian theology, and whom we now know to have been a deeply apocalyptic theologian, perhaps most profoundly so in his struggle with a primitive Christian Gnosticism. This is most clearly recorded in his Corinthian correspondence, a correspondence that cannot possibly be understood as a coherent whole. If here as elsewhere Paul's deepest ground is the crucified Christ, that ground is absent in Paul's ecstatic celebration of eternal life in 1 Corinthians 15, and it is precisely here that Paul's own language is most pagan or Gnostic. This is the Pauline language that most deeply influenced Christian orthodoxy, and despite that orthodoxy's apparent victory over Gnosticism, Christian orthodoxy has never succeeded in negating or transcending a Gnostic horizon, a purely pagan horizon that has never been more powerful than it is today.

The prophetic revolution of Israel created the ultimate goal of an absolute future, an absolute future which is finally apocalypse itself, and this revolutionary movement towards an absolute future is an inversion or reversal of the archaic movement of eternal return. Nothing is more characteristic of a genuine paganism than is the movement of eternal return, and while this movement was reborn in Judaism, Christianity, and Islam, its most powerful expression occurs in Christian orthodoxy itself, which at this crucial point truly parallels all forms of Gnosticism. But genuine Gnosticism is inseparable from a Judeo-Christian-Islamic horizon, it is never found as such in the East where a truly backward movement is impossible, if only because in the East all ultimate distinctions between past and future disappear. Indeed, if it was Christianity that created Gnosticism, this could be understood as a reversal of an absolutely apocalyptic movement, one only possible for a Christianity that was born as an absolute apocalypse. That apocalypse is in deep continuity with the prophetic revolution, most clearly in reversing every distinction between high and low, a reversal which Nietzsche outlined as the slave revolt of morality, and which he knew to be most profoundly embodied in Christianity. Hence Nietzsche could know the uniquely Christian God as the deification of nothingness, "the will to nothingness pronounced holy."[3]

In this perspective, only the uniquely Christian God is an absolute No-saying, and only a uniquely Christian ethics is a true and pure ethics of *ressentiment*. If Nietzsche only discovered *ressentiment* after he had discovered the death of God, that is because he discovered the death of a uniquely Christian God, hence one unknown apart from a Christian horizon. Already Paul could know the death of God in the Crucifixion, a death apart from which no absolute sacrifice is possible. A renewal of that death is at the very center of a uniquely Pauline ethics, an ethics revolving about a continual sacrifice of one's innermost "I" or selfhood: an ethics that can be understood as a purely apocalyptic ethics. Here, a new Adam can only be understood as a consequence of the death of the old Adam, but if that death releases an absolutely new imperative which is an absolutely new indicative, then every distinction between the imperative and the indicative disappears, but only as the consequence of an actual ending of an old world or old creation.

Remarkably enough, there is a realism in Pauline ethics which soon disappears from the great body of Christianity, a realism inseparable from an apocalyptic horizon, a horizon which itself all but disappears from Christianity, except insofar as it is recovered by truly revolutionary movements. Alone among the great religions of the world, Christianity almost wholly transformed itself in the first three generations of its existence—but Christianity alone was born with a profound conflict at its very center, a conflict between its apocalyptic and its non-apocalyptic or primordial poles, a conflict fully manifest in the New Testament.

No tradition has so profoundly transformed itself in the course of its history as has Christianity, but no other tradition embodies such deep dichotomies within itself as does Christianity. These dichotomies manifest fully within the ethical realm in a Christianity that has been profoundly conservative, even reactionary, and profoundly revolutionary at once, a Christianity which has been simultaneously destructive and creative. Of course, the scale of these dichotomies continues to diminish within modern Christianity, as does the life and power of Christianity, but with the ending of Christendom such dichotomies pass into the greater body of humanity, and uniquely and profoundly Christian hetero-doxies have become embodied in our new world. This is clearest in philosophy and the imagination, as in Hegel and Nietzsche, and in Blake and Joyce, but it is also manifest in our uniquely modern political and social revolutions, and perhaps even in modern science and technology. Certainly forward movement is manifest throughout modernity, beginning with the prophetic revolution of Israel, and ultimately embodied in Christianity. If forward movement has apparently now ended in all manifest or established Christianity, this itself is a deep transformation of Christianity, one that perhaps makes possible its transmutation into a fundamental ground of modernity.

Nothing is clearer in Wyschogrod's work than that she calls out not simply the groundlessness of all established ethics, but the very vacuity of our given ethical categories, thus placing in question all of our ethical language, and inevitably raising the question of whether any ethical language at all is possible for us. This issue, regarding the very possibility of ethical language, can be concretely observed in many of our common presumptions. It is commonly assumed, for instance, that Heidegger is not a genuinely ethical thinker, despite his profound impact upon Levinas, and despite the apparent truth that *Being and Time* embodies the deepest and most powerful ethical language of any twentieth century philosophical work, and is unique in Western philosophical literature in the very primacy and centrality of this language. Is it because Heidegger writes with a deep and extraordinarily difficult language that it is presumed that his could not possibly be an ethical language? Can only a simple language be an ethical language? And despite the dominant presumption that modern ethics transcends theology, is there a lingering, if unconscious, doubt that a non-theological language could be a genuine ethical language? *Being and Time* is bereft of all explicitly theological language; perhaps the category of God is more wanting here than in any other philosophical work. Yet recent analysis draws forth the profound theological ground of *Being and Time*, and it is now apparent that Heidegger is a deeply Pauline thinker, most clearly so in his primary focus upon an absolute death, and an absolute death that is an apocalyptic death.

Just as Paul's ethical thinking is now alien to virtually everyone, the same could be said of Heidegger, and of Nietzsche, too, and it has even become true of Spinoza. Is this not a sign of our profound alienation from a genuine ethical thinking? Now it is true that Heidegger, in withdrawing from the language of *Dasein* in his later work, withdrew from all manifest ethical thinking, but this can be understood as a reflection of an ultimate or apocalyptic crisis, one central to Heidegger throughout his major thinking, but only all-consuming in his final thinking. So, too, the death of God is more primal for Heidegger than for any other twentieth century philosopher, yet the death of God in modern thinking and vision is an apocalyptic death, and it ushers in an absolute apocalypse. Certainly Heidegger knows that apocalypse, even if he is reticent in speaking of it, yet he gives us a profound witness to it in his critical investigations of modern German poetry, just as he does indirectly in his investigations of modern technology, and this has deeply affected Wyschogrod. Perhaps it is only in an environment of all-consuming contemporary technology that we can directly see such an apocalypse; even if it is a deeply negative apocalypse, it is nevertheless an apocalypse, and one whose overwhelming impact is undeniable.

Now if Paul's apocalyptic thinking ends every possible distinction between the indicative and the imperative, and does so as a consequence of the advent of an absolute apocalypse, does our contemporary technology also embody such an advent? Paul's profound hostility towards what he was the first to know as "Law" is a hostility towards an imperative that is and is only imperative, one wholly other than the Torah of Judaism, and one released only by an apocalyptic ending of history. Is not such a "Law" manifest to us today, and is it not a fundamental force behind our pervasive anarchism, an anarchism inexplicable in our common understanding, and even inexplicable in our established philosophical thinking? Paul could know a pure imperative that cannot possibly be obeyed, one inducing an ultimate and even absolute guilt, and a guilt wholly other than any possible fault or failure. While this profound guilt has seemingly disappeared among us, still, what if the only genuine imperative that we can know is beyond all possibility of obedience, and beyond all possible appropriation? But if a totally technological world is now our destiny, does not such a world end every possible imperative, or end every imperative not embodied in itself? Then every other form of the imperative would be wholly alien and lifeless, very like that "Law" which Paul knew. Just as Paul and the Augustinian tradition could know a faith liberating us from all "Law," is our new technological world liberating us from every imperative that is simply and only imperative?

Wyschogrod can know this destiny as a profoundly a-ethical or anti-ethical world, indeed, the most a-ethical world in history, and itself a decisive sign of our history having come to an end. But just as ancient apocalypticism could know its own historical world as an absolutely anti-ethical world, a knowledge nowhere more present than in Paul's thought, is this condition necessary for an apocalyptic ethics, or an apocalyptic life? Note that to know that the world is anti-ethical in this sense is to know that the world has come to an end, and in full apocalypticism the ending of the world is the ending of the old creation, the ending of the cosmos itself. Yet Paul attains a genuine realism in his apocalyptic faith and action, one going beyond even the Qumran communities, and going beyond them in engaging the fullness of a collapsing history, thus making possible the historical victory of an originally tiny Jewish apocalyptic sect. Nothing is so apocalyptic in Paul's writing as his Corinthian correspondence, but this is just where his fullest ethical writing occurs, where he elucidates a truly new and apocalyptic ethics, one grounded in the realization that "everything has become new" (2 Cor. 5:17, NRSV). Ever since Schweitzer, New Testament scholarship has narrowed the distance between the ethics of Jesus and the ethics of Paul, for both are apocalyptic ethics, or ethics of the Kingdom of God, and now even the Sermon on the Mount can stand forth as a realistic ethics as a consequence of the advent of the Kingdom of God.

It is tempting to think that such realism could only be fantasy, just as an apocalyptic advent is fantasy, but we know the overwhelming consequences of the enactments of apocalyptic advents, not only in the ancient world but in the fullness of the modern world. If postmodernity is either the ending or the consequence of the modern world, it, too, is apocalyptic, perhaps above all technologically, and if our destiny now promises to be a totally technological destiny, here we can see a full reversal of the apocalyptic ethics of the New Testament, a reversal preserving an original apocalypticism even as it inverts it. Is everything even now becoming new, are we not being called to a truly new creation, and a new creation arising out of the ashes of an old world?

Yes, this new Adam could only be the consequence of the death of an old Adam, a death fully enacted in the late modern world, and if now the world itself is inseparable from a death-world, nothing could be more realistic for us. Hence the pervasive numbing of our world, the diminution if not collapse of everything which we once knew as sensibility, the virtual ending of everything that we once knew as the imagination, and a new politics and a new society of emptiness and illusion. Yes, a brave new world, and a seemingly passionate religious world, even if it is the most fundamentally illiterate religious world in our history, one in which theology has all but disappeared, and one in which a religious thinking or imagination is apparently impossible. Kierkegaard, Nietzsche, and Dostoyevsky foresaw this, and a host of other visionaries as well, but who could have foreseen the brute realism of our vacuity?

Perhaps Edith Wyschogrod is now the primary thinker engaged with this crisis, or ethically engaged with it, but is this finally a quixotic venture, or even an illusory one? Realists among us might think this, but if she is forcing us to rethink ethics, this is surely a genuine blessing, and it does raise the possibility of a new ethics for us, even if this could only be an absolutely impossible ethics. Could that very impossibility be a decisive clue? After all, an apocalyptic ethics has always been an impossible ethics, and yet it has nevertheless not only been indubitably real, but has profoundly transformed our history and consciousness. "Be perfect" is a summary of the Sermon on the Mount, but this call is not a true imperative: it is an imperative that is an indicative, or an imperative reflecting an absolutely new world. And in the perspective of that imperative, every other imperative can be known as what Paul knew as the "Law": the Law of God, yes, but a Law which is now a curse. If we are coming to know every ethics in our history as either empty or a curse, this crisis could be a genuinely apocalyptic crisis, or a darkness that is finally light. If we can but name our darkness, we can be open to that light, and surely Wyschogrod has decisively named it; if we cannot yet know a new ethics, we can know what it is not, and it is not anything which we can actually know as ethics. But that, too, may well be a blessing, and a blessing that we do not deserve, but if a genuine blessing is a grace, it can only be a free and unconditional grace.

If there is one topic that Wyschogrod has centered upon throughout her work, that could only be death, and even an absolute death. Thereby she is in continuity not only with Hegel and Heidegger, but also with our deeper imaginative traditions. While she seemingly ignores a biblical ground in these investigations, we may presume that one is nevertheless implicitly present, and it could be enlightening to draw forth such a presence. Heidegger's deep impact upon Wyschogrod is clear, so it is appropriate to remember that Heidegger was actively engaged in Bultmann's seminar on Paul while writing *Being and Time*, just as it is fundamental to note that Heidegger's lectures on the phenomenology of religion in 1920 called forth the apocalyptic Paul, and this at a time when New Testament scholarship had not yet discovered that identity. Nowhere in the Bible is an absolute death more primal than it is in Paul: Not only is the Crucifixion for Paul the sole source of redemption, but it is the inauguration of apocalypse itself, an apocalypse which alone makes possible an absolutely new life. The advent of apocalypse is the ending of a world that *is* world, so that being in action is the expression of being made free from the world, through suffering and dying with Christ. Nothing is more primal for Paul than dying with Christ; only that dying makes possible a sacrificial life, but in that dying Christ lives in us, and that life is both a free and an absolute grace.

Is it possible to believe that this profoundly Pauline motif did not fundamentally affect the Heidegger of *Being and Time*? If authentic existence is "being towards death," is that not an echo of Paul, an echo resounding throughout this work? Nor is this primal thesis isolated from the ultimacy of fall and guilt, which are called forth here as they are in no other philosophical work, creating the condition that makes being-towards-death possible, and if *Dasein* is essentially being-in-the-world, the basic mode of *Dasein*'s being is *Sorge* or solicitude. *Sorge* is inseparable from the facticity of being-in-the-world, but also inseparable from fall and guilt, and that is the condition in which *Dasein* realizes itself, for *Dasein* is futural in its very being (325). Such an understanding of the primacy of the future also bears a Pauline echo, and whether Heidegger understood it or not, it is also an echo of the prophetic revolution, and if Hegel and Heidegger are those philosophers who most ultimately embody an absolute future, it is just thereby that they are truly apocalyptic philosophers. Yet what we can understand only as ethical thinking is primal in Heidegger's ontological thinking as it is not in Hegel's, and even if this only occurs in *Being and Time*, its occurrence is crucial because that is Heidegger's most influential work.

No philosopher has such an absolutely negative apprehension of the condition of the world as does the later Heidegger, and here he does truly differ from the early Heidegger. Even Wyschogrod's negative judgments pale in this perspective, and if this is an ultimate philosophy of ending, it is thereby open to an absolute or apocalyptic beginning. Heidegger's primal word for that beginning is *Ereignis*, a truly untranslatable word, but it is tempting to correlate this word with the most untranslatable of all Christian turns of phrase, *the Kingdom of God*. We know that *Kingdom of God* is at the very center of the words and praxis of Jesus, but we also know that nothing has been more ultimately transformed in Christianity than this center, and most transformed in the dominant Christian apprehension of God. This is an apprehension against which Heidegger deeply rebelled, as is most manifest in his posthumously published *Beiträge zur Philosophie*, but this is the very work in which he most fully calls forth *Ereignis*, where Being itself is finally known as *Ereignis*. Yet it is so known only against the transcendent God of Christianity, for Heidegger places a deep emphasis in *Beiträge* upon the abandonment of Being, an abandonment that first happened in Christianity, with its absolutely transcendent God, an abandonment in which Being abandons beings, but this abandonment is the fundamental event of our history, and one that is now being reversed in the apocalyptic advent of *Ereignis*. Could this be an apprehension of the Kingdom of God, or an apprehension of apocalyptic Godhead, one truly reversed in Christian orthodoxy, and only called forth in the most radical Christian heterodoxy? Perhaps Heidegger can best be understood theologically in the context of such heterodoxy, and if Heidegger is our only major philosopher who was initially a truly orthodox Christian, was his life work an ever more gradual but an ever more decisive reversal of that orthodoxy?

Indeed, is it possible that a truly new ethics is only possible for us through such a heterodoxy? It is commonly thought that ethics is the simplest of all disciplines, that everyone knows what ethics is, and that all share a common conscience. But could the very opposite of this be true? Could it be that here lies one of our greatest illusions, and that nothing is a deeper mystery to us than ethics? Wyschogrod's analysis would certainly sustain such a judgment, so that if a genuine ethics, or a genuine ethics for us, is wholly other than everything that we commonly know as ethics, and can only be real with the collapse or deconstruction of that ethics, then such deconstruction is fundamental to the possibility of ethics itself. No one has more profoundly deconstructed our ethics than Nietzsche, but no other thinker has so deeply or so purely called forth an absolute affirmation or an absolute Yes-saying, and an absolute Yes-saying to the depths of our darkness. Nietzsche's understanding of *ressentiment* is an understanding of a No-saying that is the very opposite of such Yes-saying, a *ressentiment* wholly isolating and enclosing its enactor, thereby giving birth to everything that we know as selfhood. Such selfhood or self-consciousness is our deepest prison, and it is the source of our deepest hatred and violence, yet it is ended with the death of God, or ended in its deepest ground, even if this death, the most all important event in history, is the source of that nihilism which has overwhelmed us.

The truth is that no ethics can be actual or real for us which cannot act or be enacted in a nihilistic world, hence once again the importance of Paul, for he surely knew his historical world as a nihilistic world, and his ethics is finally meaningless apart from that horizon. Indeed, it is the very collapse or ending of that historical world which makes possible Paul's apocalyptic ethics, so that we must inevitably ask if something comparable could be true for us. Could an apocalyptic ethics of any kind be real for us, and is such an ethics essential for Wyschogrod's quest? If a truly new ethics could only arise for us out of the ending of our ethical worlds and horizons, then an ultimate ending is essential for such an ethics, and that ending could only be an apocalyptic ending. Yet a truly apocalyptic ending is inseparable from an apocalyptic beginning; a genuinely apocalyptic ending of the world is inseparable from the advent or dawning of an absolutely new world, for here the advent of a new creation is inseparable from the ending of an old creation. Hence genuinely apocalyptic seers who envision or enact the ending of an old world thereby enact the absolute beginning of a new world, and just as this occurs in Hegel, Nietzsche, and Heidegger, so does it occur in Dante, Milton, Blake, and Joyce, all of whom are thereby in continuity with Paul, even if the new beginning entails a reversal of a uniquely Christian consciousness and history.

Is not such a reversal essential to any genuinely apocalyptic enactment? In this perspective, we can see why Christian orthodoxies are so opposed to apocalypticism, but so, too, are Jewish and Islamic orthodoxies, and if our deepest heterodoxies are apocalyptic heterodoxies, this can be understood as being essential to genuine apocalypticism, with the consequence that an orthodox apocalypticism could not possibly be a true apocalypticism. All of our apocalyptic visionaries, even Dante, have been condemned by our ecclesiastical authorities, and just as Joachism was the gravest theological threat to the medieval Catholic world, modern apocalypticism has been the ultimate threat to the modern Christian world. Perhaps the ultimacy of this threat is most manifest in the ethical realm, for genuine apocalypticism not only ultimately challenges all established authority, but all given or established values as well, inevitably calling for a reversal of all such values, hence assaulting every given principle or identity. For what Hegel knows as the "given" is the ultimate enemy of apocalypticism, a given comprehending every established ground, and only a reversal of that given makes possible a genuine apocalypticism, or a genuinely apocalyptic ethics. Hence an apocalyptic ethics is a truly subversive ethics, and its enactment is inevitably a profound assault upon our most deeply cherished "ideals," or upon our most deeply established mythology or religion, and finally a profound assault upon everything that is given to us as God.

All of our apocalyptic thinkers and visionaries have assaulted God, or our most deeply given God, hence the ultimate offense of genuine apocalypticism, an offense first known by Paul, but one which is ever more fully enlarged in subsequent apocalypticism. Is this a fundamental reason why Wyschogrod is so reluctant to employ the word *God* in her own discourse? Is she fully aware of her own apocalyptic ground, but disguising it theologically, even if she commonly employs it in her critiques of our world? Certainly the death-world for Wyschogrod is an apocalyptic world, one realizing the end of history itself, and ushering in a final darkness which is most manifest to us in the ethical realm. Yet is it impossible to speak of God in our darkness? And is that a fundamental reason why our ethics is in crisis? For despite a common confidence that modern ethics has wholly left theology behind, does not theology recur in our greatest ethical thinking, even if it recurs in disguised and cryptic forms? This is surely true of Nietzsche, and of Heidegger, too. Nietzsche's ethics is simply impossible apart from a proclamation of the death of God, and while Heidegger brackets all God-language in *Being and Time*, he is clearly profoundly affected in that work by both Kierkegaard and Paul. Indeed, can Nietzsche's eternal recurrence or Heidegger's *Ereignis* truly be understood non-theologically? Is not each either a call to or an enactment of a final redemption, and a final or apocalyptic redemption that was born with Christianity? True, both Nietzsche and Heidegger ultimately assault the uniquely Christian God, but is not that assault a theological assault, and an assault in the service of what can only be known as redemption?

Can we truly know the darkness of our world without knowing the darkness of God? And can we truly know the emptiness of our ethics apart from knowing the death of God? While Wyschogrod is open to the death of God, she seldom employs it in her ethical analysis, and we must ask if the new ethics that she seeks can be realized apart from a theological ground, even if only a negative theological ground. It cannot be denied that Levinas is a theological thinker, and while he has a Jewish reluctance to write the word *God*, that Infinite which is his deepest ground is clearly God, a ground which Wyschogrod, too, accepts, but has that ground yet been actually realized in her ethical thinking, and must not this occur if she is to effect a breakthrough to a new ethics?

At most the late Heidegger is only on the threshold of a new ethics, and perhaps this is true of Wyschogrod, too, and while such a threshold is overwhelmingly important, it cannot indefinitely be sustained, just as it cannot stand alone. This is a threshold that must be passed, and even if this will entail innumerable missteps and bypasses, and innumerable labyrinths as well, we are certainly called to such a voyage, and most clearly so called by Wyschogrod herself. Yet such a calling demands that we free ourselves of all restraints, most certainly including our deepest inhibitions, and perhaps the deepest of all inhibitions in thinking today is the refusal of theological thinking. This is clearest in theological ethics today, an ethics bereft of all actual theological thinking, but it is manifest throughout the whole spectrum of our world, a world that is truly in crisis.

Perhaps our deepest theological restraint derives from our truly contemporary condition, a condition which is not only a nihilistic condition, but in which our only possible genuine theological thinking would be a truly heterodox thinking, one wholly inverting everything that is given to us as theological thinking. Hegel is the great model of totally heterodox thinking in our world, and Hegel is alone philosophically, unless he is rivaled by Nietzsche in creating a comprehensive thinking which is a purely and totally theological thinking, as most clearly manifest in his primal category of an absolute self-negation or an absolute self-emptying. That self-emptying or self-negation, as Hegel's own language reveals, is inseparable from a Pauline kenosis, or the absolute sacrifice of Christ, and it is all too significant that Hegel's is our only philosophical language which decisively embodies the full spectrum of Christian dogma, moving from creation through Fall, Judgment, Incarnation, Crucifixion, and Resurrection or Apocalypse. Yet the center of Hegel's philosophy is the Crucifixion or the death of God, a death of God that Hegel was the first to know, and this can be understood as that revolutionary breakthrough that first made possible a fully or purely apocalyptic philosophy. Thus we have the paradox that our most totally heterodox thinker is seemingly our fullest or most totally Christian thinker, hence Hegel has become the deepest enemy of the whole world of theology, and an all-too-partial theological incorporation of Hegelian thinking has inevitably issued in grave and deeply threatening heresies.

Yet the truth remains that Hegelian thinking is most profoundly grounded in an absolute self-negation or self-emptying, one that can be understood as being not only grounded in but only made possible by the absolute sacrifice or the absolute self-emptying of Christ, and if it is not until Hegel that thinking can comprehend this sacrifice, that not only entails a revolutionary transformation of thinking, but a revolutionary transformation of theology as well. Here lies the deepest ground of Hegel's ultimate heterodoxy, one inseparable from the death of God, and inseparable from the death of God in the absolute sacrifice of Christ, a death ending absolute transcendence itself, and inaugurating an absolute immanence that is a final and apocalyptic immanence. Consequently, the death of God and an absolute apocalypse are inseparable, and just as Paul knows that the Crucifixion inaugurates apocalypse, Hegel knows this absolute death not only as the ultimate center of history, but as the ultimate center of thinking itself. Hence a truly apocalyptic philosophy is not born until Hegel, a birth demanding a total transformation of historical Christianity, and thus demanding a pure and comprehensive heterodoxy as the innermost necessity of Christianity itself. Yet in Hegelian thinking, Christian thinking for the first time becomes a universal thinking, as the sacrifice of Christ becomes the ultimate ground of thinking itself, and even the ultimate ground of consciousness itself.

Nevertheless, Hegel was never able to incorporate this thinking into a full and genuine ethical thinking, and perhaps Hegel's ethical legacy is the impossibility of a purely or genuinely ethical thinking, an impossibility that is even manifest in Kierkegaard and Marx, who can be known as his deepest inheritors, unless this is true of Nietzsche and Heidegger. Accordingly, Wyschogrod's ethical dilemma was born with the fullness of modernity. Its postmodern expression is in full continuity with this source; the great difference is that originally it was only manifest to a few, and now it is universally actual. Can our ethical dilemma constructively be approached by seeking a purely heterodox ethics? Marx and Nietzsche certainly accomplished this, but now their revolutionary thinking is once again and even more comprehensively forbidden, and it appears to be hopelessly removed from the brute actuality of our condition. Is there no possibility of a truly heterodox ethics that could be actual for us? And could it be actual apart from being an apocalyptic ethics—Hegel, Marx, Nietzsche, and Heidegger are all apocalyptic thinkers, and their ethical thinking is surely impossible apart from their apocalyptic thinking— could that be true for us? Yet it is Hegel among these thinkers who is the least ethical thinker, as comprehended by Levinas, unless an ethics is implicitly present in his deeply theological thinking, one wholly alien to Levinas, and perhaps alien to us all.

Once again we encounter a theological challenge, and a theological challenge ever more fully manifest as an ethical challenge, a challenge to fully conjoin ethical and theological thinking. This seems impossible today, but that impossibility may well be the only possibility of ethics for us. If this challenge can be broached by a new apocalyptic thinking made possible by our comprehensive nihilism, it cannot occur apart from a full opening to our nihilism, one that Wyschogrod has given us as a genuinely ethical thinker. But nihilism must not only be reversed by a new ethical thinking, it must be incorporated to make such a reversal possible, and if it is Nietzsche who knows this most profoundly, it is Wyschogrod who seemingly knows this most concretely, hence her immersion in a postmodern nihilism, an immersion necessary for ethical thinking today. Such an immersion is necessary for apocalyptic thinking today, but a comparable immersion has occurred throughout the history of apocalypticism, and even occurred in our purest apocalyptic thinkers and visionaries. Yes, we are asleep in our apocalyptic darkness, but we are called to wake, and we can awaken only by passing through that darkness, only by making that darkness our own, for only then can we reverse it, and only then can we know a light that is only possible within it, and only possible as the light of darkness itself. Then perhaps we can truly say Yes, and say Yes to that darkness which is finally light, or that darkness which is finally God, and whose absolute Yes is now only hearable by us as an absolute No.

Here, saying and unsaying become all important. Wyschogrod integrally conjoins these acts in her *An Ethics of Remembering*,[4] and in chapter 4, appropriately entitled "Wired in the Absolute," in response to the problem of speaking about the Holocaust, she speaks of a silent "saying" anterior to speech, and proposes that such saying is an unspoken covenant between speaker and hearer, promising that her language will be marked by alterity. Surely there is no greater problem for Wyschogrod than the meaning and the reality of alterity, as these appear to be vanishing among us, and that very vanishing poses an ultimate call. For Wyschogrod the ultimate ground of alterity is the Infinite, but can we say "God" in response to that ground, and can this be only a silent saying anterior to speech? This kind of saying could account for Wyschogrod's apparent silence about God, but if this is a silence evoked for us by the death-world, must we only speak silently about God because for us to speak openly or decisively about God would necessarily be a speaking of an absolute No? And not only an absolute No, but an absolute No wholly removed from an absolute Yes, or before which an absolute Yes could only be wholly silent and unsaid? Have not our most powerful Jewish thinkers taught us that to speak of God in response to the Holocaust could only be to speak with an ultimate blasphemy, and did not Kafka realize this even before the Holocaust occurred, thereby realizing and making absolutely concrete that ultimate catastrophe which our existence has become?

Yet Wyschogrod intends finally to evoke an absolute gift, and in the conclusion of *An Ethics of Remembering*, she affirms that exteriority in its ethical sense cannot be envisioned exclusively in terms of the cataclysmic, but rather must be envisioned in its doubleness both as cataclysm and as an exteriority that is the prelinguistic "saying" that precedes language as a concrete act of communication. Can only a prelinguistic saying evoke an absolute gift, or evoke an absolute gift for us, and is this a silence that is the only possible grace for us, and a silence that alone makes possible an ethics for us? But is this an apocalyptic silence or a primordial silence: Is it a consequence of our history and consciousness, or is it absolutely prior to any possible consciousness and history? This is an ultimate theological question, and it poses the further question of whether the only possible way for us is a way of eternal return, and an eternal return to an unspeakable silence. Is this all that we can know as a true or absolute gift, and is it this silence alone that could make possible for us an actual ethics, or an ethics that we could actually enact? Modern Jewish scholars and thinkers have given us extraordinarily astute critiques of Christian apocalypticism, unveiling it as being wholly unreal but ultimately destructive in that unreality, and one can only wonder if this would not be true of any possible primordial way for us. Wyschogrod is virtually silent about how a primordial way could be actual for us, but she nonetheless evokes it, and even evokes it as an ultimate gift.

Is this our only way of being truly silent about God, and thereby a way to a genuine ethics only possible as a consequence of catastrophe? If only thereby it would be an apocalyptic way, unless following Lurianic Kabbalism we could know an absolute catastrophe as an absolutely primordial catastrophe, or an absolutely primordial Fall. Even Milton knew such a Fall, and Blake and Joyce, too, just as it is essential in Hegelian and Nietzschean thinking, so is it possible that there is finally no possible distinction between apocalyptic and primordial ways? If this is true, then perhaps a new ethics could be a truly universal ethics, and even if this universal ethics is only made possible by an absolute catastrophe, that is the catastrophe which is now our deepest ground, and the only possible source of an ultimate gift for us. Wyschogrod has silently named that source as God, but that is nonetheless a genuine naming, and even if this is a naming anterior to speech, it is a naming making possible a genuinely ethical speech, and the only possible ethical speech for us. Could such speech only be actual for us as silence, and the deepest possible silence, and only thereby the deepest possible grace for us?

The Empty Suitcase as Rainbow

MEROLD WESTPHAL

In her project of revisioning moral philosophy, Edith Wyschogrod takes a decisive turn from moral theory to hagiography, from abstract analysis and argument to concrete life stories. The negative motivation for this turn is a critique of moral theory. Two elements of this critique strike me as especially forceful. First, moral theory depends on arguments that do not persuade those outside the hermeneutic circle within which the arguments occur. Thus she points to "the circularity of standard modes of rationality."[1] The problem is that "background claims . . . cannot be agreed upon. If there is no common frame of reference, no cultural consensus in terms of which these disputes can be settled, the disputants can only go on arguing without altering moral dispositions or generating moral actions."[2]

In speaking of the failure to alter moral dispositions or to generate moral actions, Wyschogrod makes a second, powerful point. It is not just that moral theory does not produce agreement and consensus, but that "moral theories do not result in moral actions."[3] Epistemically speaking, moral theory does not give us the knowledge it promises, and pragmatically speaking, it does not give us the goodness we need.

We are greatly indebted to Wyschogrod for the bold suggestion that stories of saintly lives can help us with these problems, and for the lucid and learned way in which she develops this hypothesis. But it is not immediately clear that the turn to narrativity in general or to saintly narratives in particular will solve these problems. After all, narratives, too, have their points of view, their presuppositions, which are not necessarily shared by all readers. For example, one of the most moving hagiographic narratives to come out of the Holocaust is Philip Hallie's *Lest Innocent Blood Be Shed*. Written by a Jewish moral philosopher who has turned to narrative, it is the story of Le Chambon, a village in southeastern France whose three thousand poor inhabitants, at great risk and cost to themselves, saved the lives of as many as five thousand refugees, mostly children and mostly Jews, either by hiding them in and around the village—first from the Vichy police and then from the Gestapo—or by helping them to escape to Switzerland. It is a deeply moving and inspiring story, none the less so for being true. But in the concluding chapter, while admitting that his narrative is a form of moral praise, since he shares the presupposition of the Chambonnais that "human life had no price; it had only dignity,"[4] Hallie points out that not everyone would interpret the facts of his story that way: "The Nazis had other presumptions about the preciousness of human life." As the handbook of the Hitler Youth states it, "The foundation of the National Socialist outlook on life is the perception of the unlikeness of men."[5] If for every argument there is a counterargument, this is not least so because for every presupposition there is an alternative presupposition.

Nor is it clear that narrative passes the pragmatic test that theory fails. On the side of theory, I can be inspired by Kant's analysis of the good will, by the ideal of treating all people as ends in themselves and not merely as means to my (or our) ends, and by the idea that a person has a dignity but not a price. But that inspiration may prove impotent when it comes to my attitudes and actions. As a student I may sell my soul to the devil, proving that my price trumps my dignity, by cheating on an exam or paper about Kant's ethics so as to get the grades I need to get into law school. As a teacher I may give brilliant lectures on Kant's ethics without ceasing to view those around me, both at work and at home, primarily as means to my ends.

But the inspiration that comes from hagiography, be it the story of Mother Teresa or of the Chambonnais, may prove equally impotent. A passage from the New Testament comes to mind.

> But be doers of the word, and not merely hearers who deceive themselves. For if any are hearers of the word and not doers, they are like those who look at themselves in a mirror; for they look at themselves and, on going away, immediately *forget* what they were like. But those who look into the perfect law, the law of liberty, and *persevere*, being not hearers who *forget* but doers who act—they will be blessed in their doing. (James 1:22–25, NRSV, emphasis added)[6]

James, of course, is speaking about reading the Bible, but he might just as easily have been talking about the imperative force of stories about saints. One can be inspired one moment, seeing oneself in the narrative mirror and feeling called to radical responsibility, and in the next moment revert to what Kant calls the "dear self" [*das liebe Selbst*], neutralizing that imperative force by a certain forgetting in the service of self-deceptive self-interest.[7]

This is not to deny that the lives of saints can influence us. As Elie Wiesel writes, "Often because of one story or one book or one person, we are able to make a different choice, a choice for humanity, for life."[8] But it is not automatic. Jesus' parable of the sower comes to mind.[9] Only the seed that fell on good soil produced a harvest. The seed that fell on the path, or on rocky ground, or among thorns did not. We need to ask about the good soil in which the seeds of hagiographic narrative can be productive.

Since Kant obviously expected moral theory to influence our attitudes and actions, we might first ask, if only for purposes of possible comparison, how he thought it might do so. He is emphatic that it is not by teaching us the difference between right and wrong, good and evil. The concept of the good will "already dwells in the natural sound understanding [*dem natürlichen gesunden Verstande beiwohnt*] and needs not so much to be taught as merely to be elucidated [*aufgeklärt*]."[10] Thus, "we do not in the least try to teach reason anything new but only make it attend [*aufmerksam macht*], as Socrates, to its own principle—and thereby do we show that neither science nor philosophy is needed in order to know what one must do to be honest and good, and even wise and virtuous."[11] The reference to elucidation and to Socrates' doctrine of knowledge as recollection suggest that what moral philosophy adds to prephilosophical moral common sense is knowledge, critical, reflective knowledge, perhaps as distinguished from uncritical, unreflective knowledge (mere opinion or belief). But the reference to *Aufmerksamkeit* is doubtless the key to the efficacy of this knowledge. It signifies attentiveness, alertness, watchfulness, and vigilance, thus suggesting that more than cognitive clarity and certainty are involved.[12] The formula might be this: arguments without attentiveness fail to influence attitudes and actions.

Other portions of Kant's text point us in this direction. Though we know what we need to know without philosophy's help, morals "are liable to all kinds of corruption"[13] and innocence is "easily led astray" by an internal "counterweight to all the commands of duty" in the form of our own "needs and inclinations, whose total satisfaction is summed up under the name of happiness."[14] So what we need is not just clarity but vigilance, the *habit* of remembering what we know about right and wrong at the crucial moment, rather than conveniently forgetting it (the rocky soil, perhaps) or allowing our desires to convert what we know into "perplexity" and "ambiguity"[15] (the thorns, perhaps). But such a *habit* is not obviously the product of reading the *Grundlegung* and understanding it, of doing well in Ethics 101, or of writing the best paper in a graduate seminar on deontological ethics from Kant to Korsgaard.

What Kant's argument calls for, though he doesn't seem to realize it, is something more like a spiritual discipline than philosophical reflection. Such a practice would need to include at least (1) a regular habit of reminding myself of what I know, so as to make it harder to forget it in the moment of (self)temptation, and (2) a regular habit of self-examination in which, with the help of a hermeneutics of suspicion, I seek to bring to the light of day the hidden tricks with which I most effectively manage to deceive myself. Such a practice might very well need to be communal as well as private.

Wyschogrod also points us in this direction. She writes that to understand a saintly life is to be "swept up by its imperative force. The comprehension of a saint's life understood from within the sphere of hagiography is a *practice* through which the addressee is gathered into the narrative so as to extend and elaborate it with her/his own life."[16] There are three key elements in this passage, which we might think of as essential minerals in the soil in which the stories of saints can be fruitful.

First, there is the idea of a practice. This notion is long since familiar to those who speak the language of spiritual disciplines.[17] In the context of virtue ethics, Alasdair MacIntyre has given a careful conceptual analysis of the notion of a practice.[18] In either context, it is clear that saintliness is not simply a matter of theoretical insight.

Second, there is the notion of an essential passivity. I am to be "swept up" and "gathered" into the story by its "imperative force." This force is not the power of the better argument. Mixing his metaphors with poetic abandon, Plato talks about being "knocked out" by an argument and presents it as a "countercharm" to the spell cast upon us by poetry.[19] He even attributes "imperative force" to arguments when he introduces a short sermon with the words "Let us fancy, then, that we hear our present argument exhorting us in tones like these."[20] But stories are not arguments, and their force must be of a different sort.

Nor is the passivity in question that to which Levinas points us, in which the call of the Other as the face, or the saying in every said, is always already prior not just to my agency (intentionality) but even to my apperception (identity). For what is at issue is not the influence of the

Other upon me, but the influence of some other Other that enables me to see and to hear that first Other from the standpoint of responsibility rather than merely that of enjoyment, dwelling, fecundity, *conatus essendi*, and so forth. That first Other and the other Other, whom Levinas calls the Third, are always present to me. But the saintly Other embedded in a story may or may not be present to me, and even when the saintly Other is present, I may forget the "imperative force" of the argument before it can make any real difference in my life. Like God in Augustine's *Confessions*, the saintly Other is one toward whom and away from whom I can turn my attentiveness. The practice(s) already referred to are the deliberate attempt to put myself in the presence of saintly Others and thus render myself vulnerable to the "imperative force" of their stories.[21] We should remember that, especially in the Buddhist and Christian contexts to which Wyschogrod refers, reading the lives of saints is either part of or an extension of reading scripture. It is not reading for relaxation or excitement but a special spiritual discipline. Passivity and activity would seem to be mutually implicative.

Thirdly, there is what Kierkegaard's Climacus calls truth as subjectivity. It will be recalled that his definition goes like this: "*An objective uncertainty, held fast through appropriation with the most passionate inwardness, is the truth*, the highest truth there is for an *existing* person."[22] The reference to objective uncertainty is a reminder that so far as theoretical knowledge is concerned, we have approximation at best. This theme is echoed in Wyschogrod's point about the epistemic weakness of arguments. But for Climacus, the emphasis is on appropriation, on the way in which what I believe effectively shapes my attitudes and actions.

Wyschogrod points us in this direction when she speaks of the consumer of hagiography as the "addressee."[23] The story about the saint is about the reader as well. As with the icon, I do not so much gaze at it as find it gazing at me.[24] It is about what the saint has been and what the reader is to become. This takes us beyond the Kantian "elucidation" [*Aufklärung*] of a principle to the point where the reader is "to extend and elaborate [the story] with her/his own life."

No doubt in the chemistry of the good soil for stories of saints, these three minerals—practice, passivity, and truth as subjectivity—interact in such a way as to require one another. As with the three-legged milking stool (to mix our own metaphors), to take one leg away is to invite disaster. I am to see that saintly lives call me to conversion (subjectivity), and that to this end I need to sustain my attention toward them as addressing me (practice), so as to be moved by their "imperative force" (passivity).

In order to explore these themes more closely and concretely, and to see if other themes emerge, let us turn to *Lest Innocent Blood Be Shed*. In one sense it is a perfect example of Wyschogrod's "argument," for she is writing philosophy, not hagiographic narrative. In another sense the Chambonnais exceed her conceptual frame, and it is this combination of fit and misfit that makes them especially interesting to me. Wyschogrod gives an essentially secular definition of the saint. Saints are "those who put themselves totally at the disposal of the Other." More specifically, a saintly life is defined "as one in which compassion for the Other, *irrespective of cost to the saint,* is the primary trait."[25] According to her full and formal definition, the saint is *"one whose adult life in its entirety is devoted to the alleviation of sorrow (the psychological suffering) and pain (the physical suffering) that afflicts other persons without distinction of rank or group or, alternatively, that afflicts sentient beings, whatever the cost to the saint in pain or sorrow."*[26] Wyschogrod acknowledges that linguistically speaking, there is a link between saintliness and religion that is not captured by her definition. In the Christian tradition, this typically involves theistic belief and, we might add, practices. Since her definition overtly includes Buddhist saintliness, we doubtless need also to speak of a religiousness that is not theistic, or at best quasi-theistic (in relation to one Buddha or another). However, she says, "my account of who saints are does not mandate any given religious or cultural context, even if saints have traditionally emerged within specifiable theological and institutional frameworks."[27] So her secular definition is an extended, perhaps even metaphorical, usage.

In defense of her definition, Wyschogrod immediately begins talking about mysticism and argues that "not all saints are mystics nor are all mystics saints . . . the mystical aspect of experience is functionally distinct from the radical altruism that is *constitutive* of saintly praxis and depends on the *need* of the Other."[28] There is a point to this secular, metaphorical definition of saintliness. We are tempted to speak of the infinite responsibility involved in radical altruism as the supererogatory, above and beyond the call of duty. By contrast, Kierkegaard and Levinas argue that it is simply our sacred duty in the face of the Other. But whether we use the language of moral heroism or not, it is a matter of empirical fact that such saintly action sometimes occurs apart from religious belief and practice.

At least on the surface. There are at least three ways in which secular saintliness may involve religious influences. The story of the civil rights movement associated with Martin Luther King Jr. is largely a beautiful story of cooperation between secular Jews and devoutly Protestant African Americans. Those secular Jews, some of whom, perhaps many, did not believe in a personal Creator or participate in the practices of a synagogue, were for at least part of their adult lives saints in Wyschogrod's sense. But might their immediate secularity have been religiously mediated in various ways?

First, they may well have been inspired to engage in nonviolent resistance on behalf of those suffering personal and economic oppression by Gandhi and King, whose religious inspiration is patent. Second, their intolerance for injustice may have been formed by Jewish traditions (1) whose biblical origin is undeniable, (2) from whose religious sources they were estranged, but (3) by which they were nevertheless influenced in ways of which they were not necessarily aware.[29] Third, the Bible says that we are all created in the image of God, the God who is passionately on the side of the poor and oppressed, the widow, the orphan, and the stranger. Secular saintliness may testify to that createdness (the *imago Dei* in the saint responding to the *imago Dei* in the Other) just as religiously supported oppression or indifference attests to our fallenness.[30]

While all of this may well be true, it is not what I wish to argue or what concerns me about the secular definition of saintliness. Wyschogrod virtually equates religion with mysticism and then affirms that "not all saints are mystics nor are all mystics saints." This is doubtless true whether one's account of what is constitutive in saintliness focuses on the horizontal relation to the human Other, or the vertical relation to God, or to the combination of both.[31] But it is also misleading in the sense that it leads our attention away from the religious dimension of saintliness that is built into the very concept "saint" before its secular redefinition. The dichotomy between mystical and secular is what logicians call an incomplete division, since it does not exhaust the possibilities. Since Wyschogrod is not proceeding deductively, we don't have the fallacy of incomplete division, but perhaps we do encounter an analogous lack of conceptual clarity. For there are varieties of religious belief and practice that are not happily described as mystical but that may be very relevant to our question about the soil in which saintliness, in her sense of radical altruism, flourishes. If we bracket the religious under the heading of mysticism, we direct our attention away from an important set of influences that may be important both in producing saints (in Wyschogrod's worldly sense) and in giving them power to affect our own lives. My concern is not to argue that all radical altruism is always somehow religious, but to open a space in which to explore the link between non-mystical piety and worldly saintliness.[32]

So I turn to Le Chambon. The Chambonnais at once exemplify and exceed Wyschogrod's definition of the saint. At least during the course of

World War II, they made of Le Chambon an astonishingly safe haven for thousands, mostly children and mostly Jews, fleeing from the cruel violence of the Nazis and their Vichy collaborators. Their village became a city of refuge like one of those described in Deuteronomy, which offered shelter "lest innocent blood be shed in your land which the Lord your God gives you for an inheritance, and so the guilt of bloodshed be upon you."[33] At great cost and risk to themselves, they placed themselves at the disposal of those who were frightened, hungry, homeless, and in mortal peril.[34] Their saintliness could hardly have been more worldly. And yet it retained the verbal link between saintliness and the overtly religious,[35] making it far more than a semantic issue. That link was constitutive of their creative and costly compassion. I want to explore that link under three headings: piety, proclamation, and passivity.

The overwhelming majority of the Chambonnais were of Huguenot heritage, French Calvinists. Their leader was the local pastor, André Trocmé. He was "a passionately religious person" whose "belief in God was at the living center of the rescue efforts of the village."[36] His was a "person-to-God piety" that made him find the social gospel as he encountered it in his studies at Union Theological Seminary in New York, in spite of its ethical, worldly focus, seem "too rational for his deeply devout mind."[37] His desire, as expressed in his own notebooks, was "not to be separated from Jesus" and, when he once seriously considered trying to assassinate Hitler, he decided against it because, again in his own words, "I feared separating myself from Jesus Christ, who refused to use arms to prevent the crime that was being prepared for him."[38]

This notion of union with Christ is doubtless what Hallie has in mind when speaking of the "deep streak of mysticism" in Trocmé and of what he himself called the "abyss of mysticism" from which Magda, his wife, helped him to draw back. But his is not the Neoplatonic or Asian mysticism in which the many are dissolved back into the One beyond language and difference. It is the mysticism, if that is the right term, of a deeply personal I-Thou relation. Buber sharply distinguishes the latter from the mysticism of *Versenkung*. He writes: "What has to be given up is not the I, as most mystics suppose: the I is indispensable for any relation, including the highest, which always presupposes an I and You. What has to be given up is not the I but that false drive for self-affirmation."[39]

Trocmé's piety was shaped by saintly influences. Early on there was Kindler, the German soldier he met as a youth during World War I. A conscientious objector, he had received permission to serve even in battle as an unarmed telegrapher because "I shall not kill your brother; I shall kill no Frenchman. God has revealed to us that a Christian must not kill, ever. We [a reference to the sect to which he belonged] never carry arms."[40] But by far the greatest inspiration came from Jesus Christ, who was more but not less than a saintly influence that shaped Trocmé's thoughts and actions decisively as Trocmé became the leader of nonviolent resistance to violent injustice. He was motivated by belief in "a life-and-death ethics that God, through Moses and Jesus, had commanded men to follow."[41] But it wasn't just a matter of a divine command. It was especially the example of Jesus. He believed not only that "in the Bible God told us not to kill our fellowman" but also "gave that commandment utter clarity in the life and death of Jesus Christ."[42] He believed

> that God had shown mankind how precious man was to Him by taking the form of a human being and coming down to help human beings . . . that Jesus had demonstrated that love for mankind by dying for us on the cross. And if these beliefs sounded too mysterious, he knew that Jesus had himself refused to do violence to mankind, refused to harm the enemies of his precious existence as a human being. In short, Jesus was for Trocmé the *embodied* forgiveness of sins, and staying close to Jesus meant always being ready to forgive your enemies instead of torturing and killing them.[43]

What moved Trocmé most was the *example* and the words of Jesus, and to be with Jesus meant "imitating Jesus's example and obeying his words."[44]

Because Trocmé had Kindler and, above all, Jesus Christ as saintly influences, the Chambonnais had him as a saintly role model to inspire their own dangerous devotion to the despised and endangered.[45] He was, we might say, the saint whose life influenced his family and his congregation to become a city of refuge. He not only "set an example" for the Chambonnais, but he "generated impulses" toward "imitating Jesus' example and obeying his words." He inspired their caring with his own, "not by command but by contagion." Even at home he "expressed his morality by embodying it."[46]

Hallie believed that goodness had happened in Le Chambon and he wrote his book in the attempt to "understand that goodness face-to-face."[47] He asks a question that Levinas all but completely ignores, as if it is obvious that ought simply implies can: "How did a life-and-death ethic become incarnate across the whole commune of Le Chambon?"[48] We might say that for Trocmé himself, a large part of the answer was a piety based in *imitatio Christi*, personal devotion to Jesus as the savior who in life and in death embodied nonviolent forgiveness and compassion. As he himself became an analogous embodiment, he inspired[49] a whole village to become embodied goodness.[50] As societies, including their moral philosophies, become increasingly secular, the possibility of radical altruism doesn't simply disappear, but this soil in which saintliness can grow is increasingly eroded away.

In stressing the importance of the body of the saint, Wyschogrod writes, "Not proclamation or argument, but the flesh acquires general meaning."[51] This linkage of (religious) proclamation to (philosophical) argument and the joint dismissal of both represents another way in which the Chambonnais are misfits in relation to the secular definition of saintliness. By whatever name one designates proclamation, whether preaching, teaching, or kerygma, it played a crucial role in the goodness that happened in Le Chambon. The previous section emphasized embodiment, but not an embodiment cut off from discourse. For Trocmé himself, staying close to Jesus meant "imitating [his] example *and obeying his words.*"[52] The pastor's sermons were the soil in which saintliness grew, or at least an indispensable mineral in that soil, along with his example.

The weekly sermon was a big deal in Le Chambon. Magda Trocmé writes, "On Sundays the sermon was something very important, because at that time there were no movies, no special lectures. The sermon was something that everyone wanted to hear"![53] Without even mentioning television, the pastor's wife invites us to compare the moral formation of those who regularly expose themselves to biblical preaching with those whose world view is primarily shaped by today's media.

Of course, this wasn't just any preaching.[54] Pastor Trocmé's favorite texts were the parable of the Good Samaritan and the Sermon on the Mount.[55] He preached resistance to violent hatred of the Nazis, but not by fighting fire with fire. His commitment to nonviolence meant that this resistance could not just be a counter-violence.[56] And he preached obedience to the state *unless* such obedience meant violating a conscience informed by the law of God.[57] Both the context and the pastor's own deep conviction testified that the ideas set forth were not just the cream of his culture's crop but commands of God.

The Sunday morning sermon was not the only mode of proclamation in the parish. Trocmé established thirteen Bible study groups whose thirteen leaders were known as the *responsables*. He met with this group every two weeks (and one-on-one on a weekly basis) to discuss a biblical passage relevant to their situation. They would then lead discussion of these passages with thirteen groups of parishioners, which included many young people. The focus of these discussions would be nonviolent resistance to evil. Trocmé writes, "It was there [in these groups], not elsewhere, that we received from God solutions to complex problems, problems we had to solve in order to shelter and to hide the Jews . . . Nonviolence was not a theory superimposed upon reality; it was an itinerary that we explored day after day in communal prayer and in obedience to the commands of the Spirit."[58] These groups became the "nervous system" of the village: "When the Germans conquered France these groups and their leaders became the communications network and the moving spirits of a village committed to the cause of saving terrified foreigners from their persecutors."[59] No doubt this part of the story was due in large part to the fact that when he was growing up, Trocmé experienced prayer and Bible study not restricted to Sunday mornings, but part of daily life, both in his home and in the Union of Saint-Quentin, a Protestant youth group to which he belonged.[60]

In the Christian context in which the Chambonnais worked, proclamation is the setting forth of the word of God, and to be influenced by proclamation is to listen, to be attentively vulnerable to the Word of God. Karl Barth's threefold analysis is helpful at this point. There is the preached Word of God, which points beyond itself to the Bible, which is its basis. The Bible, as the written Word of God, points beyond itself to Jesus Christ. As God incarnate, he is the revealed Word of God.[61]

We can now see Pastor Trocmé as the middle term in the proclamation that helped make goodness happen in Le Chambon. He was both its product and its producer. As he prepared to preach and to lead the discussion of scripture with the *responsables*, he was listening to the revealed Word of God (Jesus Christ) as witnessed to in the written Word of God (the Bible), or, we might say, he was listening to the embodied Word of God[62] as pointed to in the preaching of the prophets and apostles.[63] In relation to the congregation, of course, he was himself the preacher. They listened to his proclamation, which pointed back to Jesus Christ through the witness of the Bible. Together they were shaped by the proclamation of the Word of God, by listening to the voice of God.

I speak here of Christian proclamation for the obvious reason that Le Chambon was a Christian community. No doubt similar analyses can be made, mutatis mutandis, for other religious communities.[64] We would do well not to dismiss proclamation too quickly if we would see more saintly behavior in a very unholy world. For it just might be the case that saintliness is to a very large degree a matter of whose voice I (and we) are vulnerable to as attentive listeners. The cacophony of voices in the secular "cultures" of modernity and postmodernity is not likely to be productive of saintly lives.[65]

Earlier Wyschogrod (along with MacIntyre and various traditions of spirituality) called the concept of a practice to our attention. Here we can see that both the pastor and his congregation were engaging in a practice crucial to their saintly behavior insofar as they deliberately and regularly turned their attention to the Word of God, not as an object to be apprehended (intellectually) or appreciated (aesthetically) but as a subject, a voice whose "addressees" they were. Doubtless their interpretations did not rise above the level of approximation. But instead of anathematizing those with different interpretations of scripture and of the Incarnation at its center, they focused on appropriation, on being "doers of the word, and not merely hearers who deceive themselves" (James 1:22).

I turn now to my final theme: passivity. Earlier I distinguished the passivity to which Wyschogrod points, that of being "swept up" and "gathered" into the story of a saintly life by its "imperative force," from the passivity to which Levinas points, in which the call of the Other as the face or the saying in every said is always already prior not just to my agency (intentionality) but even to my apperception (identity). The latter involves the influence of the Other upon me while the former involves the influence of some other Other that enables me to care about that first Other and not just about myself and "my own." Now I want to call attention to a powerful intertwining of the two in the story of the Chambonnais.

In the story of the saints of Le Chambon, Levinasian passivity gets expressed in the language of necessity. Hallie found the Chambonnais consistently reluctant to use the basic vocabulary of moral praise and even more so the language of supererogation. They simply did what had to be done and typically replied to Hallie, "How can you call us 'good'? We were doing what had to be done. Who else could help them? And what has all this to do with goodness? Things had to be done, that's all, and we happened to be there to do them."[66] Thus one of the women whose home became a city of refuge said, "Look. Look. Who else would have taken care of them if we didn't? They needed our help, and they needed it *then*" and even the children saw "what the rest of the Chambonnais saw: the *necessity* to help that shivering Jew standing there in your door, and the necessity not to betray him or her to harmdoers."[67] Hallie presents Magda Trocmé as holding that it is better "to open the door than to keep it closed. And the reason that it is better is simple for her: that person there—that pursued, terrified person before her—needs help, not a closed door. *That person's need* is the basis of ethics."[68] Incarnate need here gives rise to the necessity of an action of which, by virtue of that necessity, the agent is more nearly passive than active. Thus Édouard Theis, the assistant pastor who had been arrested by the Vichy police along with Trocmé and a third helper and then, while later fleeing arrest by the Gestapo, became active in the Cimade, the underground railway that smuggled Jews into Switzerland, said of his "heroics" (not his term by any means), "It was not reasonable. But you know, I had to do it anyway."[69]

This necessity is not that of coercion any more than the corresponding passivity is any kind of quietism. In Kierkegaardian language,[70] this necessity is the kind of spontaneity usually associated only with self-love. Neighbor-love in the sense of radical altruism must be commanded precisely because while romantic love and friendship are naturally spontaneous, this overcoming of self-love is not. But it can *become* so, can become, like the faith to which it is linked, a second immediacy, and that is the goal of ethical formation. It would seem that the Chambonnais had reached this level of moral maturity,[71] for they said that it was "the most *natural* thing in the world to help these people."[72] Hallie writes that if we would understand this story, "we must see how *easy* it was for them to refuse to give up their consciences, to refuse to participate in hatred, betrayal and murder, and to help the desperate adults and the terrified children who knocked on their doors in Le Chambon."[73]

Natural? Easy? Hallie says that to understand this part of the story, "we must also see the many elements that came together to make these things happen."[74] His narrative makes it clear that the practice of exposing oneself to proclamation was one of the most important of these elements. One of the women who helped, whose husband was a Communist from whom she had to hide the fact that many of the refugee children in their *pension* were nonpaying guests in hiding, acknowledged that following the Trocmés was dangerous, but said, "Oh, well, it was a matter of conscience. Whatever they asked for was just what my conscience would want. Why—I just could not have done anything else but help them and the refugees!" When asked about this conscience, "she said that the most important influence on her thinking was the story of the Good Samaritan and the commandment to love one's neighbor as oneself."[75] She embodied Levinasian necessity/passivity. In the presence of the need of the Other, she could not help but help. But this passivity was mediated, as was typical of the Chambonnais, by the passivity of sustained vulnerability to proclamation and thereby to the other Others, in this case Jesus and Pastor Trocmé, who helped make it "natural" and "easy." Their influence, both by example and by words, helped to fashion consciences that were extraordinary indeed, at least in the historical, statistical sense, even if morally speaking, those guided by those consciences only did what had to be done.

From early on the Trocmés knew that their work was dangerous. Against the possibility that André Trocmé might be arrested and deported to a concentration camp in Central Europe, Magda Trocmé kept a suitcase packed with warm clothes. In early 1943, Pastor Trocmé and two close associates were indeed arrested by the Vichy police.[76] But alas. The suitcase was empty. That empty suitcase is a perfect symbol for the saintliness of the Chambonnais. On the one hand it signifies the mortal danger in which they worked, especially after the Germans moved south in 1942 into what had previously been "Free" France under the Vichy regime. The Gestapo was quite capable of massacring a whole village they found to be resisting German rule. On the other hand, it signifies the self-sacrificial generosity of the entire enterprise, for the clothes had obviously been given away to refugees in need.

But the gift given by the Chambonnais was not just the clothes they gave to refugees, or the food, housing, and hiding. Their gift was a gift that keeps on giving. After his book was published, Hallie received a letter from a seventeen-year-old girl. Her parents gave the book to her when they saw how depressed she was becoming while studying the Holocaust. She wrote, "I have finished the book now, and I wish I could tell you how much it has helped me. Every time I will look at your book in my bookcase, it will be like hearing . . . two words . . . Don't cry!"[77]

For Hallie this is an especially precious letter; for it reflects his own situation. As a moral philosopher who had been studying human cruelty, he was himself in despair. "My own passion was a yearning for realistic hope. I wanted to believe that the examined life[78] was more precious than this Hell I had dug for myself in studying evil . . . I needed this understanding [of how goodness happened in Le Chambon] in order to redeem myself—and possibly others—from the coercion of despair."[79] If only war and prejudice and cruelty were possible, "then life was too heavy a burden for me. The lies I would have to tell my children in order to raise them in hope—which children need the way plants need sunlight—would make the burden unbearable."[80] Having rescued many Jews from deportation and death, the Chambonnais rescued the teenage girl and the philosopher from despair.[81] Hallie's symbol for this is the rainbow, which comes to him from two sources. He was lecturing in Minneapolis a few years after the appearance of his book. In the discussion a woman rose and said, "Well, you have been speaking about the village that saved the lives of all three of my children." After a stunned silence, she added, "The Holocaust was storm, lightning, thunder, wind, rain, yes. And Le Chambon was the rainbow." Hallie comments:

> We understood each other. We understood that the rainbow is one of the richest images in the Bible. The rainbow is the sign God put up in heaven after the great Flood. The sign meant: "never again shall all flesh be cut off." In His explanation of the rainbow, God repeated the phrase "never again," and ever since the Holocaust, Jews have been repeating that phrase.
>
> The rainbow reminds God and man that life is precious to God, that God offers not only sentimental hope, but a promise that living will have the last word, not killing. The rainbow means realistic hope. For that woman whose three daughters were saved by the villagers of Le Chambon, history is not hopeless, because of the unshakable fact that lives were saved in Le Chambon . . .
>
> The story of Le Chambon gives me an unsullied joy.[82]

Hosting the Stranger and the Pilgrim

A Christian Theological Reflection

GRAHAM WARD

Under the Immigration Act in Britain, it has been estimated that in 2007, up to 25,000 people were detained at places throughout the country known as Immigration Removal Centres (IRCs). Currently, the government plans to increase IRCs and "holding facilities" by 60 percent in the coming years. In the same year, 4,200 foreign prisoners were deported along with 63,140 illegal immigrants. In the first quarter of 2008, government statistics refer to 2,305 people being held, 1,980 of whom were men and 35 of whom were children. The situation is no better elsewhere. In the United States, Immigration and Customs Enforcement detained 311,213 people in 2007, and as tighter border patrols come into force Amnesty International now speaks openly of "Fortress Europe." In their report to mark World Refugee Day and the start of Refugee Week on June 20, 2005, examining the treatment of migrants and asylum seekers not only in Britain but also in Spain and Italy, they conclude:

> The reports show some common trends in the three countries. Unsatisfactory medical care, and unhygienic and harsh living conditions in detention centres, expose individuals (in particular children and vulnerable people) to traumatic experiences. The reports also noted the ill-treatment of individuals detained at reception centres and excessive use of force by police carrying out deportations. Border guards are poorly trained and the process of deciding asylum claims is often unfair and inefficient . . . It is difficult for the asylum

seekers to obtain the legal advice they need to challenge the legality of their detention or expulsion orders. In Spain, AI fears the right to seek asylum is in danger of extinction. People fleeing grave human rights violations are being prevented from reaching the country to seek protection. In Italy, foreign nationals detained in temporary holding centres have been physically assaulted by law enforcement officers and supervisory staff, and subject to excessive use of tranquillisers.[1]

Stories emerge from these IRCs and reception centers of rape and suicide, hunger strikes, uprisings, racism, harassment, overcrowding, imprisonment without trial, and the suspension of that axiom of democratic freedom, habeas corpus. For example, at a removal center in Colnbrook, UK, during the period January to August 2007, twenty-three incidents of assaults on staff and twenty-two incidents of assaults on detainees were recorded.

In honor of the work Edith Wyschogrod has done in the field of ethics and politics and as a continuation of her abiding concern with the stranger and the other, with human atrocities and death camps, and with the problem of the place from which one speaks about these victims, I want to conduct a theological reflection on hosting the stranger and the pilgrim. I need to add that the essay is explicitly political, that is, polemical—not necessarily with respect to Wyschogrod's work (for which I have the highest esteem), but with respect to the ethical demands the plight of migrants makes upon all of us. Throughout Derrida's essay for Levinas *"En ce moment même dans cet ouvrage me voici,"* where Derrida conducts a polyvocal examination of his own response to Levinas, one phrase (ultimately Levinas's) acts as a refrain throughout: *il aura obligé.* It is a complicated future anterior, translated awkwardly into English as "he will have obligated."[2] But the French plays on the personal pronoun *il*—it raises the question of who or what is obligating. It refers back, for Levinas, to *illeity*—that which constitutes the wholly otherness of the other and which renders me always and only in the accusative: *me voici.* Another English translation, slightly archaic but one I think Levinas would have approved, would yield "it will have beholden," that is, held (me) captive, claimed (me) as hostage. I emphasize the phrase here because there is a summons in Wyschogrod's writing that obligates, that calls me to respond. And because I speak from another place (as a Christian theologian), a place which is not Wyschogrod's but which is not at all transparent to myself either, my response cannot reiterate Wyschogrod's speaking. I speak otherwise, and that otherwise may indeed contest Wyschogrod's voice.

I know she is not afraid of such contestation. Her understanding of what it means to be heterological, to write heterologically, ensures a recognition that neither her writing nor my own stand monolithically. "The heterological historian realizes that the historical artifact she has fabricated is inherently incomplete: there is always some condition that threatens her narrative, calls it into question . . . [This] is the heterologist's recognition that her narrative requires the supplement of the cataclysm."[3] To be truly ethical, to be truly responsible, we must interrupt. For the written text finds a place, becomes itself a place where what is said is given a stability by becoming a matrix of interrelated themes, a thesis, and that place has to be unsettled for both the writing and the writer to regain something of what Wyschogrod calls the non-place of the ethical. The displacement always carries the possibility of a negative violence.[4] But I am confident that Wyschogrod also recognizes that the issues here and their calls to respond—mass human extermination, of the systematic violation of some human beings by other human beings—are more important than whether two academics agree or disagree with each other. We can contest because we are obligated prior to any contestation—obligated by the summons to bear witness and speak, obligated to hear our own speaking interrupted.

I want to begin my reflection on the migrant by turning to a strange father from whom Judaism, Christianity and Islam emerged, and a midrash on his journey into exile found in the Christian scriptures under the title of the *Letter to the Hebrews*. It is a letter that traditionally has been attributed to St. Paul; whether this is so or not is irrelevant for what I wish to pursue. What I think is evident from the *Letter* is that the writer understands what I will term the fierce spirituality of being a migrant, that body which is marked by a wandering. The author is certainly a *Wandersmann*. Listen:

> By faith Abraham obeyed when he was called to go out to the place which he would *afterwards* receive as an inheritance. And he went out, not knowing where he was going. By faith he sojourned [*par-ōkēsev*] in the land of promise as in a foreign country [*hōs allotrian*], dwelling in tents with Isaac and Jacob, the heirs with him of the same promise; for he waited for a city which has foundations, whose builder and maker is God . . . Therefore from one man, and him as good as dead, were born as many as the stars of the sky in multitude—innumerable as the sand which is by the seashore. These all died in faith, not having received the promises, but having seen them afar off, they were assured of them, embraced them, and confessed themselves strangers and pilgrims [*xenoi kai parepidēmoi*] on

the earth. For those who say such things declare plainly that they seek a homeland . . . that is a heavenly country. Therefore God is not ashamed to be called their God; for he has prepared a city for them. (11:8–16)

We observe that Abraham comes from a long line of wanderers, but at the heart of this wandering is a curious dialectic. It begins with the expulsion from paradise and continues with Cain, who is condemned to be a fugitive and vagabond upon the earth. But it is Cain who also builds the first city. The narrative dialectic throughout the Hebrew Bible and throughout the Acts of the Apostles and the missionary church is one of migration and community-construction. The wandering always involves a searching and a desiring—for refuge, for the promised land, for Jerusalem, for the heavenly city, for the kingdom of God. And the community-construction is always subject to the contingencies of time and the specificities of place: a tent in the desert, a city open to being conquered, a community vulnerable to persecution and diaspora, a church whose boundaries are invisible and which, in its central liturgy, gathers together around a bread which is broken and distributed.

What is to be made of this, theologically, but that as creatures of time, embedded always in places, we are by nature restless until we find our rest in God (to quote Augustine). Made in the image of God, we are wanderers and builders of temporary habitations. But if this is so, then if this condition is written into the nature of being human before and in God, it is grace. It is a gift to us, for from it will issue our redemption. Why? We return to Abraham: because we are stretched out towards a future hope in faith. And anyone who knows what such a stretching out means, anyone who knows what it is to live in that condition, given over to the grace of God in a radical dependency, will understand why I call it a "fierce spirituality." To live for a promise that is not received, to confess you are a stranger and pilgrim on the earth, to set out not knowing where you will end up, for a place which will be received only retrospectively: that is not easy. But I suggest nevertheless that this is our human condition as God has graciously fashioned it. Yahweh says to Abraham at the beginning of their relationship, "Get you out of your country, from your kindred and from your father's house, to a land that I will show you" (Genesis 12:1). So Abram (at that time) departs; he journeys into ever deeper exile. From Ur of the Chaldees to Haran, to Bethel, to Egypt, to Canaan, to Hebron, to a place, we are told, between "Kadesh and Shur," to Beersheba, to the field of "Ephron the son of Zohar the Hittite" near Mamre, where he was buried. The Palestinian poet Mahmoud Darwish writes: "We travel like other people, but we return nowhere. As if travelling is the way of clouds."[5]

Allow me to return to that phrase used in the *Letter to the Hebrews*, "strangers and pilgrims on the earth." I return to it with what to my mind is Wyschogrod's most difficult and searching book, *An Ethics of Remembering*. There she narrates a story of a chance encounter in New York City with a homeless man called Billy Joe. Although Billy Joe is evidently injured and in need of medical treatment, he does not respond to Wyschogrod's offer to drive him to the hospital. Instead he walks on and asks her only to remember his name. Named, he is but nevertheless a figure for the other, the one outside the systems of social exchange: a stranger and a pilgrim on the earth. His having a name, his naming himself, does not make the other familiar. Rather the name intensifies the mystery of who Billy Joe is. Not that I wish to wrap his situation in romantic narratives by employing the language of "mystery." All I am attempting to point out is a certain depth of human otherness and even incomprehension that opens with the passing of this stranger. His momentary pausing before a loaded furniture van in a New York street and his encounter with an internationally known philosopher raise questions about what is it to be (and who it is that is) a stranger and a pilgrim on the earth. Is there a logic binding the stranger to the pilgrim? Is the stranger always in a sense a pilgrim, and the pilgrim a stranger? What renders the stranger strange? What sets the pilgrim adrift in "the way of clouds"? And what otherness is figured in this stranger and this pilgrim?

The Greek opens up some possibilities I wish to develop. *Xenoi kai parepidēmoi* brings together two resonant words that only to a certain extent are synonyms. *Xenos* (the singular form) bequeaths to us the word *xenophobia*, the fear of foreigners. For that is what the stranger is, one who does not belong to this collective (this city, this state, this nation, this race): *Xenē* is a foreign country, *xenos* is he who has his home elsewhere, or nowhere. The stranger is someone who is not known, who has no relations, no acquaintance, no ties with other members of the community. In Greek it can sometimes be used as a synonym for a mercenary: existing outside the network of reciprocal responsibilities, familial duties, customs and even laws, the foreigner threatens to plunder, steal, smash social bonds asunder. But in Greek *xenos* can also be used as friend or guest. It can take this connotation because it occupies a place in the semantic field of *xenia* (hospitality) and *xenios* (hospitable); they share the same root. *To xenion* is the gift given by a guest to a host; the verb *xenoō* means both to be in foreign country and to be a guest, or to be entertained as a guest. *Xenos*, then, can be either friend or foe.

The translation of *parepidēmoi* (singular: *parepidēos*) as *pilgrims* reinforces how the strangers have left their home or have no home. The English translation lacks something of the ambivalence of the Greek. It is a rare word in ancient Greek and is found only three times in the New Testament. The more usual Greek terms would be *odoiporos* or *pros-epidēmos* (traveler) or *planēs* (wanderer) or *metanastēs* (one who has left his home). *Parepidēos* is a combination of *para* and *epidēos*—where *epidēmos* can describe either the one who stays at home (and is nonmigratory) or the one who is residing in a place as an alien (the migrant). In the Septuagint translation of the Hebrew scriptures, it is found once in relation to Abraham (Gen. 23:4), when Sarah has died and he is trying to buy from the Hittites a plot for her to be buried in; it describes his status as a resident without the rights of citizenship. *Parepidēmoi* are transitory people situated in places that are in-between. They are occupants of a no-man's-land.

Both strangers and pilgrims are people in transit, like Billy Joe, like Abraham; they are people belonging to a diaspora. They are temporally attached to a place, where they are to be welcomed or they are to be shunned. In Wyschogrod's account of Billy Joe, there are, significantly, two descriptors for the stranger (the irony of which I do not doubt she is alert to). One precedes the other. The first is Wyschogrod's "an old, homeless, African-American man," and the second is his "my name, Billy Joe."[6] The movement is from the anonymity of the other to a self-identification and attestation. In the passage from the *Letter to the Hebrews*, there is an opposite movement, from the singular identification of Abraham to the generality of "one man" to the amorphousness of "these" who are "strangers and pilgrims." The two movements invoke for the heterological historian the question of who is naming and the double meaning of the Greek *epidēmos*. For who calls oneself the stranger (or the guest)? Who calls the foreigner foreign, who names the migrant, the resident, the one who is residing temporally among foreigners? Before attempting to answer that question, let me recall an encounter of my own.

I had the privilege of lecturing on one occasion at Ben-Gurion University in Beersheba. The Jewish woman who was my host, a professor in the Department of Foreign Literatures and Linguistics, invited me to her home in the suburbs one evening. The home was richly decorated, aesthetically combining the contemporary and an Eastern European past, giving a sense of the profundities of the ancient that one feels in that part of the world. The garden was beautifully laid out and floodlit, with well-established palm and olive and fig trees set among a rockscape and encircling a lawn. I made a comment about how quiet and restful the place was. My host smiled, indulgently, "If we had a half an hour to leave this place, knowing we would never return, we are already prepared. All the essential documents and financial resources are ready to hand. We don't know the future here; but we have learned from the past to be prepared."

Culturally, to be a refugee or a migrant or an asylum-seeker today may seem very different from being a stranger and a pilgrim in the line of Abraham. However, I maintain that there are similarities, and it is the similarities that make for theological reflection. For the asylum-seekers of old and of today, the physiological movement and geographical displacement spatialize a fundamental relation to time: place is fluid, residence is temporary. The analysis of temporality is at the heart of Wyschogrod's investigations in *An Ethics of Remembering*. Time, as my Jewish hostess revealed to me, destabilizes all notions of home. We are all time-travelers; but the wanderer, like Abraham, lives the ec-stasis of temporal being. Wyschogrod paraphrases Heidegger: "Life is lived in anticipation of death, not as something not yet present—death will never be present to anyone— but *rather as not being able to be anywhere*."[7] Furthermore, for both today's migrant and yesterday's stranger and pilgrim to give up the futural longing that is hope is to be utterly lost. They "declare plainly that they seek a homeland" that God "has prepared." There is what Kierkegaard would call a dialectic with despair.[8] They inhabit and acknowledge the insecurities of their situation, and yet always recognize the imperative to move beyond despair and to begin journeying towards something better, some promise—of asylum, of a future elsewhere, of a fantasized return. For strangers and pilgrims then and now, there is a notion of the transcendent, of a horizon beyond oneself. For no one is the exile self-imposed. One does not elect to leave one's country, one's family, one's culture, the internalized maps that have organized one's life. No one wills displacement. One has to be compelled by powers and sovereignties beyond oneself, or a calling from deep within oneself greater than oneself. And we cannot shun the implications of this theologically: God commanded Abraham to get out. Often our theologies—I think particularly about our Trinitarian and Eucharistic theologies as Christians—are composed like candies to offer as comforts to children who cannot abide in what Kierkegaard names elsewhere as anxiety.[9] In a thousand ways we continually wish to domesticate, to make familiar, and anthropomorphize God, to secure ourselves, to attain some form of permanence as a charm to ward off temporality and transience. But the God of Abraham, like this "fierce spirituality" he calls us to, always takes us beyond ourselves, to places we cannot name (or can name only contingently), into experiences of which we cannot easily discern the goodness, justice, beauty, or truth.

On the basis of this theological anthropology and the practices of living it brings about, then, we who stand in the traditions of Abraham, whom Levinas names "the patriarch of the universal humanity,"[10] should be able to recognize the stranger, the fugitive, the refugee, the pilgrim. For these figures are integral to who we are ourselves; each human being borne on the tides of temporality is, simultaneously, host, foreigner, guest, and resident. And for those of us who are Christians, who hold ourselves to live *en Christō* and who hold Christ to be the perfection of what it is to be human, Abraham cannot be left behind. For Luke's Gospel narrates how "it happened as the disciples journeyed on the road, that someone said to Jesus, 'Lord, I will follow you where you go.' And Jesus said to him, 'Foxes have holes and birds of the air have nests, but the Son of Man has nowhere [*ouk echei pou*] to lay his head" (9:57–8). And *pou* is an adverb, not a noun; it does not designate a place, a *topos*, but the characteristic of not being in possession of, of being dispossessed. *Pou* also means "at any time." So an alternative translation here might be "the Son of Man has nothing, ever."

Let us return again to Abraham the migrant, and to answer the question about the naming of the stranger or the guest, let us examine a particular incident in the Genesis narrative when he is at rest: when the caravan has stopped, the tents have been staked into the ground under the terebinth trees at Mamre, the household furniture has been unpacked and the animals are grazing. Derrida calls this "the great founding scene of Abrahamesque hospitality,"[11] but fails to analyze it in any depth. Abraham

> lifted his eyes and looked, and behold, three men were standing by him; and when he saw them, he ran from the tent door to meet them, and bowed himself to the ground, and said, "My Lord, if I have now found favor in your sight, do not pass on by your servant. Please let a little water be brought, and wash your feet, and rest yourselves under the tree. And I will bring a morsel of bread, that you may refresh your hearts. After that you may pass by, inasmuch as you have come to your servant." And they said, "Do as you have said." So Abraham hastened into the tent to Sarah and said, "Quickly, make ready three measures of fine meal; knead it and make cakes." And Abraham ran to the herd, took a tender and good calf, gave it to a young man, and he hastened to prepare it. So he took butter and milk and the calf which he had prepared, and set it before them; and he stood by them under the tree as they ate. (18:2–8)

The paradox of Abraham's journeying into deeper exile, his abandonment onto God, is that it brings him wealth. The more he journeys, the more his flocks grow and his gold and silver accumulate. God blesses Abraham in his radical dispossession. But there is a deeper paradox that issues from this passage: being a foreigner and a wanderer does not prevent Abraham from also being a host. In fact, it is being a stranger himself that makes him welcome other strangers extravagantly. And welcome them not as lord and patriarch, but as servant, as one who has been looked upon favorably by those who are tired and hungry, thirsty and homeless. It is the recognition of their common situation that enables one to act as host and the other to act as guest. Both submit to a situation. To be a guest is to place oneself into the hands of another, in humility.[12] The proud and self-sufficient cannot be guests; they are too resentful of the submission to the other that is necessary. They cannot receive, and if they cannot receive they cannot be saved, for they wrestle ultimately with the grace of God. They fight against the experience of radical dependency, and yet it is in that very experience that God would meet them as he meets Abraham.

The migrant has to learn how to be a guest, because the danger of always naming oneself the foreigner or the wanderer is that one becomes ever more self-reliant. One becomes wrapped up with one's own survival, encircled in the self-pitying thoughts of one's dispossession. One becomes a fortress against the ever-expected assaults of an enemy—the host as *hostis*.[13] This is Edward Said, himself a Palestinian exile: exile is marked "by the sheer fact of isolation and displacement, which produces the kind of narcissistic masochism that resists all efforts at amelioration, acculturation and community. At this extreme the exile can make a fetish of exile, a practice that distances him or her from all connections and commitments."[14] The exile becomes arrogant: believing in one's own superiority when one is strong, or looking down on what one considers to be the mediocrity of people's very ordinary dwelling. To become a guest is to understand that no one is ever totally dispossessed. Though exhausted and hungry, thirsty and homeless, there is still something to give: you give yourself into the hands of the other, who receives you as a gift. That is how Abraham receives the three foreign men—as gifts: "if I have now found favor in your sight, do not pass on by your servant."[15] And he, in return as host, gives back without demanding or requiring any exchange. He does not discharge what Derrida calls the "sovereignty of the host"[16] who rules within his own domain. Theologically, each of us made in the image of God is a wanderer and a migrant; and yet, given over continually to the grace of God, we are forever oscillating between being a host and being a guest. We live in the circulations of a giving and reception that exceeds us all. We are constituted here as embodied souls; for to be embodied is to be open continually through our senses to the world. And what is it to sense but both to give ourselves over to seeing, hearing, touching, smelling, and tasting, and to be offered that which we see, hear, touch, smell, taste?

It should come then as no surprise that this scene from the life of Abraham has passed down through the Christian tradition as an icon of both Trinitarian and Eucharistic communion. One can think in the first instance of Andrei Rublev's icon of Trinitarian relations. The scriptural basis for such an association lies in the singular invocation by Abraham of "My Lord," on the appearance of the three figures, which picks up the authorial preface to the story in 18:1: "The Lord appeared to Abraham by the oaks of Mamre." Rublev's theological emphasis is upon community, the intra-Trinitarian love that constitutes the ecclesia as the city of God and institutes the agapic feast. We must be careful here: too many theologians attempt to resolve the tensions of present social relations by referring them to the perfections of Trinitarian relations, and in a Eucharistic idealism that displaces all notions of sacrifice, the mass becomes a theological placebo that placates rather than challenges. Elsewhere I have drawn attention to a pathos within Trinitarian relations, the suffering of distance and difference that is not to be erased, for it is the very essence of kenotic love.[17] Similarly, with respect to the Eucharist, to resist the anodyne abstractions of "community" and "body," we must recall always that the bread Christians are given is a broken bread that sends them out into the world. The dynamic of the Eucharist is not just centrifugal; it is also, and this returns us to our in-transit nature, centripetal.

While placing, then, this theological anthropology in the framework of doctrines of the Trinitarian God and the Church, theology must resist the temptation to vaporize the concrete and suck human situations out of history. The fact is, the vast majority of the refugees and exiles, the foreigners and *Gastarbeiter,* are the products of totally human processes: warfare, global capitalism, colonialism and political tyranny. And while Edward Said can call these processes brutally secular, they are rooted in a religious heritage and have been often sanctified in the past by religious authority.

While we cannot handle Trinitarian relations and the Eucharist as magic wands, nevertheless these teachings structure the character of Christian hope. This is very important today, because the unprecedented rise in refugees, exiles, and homeless and stateless peoples finds an echo in the growing popularity of ideas like kenosis, exile, and the nomadic among some postmodern philosophers: for example, Michel de Certeau,

Gilles Deleuze, Jean-Luc Nancy, Emmanuel Levinas, Gianni Vattimo, and Jacques Derrida.[18] Allow me to develop what is at stake here with reference to Levinas. I chose Levinas for three reasons. First, he too treats the Abrahamic narrative (and the Mosaic) as furnishing a prototype. Second, his own thinking is rooted in the experience of being part of the Jewish diaspora in twentieth-century Europe, of being a survivor of a prison camp and an intellectual living in the social and cultural aftermath of the Holocaust. Third, he more than any other thinker has influenced Wyschogrod's work, and it is at this point where, possibly, we begin to interrupt each other's thinking. Alongside Maurice Blanchot, he facilitates Wyschogrod's exploration in *An Ethics of Remembering* of what she terms a "community of hospitality,"[19] a "community where intemperate generosity prevails."[20] But I find myself critical of certain trajectories in Levinas's philosophy, though I recognise that easy judgments can be offered from an armchair. Furthermore, I find that Wyschogrod's analysis of the possibility of this community evades the theological questions that her appeal to "an unsayable transcendence"[21] begs.

What characterizes the philosophical thinking of Levinas is his devastating critique of totality: the going out from and the return to the Same in some Hegelian feedback loop, what he determines as the metaphysics of Being. This takes narrative form in the story of Ulysses, "whose adventure in the world was only a return to his native island."[22] What Levinas's phenomenology explores is a concrete diachrony—the wounding mark or trace of the infinite, the transcendent, an exteriority that forever disrupts this return to the homeland of the Same and therefore totality. His is a thinking oriented towards the other, the wholly other, a

> departure with no return, which, however, does not go forth into the void, [but] would lose its absolute *orientation* if it sought recompense in the immediacy of its triumph . . . As an orientation towards the other . . . a work is possible only in the patience, which, pushed to the limit, means for the agent to renounce being the contemporary of its outcome, to act without entering the Promised Land.[23]

The orientation towards the other, in which oneself is hostage to the other, totally responsible before this other, accused in the eyes of the other, means for Levinas that we forever live beyond ourselves. Oneself is always for-the-other. This is the basis for ethics for him, as it was for Kierkegaard, with whom Levinas shares so much (not least an understanding of dialectic). The infinite distance of the wholly other does not proceed simply to an ethics of moral prescriptions, but rather to an ethics commanded by a Good beyond being whose infinity calls all our human productions and fabrications into question. We are summoned to live beyond our home-making, beyond our own autonomy and its sense of universalized duty. In fact, the ego is never synonymous with itself. Like Kierkegaard's claim that man is not yet a himself,[24] Levinas's self, adrift in time, is always displaced, wandering from city to city of refuge. This wholly other in whose wake we follow is recognized in the face of the stranger, the widow, the orphan, and it calls each of us in turn to "go forth," even if that going forth is not "into the void." There is redemption only in this movement out to the other, only in this obedience to the calling. In a piece entitled "*Pièces d'identité*" Levinas writes: "A Jew is accountable and responsible for the whole edifice of creation. Something engages man even more than the salvation of his soul. The acts, utterance, thoughts of a Jew have the formidable privilege of being able to destroy or restore whole worlds."[25] I believe the same vocation holds for the Christian also.

Unfortunately to my mind, certainly more among Protestant than Catholic, concern with the "salvation of one's own soul" has been more important than being "responsible for the whole edifice of creation" (in Levinas's terms). But what is foundational for Levinas is that being in exile before the other, allowing the call to cause us a radical disquiet, is the condition of being human that demands our welcoming, our being received and our being hospitable. It demands a risking with respect to the other that fissures liberal humanist notions of autonomy, demanding an ethics in excess of Kant's deontology, Mill's utilitarianism, and Rorty's pragmatism. Given the growing plight of dispossessed persons, it demands that we leave the safe havens of our self-conceived sanctities and risk maybe the charge of heresy, maybe the disfavor of those we most wish to win approval from, in order to take up what, in Christian terms, might be viewed as the great cross of this "responsibility." I am reminded of a sentiment expressed by Paul Claudel in his essay "*La Sensation du Divin*": "our entire religious life is our *attention* to the particular *intention* God had when he called us into existence."[26] This is a work, as Levinas points out, of patience. "[A]s responsible," Levinas writes, "I am never finished with emptying myself of myself. There is infinite increase in this exhausting of oneself, in which the subject is not simply an awareness of this expenditure, but is its locus and event . . . *The glory of a long desire!* The subject as hostage."[27] Here the ambiguity at the root of the word "host" emerges, and emerges in a way that illuminates Abraham's servitude in the presence of the three strangers. The "host" is "hostage" to hospitality; s/he can do no other without denying the very substructure of being human (that being-with, that mutual recognition). But in receiving that hospitality the host can become *hostes*, the enemy that provokes hostility.

If I am critical of Levinas, and even more so of other modern philosophers of the kenotic or endless self-emptying, my critique rests upon a twofold basis. First, there is a tendency to fetishize the other, and, in doing so play down the shared relations that qualify the degree of alterity in every encounter with another person. There are webs of affinity and identity that cross the greatest cultural divides. Even in the recognition that this other is a widow, an orphan, homeless commonality is established through notions of family, bereavement, ownership and the lack of it. The other is never wholly other. Levinas would answer that the other person bears the trace of an infinite alterity, *illeity*, and this is perhaps a difference between Judaism and Christianity.

For in Christianity, the Word being made flesh, God becoming human in Jesus Christ, means that however much God remains beyond all our thinking, imagining, and wording, because he shared in what it is to be human that we might share in what it is to be divine (Athanasius),[28] the infinite difference has been crossed, by God himself. Transcendence is not entirely unsayable, because there has been a revelation of God's inaccessible hiddenness in Christ. Furthermore, that revelation then is generative of both now and what will be. And maybe it is because of this theological framing that the Christian scriptures (like *The Letter to the Hebrews*) use the phrase "strangers and pilgrims" to describe the saints, those who are part of the community, a community still on its way, still being performed. Possibly this relates to what Wyschogrod describes as a "community [that] is the gift of that which is not yet."[29] And when the Christian scriptures give an account of people outside of the community (as in the parable of the Good Samaritan in the Gospel of Luke) it does not speak of foreigners but neighbors. The neighbor, according to the parable, can indeed come from outside one's own ethnic grouping and be unknown prior to the encounter, but in the encounter each is brought near the other, given the gift of the other's presence that each might work out his/her salvation through that encounter. The philosophical difficulty with the fetishization of the other, the wholly other, is there can never be any knowledge, understanding, relation with such an other. "If a lion could talk, we could not understand him," quipped Wittgenstein.[30] The possibility for communication is the condition for the impossibility of a private language. The cultural difficulty of fetishizing the other, at the moment, is that the other whose actions we do not understand, the one who is being wrapped in the impenetrability of such an alterity, is the terrorist. I write in the week following the London terrorist attacks, and this morning's paper has several pages devoted to picturing and naming those who were the suicide bombers. Their neighbors, colleagues, and friends are speechless with incomprehension. In their encounter with the other, they are already trying to find those others who made them other. The widow, the orphan, Billy Joe is perhaps the acceptable side of a Levinasian alterity. The question raised here is that of who produces the other. Who names the other as other and manufactures alterity, and on what grounds? Again, Wyschogrod may be pointing to something of the scepticism of fetishizing alterity when she writes: "The community whose non-ground is hospitality is one of peace, but it must remain attentive to the potential violence of an alterity whose every existence is proscribed and, as such, coercive."[31]

Second, and as a corollary, I am critical of a lack of Levinas's attention to receptivity such that kenosis constitutes the basis for sociality. I am unsure a "community of hospitality" is possible if founded only upon kenosis. As with Abraham at Mamre, the host must receive her guests and the guests must receive the hospitality offered. For Levinas, this omission is explicable in terms of the attention given to receptivity in Kant and also, in Husserl's phenomenology, to how the self constitutes its transcendental ego. Levinas turns his attention to examining that which is prior to receptivity: being obligated or *sub-jectum* to the other. Levinas is also wishing to describe an economy, a work towards the other, that "requires the ingratitude of the other"; since gratitude would be the "return of the movement to its origin."[32] In other words, in Levinas's understanding of the economy of the gift, there cannot be mutuality or reciprocity. The economy envisaged, and Levinas is emphatic about this, is "a one-way movement."[33] And that emphasis accords neither with the Christian understanding of grace and a co-operation with it, nor with what Levinas examines in *Totality and Infinity* as the phenomenology of eros.

Allow me to unpack this somewhat, for much depends on it that will return us to what I am defining as the structure of hope that characterizes my own account of being in exile. For what this other brings or evokes is desire; "desire for the other"[34] is key to Levinas's account of oneself, one's neighbors, God and ethics. The other is recognized in the economy of the desire it evokes. But sociality is not simply desire *for* the other; it is also the other's desire for me. Levinas conceives that in the unending emptying of oneself, in the way the other empties me, I discover "ever new resources. I did not know I was so rich."[35] But from where can these resources spring if the ego is always a hostage, always accused? They can only come from that which is continually being given, such that what I am being emptied of is that which I am being given. That is, such sociality, which moves beyond ourselves and an economy of mutual exchange and into a permanent journeying towards the other, is only possible within an economy of a transcendent giving through which I am constituted, in the transit of its grace. Only then can my desire for the other not be an appetite that having the other would satisfy, but an infinite generosity, beyond appetite and beyond even attraction. There are alternative economies of the gift that do not figure mutuality in terms of a return to the same. This is an economy of the gift that Levinas inherits from Marcel Mauss, in which giving incurs a debt to be repaid. Giving is fundamentally associated with exchange, so nonreciprocity is needed to forestall a return. But the economy of giving I am outlining with respect to the host and the guest is not about exchange. Abraham does not give to the strangers because he will get something in return; neither does he set up altars to worship God because God will reward him. God's promise to Abraham remains. It is not conditional on Abraham doing anything. Being faithful is an orientation of being towards God; it determines but is prior to action. Faithfulness is not part of an exchange system. It is excessive to any system since, when nothing appears to be given and one has to live for a future in which others and not you will enter the Promised Land, faithfulness remains.

The giving that operates between oneself, other people (*autrui*) and God as wholly other (*autre*) transcends exchange understood as a symmetrical reciprocity. Levinas is right to point out how we do not own ourselves, but I believe his understanding of God as wholly other is wrong. It is a God who is always absent, whose mark upon creation is only a trace of his passing on ahead. It is a God who does not return the finitude of one's desire with the infinity of his own. For, in order to remain God there must be indifference to our continual attention to his intention in creating us. Is this why Wyschogrod evades the theological question, laying it neatly aside as apophatic discourse? Now while, as I said above, I hold to the importance of the apophatic tradition in cutting through our projections and fetishes of God, nevertheless I would maintain that the finitude of our desire for the other is only possible on the basis of the infinity of the other's desire for me, and that it is only on that basis of participation in that divine erotic giving, that each of us is able to give to each other. We are gifts to each other in an endless economy of God's grace whereby we are given in order to give.

We might then supplement Levinas's phenomenology of having been obligated (*il aura obligé*) with the phenomenological investigations into listening, speaking and vocation in the work of Jean-Louis Chrétien.[36]

And it would be important to do in order to avoid reducing my critique of Levinas (or Wyschogrod) to a set of theological differences between Judaism and Christianity.[37] Chrétien has explored how listening also begins in a radical dispossession.[38] The dispossession occurs because "[l]istening to the other does not simply meaning listening to what he says, but what it is, in the world or, in other words, to which his words are replying—what is calling his words, requesting them, menacing them or overwhelming them."[39] Listening demands being radically exposed. But where Chrétien differs from Levinas is in describing this exposure as a "hospitality of silence." The silence of listening draws us into a transcendent intimacy. "I listen and have the ability to listen because I am called," he writes,[40] called as all things are called to be, ex nihilo by God. Voicing, responding, is always paradigmatically prayer in which there is an interlacing of human and divine calling. Voicing is necessary, he argues, because it is actually "[t]he voice [that] shows the invisible that calls, summons and assembles."[41] In voicing, the Word that calls all things to be is made flesh in us. Both listening and voicing are then, for Chrétien, the foundational forms of welcoming and hosting. In a way that approaches, though it does not coincide with, Levinas's understanding of the human being's responsibility for all creation, Chrétien offers an account of naming (and an interpretation of Adam's acts of naming) as voicing of the Word's indwelling truth in the very nature of things. His naming is a reception of the gift of life, for the gift "begins only where it finishes, where it is received."[42]

Now why has this investigation into Levinas's thinking been important? Because this account of the endless journeying into exile, this account of kenosis in which one is always a stranger, is very popular among postmodern philosophers. With de Certeau and with Levinas it is developed in a theological context such that Levinas can remark that this "departure with no return . . . however, does not go forth into the void." It is the theological context alone that saves this journeying from nihilism. Nihilism issuing from an account of being in exile can do nothing for the plight of the refugee. The work of Derrida, Vattimo, and Deleuze simply announces that we are all dispossessed persons and in a continual state of being dispossessed; we are all nomads. The corollary of that is confronting the refugee with the claim: "You are nothing special. You merely give poignant expression to the condition of being human." While there is some truth in that, as I have argued above, that is not the whole of the story. As Edward Said has pointed out, "To live as if everything around you were temporary and perhaps trivial is to fall prey to petulant cynicism as well as a querulous lovelessness."[43] That is not a recipe for sociality; only for indifference, accelerated social atomism and social disaffection. Abraham journeys into deeper and deeper exile, but always within the context of God's grace and promise towards him. He journeys within the economy of divine giving, of divine loving that is not impassive to Abraham's desire to be faithful. It is this participation that enables him, in exile, to be the host, to welcome the stranger into all the temporary conditions of his own dwelling. Let me put this in another way: Abraham can befriend the stranger because he knows that his true dwelling lies in God's love for him, and the stranger can accept and return Abraham's friendship for exactly the same reason. The economy of friendship is excessive to, because prior to, economies of exchange. In such an economy, to give hospitality also requires us to recognize how we are receiving hospitality; the reception of what is given is also a hosting in oneself of the other. There is no superiority between host and guest. For to host is to allow the guest to be as oneself, and to be a guest is to receive the host as oneself. True justice only operates in obedience to the economy of friendship that recognizes the question in every encounter, "Who is the stranger?" and realizes the answer is, "Neither of us, while we have each other."

In the early 1990s, I was serving as a curate in a large city parish in southwest England. The priest in charge of the parish was away on holiday. It was the summer. I received a telephone call from the churchwarden. "Two Romanian families, with their children, have established themselves in the church, called in the television and radio people, and have declared sanctuary." I rushed across and walked into the midst of several TV cameras, photographers, and radio mikes. Every one of them was greedy to know what I was going to do. They themselves made no response; they were only greedy to feed off the recorded responses of others like myself. There in a corner I came across the families huddled together. They were two young couples and their children. They had come across on a "holiday tour" with all they could carry and declared themselves in need of political asylum. The city had placed them in a detention center (at that time they were not locked or walled in) and they had left there to declare sanctuary in the church. They had been made to realize by the authorities that they were not wanted. They were an embarrassment. They were an inconvenience. They should get back on the plane and return. It is a long story, eventually with a happy ending. But they found no welcome, only suspicion and incomprehension. What on earth could make people uproot themselves from their families, traditions, and geographies and throw themselves on the mercies of strangers? But some people don't have the luxury of choice; to continue living is not a matter of choice. What comes back to me more than their faces is the crowd of media people, hungry for a story but with no real compassion. What comes back to me also is the churchwarden who pushed a bunch of twenty-pound notes into my hand and, with tears in his eyes, asked me to help them in any way I could.

I offer this reflection on the teachings of the Christian faith not to bring comfort, but to help further that thinking and dreaming necessary for a "community of hospitality." I return to the coarse grain of real situations involving real people who hurt and suffer, in order to resist dissolving genuine social problems into accounts of intra-trinitarian love and eucharistic worship. The faith that holds firm to that intra-trinarian love and eucharistic worship expounds a radical vision, and my examination of two Abrahamic pericopes narrates such a vision. It is a vision that passes judgement on all our practices and socialities. Consider the situation we currently confront in the West. Many countries face unprecedented waves of migrants: exiles from new nationalisms, exiles from wars we have fought (some more than others) on foreign soils, exiles from past colonial exploitations caught up in the continuing allure of our high standards of living, exiles from our increasing need for cheap labor. Faced with dispossession on such a scale, the teachings of the Christian faith on hospitality, justice, and the economy of friendship speak like the blood of Abel, revealing our poverty of genuine goodness, the paucity of our love, the immensity of our fear of giving, our fear of our loss of standards to which we have grown accustomed. I would like to suggest that the current waves of immigration offer us the chance to reform radically the way we conduct our lives. They are a graced opportunity for a massive redistribution of wealth and power. Such a suggestion in such a cultural climate is prophetic. There are no comfortable theological words, only the conviction that in the light of this theological reflection, our modern ways of living in the West are cruelly wrong because our priorities are wrong. To return to what I said earlier about the economy of the gift, the majority of people's priorities are rooted in economies of exchange, economies of the quid pro quo, economies of credit and debt. Even our love relationships can be locked into such economies. No true or just sociality can emerge from priorities rooted in such economies. Hence migration has become for us a "problem." But it is not a "problem" when seen in the light of faith; it is an opportunity. And the theologian's task, I believe, in contemporary politics is to challenge the social and economic systems that would reject such an opportunity and wish to continue playing the paternalistic power game of donor and donee. The theologian should do this not because she or he has the answer to the situation, but because the critical intervention of the theological vision of justice into the contingencies of policy-making constitutes a productive dialectic that continually asks the politician, "In whose name are you doing this?" For, as the story of Abraham reminds us, some in entertaining strangers have entertained angels unawares. And Billy Joe, your name will be remembered.

"God," Gods, God

ADRIAAN T. PEPERZAK

> The relation to an unalloyed transcendence can only be expressed in contemporary discourse as an erotics. . . . The attempt to establish God's necessary existence can be seen as the coming to consciousness of the desire for a God who may be invoked in prayer but whose name resists explication. . . . Efforts to show what cannot be said in phenomenological terms . . . express both a fundamental category mistake and an ineradicable hope.
>
> **Edith Wyschogrod**[1]

Gedanken sind frei. Thoughts are free. Thinking is autonomous. Philosophers are free because they are able to receive, accept or refuse, distance, display, suspend, or focus on all that exists or has been thought. But philosophy is never first (except, *perhaps*, in a quite abstract sense of being first), because, before beginning to practice it, philosophers have already been educated, formed, accustomed to a particular language and culture, become part of an ongoing history, and set on a certain path.

Primum vivere, deinde philosophari. Emerging from a life that already has solved the basic problems of its survival, philosophy comes late, as a reflective activity, *a posteriori*, re-turning—in memory—to decisive adventures, experiences, influences, authorities and traditions that grant it a certain style and content. However, philosophy does not only listen to the already-practiced lives of individuals, communities and cultures; it also questions and critiques them, including the thoughts that have emerged from them. Indeed, all customs, experiments, thoughts, and lives need critical testing, but this again is influenced by inherited or amended methods and criteria that have been tried out in lives and philosophies of the past.

Traditional histories of philosophy have emphasized the influences of former philosophers on later ones, but an insight into the complete situation from which a philosophy emerges demands a much wider scope: social psychology, sociology, psychoanalysis, and many kinds of cultural study are required for drawing a somewhat adequate, albeit still simplified, picture of the many ties through which particular philosophers, trends, schools, and traditions are bound to the space and time in which they appear. No thinking exists without being marked by its past history and actual surrounding, even if the thinkers' memories encompass only a small part of the filiations that scholarship can detect in their meditations.

The initiation of newcomers to philosophy follows patterns that have become familiar as standards for continuation. In our time, these standards are for the most part typically modern, even if many teachers insist on renewal and originality. We can debate the extent to which a thinker is able and allowed to propose an entirely new or a very old sort of thinking, but if such thinking does not connect with any element of the memory that dominates the philosophical actuality, it hardly can be integrated into its ongoing history. Sometimes, however, an old thought, forgotten or deemed a fossil, is reanimated by thinkers who claim that it has been misunderstood or distorted before it was discarded. The multiplication of renaissances in Western history is an illustration of such revivals, but we must also recognize that each rebirth is at the same time a thorough transformation of the repressed or forgotten past. While studying the history of philosophy, one gets the impression that almost all renewals in philosophy had the structure of a revival produced by the cooperation of a refreshed memory with a (re-)creative imagination. Once a new stage has been set, the machinery of definitions and argumentation can play its game, but the style and climate, and even the content at stake, have changed dramatically.

Are we today involved in the birth pangs of a new epoch of philosophy? If so, to what extent can we speak of a revival or renaissance of any still-promising past? Depending on one's preferences and perspective, the answers will differ widely. Some will contend that the birth of the modern sciences was a new start of Western or even of all human thought. Others, who instead are saddened by the exorbitant influence of scientific questions and patterns on philosophy, may complain or exult when they interpret our epoch as the radical secularization of a contemplative trend, which until recently had not lost its religious and theological interests. Yet more others might see all modern and postmodern attempts at secularization as still driven by a search for "a God (or god) who can save us." And who is willing to examine the conjecture that some revival of a longstanding, at once humanist and God-friendly, tradition is still possible without falling into nostalgic atavisms?

Regarding religion and faith in God, the contemporary situation of philosophy is exceptional. It is difficult to deny that the history of Western thought from Parmenides to Hegel was dominated by a horizon that one could roughly characterize as "theo-logical" or even—if one is allowed to refuse Heidegger's interpretation of *on*, *theos*, and *logos*—as "onto-theo-logical."[2] From Feuerbach to Sartre, the most famous philosophers have worked hard to remove God from the philosophical scene, but even they remained fascinated by the God they rejected. However, one of the striking features of the (real or methodological) atheism that dominates—at least a part of—today's philosophical mainstream is a peculiar conception of the God who is criticized, doubted, or fought. Whereas God still figured as the cornerstone in the thought of Descartes, Spinoza, Leibniz, Kant and Hegel, the postmodernism of Feuerbach, Marx, Nietzsche, Freud, and Heidegger saw the God whose existence they denied as a highest entity that was not only different from, but also hostile and damaging to the humanity of this world and its history. The God who had presided over Western history and culture was accused of enslaving, stealing, sickening, and alienating the most splendid of human powers and possessions.

If anything is clear about theology from Plato and Justin to Hegel, it is its constant refusal to see God either as a being among, above or outside other beings, or as the essence (*ousia*) or being(ness) of all beings. God could not be identified as any one of the following: a being, the highest being, the universe of all beings, the summit of the universe, the being (or "beingness" or "essence") to which all or some beings owe that and what and how they are. Indeed, any of such identifications would make God finite instead of respecting God's infinity.[3] Neither summit nor totality, the God of the religious and philosophical traditions of the West does not fit in any all-encompassing horizon that would permit us to assign a place to him/her/it within a spatiotemporal or ontological network or universe.

The history of theology from Plato through Philo, Clement, Augustine and Aquinas to Scotus and Cusanus has been oriented toward a progressive clarification of God's absolute infinity.[4] This concept has remained central in the memory of all thinkers who understand that all and any finitization radically transforms the meaning of the word *God* into the name of one or more idols or of their gathering in some kind of pantheon.

The homonymy of the word *God* may have played a role in the corruption of classical theology, but a little study of the mutual implications of the simultaneously positive and negative theologies developed by ancient and medieval thinkers is sufficient to realize that the infinite can neither be opposed to, nor coincide with, any formation or transformation of any universe or part of it. The incomparability and the non-dialectical incomprehensibility of God, which follow from God's infinity, are inherent to the theological tradition developed by the Greeks and integrated by the great Jewish, Christian and Muslim thinkers until Hegel. This tradition is not well known among post-Hegelian enemies of "God," but even so the classics of theology would agree with their criticism of any "God" who takes away from humans what he or she or it monopolizes for him- or her- or itself: truth, power, independence, pleasure, health, authenticity, freedom, responsibility, and so on. Such a "God" would indeed be no more than a special kind of god, and on top of that, a malevolent one. In any case, no god can surpass the level of a finite entity that, with other finite, godly or ungodly, entities would compose an equally finite totality. All philosophers who deny the claim that such finite gods (or such a "God") can save humanity will be embraced by the heirs of classical theology for their hostility toward one or more pseudo-Gods, because it implies an anti-idolatrous stance. Indeed, no finite "God" is more than an idol, especially if it diminishes the greatness of humanity. A philosophically educated theologian will note, however, that the true, infinite, and consequently unique God is simply ignored as long as the idea of the infinite in its radical, incomparable and nonsublatable otherness has not invaded the scene.

Insofar as atheism is neither a protest against the absolute God of ancient philosophy and the Abrahamic religions nor a return to pagan gods (such as the gods of Hölderlin and Heidegger), but instead a late version of prophetic anti-idolatry, even an heir of the theological tradition can understand why atheists from Feuerbach to Freud accuse their "God" of impoverishing, debilitating, and alienating their human rivals. One can only agree with this negative part of their critique, but the question of the absolute and infinite God has not been broached by it.

Any opposition between a highest being and lesser beings creates a competition. As the most powerful of all finite beings, the hostile "God" is the most dangerous competitor. According to a tragic world vision, he is even envious. If finitude is the ultimate horizon, we still have a choice: destroy *all* idols, including "God," or else venerate one or more of these finite gods. By proclaiming a supreme god or the quasi-divine pantheon to be the ultimate reality, one converts it into an absolute without trans-forming it into anything infinite, but the destruction or exclusion of any nonfinite God restricts the situation of humanity to an utterly finite universe, which neither can be given, nor gratefully received. The alternative, a finite universe thoroughly purged of all gods and idols, leaves humanity to itself, but must answer the question of whether humans are absolute enough to replace the ancient gods, including the supreme "God" that has absorbed their powers.

Nietzsche seems to be the one who, better than most deniers, has intimately experienced the decisive depth of faith in one God, as well as the catastrophic loss that followed its agony. The dominant culture now proclaims an absolute solitude of human self-realization without even a tragic kind of consolation for its own mad and murderous destruction of the world and humanity itself. Zarathustra's wrath against the vulgar atheism of laughing intellectuals is one of the last expressions of the two-thousand-year-old conviction that the question of God is the most serious question of all or nothing. But even his "God" had many finite—tyrannical, cruel, moralistic, and sickening—features. This might be one of the reasons why Nietzsche did not give up his search for a more authentic Absolute, while experimenting with names and attributes that echoed former attempts.

Nietzsche's restless search expresses a most profound *pathos*, no less intense than Plato's *erōs*. Anyone who is familiar with the search for God as described by Gregory of Nyssa, Augustine, Dionysus, Bonaventura, Ruusbroec, Teresa of Avila, John of the Cross and many more, will be struck by the affinities between their drivenness and the Desire[5] that drove Nietzsche from one experiment with life to the next, never satisfied, always motivated to transcend each answer that was provisionally accepted. A Christian who has been fed and formed on biblical, spiritual, mystical practices and literature of the last twenty-five hundred years can hardly resist the temptation to interpret not only Nietzsche's restlessness, but the entire history of Western culture, as an ongoing quest for God, who then appears as the absolute "Sought"[6] of the most profound Desire that resists eradication.

If such a Christian is a philosopher and feels constrained by the methods of modern epistemologies, he/she might believe that one first should prove the existence of God before engaging in an extensive discussion with one's unbelieving colleagues. If one is impressed by the power of Desire that even atheists seem to experience in being disappointed time and again during their reaching out, one might feel obliged to prove

1. that the most basic desire of human individuals is a desire for some kind of encounter or union with God;

2. that the desired God is not a fata morgana, but indeed exists;

3. that the desired union is possible and does not surpass the human capacity for receptivity.

However, if God is indeed infinite, it is impossible to prove his/her/its existence by any syllogism or other logical operation in due form, because no linking of finite concepts can yield any concept of the infinite.[7]

As long as philosophy remains confined to argumentative structures without reference to improvable suppositions, one cannot insert God into its texts. The suppositions that modern and postmodern philosophy admits are officially restricted to logical principles and sensible (or material) evidence, but historical research detects many more assumptions, hypotheses, influences, and authorities behind the theories that have emerged since Descartes. Since postmodern writers have abandoned the conviction that the idea of the infinite is originarily given in human consciousness, however, they broke the last link of philosophy with the premodern trust that God was at the same time radically different from and fundamentally necessary for all that exists and can be thought.

The all-important existence of God cannot be demonstrated if God is not already present in human consciousness, albeit in an unrecognized mode. Indeed, the demand of a deduction from anything else (which would result in a finite "God") would only confirm its impossibility. At the same time, however, the demand of a demonstration expresses an overrating of philosophy (in its modern conception): Faith in God cannot emerge from standard methods of modern thought, but only from life itself. In its search for truth, a lived life not only reflects, but also—more intensely and more seriously—experiences, tests, and evaluates its own manners of dealing with the existential problems that are at play in its half- or still-unconscious experiments with the world and itself.

Living a life is first of all becoming experientially and experimentally acquainted with its needs, desires, experiences, affections, mistakes, confusions, clarifications, possibilities, and impossibilities. The experience of being alive and driven to probe this very experience implies that one tries to find out what living asks from the one who lives it and how it fits into the universe. My life has to deal with itself and all the available or discoverable capacities, secrets, puzzles, and mysteries that surround and inhabit me, the drives that motivate me and the qualities of their goals, the coherence of my affections and responses, and my dependence on a multiplicity of influences that I cannot avoid.

From the outset, life's ongoing self-experiencing is framed by drills, education, acculturation and advice. Parents, educators, ancients, and exemplary persons shower their wisdom on every baby, child, and adolescent to foster their quest for a meaning and a style of life that seems to fit the unique destiny for which they happen to be responsible. Belonging is one of the main conditions for becoming someone: belonging to a family, a language, a culture, and therewith to particular mores, communities, traditions, histories, and views. Narratives are attempts to arrange the memories that individual lives experimentally and experientially produce. They are characterized by an existential kind of coherence that is not completely evident in itself. While remembering or telling our stories, we may sense that certain experiences are relevant, even crucial, for our growth, although we cannot explain why. Sometimes we remain fascinated, even obsessed, by such experiences; they may trigger specific affections, images, thoughts, and other stories, but even then we may continue to wonder why we are impressed by them. It happens that a remark, a letter, or a poem resonates with our memory of such an experience and reveals some of its meaning. A kind of recognition or anamnesis may occur and lead to the conviction that the remembered experience touched upon the core of my being, my search, my life.

These hasty notes are, of course, clearly insufficient to indicate how an analysis of life's ongoing self-discovery should proceed, but they strongly suggest that we cannot continue to talk and write about the capabilities of philosophy unless we acquire more insight into its connections with the existential way of discovery that precedes and accompanies all reflection.

An abundant, subtle, and detailed literature about human self-discoveries exists. Insofar as it concentrates on life's own self-clarification with regard to the most serious questions, this literature is religious. Often it concentrates on conversions from one manner of existence to another. Plato's rendering of Diotima's address, Gregory of Nyssa's *Life of Moses*, Augustine's *Confessions*, Bonaventura's *Itinerary of the Mind to God*, John of the Cross's *Ascent of Mount Carmel*, and Teresa's description of the seven abodes of the *Interior Castle* are only a few examples of the many reports on spiritual journeys, ladders, or ascents in which seekers of God have engaged. Even Hegel's *Phenomenology of the Spirit* can be read as a modern, secularized version of such a journey (he called it a report about his *Entdeckungsreisen*), but his book summarizes life's adventure in the form of conceptual knowledge, whereas his predecessors were convinced that such knowledge can only be a partial summary of a more profound, visceral, and primarily affective history, whose secrets surpass their (onto-)logical transcription.

After reading the most authentic of spiritual journeys, one can try to sketch a kind of guide or itinerary for others who are tempted to engage in similar quests, and this is what some of the authors just mentioned did. However, the structure and dynamics of seeking God are quite different from the intellectual methods recommended by modern epistemology. Philosophical training is not a requirement for the journey itself, although it may play a (subordinate) role in the offered narratives. Philosophers who take them seriously will consider their phenomenological retrieval an urgent desideratum, however, and it is not forbidden to hope that this again will result in masterpieces of existentially authenticated philosophy and theology.

A few preliminary remarks about such phenomenologies can be made. Since God is not a phenomenon, but necessarily hidden (which does *not* necessarily entail absence), seeking God is not the search for an object that we, mortals, one day may feel, imagine, or conceptually grasp, although this has not yet happened. However, though completely invisible, unfeelable, inaudible, and incomprehensible, "the sought" is given and present in the phenomenon of its being missed: the human erōs (or pathos) that drives and motivates and possesses, or even obsesses, the human mind and body. The experience from which the seeking of God takes its departure is a suffering lack, whose suffering urges the subject to open up and reach out to the still hidden Sought or Desideratum. What and how the missed and sought—the ultimate Beloved—is, cannot (yet) be said or known, except that it is the most important and serious of all that one has to be in touch with to live a meaningful life. When, at the beginning of their search, certain travelers call their utmost beloved "God," they have borrowed this word from others who spoke or wrote about God's lovability, but its real, vital, visceral, and fully experiential meaning must become concrete and further unfold on the way. Many adventures might be necessary, and many stations can be distinguished in most travel reports: It seems to be the rule that even those who are well prepared through pious and theological initiation need to pass through several stages before they realize how the sought transforms its initial hiddenness into more adequate, deeper, at once more luminous and darker, modes of presence and reserve.

Since the ultimate Desirable is not a phenomenon, seekers have only their own corporeal, cultural, and historical existence in the world, partially shared with others, to search for signs of God's presence in it. The sought itself can reveal itself neither as a part or the whole of the universe, nor as a wholly unworldly something; it can only be approached by our involvement in the spatiotemporal, worldly, human, mortal, and finite reality. Human progress in discovering what primarily and ultimately fascinates, possesses, and obsesses human minds through its mysterious attraction (*hōs erōmenon*) is possible only through a radical transformation of the existing universe, i.e., through the two-sided reality of a new manner of worldly phenomenality in connection with a new manner of human relating. For example, a stage dominated by my conquest of power is followed by the emergence of an attitude that prefers humility and peace over mastery. Or a period in which I am primarily concerned about my own fame is followed by silent withdrawal from the public scene to be free for sustained meditation. Of course, the stages of a life cannot be reduced to such sentences as used here; each stage is a complicated ensemble of corresponding phenomena and motivations that demand refined descriptions. One could mention here Kierkegaard's analyses of several stadia. The main point is, however, that each period of an existential journey reveals a particular light and climate and mood that permit the phenomena of the earth to shine in a characteristic way, thanks to the seeker's appropriate stance. To show how fundamental changes of a person's being-in-the-world express changes in that person's relation to God, we could start with a religious interpretation of Socrates' referral to the light through which the Good allows us to admire and welcome the being (*ousia* or *idea*) of all beings. The Good frees and shines. It illuminates and attunes. Indeed, the Good illuminates the interior of the cave very differently than its outside. But in neither case does the Good itself shine directly into our eyes.

The presence of God is always mediated through a characteristic configuration of the world. The Sought is referred to, approached, presented, proposed, proclaimed as the secret that induces the emergence of a peculiar constellation of appearance and human acceptance of the phenomenal universe. In this sense "God" is always the "God" of a particular (figure of the) world. But how different does this "God" appear in the many pious and impious worlds! Doesn't the polysemy of the word *God* return here on the level of a quest for the (or a?) true God? "The God of our fathers," "the God of the crusades," "the God of our nation," "the God of America," "the God of war and conquest," "the God of philosophers," or the Dollar-God, Democracy as God, the constraint-free dialogical Community or absolute Science as God? Are we back at point zero of a desperate idolatry? In all such expressions, the *of* that links the human universe to God or "God" indicates a presence that is simultaneously revealed and hidden. Some of them are clearly worse than others, but why? Isn't it principally the peculiar character of certain repulsive worlds thus attached to "God," that prompts our aversion? How could one nation, with all its injustice, or how could money ("the mammon") be adored as the hidden presence of the Divine? Even highly praiseworthy ideals, such as theology ("the God of the theologians") cannot be proclaimed accurate revelations of God.

But what if we interpret all such names and phenomenal ensembles as masks or metaphors that grant us at least primitive and provisional attempts at naming, while at the same time urging the seekers to replace them with less inappropriate masks? New masks could then suggest less partial and less ugly "Gods," who—together with a stiff dose of negative theology—may offer better glimpses of God, and the various stages of the quest might be understood as a series of approximations, whose different degrees of adequacy are meant to keep the quest for God on the right track. If so, the phenomenology of God's masks would continue to be driven toward better constellations of affective, practical, and intellectual mondialization and incarnation, without ever stopping at any mask or metaphor or name. For stopping—embracing any worldly constellation as final—would be blasphemous by falling into idolatry. Then the search would end before it has reached the point where the ineffability of the infinite Other liberates the seekers from misinterpreting their orientation. Instead of letting them wander within the human-all-too-human labyrinth of incessant approximations, the one unnamable God burns all idols by being loved (*kinei hōs erōmenon*) as nothing special, because it is too overfull to be distinguished.

The search for ultimate meaning, the erotic journey toward the infinitely lovable, issues a collective and personal history from doubtful "Gods" to the hoped-for absolutely real God. So long as God is still narrowed, imprisoned, diminished, or reduced to anything else, all figurations and transfigurations of God are masks, caricatures, overrated gods. So long as anything else than "Nothing of all that" (the absolute contrary of nothing and therewith the overabundant wealth of the noncompeting infinite) is presented as the true Name, we stare at traces, images, or concepts, and—if they are deemed to be the end of the journey—at hopeless idols. Only continued seeking, driven by a pathos whose intensity augments the more it advances in proximity, can excuse and relativize all comparisons, while hoping to become free enough to verify its initial certainty that God cannot be confused with any of the desiderata that mimic infinity.

But what about the identification of devotion to God with concern and love for the human Other? Hasn't the latter swallowed up the entire moralism of the religion that once dominated Western culture? If it is true that the humanist ethos of unlimited philanthropy encompasses all the meaning that a human life needs to be a success, could we still accuse it of being idolatrous? Or may believers interpret it as an expression of unconscious piety and love of God?

Many contemporary atheists assure us that they do not need any religious education to adhere to an ethics of cosmopolitan benevolence and fraternity. Their conviction seems confirmed by certain words of Jesus, Paul, and John.[8] Moreover, one can point out that many persons and nations who claim to be faithful are crooks and criminals, whereas many unbelievers are heroes of charity. If, indeed, true love of all human beings implies true religion, then the question of theism versus atheism seems to be moot, at least insofar as we are concerned about good behavior and peace.

It has indeed been the constant tradition of Christian faith that the encounter with God coincides with encountering the neighbor (i.e., any human other, the proximus or first comer), if the latter encounter is motivated by sincere love. To love the human Other realizes and *is* to love (the hidden, but then more than ever present) God. After many theologians, the philosopher Emmanuel Levinas has written the most sophisticated commentary of our time on this central and all-encompassing command.

However, do we know what love is, what it demands, how it is motivated and how it works? Does our question about God now shift to the question of authentic love, concern, compassion, self-sacrifice, sharing in suffering, and so on? Certainly. But it is not sure that these questions can be separated. In any case, both suggest the staging of an entire program of phenomenological reconnaissance regarding the double presence of the human Other's speaking face and the silent word of God.

Again, a few provisional remarks cannot suffice, but must at least attempt to indicate a possible orientation for further meditation. To begin with, the simple question of what proximity, as concern and responsibility for the Other, demands from me, is not easy to answer. Of course, I must protect you against death by fulfilling your basic needs, but this does not suffice for realizing the meaning of your destiny. You have also needs that cannot be satisfied without affective, practical, and intellectual formation on all essential levels, including the most serious, which I have called *religious* in a wide sense that may encompass certain forms of atheism.

In any case, love of my neighbor cannot be reduced to respect for human rights and twentieth-century ideals of democracy and justice, especially not if these are tied to the arbitrary choices from innumerable possibilities that are imputed to emancipated subjects. A thorough critique of those ideals is necessary to show that the kind of rights, duties, and competitive claims that go with them cannot prevent warring and destruction, and that they, even without corruption, fall far short of love in any serious sense of this word.

Perfect dedication to the Other cannot refrain from asking: How can I help you, unique Other, at accomplishing what you are meant to be? That is: How can I express my (co)responsibility for your obedience to your own Desirous destiny? Education, sharing wisdom, philosophical dialogue, art, and so on . . . Yes! But will these offer you more than admonitions to be concerned about others and dedicate your life to them? That is, of course, splendid advice, but doesn't it disappoint you by only repeating that you too, like me, must be responsible for the Other—without telling what, in the end and most profoundly, the Other needs in order to celebrate the good fortune of being alive in dedication, gratitude, and hope? If, as many testimonies from all times emphasize, a human individual is capable of enjoying an infinite presence in earthly forms, would the eagerness of human Desire then not urge us to discover whether indeed and how such a possibility can be realized and shared with the others whom we love?

Whatever we will discover by *reflecting about* human relations with God, world, society, history, others, and oneself, it will never surpass the level of thematized, and to this extent, objectified and distant, truth. However, all sentences and theories *about* God, the Other, and myself betray God's, your, and my most authentic truth, for this truth cannot show up within the horizon of any overview. The only opportunity to welcome and transmit the most serious and basic truth lies in being confronted face to face or in responding to a direct address.

With regard to the human face, Levinas has shown how radically its revelation differs from any panoramic phenomenality of objects and totalities. To distinguish your facing me from all other phenomena, we may begin by calling it *absolute*, but *infinity* must be reserved for referring to God, if we want to avoid the confusion of two (not altogether infinite) infinities. Though absolute and absolutely irreducible, you are—and I, as your you, am—too finite and relative in our commitments to a discursive and distributive multiplicity, and therewith too dissimilar from God, to be called *infinite*, even if this predicate might evoke at once the coincidence of two basic devotions and the impossibility of reducing God or you to a theme. To recognize that the human Other is neither a means or transitional stage nor an end that can be subordinated to any other end, it is neither necessary nor possible to delete the abyssal dissimilarity between Godhead and humanity. The finitude of the human Other's "height" does not restrict it to a remembrance of God's immemorial past; its absolute grandeur shines when it is approached as corporeal "epiphany" of the other Other, whose infinity hides and reveals its superior humility in the faces that speak to me.

No debate about the appropriateness of such predicates as *high*, *other*, *absolute*, or *infinite* can teach us how to avoid reducing you, God, and myself to objects, themes, topics, or otherwise interesting subjects of reflection. However, each facing face summons even philosophers to outstrip examination and analysis by welcoming a presence whose absolute and infinite significance deserves absolute devotion.

PART **II**

Practices of Influence

The Name of God in Levinas's Philosophy

ROBERT GIBBS

"Philosophy is called to think the ambivalence—"

Emmanuel Levinas

Levinas testifies to one of philosophy's primary vocations. A vocation, because philosophy *is called.* Like all responsibilities, philosophy's is a response to a call it does not initiate. Philosophy is not like a God who is self-causing. But what is the *ambivalence* that is in question? Given my title, one can hardly be surprised that the ambivalence concerns God— concerns the way God can appear in thought, can appear by being named.[1]

Levinas is hardly unique in asking the question of how the name of God can refer to God. But he focuses on how philosophy must criticize itself, emphasizing that it not only uses the name of God, not only says the name, but also must unsay that name.

> God—proper noun and unique never entering into a grammatical category, does it enter into the vocative without problems? It is thus non-thematisable and even here is a theme only because in a Said, everything, even the ineffable, is translated before us, at the price of a betrayal that philosophy is called to reduce. Philosophy is called to think the ambivalence, to think in multiple times, even if called to think by the justice that synchronizes again in the Said, the diachrony of the difference of the one and the other and remains the servant of the Saying that signifies the difference of the one and the

other and the one for the other, as non-indifference *for* the other—philosophy: wisdom of love in the service of love.[2]

Philosophy is called to diminish the betrayal of translation. To name God is to betray the ineffable, the unique God. Surely, one might recognize that theology has a great interest in this one word. The one word that seems to defy our world of words. But we call upon philosophy because the validity of mundane language is also in question here. Philosophy can defend other words, or at least can justify the use of words in response to the challenge that the word God poses. Levinas explores this as the tension between the saying and the said, in which every said is a betrayal of a saying: semantic meaning is a betrayal of pragmatic meaning. More specifically, the task of discussing transcendent responsibility is in tension with that responsibility. And most specifically, to name that responsibility *God* is to risk the idolatry of worshipping knowledge at the expense of the responsibility toward others. Philosophy is capable of the loyalty to others, even at the expense of God. Philosophy shall remain the servant of the saying, even when called in by the demand for justice.

The above text from *Otherwise than Being* may serve as our mandate here, a call to which we respond. But how can we configure the question of thinking about God, or perhaps better, how can we reduce the betrayal in translation? I do not think that Levinas's work should be interpreted as moving from a too-comfortable thematic account of God to a post-theological position. In what follows I will trace a kind of continuity in his philosophical works, and between them and his Jewish writings. *God* is not examined as a word or semantic event in *Totality and Infinity*, but en route to *Otherwise than Being*, Levinas discovered not only the trace and *illeity*—his neologism of some import—but also discovered that the dialectics of absence and presence can be performed in writing. Our concern, then, will turn to the question of programmatics, the pragmatic meanings in writing (and of course in reading, but also in effacing). A text from 1969, "The Name of God according to a few Talmudic Texts," collected in *Beyond the Verse*,[3] will lead to a focused engagement with the specific and philosophically significant practices of the Name of God in Jewish tradition.

I. The Infinite

The most obvious place to start is at once the hardest for current philosophy: the God named The Infinite. One of the puzzling gestures in Levinas's work is his embrace of Descartes, the thinker that Heidegger and others most criticize for the origin of modernity. There are certainly other philosophers and theologians who could serve Levinas well, but still he returns again and again to Descartes, and especially to the third meditation. What he discovers there is a God who comes to mind, a God who overwhelms phenomenology, even the protophenomenology of Descartes. To define knowledge by the structure of my ideas about reality grants me control of what reaches me. Levinas interprets Husserl's theory of intentionality as a transcendental subject totalizing all that is real. But Descartes's search for certitude bumps up against an idea that exceeds his own powers of thought: the idea of the infinite. In a refrain familiar to Levinas's readers, he announces that in thinking the idea of the infinite, I think more than I can think. The transcendental subject is burst by the idea of the infinite, and finds its foundation beyond itself. Indeed, to find my foundation in what breaks me apart is hardly to rest on my foundation. Rather it is to have found my undoing—the moment beyond my intentionality. Far from being a concept or a theme that I can control, or even think, the infinite appears as what cannot be thought, as what cannot become a phenomenon for me.

Our concern, however, is with the name of God, with the way that God comes to language as much as to mind, and so it is noteworthy that Levinas quotes Descartes in *Totality and Infinity* in the section entitled "Language and Objectivity." The Infinite interrupts language in the task of naming and rendering the world objective. Communication is not constituted solely for the transcendental subject who thinks of and names the things before it in the world. Rather, the act of using language itself depends on an ethical relation to another. Only because of the claim made against me, made by the other person and made in my mind by the idea of the infinite, do I make the world objective at all. In Levinas's writing, Descartes's text interrupts in order to destabilize the role of language in knowing the world. Descartes's account of the infinite bursts the I who thinks, and leads me to name the world in giving it to others.

Perhaps still more puzzling is that this infinite is conformable with atheism. The theme of atheism is vital to the logic of exposition in *Totality and Infinity* and recurs in the later works. The self that thinks the world is free, free most of all from any mode of participation or connection to what it thinks. It stands over against its world. Atheism is the measure of human independence from God, insofar as the human will is free to deny God. To affirm God is not to refuse atheism. Not only can God never be a power over us, but the existence of God also is not affirmable in the way that a tree or a rock is. The possibility of the relation to the infinite that Levinas calls ethics is a radical separation.

Once again, moreover, we find the theme of language obtruding in the midst of the exposition of atheism:

> The idea of the infinite, the metaphysical relation, is the dawn of a humanity without myths. But the faith purified of myths, monotheistic faith, itself supposes metaphysical atheism. Revelation is discourse. A being fit for this role of interlocutor, a separated being, is needed in order to receive revelation. Atheism is a condition for a veritable relation with a true God *kath'hauto*. But this relation is also distinct from objectification as from participation. To hear divine speech, does not revert to knowing an object, but to being in relation with a substance that exceeds its idea in me.[4]

One's relation to God is linguistic, but not as an object of the discourse. But the claim of atheism also makes language possible: only an independent interlocutor can be truly addressed in speech. Levinas recognizes that both objectification and participation fail to make discourse (and hence, revelation) possible. To be an addressee is to be disconnected from God—to be an atheist, particularly in the metaphysical sense of theism. Speech does not unite the speaker and listener in a network of participation, but addresses what is other and free, free enough to refuse to listen.

For Levinas, however, God is not the interlocutor of revelation, nor does the infinite speak or chant. Rather, people do. The analogy of God and humans in *Totality and Infinity* has often been misinterpreted, as though the face were an image or even an icon for God. For the infinite "appears" in the face of the other person, and Levinas plays often enough with capitalizing that Other Person (*Autrui*); even his term *visage* bears with it not only the sense of face, but also the possibility of meaning God's face or countenance. An important concern arises as to whether Levinas depends on theology to do the work for his ethics, and if so, whether this compromises the claims for ethics. If the infinite happens in the face of another person, in listening to the other's instruction, is not the authority of the other person eventually resting upon a doctrine of incarnation?

This hope for a material image of God, the Infinite, in the other person (and so, by a transitive analogy, in me) guides many readings of Levinas—indeed, allows theologians to rush in. Never mind that Levinas states that "theology imprudently treats the idea of the relation between God and the creature in terms of ontology."[5] The habit of ontological thinking links humanity to God through an analogy of being, just the sort of analogy that his atheistic theme is supposed to guard against. The self is separated and free of God, and God is not only unreachable by means of analogy, rather God would be betrayed by any analogy. What is like us can be thought and so is finite. Levinas's claim is much more subtle than one which sees an image of God's face in the human face. The decisive sentences are in the same section which promises atheism:

> There can be no "knowledge" of God separated from the relationship with men. The other person is the place itself of metaphysical truth and is indispensable for my relation with God. He does not perform the role of mediator. The other person is not the incarnation of God, but precisely by his face, in which he is disincarnate, the manifestation of the height in which God is revealed.[6]

Levinas claims not only that we are not the incarnation of God, but also that the other person becomes *disincarnate*—the condition of being inaccessible as a phenomenon in the world. The authority of the other person arises not because we see God in his face, but because he sees me, and so originates speech that I cannot foresee. The authority of address rests with the other person because the reach of my own intentionality is exhausted when he addresses me. If this required an ontological prop, then Levinas would still fall prey to a totality he strives to burst. The authority of the other person transpires in my being addressed, and in that moment the infinition of responsibility happens. God does not appear because God cannot. The height of the other person happens, but without becoming an entity. A sublime height, sublime beyond reason, much less representation. But as I am changed in responding, invested with more responsibility than I can choose, the revelation of God happens. It is not the other's physiognomy. It is also not in a space between us. It is in the vector pointing up beyond my intentional range. It has no end, no object, but is rather infinite and unimaginable.

II. Glory and the Word

But the call to philosophize, to theorize about just these relations between terms that cannot be made thematic, the relations that exceed being, requires a justification. While the infinite is not a phenomenon, the discourse about the infinite, even if it should avoid representing that God, itself produces a phenomenon. What is the status of that discourse? For Levinas in *Otherwise than Being*, the best reason for such discourse is to glorify God. Talking about God can be a witness of the Infinite. While the need to give a sign originates in relation to the Infinite, in nearness to another person, there is a further responsibility to give a sign of giving signs: or in Levinas's terms, to say the saying.

The Infinite is not *before* its witness, as though outside or "on the other side" of presence, already past, out of reach; a reticent thought too lofty to push itself to the front row. "Here I am in the name of God" without referring directly to His presence. "Here am I," just that! In the phrase where God comes to be involved with words for the first time, the word God is still absent. It does not in any way state "I believe in God." To witness to God is precisely not to state this extra-ordinary word, as if the glory could be accommodated in a theme and be posited as a thesis or made into the essence of being.[7]

This saying of saying is the glorification of God, but in it God does not appear. We have a glorifying, and we have a witness to the glory (me), but the witness does not produce evidence, does not produce God. This witness is found in the saying "Here am I"—a disposability for the other, announcing the vulnerability of all speaking. Levinas at times will accentuate that the "Here am I" will itself lack the implicit phrase "in the name of God" in order to witness, because God cannot be the presentation of God as a theme for discourse or an essence intuited. For Levinas, witness to God, in the first instance, occurs with any use of the word *God*. Indeed, the most popular form, "I believe in God," is not only lacking, but cannot *in any way* be stated. For that statement is a proposition that would require God to be a matter upon which one articulated qualities or even essence. God is not the object of my intention. The word is, in this way, best left unsaid.

Thus, witnessing requires a specific relation to what it witnesses, and Levinas invents a new term: *illeity*. Witnessing to the infinite is a witness that allows what is witnessed to be detached from the act. It is, in the strongest sense, a dative—not the direct object of my speaking, but the indirect object: "A plot that connects to what is absolutely detached, the Absolute—a detaching of the Infinite in relation to the thought that seeks to thematize it and that tries to hold it in language in the Said—and that we have called *illeity*."[8] The consonance with Descartes's infinite as the thought that thinks more than it can think is significant. Here it is a thought trying to thematize what it cannot. What is further developed here is the place of language. But the double grasping of thought and language is not itself shocking. The illeity, in short, is a more specific reference to the escape (the detaching) of God from our efforts to know and to name God. The third-ness of *il* reflects the impossibility for God to become an interlocutor, the very failure of direct address. As such the *il y a* in Levinas is quite other—it is the chaos, the *tohu-vavohu* of the creation narrative, which opens up a kind of existence with entities. *Illeity* represents an excess of the infinite, not the suspension of determination but the withdrawal of it. While one cannot address the *il y a* because no entity, much less person or face, arises in it, the infinite exceeds as He, as more face than we can face. The increase in reflexivity about our own discourse, if it is a genuine increase, is that the discourse of Levinas's own thought is now held in check. (But one can wonder if the discourse of the Infinite in *Totality and Infinity* was really any less self-conscious of its own limitation, and its own inclination to attach God to discourse.)

Levinas proceeds to claim that God's disappearance from language itself is the foundation of both Justice and Writing. Without developing the relation to the third person in detail (a theme I have explored elsewhere[9]), let me note that the infinite responsibility I bear for the other whom I am near is translated and betrayed in a social context with the third person—that is with a "real" society, with conflicting needs and responsibilities. Justice emerges from the prior responsibility as a new responsibility to limit the extreme responsibilities I have with one other person, given the need to give each her due.

But in *Otherwise than Being* the relation to the third person yields both a translation and betrayal of illeity, a relation in which I also become an other person for others. Without the third, I am not other for the others, but asymmetrically bound to respond for the other person. To install me as equal, as ethically invested with a proper self-interest, nevertheless depends on more than the third human. Somehow God is engaged in this story. Levinas writes: " 'Thanks to God' I am an other person for the others. God is not 'implicated' as an alleged interlocutor: the reciprocal correlation connects me to the other man in the trace of transcendence, in *illeity*."[10] Were God summoned, or even subject to subpoena, I would be bound only to God. But God's absence sends me back to society, becoming one among the others. But if God had not so called me, bound me to a specific other person, I would not need justice—that is, I would have no ethical desire for society. The withdrawal of God, signified by *illeity*, allows for others to address me as an other, allows for justice to become binding on all of us.

This drama of absence is rendered programmatic precisely in the account of law and a written book. In other places, I have been able to develop Levinas's account of writing and philosophy from *Otherwise than Being*, but here I wish to merely indicate its scope and import.[11] The point of departure is justice: the need in society for contemporaneity and co-presence of each member is bound to a said that does appear—a book, even a book of law. For mutual access to the terms of shared responsibilities, we need a said that is stable and phenomenal. Levinas does not opt only for stone tablets, but the process of working out justice cannot be performed solely in saying. The stabilization of a said is not itself justice, but is one aspect of the working out of justice. The saying must still be allowed to interrupt the said, even as the said retells the saying into its narratives and norms.

When Levinas discusses how books work, especially law books, he claims that they are "interrupted discourse catching up with its own breaks."[12] A text, like a textile, is made of knotted threads, discourse in which the saying appears through the said. One can read a text to find the places where the said was ripped by a saying and mended. The mending leaves traces of the rip. The rip, however, is another's voice, another saying that pierces the text of said. But while the book catches up all the interruptions, there is a writing and a reading that exceeds the written book. The writing is for a reader. The book calls to other books, as Levinas says.

Our concern is more limited: the book as a complex said requires the detachment of the absolute. The sovereign establishes the rule of law at the cost of presence and irresistible power. Moses exhorts the community to follow the commandments after his death, and God commands in unintelligible thunder, in order to leave the sacred text—a text that was broken, rewritten, and then enthroned in the ark—or, if you prefer, in order to leave the rule of parliaments, congresses, constitutions, and the fundamental principle that no ruler is above the law.

But to refocus on the question of the name of God, beyond the problem of giving the law, we find more than reticence over saying the name. For Levinas realizes that the word—God—is not simply another name. He calls it "an overwhelming semantic event."[13] On the one hand it names the illeity, the absence that God has to be, but on the other hand, by naming God it fixes God in the said. God overwhelms semantics—not irrefutably, but by disrupting the hegemony of the said and the present. God does not name a member of a genus, nor for that matter is its uniqueness at home in the network of semantic terms. To say the word God is, rather, to say that the said cannot contain what I say. Of course, this excess can be recouped in a strong and brilliant analysis of the word *God*, even in this slightly lengthy essay on the name of God in Levinas.

> Revelation of the beyond being is of course maybe only a word; but this "maybe" belongs to an ambiguity where the anarchy of the Infinite resists the univocity of an origin or of a principle; belongs to an ambiguity where an ambivalence and an inversion is stated precisely in the word God, the *hapax legomenon* of vocabulary.[14]

Why is God the hapax legomenon of vocabulary? A hapax legomenon is a unique use of a term—and when a philologist applies the term it usually carries the sense that the semantic map cannot secure a meaning for the term. God is unique among words, a place where the beyond of being leaves its enigmatic presence, a trace without evidence. God (*Dieu*) is a term that cannot be known.

III. The Unsayable Name

I could not actually speak the name of God in Hebrew, the term that "God" and "*Dieu*" translate. I could not say it, because it is only written. It is never pronounced now, and it was only pronounced in the Jerusalem Temple once a year by the High Priest. It is a capital offense for anyone else or at any other place or time to pronounce it. The letters *yod he vav he* are the four letters used to write the name of God, and so it is called the Tetragrammaton. But of course that is only what it is called in Greek, or with reference to its Greek roots. And what is it called in Hebrew? *Hashem*, literally "the Name." Or at times "the stated name"—read: unstatable name. Additionally, in proclaiming the written name Jews make use of a euphemism, in this case another name of God—"*adonai*," my Lord. The gap between the written and the oral names itself creates an odd disruption of both speech and writing. But of course the Name is written, in the Bible and in holy books. But even writing it becomes difficult, and so the later texts have recourse to an "abbreviation": *yod he*, and then *yod yod yod*, and even *yod yod*. Or euphemisms, which abound: "master of the universe," "the Holy one, Blessed be He," and so on. Here is a written word that is not a sign of a spoken word. Is it a word at all?

You might suspect that I have stacked my deck. That the transition to Jewish thought is made too easy, but perhaps the translation between Jewish sources and philosophical concepts is rather just what is at stake. For Levinas developed a rich and challenging account of The Name in an essay written in 1969, before he developed his account of writing and even before his discussion of *God* as overwhelming semantic event in 1972. The question of the name of God occupied him not merely in relation to the conceptuality or the adequacy of thematics in naming God, but rather through a consideration of the practices of the rabbinic sages of the first six hundred years of this era (and indeed in traditions of practice that continue today). This shift from philosophical reflections on the adequacy of reflection and on signs to an exploration of rabbinic practices is not haphazard. I am not claiming that only Jewish sages perform noteworthy actions in using the name of God, nor am I claiming that Levinas's own practices in writing about God in his philosophical works are not worthy of careful reflection to display a set of proper practices for using God's name. But the Jewish sages established and refined the complexities that emerge with the Biblical text, and in so doing, became paradigmatic for philosophical reflection both on the Name and on Jewish thought.

While we might start with a series of striking parallels and anticipations of the themes of *Otherwise than Being* in this essay, especially in the account of illeity, I would rather begin with Levinas's own account of the problematic of the name.

> The Hebrew terms of the Old Testament that we are led to translate by "God" or "*Deus*" or "*Theos*," the Talmud would treat as proper names. The name of God would always be a proper name in Scriptures. The word God would be lacking in the Hebrew language. A fine consequence of monotheism, where there is neither a species of divinity nor a generic word to designate it![15]

This ontological gap, that there is a beyond being where something exceeds the schematism of species and individual, is marked out here in semantics. While the word God is a hapax legomenon for our languages, for Hebrew it is simply lacking. This lack is not made good by the proper name, because a proper name requires a set of other proper names. Indeed, the structure of the proper name itself dissolves under the weight of naming God, or perhaps, and here the point becomes more obvious, under the weight of the Name.

For what is the Name? Not merely a proper name, but the proper name for names, not in a simple iteration of passivity, but in the desire to give a name to the naming activity of names. The Name is the one name—and not the model for other names (e.g. "Emmanuel Levinas," "Bob Gibbs," "Edith Wyschogrod"). As one name it disturbs our understanding of how those other names name. That "overwhelming semantic event" is made explicit in Hebrew by calling it The Name, and so un-naming the working of all names in naming the one Name.

The impossibility of the name, even of the name of the Name, that is *ha-shem*/"the Name," appears most clearly for Levinas in the formula of blessings, a form which the sages developed, and deployed throughout Jewish life. For blessings were recited in the morning and the evening, over food, in the daily prayers, when studying, when performing a great number of everyday activities. The standard form begins "*Barukh attah ha-shem eloheynu melekh ha'olam*," which translates as "Blessed are you, O LORD, our God king of the universe." But there is a disagreement over which part of this formula is efficacious: one sage prefers the part that names *ha-shem/*"the Name" by pronouncing "*adonai/*Lord"; another prefers the part that names "king of the universe." But the issue is much more complex. First, the name "*adonai/*Lord" *is* in fact the Name, pronounced with another "name," as euphemism.[16] Hence the first sage claims that only the Name makes the blessing bless. The second piece, "our God," is another term. It is inflected from *elohim*, which also means judge. It has more than a little confusion about it, but is not the Name. And then there is the question of "king of the universe"—an uninflected name (neither accompanied by "our" nor addressed as a "you"). Levinas ducks the question of this particular disagreement.

Instead, Levinas admits that he is straying into kabbalist turf by allowing the names to become themselves an objective sphere, whereas Levinas prefers the Talmudic interpretation, where the names have pragmatic meanings that are dependent on the context in which they are used. Be that as it may, we can now see Levinas drawing near the kabbalist, who produced an interpretation of the sages' intention in formulating the blessing:

> The blessings begin by invoking God as a You. But the second-person personal pronoun is followed by the tetragrammaton . . . The formula of blessing in the second person up to the Name is in the third person in the words which are placed after the Name. The You becomes He in the Name, as if the Name belongs at once to the directness of address in the second person and to the absolute of holiness.[17]

The formula is unusual, grammatically confused. One addresses God in the second person ("as a You"), invokes a euphemism for the Name, addresses "our God," and finally shifts to "the king of the universe," the third person. But Levinas is interested in the way the Name appears. He claims that the Name itself is a hinge, translating a You into a He. I do not feel that Levinas has provided an adequate reading of either the blessing or the Talmudic text. But it also is clear that what Levinas finds is relevant: saying the blessing invokes a you who cannot remain you to me—but quickly becomes He. In speaking the blessing, the speaker translates the Name into a third person, no longer present as my addressee. The very moment I succeed in calling the other into speech ("Blessed are You"), I lose sight of my addressee, who becomes a third, or perhaps appears as *illeity*, neither present nor absent, but addressed and also inaccessible.[18] The very structure of Jewish prayer seems struck and then sealed in this mode of speaking: the directness of address convokes God only to lose God. God does not linger in my address long enough to be a theme, but retires to the third person discourse, to *illeity*, in order to prevent me from fixing God even in the addressee position.

The withdrawal of the Name becomes still more complicated when we shift from saying the Name to the realm of the written Name. For we have a double movement of address and withdrawal. The withdrawal of the author happens in writing, and then there is also a withdrawal of that withdrawal. The first, the withdrawal by writing the Name, is developed in Levinas's text by recourse to a central rule that the written name is not to be effaced. Indeed, texts with any of a set of euphemisms or abbreviations, as well those with the Name, are never discarded, but are buried or preserved, even when they are worn out and fragmentary. The prohibition of effacement marks the written name as different from all other writings, indicating that what is written about transcends the text, but also consigns the Name to an accessibility that is shared with all written texts.

> But precisely thus the ambiguity—or the enigma—is shown of this manifestation, by which it breaks off from the "objectivity" of what is perceived, from the historical, and from the world where that objectivity would enclose it. Thus a modality of transcendence is outlined. The square letters are a precarious dwelling from which the revealed Name is already withdrawn; erasable letters at the mercy of the man who traces or recopies it. Writing that is altogether ready to be confused with the writing submitted to the history and the criticism of texts, writing opened to the research into its origins and thence, contemporaneous to the history of what is memorable, where transcendence is annulled—an epiphany at the boundary of atheism.[19]

The text is vulnerable. A spoken word can go unheard; it can be retracted. My word in my speaking is in my mouth, and so is sheltered by me, and safeguarded by the very transience of vocalized speech. The performance disappears without a trace. To prevent abuse and suffering, the Name is ruled unpronounceable. Even the evanescence of speech is too risky. But that same Name is now written. To protect the writing, rules are made for the disposal of texts, but Levinas notices the vulnerability of the written word. Materially, it is vulnerable to erasure, to destruction, to abuse.

But Levinas expands the horizon: the text is vulnerable to reductive and analytic reading. It flaunts this risk by its textuality, handing itself over to those scholars who are blind to the transcendent dimension that animates it. It welcomes higher criticism by casting the Name into a written text. The text is the exposure, even the profanation, of the Name. It is an epiphany of what transcends the text in the text through the submission of the text to a world that will secure itself against the transcendence. The written name brooks atheism—and does so because it brings transcendence into its enigmatic relation with its reader. So transcendent is the Name that it can appear, then submit to its own effacement through erasure or analysis. It is not sequestered or cloistered away from the text and its vulnerabilities, but appears within the text. Writing is a risk ineliminable from writing, a risk that transcendence runs in the name of God.

But only one more step is needed: the prescription of an inscription in order to efface it—and of course this very dialectical textual tradition knows just this sort of effacement: a ritual trial known as *sotah*, prescribed for a woman accused of adultery (a type of trial suspended thousands of years ago), but still of interest to the Talmudic sages and still of interest to Levinas. What is of interest is not the trial itself, but the remarkable *écriture* in this test: the Name was inscribed, fully, in a book and then dissolved in bitter waters, which the woman drank. Levinas writes: "Isn't effacement the transcendence of the name of God in relation to all thematization, and isn't that effacement the very commandment which obliges me in relation to the other person?"[20] This effacement is not simply the not-writing of the Name; rather, it is a writing written in order to be dissolved. But the dissolution brings about a reconciliation of the husband and wife, or at least facilitates it. Levinas, following another text, suggests that God commands us to efface the Name in order to make peace between the two people: their reconciliation is more important than the safeguarding of the Name. But that is altogether too weak. This effacement is God's way of commanding and remanding us to the other person. The dissolution of the name is the emptying out of metaphysics into ethics. Only a name which was the Name and so unpronounceable and so unerasable could serve this radical function of obliging us toward the other. Only a transcendence that disappears, that even obliges us to dissolve it, not merely brooking atheism, but leading us to destroy the Name for the sake of others, is adequately transcendent.

The responsibilities that surpass honoring the Name lead Levinas to consider the responsibility to God which supplants God with the other person. Levinas explores a surprising midrashic reading: that Abraham made God wait in order to welcome his guests—and was honored for it.

And The Name appeared to him at the terebinths of Mamre, as he was sitting at the opening of the tent in the heat of the day. And he raised his eyes and behold three men stood near him, and when he saw, he ran to call to them from the opening of the tent and bowed to the ground. And he said "My Lord, if I have found favor in your eyes, do not pass by your servant. Let a little water be drawn and wash your feet and rest yourselves under the tree, and I will fetch a piece of bread . . ." (Gen. 18:1–4)

This is a confusing story. It starts, "And the Name appeared," but at what point does the Name, does God, appear? The Name is written, but the three men appear. Levinas returns to this story often in his works, but in the context of discussing the Name he refers to one Talmudic reading where there is an argument about whether a specific name used by Abraham is holy (and thus uneffaceable). The general claim is that every name he used in addressing God is holy, but the text brought as a possible exception is this one when Abraham addresses the passers by the word "*adonai*." Is he using the word merely in politeness and politics to refer to the passers by, or is he addressing God as "my Lord"? The term seems to be addressing God. But two sages disagree and proclaim it, in its address of the human, as also Holy. And this is bolstered by a general rule: "Greater is welcoming guests than receiving the face of the divine presence."[21]

The implication of this comment is that the term "*adonai*" is addressed to God and not to the visitors, and that Abraham is putting God off in order to take care of the travelers. Levinas notes:

God would have appeared to Abraham at the same time as the three passers by. He would say to Him, "*Adonai*, do not pass by your servant." He would say "Wait while I receive these three travellers" since those passing by were overcome by heat and thirst, they come before the Eternal our God. The transcendence of God is his effacement itself, but this obliges us in relation to men. Higher than greatness is humility. The meaning of Abrahamic monotheism.[22]

Levinas's views are not simply about Abraham, but about the relation of God and Abraham. The chapter begins with the *appearance* of God to Abraham. The appearance is not identical with the arrival of the three travelers, but somehow these Talmudic texts treat the travelers as a specific stand-in for God: they represent the others to whom we must attend before attending to God. God appears by yielding place to the others, or perhaps one would say God disappears, obliging us to the others.

But notice, moreover, that the somewhat odd Talmudic reading of this text points to a textual problem: where does the Name go? The "legal" problem is whether Abraham's address uses a holy euphemism, but after the eruption of the Name at the start of this chapter, it disappears until verse 13, with the promise of a child to Sarah. Indeed, no mention or reference to God occurs again until that moment. Like the *écriture* of the name in the test of the bitter waters, the Name here signals a disappearance. A disappearance, we would say, of that which never can simply appear. The trace of the absence is Abraham's address to God as "my Lord," a trace that is enigmatic in the special way of Biblical texts. Levinas discovers here just the dialectic of effacement and ethics that *illeity* names.

We have thus followed Levinas's thought through a name that is not even a proper name, much less a generic one. A name that cannot be pronounced. A name that cannot be erased, and can almost no longer be written. A name that designates an absence, a trace. God is an overwhelming semantic event for Levinas, but "God" is but a poor translation for this name. Levinas's interest exceeds semantics and even pragmatics (in the narrow sense of how the sign is used). For the use of the Name both calls toward transcendence and leaves it transcendent: but through that call and erasure, we are assigned not to transcendence but to others.

The theme here, moreover, is precisely the way that the Jewish practices and interpretations of the name of God become philosophy. In the very essay under consideration, Levinas makes his own translation in the last section of this reading of Talmudic texts, arguing for a philosophical parallel position, which he there defines as one independent of the authority of scripture and its interpretation.[23] *Otherwise than Being* offers a full elucidation of the way a text is a mended textile of knots, and how writing bears the trace of what cannot appear in writing. Indeed, even the unsaying of the said, parallel to the effacement of the name of God, is elaborated there. Illeity as a term is coined several years before this essay. It is not, therefore, a matter of a genetic sequence of concepts in Levinas. Nor for that matter should we forget that the debates in the Talmud predate both Derrida and Levinas. At issue, however, is whether we do not learn more about transcendence and writing, transcendence and God's absence, illeity and so on, by consulting a tradition of thought intimately bound up with these questions. Heidegger's efforts to cross out Being seem almost simplistic compared with a body of thought devoted to an unpronounceable and only occasionally effaceable name of God. That such ideas can be thought philosophically is to their credit, and the fact that the sources of Judaism can enrich our struggles seems not to ask much of philosophy.

That Judaism demands this exposure in philosophical discourse for itself, however, seems more than a little shocking. Levinas devoted several essays and Talmudic readings to this question. But in his discussion of the written we have already seen the key point: God is willing to be written in, precisely because God's transcendence is safe from historical criticism and other means of mishandling a sacred text. The point of writing is to expose that vulnerability; transcendence does not overpower but is humble. Is it too much to say that to expose such ideas in a general philosophical court is to witness to a transcendence that obliges us to other people—including thinking people who do not know the texts of the Jewish tradition? For God's sake, do we not first have to offer nourishment and refreshment to those who are wandering?

Kenotic Overflow and Temporal Transcendence

Angelic Embodiment and the Alterity of Time
in Abraham Abulafia

ELLIOT R. WOLFSON

Tempus Discretum and the Eternal Return
of What Has Never Been

In a number of previously published studies, I have explored the phenomenon of time in kabbalistic literature from various perspectives.[1] Needless to say, the permutations of this theme that may be gleaned from this variegated corpus are complex and multifaceted. Without denying that any attempt to represent the kabbalah as monolithic is prone to criticism, it seems to me nonetheless legitimate from the perspective of both the kabbalists' own hermeneutical practices and contemporary theoretical models to offer generalizations that are based on a plethora of specific textual sources. With regard to the notion of time, I am prepared to say in a general way that the intricate symbolic world of kabbalists defies the commonly held distinction between linear and circular time. I have, accordingly, dubbed the kabbalistic perspective by the paradoxical expressions "linear circularity" and "circular linearity," expressions that are meant to convey the dual deportment of time as an extending line that rotates like a sphere or as a rotating sphere that extends like a line. Rendered in an even more appropriate geometric figure, we can speak of time as a swerve in which line and circle meet in the sameness of their difference.

The convergence of line and circle can be thought from the vantage point of the confluence of the three modes of time in the moment: the present is determined by the past of the future that is yet to come as what has already been, and by the future of the past that has already been what is yet to come. The pattern implied in these words suggests that past and future are to be viewed not as the starting point and finishing point of a closed circuit, but rather as termini of a path that is eternally bent, to paraphrase Nietzsche's memorable locution, a path discerned anew from and in each and every moment, recurrently breaking through the cycle, beginning and end constantly refashioned by the intentional acts of retention and protention, tracks that crisscross eidetically in the midpoint of the circle whose center is everywhere and whose circumference is nowhere.[2] Alternatively expressed, kabbalists delineate time as the eternal overflow of a *tempus discretum*, the duration of the interruptive present in which past may be anticipated as future that has not yet come to pass, and future remembered as past that has not yet taken place.

The texture of temporality can be understood better if one bears in mind that the perspective I am attributing to kabbalists may be considered an explication of a well-attested tradition that the Tetragrammaton, ostensibly beyond signification, signifies the compresence of past, present, and future, or, in the widespread Hebrew locution, *hayah howeh we-yihyeh*, "he was, he is, and he will be."[3] The intent of this interpretative gloss is that within the immutable divine nature, the three modes of time are indistinguishable: he was before the time of creation, he is during the time of creation, and he will be after the time of creation, an apprehension that flies in the face of an experience of time predicated on a clear demarcation of past, present, and future.[4] How does one account for all three tenses coexisting at the same temporal interval? Can we even speak meaningfully of an interval if a being is past, present, and future all at once? Contemplation of this seemingly imponderable idea helped foster the kabbalists' notion of a time-that-is-not-time, a timeless time that ensues from the intersection of all three tenses in the moment, an equiprimordiality of past, present, and future that mimics the eternality of the divine ipseity,[5] a time-out-of-time that, at all times, is comported temporally in the here-and-now by the recollected projection of the beginning discerned from the projected recollection of the end. In this conception, the tension that may arise from the doubleness of time as stretched and punctiform, to borrow the locution of Edith Wyschogrod,[6] finds a resolution insofar as what is experienced phenomenologically as temporal continuity in reaching backward through memory and extending forward through anticipation is constructed hermeneutically in the moment that cuts the timeline by looping pastness, presentness, and futurity in a threefold bond of eternal discontinuity.[7] Time's passing, consequently, is not overcome by the dissolution of temporal transience in an ocean of eternity, but by abiding in the persistent demise of what has never been except as what is ever to come, the eternal cycle of recurring difference wherein being becomes interminably in the terminable becoming of being. In the ephemerality of time's ebb and flow lies its endurance; the one thing constant is change.

My understanding of the kabbalistic viewpoint can be profitably compared to the account of Nietzsche's doctrine of eternal recurrence offered by Gilles Deleuze:

> We misconstrue the expression "eternal return" when we take it as the return of the same. It is not being that recurs, but, rather, that recurrence itself constitutes being insofar as it affirms becoming and passing. It is not some one thing that recurs, but that recurrence is itself affirmed by the passage of diversity or multiplicity. In other words, identity in the Eternal Return does not designate the nature of what recurs, but, to the contrary, the fact of recurring difference.[8]

In another context, Deleuze repeats his contention that the idea of the eternal return in Nietzsche

> is in no way the return of a same, a similar or an equal. Nietzsche says clearly that if there were identity, if there were an undifferentiated qualitative state of the world or a position of equilibrium for the stars, then this would be a reason never to leave it, not a reason for entering into a cycle. Nietzsche thereby links eternal return to what appeared to oppose it or limit it from without—namely, complete metamorphosis, the irreducibly unequal . . . The eternal return is neither qualitative nor extensive but intensive, purely intensive. In other words, it is said of difference.[9]

I will not assess the accuracy or legitimacy of the Deleuzian reading of Nietzsche, though I am of the opinion that his perspective is defensible. What is more important for the drift of these reflections is the remarkable assonance between this interpretation of Nieztsche's doctrine of eternal recurrence and the kabbalistic stance on time and eternity that issues from the gnosis of the name *YHWH*. As I noted above, the Tetragrammaton denotes the compresence of past, present, and future. This idea, which destabilizes the triadic division of time that informs the commonsense outlook, rests on the assumption that the eternality of the divine being is instantiated incessantly in the becoming of the moment. The entwining of the three temporal modes logically suggests a sense of return, a recycling of the temporal flux, since if it is presumed that all is present in every moment, then what will come to be in any moment in some sense has already been. What is recycled, however, is not a selfsame, immutable identity; the return, the coming back, is about "complete metamorphosis," the coming to be of a future past that is "irreducibly unequal" to the past future, and hence the only constancy of being that we can speak of is the becoming of change. The name *YHWH*, as its scriptural elaboration *ehyeh asher ehyeh*, "I will be as I will be" (Exod. 3:14), drives the point home as this unusual delineation indicates that the being of the God of Israel is marked by its becoming, and hence the name does not name anything that could be named except the unnameable. All that recurs in the interminable succession of time, therefore, is a manifestation of the divine essence, but that essence is essentially inessential, that is, its essence consists precisely of its having no essence: it is what it is to become. The kabbalistic teaching resonates with the description of the "play of the eternal return" in a third passage from Deleuze:

> This return is precisely the Being of becoming, the one of multiplicity, the necessity of chance. Thus we must not make of the eternal return a *return of the same*. To do this would be to misunderstand the form of the transmutation and the change in the fundamental relationship, for the same does nor preexist the diverse (except in the category of nihilism). *It is not the same that comes back*, since the coming back is the original form of the same, which is said only of the diverse, the multiple, becoming. The same doesn't come back; only coming back is the same in what becomes.[10]

Admittedly, the core of the kabbalistic teaching was shaped in the crucible of an elitist European culture in the high Middle Ages, and thus kabbalists were well-informed of philosophical and scientific views that Nietzsche would have rejected as part of his critique of Western (or, more specifically, Platonic-Christian) metaphysics. Nonetheless, the Nietzschean perspective as presented by Deleuze is strikingly similar to what I have drawn independently from the texts penned by kabbalists, a kenotic understanding of time that parallels their embrace of an apophatic discourse.[11] That is, just as kabbalists affirmed that language in what is, paradoxically, its most restricted and most expansive sense, leads one to speak the unspeakable, to think the unthinkable, to say what is unsaid in the unsaying of what is said, so, in their understanding, the giving of time comes forth from an infinite presencing of a presence that can be present only and always in the absence of its presence, an event of presence, one might say, rather than the presence of an event, the withdrawal of withdrawal in the recurrence of the same that becomes the same in virtue of being different, a becoming that comes to be in the return of what has always never been.

Intellectual Conjunction and the Mechanics of Divine Influence

In this essay, I will turn my focus to some dimensions of the phenomenological depictions of time that may be elicited from the mystical thought enunciated by the thirteenth-century Spanish kabbalist, Abraham Abulafia, with a specific interest in elucidating what I have called kenotic overflow and temporal transcendence.[12] To date, the only aspect of Abulafia's thinking about time that has been addressed in any detail is the role of history in his messianic vision.[13] My attention will be on other philosophical dimensions of temporality as they emerge from Abulafia's compositions, though the conclusions I will draw surely have a bearing on the eschatological elements of the prophetic kabbalah.

Before proceeding to discuss the complex of themes related to this topic, it is incumbent on me to provide a sketch of the main contours of Abulafia's kabbalistic landscape. Somewhat improbably, Abulafia was able to combine the basic tenets of Maimonidean religious philosophy with esoteric doctrines and mystical practices (mediated chiefly through the works of the Rhineland Jewish pietists, but also through select treatises of Catalonian and Castilian kabbalists that either preceded or were contemporary with him)[14] to produce his distinctive understanding of kabbalah as a path, *derekh*,[15] a way to attain knowledge of the name (*yediʿat ha-shem*).[16] To cite a succinct formulation by Abulafia himself from one of his major treatises, *Ḥayyei ha-Olam ha-Ba*, composed in Rome in 1280: "Hence, you must know in truth that the emergence of these permutations from the glorious name [*yeṣiʾat ha-ṣerufim min ha-shem ha-nikhbad*] is for us the prophetic kabbalah [*qabbalah ha-nevuʾit*] whence the soul is conjoined to the name. And the receiving of the emergence [*qabbalat ha-yeṣiʾah*] is so that one may be influenced by the other [*lehiyotah nishpaʿat zo mi-zo*], and the one that is influenced [*ha-nishpa*] by it is called the Holy Spirit [*ruaḥ ha-qodesh*]."[17]

The matter of influence is crucial to Abulafia's cosmology and psychology, and hence the choice to led it guide our explication of his mystical system is warranted. I commence with the observation that these two elements may be distinguished conceptually and marked as linguistically distinct, but as a matter of experience they are inseparable. With regard to the cosmological, in a manner consonant with Maimonides,[18] the universe is described by Abulafia as issuing from and being sustained by an influx of divine intellection, the light that emanates from the First Cause (*sibbah ha-riʾshonah*), the "necessary of existence" [*meḥuyav ha-meṣiʾut*],[19] the "form of the intellect" [*ṣurat ha-sekhel*][20] that links all of reality in an unbroken chain of being. Abulafia identifies the intellectual overflow as the

Tetragrammaton, but, in a manner closer to Judah Halevi than to Maimonides, he maintained that the knowledge of this name, which is the essence of the tradition, is not grasped by speculation shared universally by all nations, but by a prophetic vision unique to the people of Israel.[21] Moreover, insofar as this name is equated with the Torah,[22] and the Torah is composed of the twenty-two letters of the Hebrew alphabet, we may surmise that implied by this identification is the belief that the vital life force of all existence consists of the "holy tongue" [leshon ha-qodesh], the "mother of all languages" [em kol ha-leshonot][23] that Abulafia considered "natural" in contrast to all the other seventy languages that are derived from Hebrew and are assigned the status of "conventional."[24]

I will cite here one of countless texts in which Abulafia affirms this rudimentary principle of Jewish esotericism.[25] Commenting on the statement in Sefer Yeṣirah that by means of the letters the Creator "forms the soul of every creature and the soul of everything that will be formed,"[26] Abulafia writes: "Indeed, each and every body is a letter [ot] . . . and every letter is a sign [ot], signal [siman], and verification [mofet] to instruct about the divine overflow [shefa ha-shem] that causes the word [ha-dibbur] to emanate through its mediation. Thus all of the world, all the years, and all the souls are replete with letters."[27] The influx that bestows vitality upon all beings of the world—classified by Abulafia in terms of the three-fold division in Sefer Yeṣirah, olam, shanah, and nefesh, rendered narrowly as "world," "year," and "soul," but denoting more broadly the temporal, spatial, and human planes of existence, each of which is constituted by the Hebrew letters—is here identified as the word (dibbur).

For Abulafia, therefore, the ancient cosmological speculation is reinscripted within the medieval worldview, yielding the belief that the intellectual efflux, which informs the cosmos, is made up of the twenty-two Hebrew letters, and these collectively are the word of God, which is also identified as the Tetragrammaton, and this, in turn, with the Torah in its mystical valence. The archaic esoteric doctrine attenuates the split between soul and body that is suggested by Abulafia's own insistence that the meditational practice of letter permutation has the goal of untying the knots of the body so that the soul/intellect may be separated from its somatic encasement.[28] I am not overlooking the fact that the corporeal body is viewed by Abulafia as an obstacle to the attainment of spiritual perfection, a point that has been appropriately emphasized by scholars. My contention is, however, that from Abulafia's corpus we can adduce that he envisioned another sense of corporeality, one that does not position soul and body in diametric opposition.[29] Viewing the body as letter, and the letter as sign that points to the intellectual overflow permeating reality, provides a theoretical ground to undergird an alternate conception of embodiment, a transposed materiality that is rooted in the belief that the body, at its most elemental, is constituted by semiotic inscription, the flesh-that-is-word garbed in the word-that-is-flesh.[30] As he puts it in *Hayyei ha-Olam ha-Ba*, "The letters are the force of the root of all wisdom and knowledge without doubt, and they themselves are the matter of prophecy [*homer ha-nevu'ah*], and they appear in the mirror of prophecy as if they were dense bodies [*gufim avim*] that speak to a man mouth to mouth in accord with the abundance of the rational form [*ha-siyyur ha-sikhli*] that is contemplated in the heart that converses with them, and they appear as if they are pure, living angels that move them."[31] In *Sefer ha-Hesheq*, a relatively short treatise that proffers a kabbalistic exposition of the Maimonidean ideal of *'ishq*, we are told that the mind (*mahshavah*) of the adept at the peak of the ecstatic conjunction with the object of his yearning

> imagines an image of the letters [*ha-mesayyeret siyyur ha-otiyyot*] that are imagined [*ha-mesuyyarot*], contemplated [*ha-muskkalot*], and thought [*ha-nehshavot*], rational thoughts replete with letters [*mahshavot sikhliyyot mele'ot otiyyot*], which are the true forms [*ha-surot ha-amitiyyot*], imagined in the image and likeness of the ministering angels [*mesuyyarot be-selem u-demut ke-mal'akhei ha-sharet*], for each letter is a vision from the prophetic visions [*mar'ah mi-mar'ot ha-nevu'ah*], and each of them is pure splendor [*zaharurit zakhah*].[32]

With regard to the anthropological, Abulafia maintained that by means of proper discipline, one can be conjoined to the effluence of intellectual light,[33] a unitive experience that, both conceptually and experientially, relates to the contemplative ideal of conjunction (*devequt*), whose epistemological and ontological contours he configured on the basis of philosophical assumptions elicited from Jewish and Muslim sources wherein the Aristotelian and Neoplatonic currents are intertwined, for example Avicenna, Averroës, Abraham Ibn Ezra, and, above all others, Maimonides.[34] In another excerpt from *Hayyei ha-Olam ha-Ba*, the experience is conveyed in the following way: "The secret of the splendor [*sod ha-ziw*] that emanates upon us from the supernal, divine Intellect [*ha-sekhel ha-elyon ha-elohi*], through it we comprehend the Active Intellect that is in us, which is called the splendor of the Presence [*ziw ha-shekhinah*]."[35] The *Shekhinah*, also designated the "Holy Spirit" [*ruah ha-qodesh*][36] or the "spirit of the living God" [*ruah elohim hayyim*],[37] is a splendor that emanates from the supernal Intellect, and serves as the means by which the soul comes to comprehend the Active Intellect that is within itself. The final words are crucial as they underscore that in the moment of ecstatic union, the distinction between outside and inside is no longer epistemically tenable.

The double mirroring to which I refer is alluded to in the following comment in *Imrei Shefer*: "This is the prophet who sits upon the throne of the Lord . . . and concerning this man it says 'and on top, upon the image of the throne, there was the image in the appearance of a human' (Ezek. 1:26), he appears to him in his image [*we-hu bi-demuto mitdammeh lo*], and his appearance [*u-mar'ehu*]—he makes visible the image of the glory of the Lord [*hu mar'eh demut kevod yhwh*], and he sees himself in the speculum [*aspaqlaryah*] that illumines the eyes and heart."[38] By means of the meditational training, the adept is transformed into the angelic guide, the Active Intellect (*sekhel ha-po'el*), personified in the figure of Metatron,[39] the demiurgic angel about whom there is intentional confusion regarding its ontic relationship to the glory,[40] the angel of the Lord (*mal'akh yhwh*), that is, the "angel whose name is *YHWH*,"[41] the intermediary[42] between human and divine[43] that assumes corporeal shape in the imagination at the moment of prophetic vision.[44] Referring to this process in *Hayyei ha-Olam ha-Ba*, Abulafia writes: "It is known that we, the community of Israel, the congregation of the Lord, know in truth that God, blessed be he and blessed be his name, is not a body or a faculty in a body, and he never materializes [*hitgashem*]. But his overflow creates a corporeal intermediary [*emsa'i ehad gufani*], and it is an angel in the moment of the prophecy of the prophet [*we-hu mal'akh be-et nevu'at ha-navi*]."[45] Or, again, as he puts it in *Sefer ha-Malmad*: "Every speech written about in the Torah that God spoke to Moses or to one of the prophets is not like our speech, which comprises voice [*qol*], breath [*ruah*], and speech [*dibbur*]. Rather, this speech is in accordance with what the ears of the prophet hear, just as the body, the form that is seen in the prophetic vision, is not like our actual body, but it is like the body seen by man in his dream."[46] The ambiguity that one may discern in Abulafia's demarcation of the object of the unitive experience as either God or the Active Intellect[47] may be explained by the fact that he viewed the latter as the visible vehicle by which the invisibility of the former is manifest in space and time. In the moment of theophanic incarnation, the line separating the two is blurred. As Abulafia himself put it in *Sefer ha-Hesheq*, "All these matters emanate from the Active Intellect, which informs the person about the truth of the substance of his essence by means of the permutation of the letters [*seruf ha-otiyyot*] and the mentioning of the names [*hazkarat ha-shemot*] without doubt, until the person is restored to the level of intellect [*ad she-yashuv ha-adam be-madregat ha-sekhel*] so that he may be conjoined to him in the life of this world in accord with his capacity and in the life of the world-to-come in accord with his comprehension."[48]

In the Blink of an Eye: Time as the *Mysterium Coniunctionis*

Following Maimonides, Abulafia portrays the imagination in negative, indeed at times in explicitly satanic terms, but he also accepts that this faculty plays a crucial role in the mechanics of prophecy (with the exception of Moses) as the angelic intermediary[49] that bridges spirit and matter, intellect and body.[50] Thus, in one passage wherein the prophetic vision is discussed in terms of a mirror or a body of water, through wordplay Abulafia links together imagination, (*dmywn*), demon (*dymwn*), and medium (*mdwyn*).[51] According to another passage, Abulafia notes that the expressions *demut* ("image"), *shem dimyon* ("name of the imagination"), and *shefa* ("overflow") all equal 450,[52] a numerical equivalence that drives home the point that the imaginal form envisioned by the prophet-mystic is the concretization—"incarnation" would not be an appropriate term as long as we understand the latter in terms of an imaginal rather than a material body, that is, a theophanic apparition that is configured as real in the specter of the imagination[53]—of the divine effluence.

Also relevant here is the grouping of the terms *mal'akh*, *adam*, and *satan*.[54] The justification for juxtaposing these three is that the human, *adam*, is situated between the two as he has the capacity to be one or the other, an elaboration of a basic postulate of rabbinic anthropology concerning the good and evil inclinations lodged within each person's heart. For Abulafia, the two inclinations, *yeṣer ha-ṭov* and *yeṣer ha-ra,* also identified by him as the good angel (*mal'akh ṭov*) and the bad angel (*mal'akh ra*), or as the scale of merit (*kaf zekhut*) and the scale of debt (*kaf ḥovah*),[55] correspond to matter and form, the imagination and intellect, both of which are sealed within the Tetragrammaton.[56] Abulafia elaborates on this twofold aspect of the explicit name (*shem ha-meforash*) in *Sefer ha-Malmad*: "In the secret of this name that is permutated front and back as HWH″Y or as HYH″W, and this is the reality of the essence of the soul in the secret of the good inclination and the evil inclination. And the secret of [the word] 'explicit' ['*meforash*'] is a witness as its numerical value is [equal to the expression] 'there is and there is' ['*yesh we-yesh*']," which is the Active Intellect."[57] The two dimensions of the Tetragrammaton, which are linked to the two permutations HWH″Y and HYH″W, troped respectively as the front and back, are attested in the numerical equivalence of the word *meforash* (40 + 80 + 6 + 200 + 300 = 626) and the expression *yesh we-yesh* (10 + 300 + 6 + 10 + 300 = 626), an allusion to the duplicitous character of the Active Intellect as good and evil. In another passage in *Sefer ha-Malmad*,[58] Abulafia expresses this idea in terms of the attributes of mercy and judgment, which, following the ancient rabbinic tradition, are correlated respectively with the names *YHWH* and *Elohim*. The mystical knowledge that "the two attributes are one attribute" [*ein shetei ha-middot ela middah aḥat*] is transmitted by the following numerological equivalences: the value of YHWH is 26 (10 + 5 + 6 + 5) and that of Elohim is 86 (1 + 30 + 5 + 10 + 40), and the sum of the two is 112 (26 + 86), which is the value of the letters that signify the number 26 (*k"w*) when they are written out in full as *k"f w"w* (20 + 80 + 6 + 6). The name *Elohim* also alludes to this secret insofar as it can be divided into *y"h ml"a*, and *y"h* can be spelled out as *yw"d h"a*, which numerically equals 26, the value of YHWH. Interestingly, at the conclusion of this discussion, which is the end of *Sefer ha-Malmad*, Abulafia mentions briefly the matter of the front and back of the divine (citing Exod. 33:23) but he considers it a "great secret" that he cannot elaborate in writing. From the context, however, as well as from other passages in his compositions, we can deduce that the terms "front" and "back" denote the polarity that characterizes the Active Intellect, a polarity that Abulafia delineates in his writings in a litany of binaries: mercy (*raḥamim*) and judgment (*din*), form (*ṣurah*) and matter (*ḥomer*), intellect (*sekhel*) and imagination (*dimyon*), male (*zakhar*) and female (*neqevah*), good (*ṭov*) and evil (*ra*), sacred (*qodesh*) and profane (*ḥol*), truth (*emet*) and deceit (*sheqer*), life (*ḥayyim*) and death (*mawet*). Just as the Active Intellect ontically displays the warp and woof (*sheti wa-erev*) of this twofold comportment,[59] so each human being[60] psychically possesses a dual potential to act in accordance with either the angel from the right or the angel from the left.[61] The goal is to actualize the angelic potential over and against the satanic, to subjugate the imaginative faculty to reason,[62] thereby facilitating the ocular apprehension of the letters *YHWH*.[63]

Note that the prophetic-ecstatic vision is predicated on a harnessing of the intellect and imagination, not the eradication of the latter by the former. This harnessing is possible because at root, opposites are identical in their difference. The point is epitomized in Abulafia's observation that the adept who visualizes Metatron in the "countenance of the living man" [*parṣuf adam ḥai*] comes to know that "death is life, and that life, too, is death, and that if the living die, the dead shall live."[64] This insight lies at the core of Abulafia's understanding of androgyny. As he writes in *Oṣar Eden Ganuz*, "Just as [the word] 'far' [*raḥoq*] [and the expression] 'and near' [*we-qarov*] in our language are numerically equal [both equal 314], so [the word] 'androgyne' [*androginos*] [1 + 50 + 4 + 200 + 6 + 3 + 10 + 50 + 6 + 60 = 390] and [the expression] 'male and female' [*zakhar u-neqevah*] [7 + 20 + 200 + 6 + 50 + 100 + 2 + 5 = 390] are equal."[65] By juxtaposing these two numerical equivalences, Abulafia drives home the point that just as the spatial difference between distant and proximate collapses in the identity of their opposition, so the gender difference between male and female, which may legitimately be translated as paradigmatic signposts for the various binaries mentioned above, is overcome in the opposition of their identity.

Textual support for this claim may be gathered from the admonition that Abulafia offers as the introduction to the third part of *Sitrei Torah*, one of his commentaries on the secrets in *The Guide of the Perplexed*, by Maimonides.[66] He begins by noting the basic axiom, which, in his view, is known to both the "kabbalistic sages of Torah" [*ḥakhmei ha-torah ha-mequbbalim*] and the "true philosophical sages" [*ḥakhmei ha-meḥqar ha-amitiyyim*], that each human being is endowed with the freedom to act one way or another. Psychologically, however, there is an efficient force (*koaḥ ha-mitʿorer*)[67] that arouses (*meʿorer*) the heart of the person "to act or not to act." This force, moreover, helps one decide between the two opposites (*hafakhim*) that seemingly compete and struggle with one another, the good and evil inclinations (*yeṣarim*), which Abulafia also refers to as "forces" [*koḥot*], "angels" [*malʾakhim*], "thoughts" [*maḥshavot*], and "images" [*ṣiyyurim*]. Abulafia here touches on the philosophical/theological dilemma that has plagued, and continues to plague, thinkers through time, that is, the problem of evil and its relation to the good. Abulafia emphasizes that one must strive to comprehend the existence of these forms (*ṣurot*), to discern their essence, to determine if they are two expressions of one reality that ought to be conjoined, or two independent realities that must be separated. Abulafia's response begins from the empirical perspective that the two forces wage an ongoing battle in the heart, interacting with and affecting one another, and thus it is reasonable to presume that "there is a time for this one and a time for that one [*yesh et la-zeh we-yesh et la-zeh*]."[68] That a discrete time is allocated for each of the impulses suggests that they are to be kept distinct. In the continuation, however, Abulafia describes the nature of that time, and, in so doing, provides a way to construe the opposites as identical in their contrariety: "it is like a small second [*ke-rega qaṭan*], as an indivisible point [*ki-nequddah bilti neḥleqet*], less than a blink of the eye [*paḥot me-heref ayin*]."[69] That the time apportioned for each impulse is no more substantial than a split second, a point that has no parts, even briefer than the blink of the eye, implies that the difference between the good and evil inclinations is minimal, even if it might seem from the psychological battle that rages within the heart that the disparity is vast, if not unbridgeable.

It is noteworthy that Abulafia chose to describe this matter in temporal terms elicited from the expression *yeshuʿat yhwh ke-heref ayin*, "The salvation of the Lord comes as a blink of the eye." Since the word *yeshuʿat* is written defectively without a *waw*, the phrase *yeshuʿat yhwh ke-heref ayin* can be read as *yesh et yhwh ke-heref ayin*, "There is a moment of the Lord that is like a blink of the eye."[70] The sensitivity of what is at stake is underscored by Abulafia's additional words of counsel, "Know this." The transposition of the expression *yeshuʿat yhwh*, "The salvation of the Lord," into *yesh et yhwh*, "There is a moment of the Lord," impels the reader to attend to the gnosis of redemption, a wisdom that is linked to the "moment of Lord" [*et yhwh*], the interlude of time that concurrently marks and effaces the difference between the spiritual and material, the intellectual and imaginative, the divine and daemonic.[71] What separates good and evil is nothing but a fracture of time, a split second, a point so infinitesimal that it cannot be divided, a duration that measures less than the blink of an eye. In Abulafia's own words: "This may be compared to the sparks of light that strike the eye as one sees it in a blink of the eye, the spark strikes him, then it returns, and it appears to him as if another [spark] has struck him, and afterwards it returns immediately in the form of the matter 'and the beasts ran to and fro in the appearance of lightning'" (Ezek. 1:14).[72]

The analogy of the spark provides the logic of the identity of opposites in their difference: there is only one light, but its varied manifestations leave the impression that the light is manifold. Abulafia explains this phenomenon by referring to the process through which the soul, which is a "heavenly, resplendent light" [*bahir shemeimi*], materializes [*hitgashem*] into a force in the body, the form in relation to the matter, and it "produces sparks of thought [*niṣoṣei maḥshavah*] in the heart, and the heart receives from it two ways of configuration [*darkhei ṣiyyur*]," that is, the good and evil inclinations, which take shape "in accordance with the capacity of the eye of the heart [*kefi yekholet ein ha-lev*]—if it is strong, it is true and it will persist, but if it is weak, it is a lie and it will fade." From the heart these sparks of soul (*niṣoṣei ha-nefesh*), which arise from the "sparks of intellect" [*niṣoṣei ha-sekhel*], spread forth to the remaining forces in the body, terminating with the physical sense (*hergesh*), the last of the cognitive faculties determinative of human nature.[73]

We may conclude, therefore, that, according to Abulafia's esoteric teaching, the roots for which can be discerned in Baruch Togarmi's *Maftehot ha-Qabbalah*,[74] from one perspective the two impulses ought to be treated as conflictual, and hence it is appropriate to speak of one as truth and the other as deceit, but from another perspective the two impulses are manifestations of one light, and hence the contrast between truth and deceit collapses. In *Oṣar Eden Ganuz*, Abulafia links this insight to the depiction of the *sefirot* in *Sefer Yeṣirah*,[75] "their end is fixed in their beginning, and their beginning in their end, like the flame bound to the coal [*ke-shalhevet qeshurah be-gaḥelet*]": "The secret of the 'coal' [*gaḥelet*] is 'truth' [*emet*], and the secret of the bond [*qesher*] is deceit [*sheqer*], as in the matter of our existence, that is, in deceit there is truth."[76]

Abulafia discerns the secret of the paradoxical identification of opposites in the uroboric description of the *sefirot*,[77] an idea that he substantiates exegetically by the numerical equivalence of *gaḥelet* (3 + 8 + 30 + 400 = 441) and *emet* (1 + 40 + 400 = 441), on the one hand, and by the transposition of *qesher* into *sheqer* (they are composed of the same consonants and thus they are numerically equivalent as well, equaling 600), on the other. The unity of the *sefirot* bespeaks the metaphysical truism that is reflected empirically in the fact that in every falsehood there is truthfulness. In another passage from *Oṣar Eden Ganuz*, Abulafia adduces this paradox from the description of the three matrix letters in *Sefer Yeṣirah*, *alef*, *mem*, and *shin*, as the "great and wondrous secret, concealed and sealed in six rings"[78]: "From them you will find the deceptive truth [*ha-emet shiqri*] [5 + 1 + 40 + 400 + 300 + 100 + 200 + 10 = 1056], as you find the truthful deception [*ha-sheqer ha-amiti*] [5 + 300 + 100 + 200 + 1 + 40 + 400 + 10 = 1056]. And thus the enlightened one [*ha-maskil*] through the power of his intellect can make the deception truthful [*ye'ammet ha-sheqer*] [10 + 1 + 40 + 400 + 5 + 300 + 100 + 200 = 1056] and also make the truth deceptive [*yeshaqqer ha-emet*] [10 + 300 + 100 + 200 + 5 + 1 + 40 + 400 = 1056], that is, the truth is divisible into three parts in the secret of *alef*, *mem*, *shin*, *emet makhriᶜa sheqer* [truth mediates deception]."[79] For the sage, truth and deception are not in binary opposition, as he knows that truth is the mediation between what is true and what is false (the three matrix letters *alef*, *mem*, and *shin* decoded as the acrostic *emet makhriᶜa sheqer*), and hence he has the capacity to ascertain the deceptive truth (*ha-emet shiqri*) that is the truthful deception (*ha-sheqer ha-amiti*).

The pietistic ideal that emerges from this gnosis is one of transformation as opposed to obliteration, the intellect guiding rather than annihilating the imagination.[80] As Abulafia puts it in the concluding sentence in his advisory note in the introduction to the third part of *Sitrei Torah*, "On account of this it is necessary for every person to have a revealed and a concealed matter [*inyan nigleh we-nistar*]."[81] From the vantage point of the soul that is not yet enlightened, the revealed and concealed must be kept apart, and thus the model of redemption entails liberating the intellect from the imagination,[82] but from the vantage point of the soul that is enlightened, the revealed and concealed are to be united, and thus the model of redemption entails transmuting good into evil. In a manner that resonates with the dyophysite portrayal of Mercurius in alchemical treatises (expressed in a number of antinomies, including the male/female binary, the spiritual/material polarity, and the divine/demonic dichotomy),[83] in the kabbalistic teaching enunciated by Abulafia, Metatron exemplifies a duplex nature,[84] a fact typified by the characterization of this angel as both the first and the last of the ten intellects, marked respectively as *alef* and *yod*,[85] and designated by the two names Israel and Jacob, the former signifying the head (*yisra'el* = *ro'sh li*) and the latter the heel (*ya'a-qov* = *iqvi*).[86] The adept who attains mystical insight discerns that the two aspects that might appear from a logical standpoint to be antinomical are in reality unified within Metatron. As Abulafia expressed the esoteric wisdom in *Oṣar Eden Ganuz*, "And the eminent secret that one must know is that his head is in the tail and his tail is in the head."[87] In *Ḥayyei ha-Olam ha-Ba*, Abulafia relates the unity of opposites to the scriptural instruction to craft the two cherubim from one piece of gold (Exod. 25:18–19): "The matter of the two cherubim is to allude to the Presence [*ha-shekhinah*], they are cause and effect, male and female, and therefore they were hammered in one body with two forms, and they saw one another, and God was between them."[88] The soul that is transformed into this angel realizes the integration of opposites in its own being and thereby imitates the divine. Abulafia refers to this gnosis as the "secret of inversion" [*sod ha-hippukh*] or as the "inversion of attributes" [*hithappek-hut ha-middot*][89] predicated on the realization that opposites are one, that the attribute of the right is the attribute of the left and the attribute of the left is the attribute of the right, since we cannot properly speak of an autonomous left that is not comprised within the right.[90]

The secret of time, therefore, is intricately linked in Abulafia's thinking with the paradoxical identity of opposites. Thus, in a discussion in *Imrei Shefer* concerning the three critical moments that determine the fate (*goral*) that befalls a person in this world—the moment of intercourse (*rega ha-shimmush*), the moment of conception (*rega ha-yeṣirah*), and the moment of birth (*rega ha-leidah*)—Abulafia notes that the "secret of the lot [*sod pur*] . . . comprises the conjunction of 'the impure' [*ha-ṭame*] and 'the pure' [*ha-ṭahor*] together."[91] Abulafia avails himself of numerology to anchor the dual characterization of time, represented typologically by the categories of purity and impurity, for the word "lot" [*pur*], which denotes the wheel of time, numerically equals 286, which is the sum of the words *ha-ṭame* and *ha-ṭahor*, the "impure" and the "pure." Predictably, Abulafia relates the identity of opposites to the Tetragrammaton: "And the secret of the name is entirely [in the word] 'explicit' [*meforash*], for it combines being [*hawayah*], the body [*guf*], the impure [*ṭame*], and that which contaminates [*meṭamme*], and to it is joined the soul [*nefesh*], which is pure [*ṭehorah*] and which purifies [*meṭaheret*]. And when you comprehend this secret you will comprehend the secret of the calf, the secret of the ashes of the cow, why it purifies the impure and contaminates the pure."[92] The choice of the ritual ordinance of the red heifer (Num. 19:1–10) to exemplify the paradox is sensible enough, inasmuch as it had the curious capacity to render the pure impure and the impure pure. For Abulafia, then, the depiction of time as the *mysterium coniunctionis* is connected to the idea of the lot, *pur*, which he articulates as the inner meaning of the holiday of Purim, a title derived from the plural of this very word. For example, in *Ḥayyei ha-Nefesh*, he writes, "The explicit name [*shem ha-meforash*] falls upon the name of the lot [*shem ha-pur*] for every revealed being. And [the word] *purim* refers to two without doubt, for there are two lots, 'one lot to the Lord and one lot to Azazel' (Lev. 16:8)."[93] The juxtaposition of the mystery of the Tetragrammaton and the secret of the lot is based on the fact that *shem ha-meforash*, the "explicit name," and *shem ha-pur*, the "name of the lot," are made up of the same consonants and, consequently, they have the same numerical value.[94] Having established that correspondence, Abulafia goes on to link the dual nature of time to the word *purim*,[95] which he connects, in turn, with the priestly tradition of the two lots that were placed on the goats, one marked for the God of Israel and the other marked for Azazel. From Abulafia's perspective, therefore, Purim instructs us about the hermaphroditic measure of time weighed in the balance of life and death, guilt and innocence, the two faces of Metatron.

In *Sitrei Torah*, Abulafia explicates the matter as follows: "And thus the 'turn of Esther' [*tor esther*] (Esther 2:15), the turn, the scale of merit or the scale of guilt [*tor kaf zekhut o kaf ḥovah*], for the scale of merit and the scale of guilt comprise the moment of the end [*et qeṣ*], and the moment [*et*] is an appointed time [*mo'ed*], as there is a moment for the appointed time [*et la-mo'ed*]."[96] Based on the numerological equivalence of the expressions *tor esther* (400 + 200 + 1 + 60 + 400 + 200 = 1261) and *tor kaf zekhut o kaf ḥovah* (400 + 200 + 20 + 80 + 7 + 20 + 6 + 400 + 6 + 1 + 20 + 80 + 8 + 6 + 2 + 5 = 1261), Abulafia derives from the figure of Esther in the Purim narrative the characterization of time as a balance on the scales of guilt and innocence. Insofar as Abulafia on occasion employs the image of the scales as a figurative representation of the evil and good inclinations,[97] it is reasonable to propose that the aforementioned depiction of Esther is an alternative way of speaking about time as the mediation of opposites. The surmise is substantiated by two other passages. The first is a description of the "elements of man" [yesodot ha-adam] in Sefer ha-Ḥesheq as "twins [te'omim] in the image of the left and the right upon which the intellect and the imagination are engraved. Therefore, I have commanded you that the intellect should prevail over the imagination and the scale of merit should offset the scale of debt."[98] The underlying temporal implication of the image of the twins is brought to the surface in a second extract from Ḥayyei ha-Olam ha-Ba:

> Even though heaven and earth were completed from one side, their seal, which is the seal of evening and morning [ḥotam erev wa-voqer], was not sealed on account of the secret of the sabbatical of the earth [sod ha-shemiṭṭah shel ha-areṣ], but the seventh day was sealed in the completion of the work, the resting, the blessing, and the holiness . . . And the essence is that the right and left are twins [te'omim], a "veritable day" [yom emet], and that is "entirely true" [kullo emet], and this is "his work" [mela'khto], "his work" [mel-a'khto], "his work" [mela'khto], "they were garbed as angels" [lav-shu mal'akhut].[99]

Abulafia strings together various images to elucidate the notion that the essence of the material creation is linked to the binary of night and day, the "seal of evening and morning," also identified as the right and left twins. Through a series of letter transpositions and numerical equivalences, Abulafia links the expressions te'omim, yom emet, kullo emet, mel-a'khto (repeated three times corresponding to the number of occurrences in Gen. 2:2–3), and mal'akhut. The full idiom connected to the latter is lavshu mal'akhut,[100] which Abulafia appropriates from a dictum transmitted in Genesis Rabbah (though it is likely that his use reflects the reference to it on the part of Maimonides as a "great prophetic secret"[101]) that seeks to explain the textual discrepancy between the appearance of the figures to Abraham (Gen. 18:2) in the form of men (anashim) and their appearance to Lot (ibid., 19:1) in the form of angels (mal'akhim): "When the Presence [shekhinah] departed from them, they were garbed as angels [lav-shu mal'akhut]."[102] When refracted through the prism of Abulafia's interpretative gaze, the term mal'akhut signifies angelic embodiment, that is, the concretization of the divine effluence in the figure of Metatron, whose body is composed of the letters of the name YHWH, which itself comprises all of the letters of the Hebrew alphabet, configured as an anthropos in the imagination. This incarnation, moreover, is referred to as God's work (*mela'khto*) in creating the universe, the temporal nature of which is manifest in the duplicity (*te'omim*) of night and day, the two aspects that jointly constitute a single "day of truth" [*yom emet*] that is "entirely true" [*kullo emet*].

One of the most striking accounts of the *coincidentia oppositorum* is offered by Abulafia through the imaginary persona of Zekhariah in *Sefer ha-Ot*,[103] a prophetic treatise composed in poetic form. The visionary relates that the "figure of the name" [*temunat shemo*], i.e., the Tetragrammaton, is engraved in his heart[104] in the "image" [*ṣelem*] and "likeness" [*demut*] that correspond to the intellect and imagination.[105] At first, he considered separating them (*lehavdil beneihem*), but he then realized that the "two are bound to one another" [*qeshurim sheneihem zeh ba-zeh*], and just as it is impossible to separate two letters that are identical, so it is not possible to separate the two forces.[106] Abulafia readily acknowledges that there is an intense battle in the heart between form and matter, spirit and body, intellect and imagination, depicted metaphorically as ink and blood,[107] but he also relates that he had the capacity to transform the lethal drug (*sam ha-mawet*) into an elixir of life (*sam ha-ḥayyim*),[108] a transmutation that is possible because life and death share a common source. The alchemical ideal is laid out in more detail in the following passage from *Imrei Shefer*:

> The one who transmits the transmission of the name [*ha-moser mesirat ha-shem*], in the secret of the two inclinations, informs his disciple initially that in the beginning of his creation he was himself one essence composed of two matters [*eṣem eḥad murkav mi-shenei inyanim*], and they are called matter [*ḥomer*] and form [*ṣurah*], or mass [*golem*] and image [*temunah*], for everything was indifferently the same [*ha-kol shawweh*]. They are also called the two inclinations sealed in the explicit name [*shenei yeṣarim ḥatumim be-shem ha-meforash*], who conceals his mysteries, and this is their sign: the good inclination [*yeṣer ha-ṭov*] and the evil inclination [*yeṣer ha-ra*].[109]

The esoteric wisdom consists of apprehending that there is one essence that is composed of two facets. The time of this realization is the split second, the indivisible point, an eternity more fleeting than the blink of the eye. In *Sefer ha-Malmad*, Abulafia provides more insight into the nature of this time by echoing the Talmudic association of the blink of the eye and twilight[110]: "We have also received that twilight [*bein ha-shemashot*] indicates that it is without time [*heyot zeh belo zeman*], for the meaning of twilight is that its moment is like a blink of the eye [*she-itto ke-heref ayin*]."[111] It is precisely in and from that site, the point upon which the secret of the world to come is dependent,[112] that one may discern the line that divides and thereby conjoins light and dark, day and night,[113] the angelic and satanic capacities of the human being. In the time of twilight, a time that is without time (*belo zeman*), the interim between life and death, opposites are identified by the difference of their identity to the extent that they are differentiated by the identity of their difference.

In a passage from *Oṣar Eden Ganuz*, Abulafia addresses this point in slightly different language: "Every enlightened person [*maskil*] knows that the human being possesses these three types of existence, as we have remarked. Hence, at times he is a human, and his actions attest that they are human actions [*maʿaseh adam*], and at times he is Satan, for his actions are satanic actions [*maʿaseh saṭan*] that are injurious to himself and to others, and at times he is an angel, for his actions are angelic actions [*maʿaseh malʾakh*] that are beneficial to himself and to others, and this is well understood."[114] In other contexts, the satanic and angelic[115] are identified by Abulafia as two faces of Metatron, sometimes portrayed as the attributes of mercy and judgment, and thus we may assume that in grouping together human, angel, and Satan, what he intends is that an individual can emulate either dimension of Metatron.[116] This symbolism may relate as well to Abulafia's portrayal of Christianity as demonic,[117] which he associates (in line with any number of medieval rabbinic figures) with its idolatrous nature, that is, the worship of the image (the term that Abulafia often uses is *demut*) of the divine body, a characterization that is based, in turn, on the assumption that the tenets of this Abrahamic faith are rooted in the imagination rather than reason.[118] In a paradoxical twist, the religion that dogmatically professes the incarnation of God in human form is placed on the level of Satan as opposed to Adam, whereas the religion upon whom the prophetic tradition has been bestowed expresses its Adamic nature by actualizing the capacity to conjure the angelic body, the anthropomorphic configuration of the incorporeal, in the imagination.[119] It is feasible, then, to surmise that the three terms, *adam, malʾakh*, and *saṭan*, signify the struggle on the psychological plane between the evil and good inclinations, which corresponds to the battle on the theological plane between Christianity and Judaism, Jesus of Nazareth and the Messiah of Israel, the seals of the sixth and seventh days of the week, the material Tree of Knowledge and the spiritual Tree of Life.[120] The threefold distinction can also be cast in temporal terms that were a commonplace in the cosmological order that Abulafia derived from Maimonides: the satanic corresponds to corruptible matter and it is thus subject to time; the angelic corresponds to the incorruptible intellect and it is thus not subject to time; the human being is a composite of matter and intellect and it is thus both subject to and not subject to time,[121] or, to put it in different terminology, the human being has the capacity to eternalize the temporal by temporalizing the eternal.

Angelomorphic Transformation and Monopsychic Integration

As a consequence of the angelomorphic conversion, the distinction between the one cleaving and that to which one cleaves cannot be easily upheld.[122] The individual conjoined to the Active Intellect, therefore, becomes cognizant, or perhaps "incognizant" would be the more felicitous term, of being part of the oneness of all the things that are contained in this Intellect,[123] an experience of ecstasy portrayed in a panoply of intensely heteroerotic images,[124] the male character assumed by the Active Intellect and the female by the human soul.[125] To receive the efflux of the Holy Spirit is to be conjoined to the Intellect, to be transmuted into Metatron, to be incorporated into the name, which is the Torah, and to be restored to the light.

Let us consider one more extract from *Ḥayyei ha-Olam ha-Ba*, which summarizes the essential aspects of Abulafia's mystical worldview:

> Both the heart and the mouth have to be circumcised, "in your mouth and in your heart" (Deut. 30:14), the mouth to enunciate [*lehazkir*] through it what needs to be enunciated [*ha-nizkar*] in the enunciation of the glorious name [*be-hazkarat ha-shem ha-nikhbad*], and the heart to contemplate [*laḥashov*] the name in the time of the enunciation [*hazkarah*], that is, the letters of the name themselves, for they are the limit of comprehension [*takhlit ha-hassagah*] . . . Therefore, the first intention is to enunciate the name of God [*lehazkir be-shem ha-shem*] in order to receive from him the overflow of wisdom and knowledge [*shefa ḥokhmah wa-daʿat*]. The second is to augment what he has received, and to rectify the doubts that are thought with respect to many issues, and to fortify the overflow until it returns more perfectly to the one who receives from what was, and he will ascend from matter to matter, and the Holy Spirit will return.[126]

Availing himself of the language of Deuteronomy and *Sefer Yeṣirah*, Abulafia depicts the two stages of the meditational process respectively as circumcision of the mouth and circumcision of the heart. The former involves verbal articulation of the name, and the latter, mental contemplation.[127] It is important to recall here that the practice promoted by

Abulafia entailed three phases: combining the letters of the name in writing, verbally, and mentally.[128] The text I have cited obviously relates to only the latter two stages, something of a departure, since it is more common to find references in the compositions of Abulafia and other ecstatic kabbalists to the first two stages of the process.[129] It is reasonable to propose, however, that the two circumcisions singled out by Abulafia reflect a distinction affirmed by the intellectual elite of his time, largely due to the impact of the ideal of intellectual worship set forth by Maimonides,[130] that is, a distinction between liturgical prayer, which is dependent on the enunciation of words, and contemplative prayer, a form of speculative meditation that is without words, the silent worship of the heart.[131] From the standpoint of the philosophically enlightened sage, traditional prayer is problematic as the words used to describe, to approach, and to elicit a response from God are literally false, and, hence, "silence and limiting oneself to the apprehensions of the intellects are more appropriate."[132]

Demarcating the limit of language was not merely a logical deduction for Maimonides, but, rather, a consequence of contemplating the divine luminosity, the flood of intellect that carries one beyond intellection: "We are dazzled by His beauty, and He is hidden from us because of the intensity with which He becomes manifest, just as the sun is hidden to eyes that are too weak to apprehend it."[133] The paradoxical gist of this statement should be evident: the hiddenness of God is consequent to his becoming manifest, that is, to be revealed, God must be concealed, for the concealment of God cannot be revealed without being concealed, just as the light of the sun is too powerful to be seen, and thus it is phenomenally visible only when it is veiled. We may take this as an alternative expression of the paradox of the apophatic perspective that Maimonides explicitly embraces in his observation that "all men, those of the past and those of the future, affirm clearly that God, may He be exalted, cannot be apprehended by the intellects, and that none but He Himself can apprehend what He is, and that apprehension of Him consists in the inability to attain the ultimate term in apprehending him." Herein lies the fundamental paradox of the *via negativa*: knowing God consists precisely of knowing that God cannot be known, a knowledge that cannot be communicated except by paradoxical dicta that extol the ideal of learned ignorance.[134] The only philosophically credible liturgical response to God, therefore, is silence, a view supported exegetically by the citation of the words of the ancient poet, "Silence is praise to thee," [*lekha dumiyyah tehillah*] (Ps. 65:2).[135]

Scholars have duly noted that a number of Spanish kabbalists in the thirteenth century opposed the extreme spiritualization of prayer that could potentially, and in some instances actually did, lead to an abrogation of ritual worship.[136] I bracket the question of Abulafia's own commitment to statutory prayer. What is most important for our purposes is his application of this philosophical issue to the meditational practice more generally. He is unequivocal on this point—one needs to vocalize the names orally and to contemplate them mentally—a position that, in my mind, parallels Abulafia's insistence elsewhere that circumcision of the flesh is a necessary prerequisite for circumcision of the tongue, that is, just as only one who bears the somatic mark of circumcision is capable of undertaking the regimen of letter combination, the goal of which is to separate the soul from the body, so, too, only one who pronounces the divine names verbally is capable of contemplating them internally.[137]

It is worth noting, moreover, that the application of the term *hazkarah* to the vocalization of the name by the mouth and to the meditation on the name in the heart is reminiscent of two types of *dhikr* that one finds in Sufi devotional practice, the verbal recitation of the names and the introspective recollection of them.[138] There are, of course, important differences. One of them, as noted by Idel, is that in Sufism the objective of *dhikr* is to achieve a state of undivided mental focus—concentrating on a point—by the repetition of onomastic formulas, whereas Abulafia's technique is based on purifying the mind by rapid permutation of consonants and vowels in constantly changing patterns.[139] To clarify the point, according to the tenets of the kabbalah enunciated by Abulafia and his disciples, there are fixed patterns to the permutations, patterns that are determined by a received number of possible pairings; the practice of letter combination, however, does not involve the iteration of the same name or even a sequence of names, but the vocalization of different combinations that follow in a rapid pace and effect the trancelike state into which the adept temporarily succumbs. Discrepancies notwithstanding, the affinity between the Abulafian *hazkarah* and the Sufi *dhikr* cannot be ignored, and one ought not rule out the possibility that the crucial meditational exercise promulgated by prophetic kabbalah, the path of the names (*derekh ha-shemot*), evolved as a modification or adaptation of the practice cultivated by Muslim mystics.

What is essential to emphasize is Abulafia's explanation of the purpose of the two circumcisions or the two stages in the meditational method. The "first intention" is to enunciate the name of God so that one may receive the overflow of wisdom and knowledge. The "second intention" is to contemplate the name so that one may augment what one has received initially, to fortify the overflow until it returns more perfectly. As a consequence of the amplification of light, the adept ascends spiritually from the world of multiplicity to the divine unity[140]—an ascent upward that is, at the same, a journey inward—and thereby restores the Holy Spirit to its source.[141] The psychological experience of union cannot be separated from the ontological assumption regarding the unity of all things in the light of the intellect (*or ha-sekhel*), which Abulafia identifies as the First Cause[142] whence the whole of reality emanates and to which it returns. Consider, for instance, Abulafia's formulation in the *Iggeret we-Zo't li-Yehudah*: "When you loosen the bond of all the *sefirot*, you will unify them of necessity, and when you unify them in the ultimate unification [*takhlit ha-yihud*], you will not find in them anything but the unity, and when you unify from the unified one [*meyyahed min ha-meyuhad*],[143] you will not find there any *sefirah* but the First Cause [*ha-sibbah ha-ri'shonah*] exclusively . . . Everything will be restored to its beginning, which is the one [*yashuv ha-kol el re'shito she-hu ehad*]."[144] Or compare the language in *Imrei Shefer*, which seems to be based, in part, on the description of the *sefirot* in *Sefer Yeṣirah*, "their end is fixed in their beginning, and their beginning in their end"[145]: "And the secret is that the first ones are the last ones, and the last ones are the first ones, and everything is his, blessed be he, and therefore he constantly says 'to me it belongs' (*li hu*). 'For the entire earth is mine' (Exod. 19:5), everything is my portion, and I am divided in all of the parts, from beginning to end."[146]

I thus concur with the assessment that Abulafia's mysticism betrays the mix of a "transformational unitive component" and a "limited pantheistic facet."[147] My own preference, however, would be to view the pantheistic facet as more than limited, though, I hasten to add, perhaps terms such as "panentheistic," "monistic," or "monopsychic," are better suited to translate Abulafia's thinking.[148] Indeed, the very possibility of the *unio mystica* rests on an ontological affirmation of the underlying oneness of all being, a unifying force that Abulafia relates to the intellectual overflow, the providential light, which actualizes the potential of all that is contingent from itself but necessary from the point of view of its efficient cause.

As an illustration of the point, I will cite from *Ḥayyei ha-Nefesh*, one of Abulafia's commentaries on the secrets of Maimonides' *Guide of the Perplexed*. Following Maimonides, Abulafia insists that "all of existence is necessitated from the existence of his essence, blessed be, from his will, which is his essence, as the wisdom of his existence decreed in the essence of his truth as it is in itself." With regard to this matter, there is a convergence of philosophy and tradition, and thus Abulafia speaks of the "rational and received unity" [*ha-yihud ha-sikhli we-ha-mequbbal*]: the oneness of God experienced mystically is a matter that is both demonstrated rationally and received traditionally. To add anything to God's essence is to be guilty of ascribing complexity (*harkavah*) to the incomposite nature of divine simplicity.[149] It follows, therefore, that all the attributes of God, such as "the form of the world" [*surat ha-olam*], "the form of all the forms" [*surat ha-surot kullam*], the "end of all ends" [*takhlit ha-takhliyot*], relate to actions vis-à-vis the world that proceed continually from his necessary existence, "for he is the cause and reason [*sibbah we-illah*], the origin [*we-re'shit*], and the first principle of everything [*we-hathalah ri-'shonah la-kol*], and in him is everything [*u-vo ha-kol*], and from him is everything [*u-me-itto ha-kol*], and he is the all of everything [*we-hu kol la-kol*], and all for every part that is contained in everything [*we-khol la-kol heleq ha-nikhlal ba-kol*], and, he, blessed be his name, is the all [*we-hu ha-kol yitbarakh shemo*]." In the continuation of this passage, Abulafia turns to the status of the one who is conjoined to the divine. He notes that it is incumbent upon every enlightened person (*maskil*) to imitate God by becoming the incomposite whole, something that is possible for the soul but not for the body, since corporeality presupposes division. "In the moment of being conjoined to the Intellect, and being separated from the body, she and he are everything [*hi we-hu kol*], and hence they are one thing [*hem davar ehad*]."[150]

When the soul (portrayed as feminine) is separated from its somatic encasement, and it unites with the Intellect (portrayed as masculine), it transcends its partiality by becoming one with the all, *kol*, a technical term that Abulafia assigns to the Active Intellect, insofar as the latter encompasses in itself everything that is contained in the First Cause (*ha-sibbah ha-ri'shonah*) or the First Existent (*ha-nimsa ha-ri'shon*),[151] and, consequently, the execution of the governance (*hanhagah*) over everything is attributed to it.[152] In the following passage in *Osar Eden Ganuz*, Abulafia combines ancient Jewish angelological traditions, the Maimonidean account of the Active Intellect, especially its designation *saro shel olam*, "archon of the world,"[153] a locution based on the title *sar ha-olam* found in older rabbinic and mystical sources,[154] and sefirotic nomenclature derived from contemporary kabbalistic sources:

> Know that all the attributes are dependent on the Holy Spirit to guide them, as it is the guide of everything [*manhig ha-kol*]. Therefore, one *sefirah*, which is the Active Intellect, is called the "all [*ha-kol*], for it is the archon of the world [*saro shel olam*]. And it is the king of the world [*melekh ha-olam*], and it is called the "Life of the Worlds" [*hei ha-olamim*] . . . and from one perspective it is possible to call it an angel in actuality [*mal'akh mammash*], and its name is "angel of the Lord" [*mal'akh yhwh*], and it is the angel whose name

is YHWH. And it is the one in whose hand are all the attributes, and the attribute of *Malkhut* is assigned the name of the tenth attribute [*meyuḥeset be-shem middat ha-eser*].[155]

Kenotic Expansion, Temporal Delimitation, and Becoming the Nothing-that-is-all

In the following passage from *Imrei Shefer*, the ecstatic ideal of mystical union with the Active Intellect outlined above is cast in language that further reflects the sefirotic terminology of kabbalistic theosophy, a framing that affords one an opportunity to attend more closely to the kenotic dimension of the ecstatic experience, a critical component in Abulafia's phenomenology of time:

> In discovering, however, that the beginning of the name [YHWH] is *yod*, we know immediately that the purpose of the intention in the existence of man is that he comprehend himself and his essence, which is in the form of *yod* according to its form . . . that is, the gathering of the thing that gathers everything [*qehillat davar meqahel ha-kol*]. And this is the secret of the Assembly of Israel [*kenesset yisra'el*], for its secret is the gathering of *yod*, the archon of God [*kenesset yod sar el*]. The perfect man [*ha-adam ha-shalem*] gathers everything [*maqhil ha-kol*], and he is called the congregation of Jacob [*qehillat yaʿaqov*]. The essence is from the all [*iqqar me-ha-kol*], the ten souls, according to the gathering [*qibbuṣ*] of the ten *sefirot* in the *sefirah* of *Shekhinah*, which is the female that is impregnated [*ha-neqevah ha-mitʿaberet*], and she receives everything from the all [*meqabbelet ha-kol midei ha-kol*], and her name is *ṣedeq* in the masculine and *ṣedaqah* in the feminine.[156]

In Abulafia's writings, the *sefirot* are identified as the separate intellects that cause the motion of the heavenly spheres.[157] Accordingly, *Shekhinah*, which is the last of the sefirotic emanations, is another cognomen for the Active Intellect. Just as kabbalists, who embraced a theosophic interpretation of the *sefirot*, spoke of *Shekhinah* as the quintessential vessel, the gradation that has nothing substantial of its own but only what it receives from the gradations above, so Abulafia describes the Active Intellect in relation to the Intellects from which it receives the divine overflow. Accordingly, Abulafia appropriates the theosophic designation of *Shekhinah* as the "Assembly of Israel," *kenesset yisra'el*, which he transposes into *kenesset yod sar el*, "the gathering of *yod*, the archon of God."[158] The *yod*, which is the tenth letter of the Hebrew alphabet but the first letter of the

Tetragrammaton, alludes symbolically to the decade of souls or *sefirot* that converge in the tenth one. Not surprisingly, Abulafia also avails himself of the kabbalistic depiction of *Shekhinah* receiving the overflow more directly from *Yesod*, the ninth *sefirah*, which is designated *kol* because it comprises the totality of the divine light within itself in the same manner that the phallus was thought to contain within itself the energy of the whole male body. Abulafia, accordingly, refers to *Shekhinah* as the "impregnated female" [*ha-neqevah ha-mit'aberet*], but, in his case, the symbolism must be interpreted allegorically as a reference to the widely held belief that the tenth of the separate intellects takes in the efflux of intellectual light from all the intellects above it and hence it is designated *kol*. Inasmuch as *Shekhinah* exhibits an androgynous character of receiving and overflowing, both masculine and feminine names, *ṣedeq* and *ṣedaqah*, are bestowed on her.[159] In the kabbalistic sources whence Abulafia derived this terminology, *ṣedeq* refers to *Yesod* and *ṣedaqah* to *Shekhinah*, but both terms can be applied to the latter.[160] What Abulafia shares in common with the other kabbalists, therefore, is the view that the last of the ten *sefirot* displays both the power to overflow, the formal principle engendered as masculine (*ṣedeq*), and the capacity to receive, the material principle engendered as feminine (*ṣedaqah*).

As I noted above, the gender dynamics of the divine-human encounter are such that the soul is feminized in relation to God. Abulafia has this in mind when he states that the perfection of human existence is realized when one is conjoined to the *yod*, that is, the Active Intellect, which is the tenth *sefirah*, designated *Shekhinah* or *Malkhut*, and one thereby becomes oneself a *yod*, the vessel that "gathers everything" [*maqhil ha-kol*].[161] Orthography is necessary to get the point fully: the *yod* is shaped like a half circle, a shape that brings to mind the image of a vessel, thus conveying the notion of gathering. As a consequence of the conjunction, the soul morphs into this *yod* and thus assumes the name "congregation of Jacob," *qehillat ya'aqov*, a scriptural designation of the people of Israel (Deut. 33:4), but here a technical name applied to *Shekhinah* as it is the intellect that comprises the overflow of all the intellects. To receive the effluence of the all, one must become a vessel, a process that rests on the paradox of concomitant constriction and expansion—by being diminished like the *yod*, the smallest of Hebrew consonants, one is incorporated into the *yod*, which is the fullness of everything.[162] As Abulafia puts it in his commentary on *Sefer Yeṣirah*,

> From this perspective it was necessary for us to vocalize the name of God in its beginning with the smallest of all the letters and the greatest of them in number—just as we are the little ones of the world,

and each of us is called a "microcosm" [*olam qatan*], and this is the secret of the world-to-come, which is suspended on the point [*sod ha-olam ha-ba she-hu taluy al nequddah*], and we are the "macrocosm" [*olam gadol*] when we comprehend the truth of the point that is renewed in truth, and its name is *yod*, and its numerical value is ten, and its form is that of a half-circle, and their secret [the sum of the name of the letter *yod* when written in full, *ywd* (10 + 6 + 4 = 20) + the word for "ten," *asarah* (70 + 300 + 200 + 5 = 575) + the letter *yod* itself (10) = 605] is the tenth majesty [*hod asiri* = 5 + 6 + 4 + 70 + 300 + 10 + 200 + 10 = 605].[163]

There is no need, in my judgment, to distinguish sharply between affirmations of the unity of all being and statements concerning the union of being with God.[164] To be united with God is possible, for all things are expressive of the divine unity, a unity that is troped more specifically as the intellectual overflow that sustains the world through the agency of the *agens intellectus*. In becoming conjoined to this intellect, the "soul that comprises all of the souls" [*neshamah kolelet kol ha-neshamot*],[165] the distinction between the one who is conjoined and the one to whom one is conjoined is effaced, since in the moment of conjunction, the intellect (*sekhel*), the act of intellection (*maskil*), and the intelligible (*muskal*) are no longer distinguishable; in fact, as Abulafia repeatedly reminds his reader, the Active Intellect and the human intellect are ontically homologous.[166] Insofar as this threefold unity is applied to God's self-intellection, it can be said that the breakdown of boundaries portends the divinization of the human, which presumes in tandem a humanization of the divine.

I suggest that Abulafia alludes to this insight when he remarks in *Sefer ha-Ḥesheq*, concerning the archon of the face (*sar ha-panim*)—identified in this context as Uriel, but in other contexts associated with Metatron—

his power speaks in the heart [*koho medabber ba-lev*], and he also shows his power in the heart [*mar'eh koho ba-lev*], for we said that the Presence of God [*shekhinat el*] is in the middle, and our intention is to speak of him, for his name is the first matter [*homer ri-'shon*], and all of the world is the first matter in the middle . . . You should be careful lest it rise in your thought that the form hinted at refers to the issue of the First Cause [*inyan ha-sibbah ha-ri'shonah*]. Rather, you should know that the matter is imagined [*medummeh*] on account of the secret of the existence of the world and of man, for the Intellect is in everything [*hu ba-kol*], and a place is not attributed to it except by way of analogy [*derekh mashal*]."[167]

That the Active Intellect both *speaks* in the heart of the visionary and *shows* its power illustrates that Abulafia acknowledged the synesthetic element of the experience: The word that is spoken assumes the form that is visually apprehended, but since the Intellect is omnipresent, it cannot be circumscribed to any particular place. What is seen in the prophetic vision, therefore, is an imaginal body, that is, a bodily form of the immaterial that is configured as real in the imagination.

Mystical gnosis of the name, which is achieved as a result of the meditational technique of letter combination (*ḥokhmat ha-ṣeruf*), entails a state of intellectual conjunction that Abulafia, following Maimonides, branded in terms of both the scriptural idea of prophecy (*nevu'ah*) and the rabbinic notion of eschatological felicity, the "life of the world-to-come" [*ḥayyei ha-olam ha-ba*].[168] Although the latter retains something of its original connotation in Abulafia's scheme, he was far more interested in utilizing the phrase—we have already cited and analyzed several extracts from a treatise that bears this expression as its title—to denote an interior state of spiritual transformation occasioned by the triumph of intellect over imagination, spirit over body, an orientation that is attested as well in other medieval Jewish philosophical exegetes, poets, and kabbalists.[169] To be sure, Abulafia does not go so far as to negate entirely the nationalistic and geopolitical aspects of the messianic ideal, but it is clear from his writings that his messianism is primarily psychic in nature.[170] Tactilely, the ecstatic experiences the illumination as being anointed with oil, and thus the one who is illumined is not only capable of being redeemed proleptically, prior to the historical advent of the messiah, but such an individual noetically attains the rank of the messianic figure.[171] The anointment also denotes the priestly status of the illuminate;[172] indeed, in the unitive state, the ecstatic assumes the role of high priest,[173] the position accorded Metatron in the celestial temple, the role of the angelic viceregent summoned by Abulafia as the object of conjunction.[174]

We may conclude, therefore, that the phenomenon of anointment comprises three distinct, though inseparable, aspects of the pneumatic metamorphosis—messianic, priestly, and angelic. For Abulafia, moreover, the matter of reception is critical to his understanding of the prophetic-messianic experience, as the enlightened mind, the soul unfettered from the chains of corporeality, receives the overflow of the Holy Spirit, which is identified in Abulafia's system as the Active Intellect, the angel Metatron, and as the wheel of letters that is the Torah scroll in its idealized form.[175] The experience of *unio mystica* may be considered phenomenologically in four ways: to cleave to the name, to be conjoined with the intellect, to be transformed into the demiurgical angel, and to be incorporated within the textual embodiment of the word of God.[176]

Life of the World-to-come: YHWH and the Compresence of Time

In another passage from *Hayyei ha-Olam ha-Ba*, the experience of conjunction with the Active Intellect is characterized in terms that contribute significantly to our understanding of the role of time in Abulafia's prophetic kabbalah.

> The comprehension of the Active Intellect [*hassagat ha-sekhel ha-po'el*] is the purpose of the life of the rational soul [*takhlit hayyei ha-nefesh*], and it is the cause of the life of the world-to-come [*sibbat hayyei olam ha-ba*], and this soul is conjoined [*tidbaq*] to God, blessed be the name, eternally and forever. And the matter [*davar*] that is called the image of God and his likeness in the person lives eternally without end in the life of the Creator who is their cause. Concerning this it says "For he is your life and the length of your days" (Deut. 30:20), and it says "You, who cleave to the Lord your God, are all alive this day" (ibid., 4:4). The one who is not conjoined to God does not live an eternal life that is like "this day" [*ha-yom*], which is perpetual [*tamid*], and thus the expression "this day" was added.[177]

As a consequence of the ecstatic union, one participates in the eternal life that is God's being. Significantly, the overcoming of time in the transformative experience is linked exegetically to the scriptural locution "this day" [*ha-yom*] in the verse "You, who cleave to the Lord your God, are all alive this day." The eternality of the divine into which one is assimilated as a result of the unitive experience is conveyed rhetorically in the expression "this day," for just as the sense of permanence communicated by this elocution is not to be understood as the mere repetition of the same, but rather as the abiding of the flux that is continuously changing, so conjunction with God results in the attainment of a pneumatic perpetuity realized in the moment that persistently alters the eternity of the past and the eternity of the future. Abulafia expresses the matter in terms of the relationship between the two names, *Ehyeh* and *YHWH*, to which he refers respectively as the "first secret" [*sod ri'shon*] and the "last secret" [*sod aharon*]. The "intermediate secret" [*sod emṣa'i*] is Yah, that is, the letters *yod* and *he* that are found in both names. These two occurrences of Yah "instruct about the secret of beginning [*ro'sh*] and end [*sof*], for the first instructs about the secret of the Yah that is primordial [*qadmoni*] and the second the Yah that is eternal [*niṣḥoni*], and the secret that is in both of them is perpetual [*tamid*]."[178] The character of time is everlasting is the present that mediates perpetually between the primordiality of the past and the eternality of the future.

The character of temporality is explored further in another passage from *Ḥayyei ha-Olam ha-Ba*:

> Know, my son . . . that the name is his essence, and the essence is his name, and the name of the unique name [*ha-shem ha-meyuḥad*] is composed of four letters, and they are, in truth, YWH"A, and they are the concealed letters [*otiyyot ne'lamot*]. Since they are beginning, middle, and end [*ro'sh tokh sof*], they instruct about the name whose secret is beginning, middle, and end, and this is the universal secret [*sod kelali*] that is called "place" [*maqom*], and it is called "time" [*zeman*], which is the "confidant" [*amon*], and this is the squared number that emerges from YHWH [that is, the sum of each of the letters of the name squared: $10 \times 10 + 5 \times 5 + 6 \times 6 + 5 \times 5 = 100 + 25 + 36 + 25 = 186$] . . . And the secret is [the word *maqom* spelled out in full as] *m"m qw"f w"w m"m* [$80 + 186 + 12 + 80 = 358$], and the all [*we-ha-kol*] that is the "name of the living" [*shem ḥai*] [$340 + 18 = 358$]. Know that it comes forth from YHWH, "male and female" [*zakhar u-neqevah*] [$227 + 163 = 390$], and this is the secret of the Presence [*ha-shekhinah*] [$= 390$], the "Almighty, and Adam, and Eve" [*shaddai we-adam we-ḥawah*] [$314 + 51 + 25 = 390$], "male and female" [*zakhar u-neqevah*] [$227 + 163 = 390$]. Therefore, it is the secret of "the image of Adam and the image of Eve" [*ṣelem adam we-ṣelem ḥawah*] [$160 + 45 + 166 + 19 = 390$], "male and female" [*zakhar u-neqevah*] [$227 + 163 = 390$], and this is 15 [*yod-he*] times 15 [*yod-he*], which is 225, and 15 [*yod-he*] times 11 [*waw-he*], which is 165, and together [$225 + 165 = 390$] they are "male and female" [*zakhar u-neqevah*] [$227 + 163 = 390$], for they were created from the combination of the name *yod-he* with the name *yod-he*, and the name *waw-he* with the name *yod-he* . . . And the secret of time [*zeman*] is *zy"n m"m nw"n* [$67 + 80 + 106 = 253$], and together they are the matter [*ha-ḥomer*] [$5 + 8 + 40 + 200 = 253$], and it is created [*nivra*] [$= 50 + 2 + 200 + 1 = 253$].[179]

The passage is a typical specimen of Abulafia's literary style and associative mode of thinking, linking together seemingly disparate ideas by linguistic transpositions and numerical equivalences. The starting point is the identification that Abulafia makes between the name and the essence, but the name that he has in mind, which he denotes as the unique name (*shem ha-meyugad*), is YWH"A, a name that consists of the four letters referred to as the "concealed letters" [*otiyyot ne'lamot*].[180] These letters, which are designated in other medieval Jewish sources as *otiyyot ha-hamshakhah* or *otiyyot ha-dibbur*,[181] are the consonants that guide one in the vocalization of words,[182] and thus they were compared by Judah Halevi to souls in relation to all the other letters, which are like bodies.[183] Three of the letters, *yod, heh*, and *waw*, constitute the core letters of the Tetragrammaton, and, consequently, various masters of esoteric lore in the thirteenth century began to refer to them as the hidden name of God.[184] For his part, Abulafia follows this tradition, and, in one place, he even refers to these letters as the "holy of holies . . . that instruct about the secret of the ten *sefirot*."[185] The numerical value of the four letters (*alef, heh, waw, yod*) equals twenty-two, and thus this name signifies the totality of the Hebrew alphabet or the Torah in its mystical essence.[186] I would suggest that Abulafia has this in mind when he describes the name as comprising beginning (*ro'sh*), middle (*tokh*), and end (*sof*). This expression, which appears frequently in Abulafia's writings,[187] and which in some contexts is related specifically to the practice of letter combination associated with the seventy-two letter name derived from Exodus 14:19–21,[188] in the aforecited context denotes past, present, and future. On occasion Abulafia makes the point of noting that the first letters of the three words, when arranged in reverse order (*sof, tokh, ro'sh*), spell *seter*, implying thereby that the three temporal modes constitute a "mystery."[189]

The secret related to the triadic structure of beginning, middle, and end is underscored further by the numerical equivalence of the terms *zeman* (7 + 40 + 50 = 97) and *amon* (1 + 40 + 6 + 50 = 97), the latter term (drawn from Prov. 8:30) signifying the demiurgical capacity that is attributed to the Active Intellect. Abulafia alludes to this gnosis in the following remark in *Sitrei Torah*: "And the secret of time [*we-sod zeman*] is the demiurge [*amon*], which comprises four letters, and in full it is *zy"n m"m nw"n*, and its secret is the fifty times [*nw"n zemannim*], and this is the secret of the jubilee, the fifty years . . . and the [word] *zeman* in full is *ha-ḥomer*, and its secret is *nivra*, for the matter is created [*ki ha-ḥomer nivra*] without doubt."[190] Further support for this interpretation may be found in the following comment in *Sefer ha-Ḥesheq*: "Uriel is the archon of the face [*sar ha-panim*], and he is in the image of matter [*bi-demut ḥomer*] before the Torah . . . and *zy"n my"m nw"n* [the letters that spell *zeman*] are also in an image [*bi-demut aḥat*], and [the expressions] 'demiurge' [*amon*], 'and the angel' [*u-mal'akh*], 'and the tree' [*we-illan*] are clear witnesses in relation to him, and he is the wise one that speaks [*ḥakham medabber*]."[191] It is noteworthy that the Active Intellect, the archon of the face, identified here with Uriel, the "wise one that speaks," is aligned with the image of time, *zeman* (7 + 40 + 50 = 97), which is further linked to the expressions "demiurge" ([*amon*] = 1 + 40 + 6 + 50 = 97), "and the angel" ([*u-mal'akh*] = 6 + 40 + 30 + 1 + 20 = 97), and "and the tree" ([*we-illan*] = 6 + 1 + 10 + 30 + 50 = 97). The depiction of the Active Intellect as the locus of time cannot be separated from its characterization as the chiasm of space. If we were to phrase this in a contemporary idiom, we would be justified in referring to the Active Intellect as "timespace" or "spacetime." This is the implication of Abulafia's reference to the square of each of the letters of the Tetragrammaton, the sum of which is 186, the numerology of the word *maqom*, "place." By spelling out this word is full as *m"m qw"f w"w m"m*, letters which equal 358, Abulafia is able to reinforce the connection between time, space, and the Active Intellect (referred to as the "name of the living," *shem ḥai* = 358). Once he establishes this connection, he goes on to make several numerical calculations (all based on the sum 390) aimed at elucidating different features of the androgynous nature of Metatron (*zakhar u-neqevah* = *ha-shekhinah* = *shaddai we-adam we-ḥawah* = *ṣelem adam we-ṣelem ḥawah*). Space and time, we may presume, are themselves expression of this androgyny, which is derived from the Tetragrammaton,[192] if we multiply by 15 the two parts of the name that correspond to masculine form and feminine matter, respectively, that is, *yod-he* (10 + 5) × 15 = 225, and *waw-he* (6 + 5) × 15 = 165; the sum of the two (225 + 165) equals 390.

Abulafia establishes an inextricable link between time and matter, or, more specifically, the "first matter," which, as we have seen above, is applied to Metatron. Thus, at the end of the extract from *Ḥayyei ha-Olam ha-Ba*, we find the observation that "the secret of time [*zeman*] is *zy"n m"m nw"n* [67 + 80 + 106 = 253], and together they are the matter [*ha-ḥomer*] [5 + 8 + 40 + 200 = 253], and it is created [*nivra*] [= 50 + 2 + 200 + 1 = 253]," and in *Sefer ha-Ḥesheq*, the Active Intellect is described as the "image of matter [*bi-demut ḥomer*] before the Torah." In light of the theoretical explanations of time that circulated in his day, it should come as no surprise that Abulafia would himself affirm a nexus between corporeality and temporality. In that regard, time is uniquely associated with the concept of a world (*olam*) that is extrinsic to the divine.[193] What is surprising, however, is that space and time are not treated by Abulafia, to use the Aristotelian system of classification, as independent qualities attributed to one substance, but rather as two conduits through which the intellectual overflow of the divine is instantiated in the chain of being. This, it seems, is the import of the reference in *Ḥayyei ha-Olam ha-Ba* to the "universal secret" [*sod kelali*] that is called "place" [*maqom*] and "time" [*zeman*].[194]

This identification of the Active Intellect as either space or time strikes me as one of the more innovative ideas proffered by Abulafia. As he formulates it in another passage from the same work:

> Therefore, it is written "But where can wisdom be found; where is the source of understanding?" (Job 28:12). The secret of 'where' [*me-ayin*] is *min d"y*, from *alef* until *yod* . . . "Where is the source of understanding?" The secret of "source of understanding" [*meqom binah*] through permutation is "he understands the stature" [*mevin qomah*], that is, "he comprehends the world" [*mevin ha-olam*], "in the midst of the place" [*bein ha-maqom*],[195] and they are numerically [equal to] *zy"n m"m nw"n*, which instructs about the created time [*zeman nivra*], and this matter [*ha-ḥomer*] is called something from nothing [*yesh me-ayin*]. When you comprehend these two aspects in truth, which are time [*ha-zeman*] and place [*ha-maqom*], you will comprehend with them the matter [*ha-ḥomer*].[196]

The two facets of the Active Intellect are portrayed in the above passage as *Ḥokhmah* and *Binah*, the former comprising the ten separate intellects, the first designated as *alef* and the tenth as *yod* (both derived from the word *ayin* , which appears in Job 28:12), and the latter the embodiment of the intellectual effluence in the material universe, an idea that is substantiated by the scriptural idiom from the same verse, *meqom binah* (40 + 100 + 6 + 40 + 2 + 10 + 50 + 5 = 253), which is transmuted linguistically into *mevin qomah* (40 + 2 + 10 + 50 + 100 + 6 + 40 + 5 = 253) and *bein ha-maqom* (2 + 10 + 50 + 5 + 40 + 100 + 6 + 40 = 253), and numerically transposed into *mevin ha-olam* (40 + 2 + 10 + 50 + 5 + 70 + 6 + 30 + 40 = 253). All of these, which can be seen as specifications of the spatial dimension, are linked further to the aspect of time as the word *zeman* when written out in full, which has the same numerical equivalence (*zy"n m"m nu"n* = 7 + 10 + 50 + 40 + 40 + 50 = 6 + 50 = 253), which is also the value of the word *nivra* (50 + 2 + 200 + 1 = 253), "created," in the expression *zeman nivra*, the "created time," a turn of phrase that underscores the fact that the temporal is assigned to matter (if the word *ha-ḥomer* were written in the defective form, i.e., without the *waw*, its numerical computation would be 5 + 8 + 40 + 200, which equals 253, the same sum as *zeman* when it is spelled out as *zy"n m"m nu"n*), the "something" [*yesh*] that issues from the "nothing" [*ayin*]. For Abulafia, therefore, the traditional formula *creatio ex nihilo* does not denote the volitional and temporal creation of being from nonbeing, but the necessary and continuous emanation of the cosmos from the intellectual overflow from the *ens necessarium*, a view that, in my judgment, resonates with the opinion of Maimonides.[197] The key point is that, in Abulafia's thinking, time and space are not conceived as attributes of matter; they are matter itself, which can be viewed as spatial from one perspective and as temporal from another perspective.

Alternatively expressed, for Abulafia, time and space are correlated with the dual aspects of Metatron, and since Metatron is the imaginal configuration of the Active Intellect, it is plausible to speak of the temporal and spatial as modalities of the divine mind. On this score, the gap between the divine and nature is significantly narrowed. As Abulafia observes in *Sefer ha-Ḥesheq*, "For nature [*ha-ṭeva*] is the act of God [*maʿaseh elohim*]."[198] One might be inclined to interpret this comment in a figurative way, but I am of the opinion that it should be taken in a more precise manner as an affirmation of the divine status of nature and the natural status of divinity, a stance that is supported by the numerological equivalence of *ha-ṭeva* ($5 + 9 + 2 + 70 = 86$) and *elohim* ($1 + 30 + 5 + 10 + 40 = 86$), which Abulafia proclaims explicitly in another passage from the same work: "Thus the secret of God is nature [*elohim sodo hu ha-ṭeva*]."[199] I would surmise, however, that just as the other binaries collapse into a twofold unity—for instance, the left is absorbed in the right—so space in its originary inception is to be viewed as a manifestation of time. That this is the tenor of the ecstatic experience is implied in the following comment in *Sefer ha-Malmad*: "His explicit name [*shemo ha-meforash*] and the soul [*ha-nefesh*] are conjoined and bound in the steadfast bond at the time of creation [*be-et ha-yeṣirah*], and this is the 'soul of Israel' [*nefesh yisraʾel*], and this is the 'beginning of time' [*roʾsh et*]."[200] The inceptual moment of creation is marked by the conjunction of the Jewish soul and the divine name, a correlation substantiated by the numerical equivalence of the expressions *nefesh yisraʾel* ($50 + 80 + 300 + 10 + 300 + 200 + 1 + 30 = 971$) and *roʾsh et* ($200 + 1 + 300 + 70 + 400 = 971$).

In the mystical state of conjunction, the soul assumes the character of the name to which it is attached, and, insofar as the name embodies the compresence of past, present, and future (*hayah, howeh,* and *yihyeh*), we can speak of the ecstatic experience as the convergence of the three modes of time in the mystery (*seter*) of the moment that comprises beginning (*ro'sh*), middle (*tokh*), and end (*sof*). To cite once more from *Ḥayyei ha-Olam ha-Ba*: "And the name YHWH in its triad [*shillusho*] [signifies that] 'he was, he is, and he will be' [*hayah we-howeh we-yihyeh*], which are *rt's* [*ro'sh tokh sof*], and time is entirely without distinction in relation to him [*we-ha-zeman kullo eṣlo shawweh*], which is not so in our case."[201] The secret of the name, therefore, is encoded in *r"ts*, an acrostic for *ro'sh tokh sof*, the beginning, middle, and end, a mystery further elucidated by the compresence of past, present, and future. Within God the three tenses merge so that there is no way to distinguish between them, which marks a crucial difference between the nature of time when viewed from the human and divine perspectives. Abulafia understands the affirmation of God's timelessness and immutability in terms of the secret of the intersection of all modes of time in the divine essence. As he writes in *Ḥayyei ha-Nefesh*:

> Since he does not fall under time, the three times are affixed to him without distinction [*be-shiwwuy*], as it is said about him, blessed be he, that he was, he is, and he will be [*hayah we-howeh we-yihyeh*], he was before man, he is together with man, and he will be after man. And so the tradition [*ha-qabbalah*] is that he was before the world, he is together with the world, and he will be after the world. And the secret is that he was in the past as he is now and as he shall be in the future without change, for nothing of his actions changes in relation to him and in accordance with his knowledge. All the more so he himself does not change, and inasmuch as his attributes are naught but his essence, his attributes do not change.[202]

When the mystery of time is viewed linearly, then we may be prone to think of the present as the midpoint that connects the past that is no more and the future that has not yet been, but when time is viewed circularly, the present would be conceived better as a spot in which past and future remain open, where beginning and end can both occupy the position of the middle. In attaining the life of the world-to-come, one emulates the motion of the Active Intellect, "whose action is in the image of a sphere that turns in a circular rotation [*bi-demut ha-galgal mitgalgel be-sibbuv iggul*], for it acts as it is, it was, and it will be [*howeh we-hayah we-yihyeh*]."[203] In this triune unity of the name,[204] the eternal is temporalized and the temporal eternalized.

By way of conclusion, we may say that Abulafia's mystical theosophy is predicated on an ontological presumption regarding time as the primal impulse of God in nature, as mediated through the light of the Active Intellect, the demiurgical angel, the soul of the universe, who maintains the balance of existence by holding together opposites in the space of their divergence. In *Oṣar Eden Ganuz*, Abulafia expounds the matter specifically as it relates to the time of the eschaton:

Thus I will inform you of something greater than this, for the secret of the scale of merit and the scale of guilt instruct about the time of the end [*et qeṣ*], and they are composed of the account of creation in the account of creation [*maʿaseh bereʾshit be-maʿaseh bereʾshit*]. In the account of the chariot, there are an additional twenty-two corresponding to the letters, which instruct about the two accounts together [*yaḥad*] [10 + 8 + 4 = 22]. And, indeed, "merit and guilt" [*zekhut we-ḥovah*] [7 + 20 + 6 + 400 + 6 + 8 + 6 +2 + 5 = 460], "the one who sees within it" [*ḥozeh be-tokho*] [8 + 6 + 7 + 5 + 2 + 400 + 6 + 20 + 6 = 460), "the script that holds on" [*ha-katuv ha-oḥez*] [5 + 20 + 400 + 6 + 2 + 5 + 1 + 6 + 8 + 7 = 460], which is the "stone" [*even*] [1 + 2 + 50 = 53) joined together with the "letter" [*ot*] [1 + 6 + 400 = 407], in the junction of "intellect" [*sekhel*] (300 + 20 + 30 = 350) and "imagination" [*dimyon*] [4 + 40 + 10 + 6 + 50 = 110], as the junction of "the angel" [*ha-malʾakh*] [5 + 40 + 30 + 1 + 20 = 96] and "the Satan" [*ha-saṭan*] [5 + 300 + 9 + 50 = 364]. Thus "holy to the Lord" [*qodesh la-yhwh*] [100 + 4 + 300 + 30 + 10 + 5 + 6 + 5 = 460] is in the image of "son and daughter" [*ben u-vat*] [2 + 50 + 6 + 2 + 400 = 460], and this is the "created light" [*or nivra*] [1 + 6 + 200 + 50 + 2 + 200 + 1 = 460], which is the "light of the limbs" [*or evarim*] [1 + 6 + 200 + 1 + 2 + 200 + 10 + 40 = 460) from which "the worlds were created" [*nivreʾu ha-olamim*] [50 + 2 + 200 + 1 + 6 + 5 + 70 + 6 + 30 + 40 + 10 + 40 = 460].[205]

I end with one final citation from Abulafia's *Sefer ha-Ḥesheq*, one that weaves together the diverse themes explored in detail in this essay. The immediate context is an exegetical meditation on the critical verse, "I was with him as the demiurge, a source of bemusement every day, toying before him in every moment," *wa-ehyeh eṣlo amon wa-ehyeh shaʿashuʿim yom yom mesaḥeqet lefanaw be-khol et* (Prov. 8:30):

The secret of "in every moment" [*be-khol et*] is "five thousand years" [*hʾa alafim shanah*] "written" [*nikhtavin*] "on the script" [*al ketav*] in the two opposites, "in death and life" [*ba-mawet we-ḥay-yim*]. Therefore it says "I was with him as the demiurge" [*wa-ehyeh eṣlo amon*] [who is] doubled [*kaful*]. [The words] "with him as the demiurge" [*eṣlo amon*] [can be transposed into] "it emanated from El and Yah" [*aṣulah me-el we-yah*], and the two of them are the bemusement [*shaʿashuʿim*]. The name of the attribute of judgment [*middat ha-din*] is El and the name of the attribute of mercy [*middat raḥamim*] is Yah. Elijah is proof, as is Enoch who is Metatron, and he is the secret of "in every moment" [*be-khol et*]. And the secret of the "moment" [*et*] is "the created light" [*ha-or ha-nivra*], which is "from the soul" [*mi-nefesh*], the "scale of reality" [*mishqal ha-meṣiʾut*].[206]

In this extraordinary text, Abulafia offers a succinct summation of his exceedingly complex conception of time. The exegetical springboard for his reflections is the verse in Proverbs that describes wisdom's intimate relation to God in images of temporality, which Abulafia applies to Metatron.[207] The passage begins with the expression that appears at the end of the verse, "in every moment" [*be-khol et*], for by attending to the nature of the moment, one can discern the character of time more generally. Numerically, *be-khol et* $(2 + 20 + 30 + 70 + 400 = 522)$ is equal to *h"a alafim shanah* $(5 + 1 + 1 + 30 + 80 + 10 + 40 + 300 + 50 + 5 = 522)$, "five thousand years," an expression likely based on the rabbinic tradition that history can be divided into six millennia, the first two corresponding to the period of chaos (*tohu*), the next two to the period of Torah, and the last two to the days of Messiah.[208] I would suggest, accordingly, that the expression "five thousand years" denotes the totality of the historical cycle prior to the messianic advent in the sixth millennium.

Abulafia expands on the quality of time by proffering three other expressions that have the numerical value of 522, *nikhtavim* $(50 + 20 + 400 + 2 + 10 + 40)$, *al ketav* $(70 + 30 + 400 + 20 + 2)$, and *ba-mawet*[209] *we-ḥayyim* $(2 + 40 + 6 + 400 + 6 + 8 + 10 + 10 + 40)$. The first two, *nikhtavim*, "written," and *al ketav*, "on the script," are alternative ways of communicating that time is a matter of inscription,[210] an idea that is a reverberation of two elemental tenets of Jewish esotericism, the semiotic nature of corporeality and the scribal role assigned to Metatron. The third expression, *ba-mawet we-ḥayyim*, "in death and life," conveys that time is a coincidence of opposites, a motif, as we have seen above, that is also linked to the twofold nature of Metatron, an idea referred to here in Abulafia's aside that the demiurge is doubled (*kaful*). This idea is reiterated in the numerical morphing of *eṣlo amon* $(1 + 90 + 30 + 6 + 1 + 40 + 6 + 50 = 224)$ into *aṣulah me-el we-yah* $(1 + 90 + 6 + 30 + 5 + 40 + 1 + 30 + 6 + 10 + 5 = 224)$, the names El and Yah designating the attributes of judgment and mercy, the two faces of Metatron, encoded as well in the word *sha'ashu'im*. The duplicity is linked to the figure of Elijah, presumably on account of his status as being both human and angelic, which is made more explicit in the figure of Enoch who, according to a much older tradition, was translated to heaven and transformed into Metatron.[211] In the end of the passage, Abulafia circles back to the beginning by noting that Metatron, the being who mediates between human and angel, is the secret of "in every moment" [*be-khol et*], substantiating the point by observing that the word *et* (70 + 400 = 470) has the same numerical value as *ha-or ha-nivra* (5 + 1 + 6 + 200 + 5 + 50 + 2 + 200 + 1 = 470), *mi-nefesh* (40 + 50 + 80 + 300 = 470), and *mishqal* (40 + 300 + 100 + 30 = 470). In this chain of numerological equivalences, Abulafia imparts his understanding of time as the moment, the instantiation of the created light, the soul of the cosmos, and the scale of existence.

Tribute to Derrida

AMY HOLLYWOOD

But the Professor was not always right.[1]

H. D.

In 1977, the Hebrew University of Jerusalem inaugurated a Sigmund Freud Professorship. They invited Freud's daughter Anna Freud to speak. Unable to attend, Anna Freud sent a paper, described by Yosef Yerushalmi in *Freud's Moses: Judaism Terminable and Interminable*, as "a sober and clear review of the possible future directions of psychoanalysis and its potential place within a university setting."[2] Yerushalmi notes his approval: "In all, it was an eminently suitable paper for an academic event." What really interests Yerushalmi, however, is not this eminently suitable and restrained academic paper, but the "abrupt and unexpected ending, in total discontinuity with what had come before, that sent a shock of amazement through the eminent audience."[3] Here are the words read in Anna Freud's name (as cited by Yerushalmi):

> During the era of its existence, psychoanalysis has entered into connexion with various academic institutions, not always with satisfactory results. . . . It has also, repeatedly, experienced rejection by them, been criticized for its methods being imprecise, its findings not open to proof by experiment, for being unscientific, even for being a "Jewish science." However the other derogatory comments may be evaluated, it is, I believe, the last-mentioned connotation

150

which, under the present circumstances, can serve as a title of honour.[4]

Yerushalmi claims that nothing in Anna Freud's writings up to this time prepares one for these lines. His book has laid out evidence from Sigmund Freud's life and letters, however, that suggests Sigmund might have uttered them, despite his repeated assertions that the universal scientific claims of psychoanalysis would be damaged by its association with Jewishness. This leads Yerushalmi to ask his hypothetical interlocutor— Sigmund Freud himself—"When your daughter conveyed those words to the congress in Jerusalem, *was she speaking in your name?*"[5]

Yerushalmi points to two documents as offering particularly strong evidence that Anna Freud is speaking for Sigmund. Earlier in *Freud's Moses*, Yerushalmi had uncovered a sentence from Sigmund Freud's *Autobiographical Study*:

> I was moved . . . by a sort of curiosity, which was, however, directed more toward human concerns than toward natural objects; nor had I grasped the importance of observation as one of the best means of gratifying it. *My deep engrossment in the Bible story (almost as soon as I had learned the art of reading) had, as I recognized much later, an enduring effect upon the direction of my interest.*[6]

This reference to his early reading of the Bible—Yerushalmi argues that Jakob Freud would have taught Sigmund to read out of a Hebrew and German Bible—was not included in the first edition of the autobiographical study (1925), but only in the 1935 edition, which appeared a year after the completion of *Moses and Monotheism* (*Der Mann Moses und die monotheistische Religion*), suggesting that work on the latter reminded Freud of the importance of the Bible to his work (in its person-directedness, if not in its methods). Immediately after citing Anna Freud's speech, in the closing paragraphs of his study, Yerushalmi cites a 1926 letter to Enrico Morselli in which Freud claimed that although he wasn't sure if psychoanalysis was the product of the Jewish mind, if it were he "wouldn't be ashamed."[7]

But even if Yerushalmi can show that Sigmund Freud might have agreed with his daughter's words, can we take this as evidence that she was speaking in his name? And why should this be so important? In *Archive Fever*, Jacques Derrida begins to ask the pertinent questions:

> Yerushalmi asks himself whether this sentence *written* by Anna is indeed *signed* by Anna. Asking himself this, he asks his spectral interlocutor (he asks himself (of) his specter who would first have

asked himself this) if his daughter spoke in her own name: as if he doubted that a daughter, above all the daughter of Freud, could speak in her own name, almost thirty years after the father's death, and above all as if he wished, still secretly (a secret he says he wants to keep, that is to say, to share with Freud, to be alone in sharing with Freud), that she had always spoken in the name of her father, in the name of the father.[8]

Yerushalmi wants Anna Freud to efface herself in order to speak the father's words, to transmit to Yerushalmi—the son—the father's secret. Moreover, Yerushalmi effaces the daughter again in order to secure the primacy of his own relationship to the father. For why ask Sigmund Freud if Anna Freud speaks in his name? Isn't Anna the only one who would know for sure if that were the case? But Yerushalmi doesn't, finally, care what Anna Freud intended, or even what she wrote, except insofar as it bears the name of the father.

Yerushalmi calls Anna Freud, as did Sigmund Freud himself, Sigmund Freud's Antigone. Derrida suggests this is the secret to Yerushalmi's reading of her words: "Yerushalmi wishes that Anna-Antigone had only been the living spokesperson, the faithful interpreter, the voice bearer come to support her dead father and to represent his word, his name, his belonging, his thesis, and even his faith."[9] To say that Yerushalmi "wishes" Anna to be a "living spokesperson" only partially describes his attitude toward Anna. Yerushalmi wants Anna Freud to be an effaceable and effaced voice so that he can have the illusion of an unmediated relationship with the father. Yet the reference to Antigone points to an even more problematic position, for Antigone supports the father only in her living death, entombed alive within a cave as punishment for burying her dead brother. Like Antigone, Anna Freud is the voice of the father, Yerushalmi's text implies, only until such a time as the true heir—Yerushalmi himself, apparently, figured as the son of Sigmund Freud—arrives and speaks in the father's name. To take the place of the son, then, Yerushalmi must kill the daughter, effacing her thoroughly so as to deny any necessary intermediary between father and son. Yerushalmi not only wishes that Anna-Antigone be the living spokesperson of the father, but also that she (like Antigone) die, ceding all authority to the future son (for, of course, Antigone's brothers are both dead).[10]

There is a further problem for Anna Freud, as Derrida suggests: Yerushalmi implies repeatedly that only the son can be Jewish. If Freud's science is Jewish, as Yerushalmi wants to argue Freud himself believed, then his heir must be a son, according to Yerushalmi's understanding of Jewishness (which, Derrida argues, is not quite the same as Judaism for Yerushalmi).[11] Yet Sigmund Freud explicitly named Anna Freud as his heir. From Yerushalmi's perspective this necessitates a "deracination" or "de-Judaizing" of psychoanalysis—hence, according to one set of potential oppositions, a universalizing of its claims that would make it "really" scientific. This is a direct threat to Yerushalmi, figured as the son, and—again in Yerushalmi's formulation—to Jewishness, which in his understanding can only be passed down from father to son. In order to prove that Freud understood psychoanalysis to be Jewish, Yerushalmi needs both to cite Anna Freud's words *and* to efface her as a legitimate heir and interpreter of Sigmund Freud's work. In fact, one might argue that he needs to stage Anna Freud's murder in order to assert his own authority, for as Derrida cogently notes, Yerushalmi does have Freud's letter to Enrico Morselli. He doesn't really require Anna Freud's words, although one might argue for a difference between not being ashamed of Jewishness and finding it to be a "title of honour." In this reading, Yerushalmi invokes Anna Freud only in order to slay her and usurp her place as the authorized interpreter of her father's works.

Derrida points to this reading in his attention to circumcision as the mark of Judaism and of Jewishness. Derrida interprets Jakob Freud's inscription in Sigmund Freud's Bible, with its reference to the "new skin" of the Bible's binding, in terms of circumcision (probably incorrectly, as Yerushalmi points out); Yerushalmi reads it in terms of Jewish knowledge, understood by him as being transmitted through an all-male tradition. For Derrida, the archive through which knowledge is transmitted and circumcision are always linked: "writing, the trace, inscription, on an exterior substrate or on the so-called body proper, as for example, and this is not just any example for me, that singular and immemorial archive called *circumcision*, and which, though never leaving you, nonetheless has come about, and is no less exterior, *exterior right on* your body proper."[12] By marking the body in its exteriority, circumcision, like the phylacteries that men (and not women, at least for the most part) wear close to their bodies, constructs a certain interiority, a certain subjectivity never accessible to women, who do not share in the mark and whose bodies are defined as unable to bear that mark.[13] Derrida suggests that writing as a form of inscription, marked by a cut or trace, similarly restricts access insofar as the pen or stylus is figured as male (the penis/pen) and that which is inscribed on is female (the Torah).[14] If woman is the silent and passive surface on which man is able to write, and through which he is able to speak, then her voice can never be heard as her own; this is the problem of Antigone and of Anna Freud.

If the mark of Judaism and of Jewishness—the sign of the covenant between God and the Jewish people and, even more, an essence of Jewishness independent of belief in that covenant and that God—is circumcision, what does it mean for the daughter to be Jewish? For Derrida, for whom circumcision is figured as the primary mark of Jewishness (perhaps because of the absence in Derrida's life of dietary laws and other bodily practices with which subjects are inscribed by and within that tradition), the exclusion of the daughter, paradoxically, becomes particularly visible.[15] And, Derrida *almost* writes, the practice of circumcision within Judaism makes manifest a larger truth—the patriarchal nature of the archive, of the tradition on which it is based, and the primacy of the son.[16] So there is a particular problem for Judaism and Jewishness: given patriarchal conceptions of what it means to be Jewish, what does it mean to be a Jewish woman, particularly a secular Jewish woman? (Derrida worries about not circumcising his sons, but what if he had had the hoped-for third child, a daughter?) This is exemplary of another problem: how is the archive constructed such that the daughter cannot speak, or cannot be understood as speaking, in her own name? And how might it be constructed otherwise?[17]

These issues frame *Archive Fever*, in which Derrida analyzes Freud's destabilizing account of the patriarchal logic of the archive *and* his reinscription of that logic in the family romance of the psychoanalytic movement. The crucial point is first raised early in the essay, characteristically, in a footnote:

> There is no political power without control of the archive, if not of memory. Effective democratization can always be measured by this essential criterion: the participation in and the access to the archive, its constitution, and its interpretation . . . Among all these questions, and in referring the reader to this book [Sonia Combe's *Forbidden Archives*], let us isolate here the one that is consonant, in a way, with the low tone of our hypothesis, even if this fundamental note, the patriarchive, never covers all the others. As if in passing, Sonia Combe asks in effect: "I hope to be pardoned for granting some credit to the following observation, but it does not seem to me to be due to pure chance that the corporation of well-known historians of contemporary France is essentially, apart from a few exceptions, masculine . . . But I hope to be understood also . . ."[18]

As Derrida's analysis of Yerushalmi's relationship to Anna Freud suggests, the problem is not simply the empirical one of the need for more women working in the archives. For even when women do speak and write authoritatively (and in what field more so than psychoanalysis?), how they are heard or read is all too often structured by the patriarchive and its logic.[19]

Even Freud, who dares to tell the story of Moses without any available archive—hence the fiction that is *Moses and Monotheism* (*Der Mann Moses und die monotheistische Religion*)—continually reinscribes the logic of the patriarchive in his work. Creating a viable future, in the case of Moses through monotheism and for Freud through psychoanalysis, depends on the ability to create an archive. Yet Derrida forces us to ask whether the generation of the archive, like its handing down, is dependent on the effacement of mothers and daughters. Freud's account of the origins of religion in *Totem and Taboo* perhaps demonstrates this logic most clearly. The father becomes divine when the primal horde of brothers kills him in order to take his women from him. Identification with the lost father and guilt over their patricidal act generate both the father God and the incest taboo. Mothers and daughters, although not dead, are utterly silent within this narrative and it is out of their silence that the speech of the father and of the sons emerges.

In *Archive Fever*, Derrida links Anna-Antigone, the archive, and writing with new forms of archival technology. Is he suggesting that virtual technologies, which cannot easily be reduced to metaphors of inscription, might offer new possibilities for women "to speak in their own names"? Virtuality does not do away with materiality or the "so-called body," as some claim, yet do we see here a certain (although certainly not unquestioned) utopic impulse in Derrida, a virtuality which might loosen signification from at least some of the constraints of bodily existence? Thus in recent years we've seen arguments that in virtual reality one's body—no matter how culturally marked and constituted—can be transcended. Edith Wyschogrod forcefully demonstrates that virtual reality will always be a reality mediated through the body.[20] Moreover, the formation of subjectivity as sexed, gendered, raced and otherwise embodied is at the heart of the chiasmatic structures of bodied existence she describes and can never be fully transcended through writing or other technologies. Hence the importance of Derrida's more radical claim that virtual technologies demand a rethinking of materiality—and so implicitly of spirituality—itself. It is not that bodies will disappear, but that some bodies may become legible in ways previously unimagined.

I have argued that Derrida makes the particularly "Jewish" problem of bodily inscription exemplary (although he enacts a constant questioning

of the very logic of exemplarity) of women's relationship to all (patri)arch-
ives and (patriarchal) traditions. He suggests a close link between the form
of the archive and the particular exclusions on which it rests, in that textuality depends on a cut inscribed in/on a surface, and the tool is figured as
male, the surface as female.[21] How inescapable are these figurations? Are
there other ways to figure writing and the archive? Can we turn to virtual
realities as new modes of archival technology, modes less dependent on
bodily inscriptions and perhaps less constrained by putative bodily differences? Perhaps these new modes of figuration will enable women to be
authoritative interpreters, readers, writers, and speakers. Yet if this sound
too utopic, Derrida also insists that there can be no archive without "*a
certain exteriority. No archive without outside.*" (And as a result, the very
thing that supports the archive also works toward its destruction.[22]) As
Derrida shows, there are dangers in the universalizing and deracinating
presumptions of certain virtual utopias, presumptions that parallel those
held by historians and psychoanalysts who want to make psychoanalysis
scientific *rather than* Jewish, as if the two can simply be opposed to each
other. Judaism and religion are two overlapping sites on/in which the pull
between the particular and the universal is enacted, but so too are the
logics of the archive (as Derrida shows) and of sexual difference.

Wyschogrod suggests, like Derrida, that the trick is to find a way to go
"virtual" without losing sight of the salience and importance of particularity, materiality, and the body.[23] Only in this way can new futures, and
new relationships between fathers, mothers, daughters, and sons—
perhaps even, as Judith Butler suggests in her reading of Antigone, entirely new models of kinship[24]—be imagined and lived. The question to
ask of Derrida is whether and how, if the universal is a movement toward
the one that always involves a particularizing and exclusionary gesture (no
matter how hidden), we can determine what would constitute more or
less just modes of universality and particularity.[25]

Thus Derrida ends his text on Freud, Yerushalmi, the Jewishness of
psychoanalytic science, and the nature of its archive with a final restate-
ment of the doubleness of Freud's practice:

> *On the one hand*, no one has illuminated better than Freud what
> we have called the archontic principle of the archive, which in itself
> presupposes not the originary *arkhē* but the nomological *arkhē* of
> the law, of institution, of domiciliation, of filiation. No one has ana-
> lyzed, that is also to say, deconstructed, the authority of the archon-
> tic principle better than he. No one has shown how this archontic,
> that is, paternal and patriarchic, principle only posited itself to re-
> peat itself and returned to re-posit itself only in parricide. It

amounts to repressed or suppressed parricide, in the name of the father as dead father. The archontic is at best the takeover of the archive by the brothers. The equality and liberty of brothers. A certain, still vivacious idea of democracy.

But on the other hand, in life as in his works, in his theoretical theses as in the compulsion of his institutionalizing strategy, Freud repeated the patriarchal logic.[26]

Derrida here is in danger of effacing the death of the daughter, the incestuous rape of mothers and daughters, in ways the rest of *Archive Fever* belies. Because of this, I think, he does not make explicit that the repetition he describes becomes inevitable, given that parricide results merely in the reign of brothers—brothers who are themselves, in the classic story of Oedipus as in Freud's primal horde, also sons. Derrida suggests that the problem with virtual reality is located at precisely the same site as its possibilities: its movement toward disembodiment, even deracination. The issues are similar with regard to the question of whether psychoanalysis is a Jewish science. To affirm this seems to demand its stake in a patriarchive and patriarchal logic that Freud at times and Derrida more consistently, if still imperfectly, both wish to eschew. Yet Derrida wants to avoid the false universalism of certain masculine discourses without departicularizing or deracinating them entirely in the name of some new, also potentially exclusionary, universalism. Thus Christianity universalizes or spiritualizes the promise of Judaism, thereby deracinating the Jewish messianic promise, while at the same instituting new particularizing and exclusionary gestures.

Sigmund Freud's insistence on repetition leads "certain people" to wonder "if, decades after his death, his sons, so many brothers, can yet speak in their own name[s]." Even the sons, then, are infected by the fate of the daughter (Haemon, Creon's son, kills himself when Antigone is put in the cave); concerning that daughter, Derrida writes that one might wonder if she "ever came to life (*zoē*), was ever anything other than a phantasm or a specter, a Gradiva *rediviva*, a Gradiva-Zoe-Bertgang passing through at Berggasse 19."[27] But of course, she was. And as for the Gradiva-Zoe-Bertgang of Wilhelm Jensen's story, Freud credits her—a fictional character, of course—with analytic skills unmatched by the "real" doctors. Zoe-Gradiva can effect a dramatic cure because she is beloved by Norbert Hanold, the archeologist, the one possessed by "archive fever." Derrida suggests that finding a site from which the daughter can speak in her own name will also save the sons, making possible (among other things) a more universal democracy. And a transformation of the archive, through new forms of technology from the telephone to e-mail, may, Derrida suggests, provide the enabling conditions in which the daughter can be heard.

Like Yerushalmi, Derrida reiterates the claim that the relationship between Judaism and Christianity is not only patricidal, but also fratricidal; it is marked not only by an Oedipal complex, but also by a Cain and Abel complex (or an Eteocles and Polyneices complex, or the problem of the primal horde) and once again I find myself wondering, "What about Antigone?"[28] The democracy of brothers is still marked by strife, especially insofar as each brother claims to speak in the name of the father; the greater the continuing authority of the father, the greater the strife. In all of this, the voice of the daughter is buried, returning only when the father and brothers are all dead and then heard only as the return of the father and his authority—or authoritative curse, in the case of Oedipus. (Note that even the possibility that she could be an authoritative interpreter *of* the father is denied.[29]) So perhaps the return of the repressed is not (or not simply) the return of the murdered father; but rather (also), that return is a screen for the effaced daughter and sister whose voice is (can) never (be) heard.

Does this mean, then, that the only hope for daughters to speak is as the returned, repressed, murdered father (who is also, of course, that God in whom Freud refuses to believe)? Are daughters left with no place to speak and to be heard? Is our place only the crypt in which, like Antigone, we suffocate? If we are always inevitably haunted, can we never speak as our mothers, brothers, sisters, colleagues, lovers, friends, ourselves? Can we never hope to speak *to* and *with*, rather than *for* or *as*, the father? Can Derrida, finally, loosen his grip on us sufficiently—can we loosen our grip sufficiently on *him*—to empty a space for other words? He did and he does, and he will in death—we will against his death—continue to do so, more than just about any other.

"But the Professor was not always right."

PART III

Channeling History

Hearing the Voices of the Dead

Wyschogrod, Megill, and the Heterological Historian

JOHN D. CAPUTO

1.

In response to a question put to Jacques Derrida by Elizabeth Clark, one of America's leading historians of early Christianity, about the relevance of deconstruction for history, Derrida said what we would expect him to say, that historians must constantly question their assumptions about history and stay open to other concepts of history and of historiography, and that is where deconstruction can help. But the first thing he said was unexpected: "I dream of being a historian." He expressed his feeling that, in a way, ever since *Of Grammatology*, "I was just doing history." That was not a bit of whimsy on his part or an attempt to please his questioner. When the audience chuckled, he added, "Really, I dream of this."[1] For the "messianic" structure of deconstruction does not only mean that it is turned always and already to the to-come, the *arrivants*, but it also means that deconstruction is a logic of haunting, or of being haunted, that it is constantly "spooked" by the *revenants*, the ghosts of the dead who give us no peace. It should not be forgotten that when Derrida spoke of the messianic, he often mentioned Walter Benjamin, for whom the Messiah is not something coming. On the contrary, we ourselves are the messianic figures; we today occupy the messianic place. We are the ones for whom the dead were waiting, the ones who are supposed to redeem them. Deconstruction is "hauntology," a way of worrying about the dead, of being spooked, of hearing the voiceless voices of the past.

Derrida's dream is perfectly serious, and the reason for this, in my view, is that the historian of whom Derrida is dreaming is the same one of whom Edith Wyschogrod is dreaming when she speaks of the "heterological" historian in *An Ethics of Remembering: History, Heterology and the Nameless Others*. By this expression, coined by one of the founding figures of a field that we today tend to call "religion and postmodernism," who has helped to shape the very space in which we all work, Wyschogrod means the historian as one who responds to the claim that is laid upon her by the past, by the dead, whose silences speak volumes to us, demanding not to be left in peace, demanding our attention, our retention, our memory, our devotion, whose voicelessness calls out to us and begs our response. The historian, to advert to the theme of this, lives under the influence of the dead and her work flows from it. We do history because we live always and already under the influence of history. History for her is thus an eros, driven by a "double passion, an eros for the past and an ardor for the others in whose name there is a felt urgency to speak."[2] The dead address us from the past but they are unable to speak for themselves. The historian is one who brings that-which-was to words in the light of this double passion, promising the dead that she will tell the truth, driven by a kind of historical necrophilia. The dead are not simply dead; rather, they lay claim to us from across the ages, interrupting our complacency with ourselves and with the regime of the present. So the work of the historian is shot through from the start with an ethical obligation, one that is analogous to the structure of our responsibility to the other in Levinas, whose work was first brought to the attention of the Anglophone world by Edith Wyschogrod some thirty years ago.

When we speak about the other, and remember the other's name, Wyschogrod holds that this act is to be treated as an "ethical placeholder" for the other's unnameable transcendence,[3] and this above all when others have been the victim of an attempt to violently erase the memory of them. The historian writes in and from the present where the present, our present, is the time of the "cataclysm," the age of bureaucratic and technologically engineered mass exterminations,[4] and she promises the murdered the truth. The historian's work is situated from the start in the space of ethics, weighed upon by the immemorial press of the dead other before writing even begins. Historical writing is "always already implicated in a prediscursive ethics before it is a conveying of facts." So the heterological historian is driven at one and the same time by a passion or eros for the claims of the dead, and also by a promise to speak the truth and to assume "responsibility for a dispassionate relation to events."[5] But the passionate disposition precedes the dispassionate one, for the dispassion, which "at first appears to suggest strictly epistemological questions," presupposes the presence of the heterological historian herself, who is writing in the present about the past, and whose passion drives the undertaking.[6]

2.

However much one may be persuaded by this line of thought about the influence of the dead, as I am, it is not without its complications. As Allan Megill says in a lucid and important essay that constitutes, I would say, a "critical appreciation" of Wyschogrod's *An Ethics of Remembering*, the first, last, and constant ethical duty of the historian is to tell the truth about the past and let the chips fall where they may. The historian who works in the present must also keep a safe distance from the present, from the passions, the persuasions, and the politics of the day, lest her work be distorted by its passing pressures. The leftish, heterodoxical causes we academic heterologists of various stripes typically advocate can function as dogmas steering in advance the course of historical research (just as right-wing causes can): "Historical investigation is prone to corruption when it is carried out under the dominance of the present."[7] If, in writing a history, one has set out to make a policy statement useful to the ethical causes one prefers in the present, the results will be "systematically distortive." Megill continues, "Similarly, history written in order to support some presumably good end in the present is all too prone to fall into various forms of special 'pleading' or 'propaganda' for an admittedly good cause."[8]

I describe Megill's essay as a "critical" appreciation in the strictest sense, where the word "critique" (from *krinein*) means to delimit or discriminate, to draws lines around and show the boundaries of a discourse. Megill does not so much reject Wyschogrod's idea of a heterological historian as he wants to situate it, to put first things first and then to give it a prompt or cue from offstage as to when it may make its appropriate entrance. He writes, "I find that Wyschogrod moves too quickly, too much on the basis of a presumed consensus about what was the case in the past . . . Before we can begin to engage erotically with the past, attempting with ardor to attend to the past's silent voices, we need to ask two questions: What do we know about the past in question? And how do we know it?"[9] Our ethical passion for the dead must be guided in advance by knowledge or it is blind. Megill does not deny that ethics is there from the start, but the ethics in question is the ethics of the historian, the one who governs the practice of "history" as a discipline, namely, truth-telling. The ethics of the *Wissenschaftler*, of disciplined and rule-governed inquiry, what we sometimes call "professional" ethics, comes first. It precedes the substantive ethico-political commitment of the historian.

So, in contradistinction to Wyschogrod's title, *An Ethics of Remembering*, Megill's essay addresses "the ethics of history-writing," where "history" means disciplined historical inquiry. History in this sense is not to be confused with "memory," just as knowledge is not to be confused with proof. What we remember is part of what we "know" or think we know. Knowing and remembering are personal; they have to do with insight and intuition and recollection, and they may be as right as right can be (or they may not). But the knowledge of the historian is based upon public rules of evidence, upon what can be documented, attested to and proven by the methods of historical research, just the way a scientific experiment can be repeated by other scientists in other places and times, which is what constitutes their results as public "objects," not personal beliefs. Memories are personal and they serve to build up the "identity" of someone in the present; history is public and it is meant to establish objective truth and requires distance from the present and personal identities. Both the prosecutor and the defense attorney may personally know a suspect is guilty as sin, but that is a long way from being able to prove it in a court of law which proceeds by way of the public rules of evidence. Indeed, even the judicial analogy has a limit, Megill says, at least the analogy to Anglo-Saxon law. The latter is based upon adversarial proceedings, in which opposing lawyers make the best case they can for the procedural innocence of their clients, a tactic that sometimes skirts perilously close to countenancing perjury. "The historian's obligation is not to speak *for* the silenced others—or for anyone else in the past. This historian ought not to be an attorney for one side or another in the past: the attorney is judge, not advocate," for "advocacy leads to subtle corruptions."[10]

So the ethics of history precedes the ethics of memory. The passion of the heterological historian for the dead must wait for the dispassionate and disciplined work of the scientific historians, for they alone determine precisely what there is in the past to be impassioned about. "The first point that needs to be made is that history's 'responsibility toward the dead' is *built on top of* the process of reconstructing the past . . . It is based on the assertion that we actually do owe a debt to the people whom we honor, because they really did act in a way that puts us in their debt."[11] Thus Wyschogrod is critical of Hayden White for holding that a prescriptive or ethical moment "emanates from the descriptive without further explanation," on the grounds that White "has not noticed that the ethical referent goes all the way down, that the alterity of the other grips the historian prior to her narration and not as inference from it."[12] But Megill thinks that White is precisely right, that prescriptives follow upon descriptives and the more discreet, the more understated and tight-lipped the prescriptive is, the better, lest the historian look like an advocate.[13] Or again, when Megill says that the judicial model of historical judgment holds if we move from the adversarial attorney to the impartial judge, Wyschogrod sides with Lyotard, who raises the question of those who have been so effectively silenced that they are deprived of the very idiom in which to state their complaint.[14]

So Megill's critique of Wyschogrod comes down to a debate about priorities, about which comes first: memory or history? The personal or the professional? The heterological historian or the objective scientist? Does the (professional) promise to tell the truth about the past precede the historian's personal commitment to the dead, and this because we have first to ascertain who the dead were and whether they deserve our honor (Megill)? Or, does the promise to tell the truth, to render the facts, presuppose the space of a "prediscursive" ethical bond to the past which has bent our head back in the direction of the dead in the first place (Wyschogrod)? The difference of opinion in this matter illuminates the modern/postmodern split, highlighting the postmodern critique of the modernist idea of dispassionate objectivity and procedural justice, a critique foreshadowed by Pascal's critique of Descartes,[15] Kierkegaard's critique of Hegel, Heidegger's critique of Husserl's pure transcendental phenomenology, and more radically carried out in our days in the works of Derrida, Foucault, Deleuze, and Rorty. Megill invokes the classical canons of truth and the modern notion of objectivity, but he wants to make room for the ethical passion Wyschogrod describes, to give it its place.[16] Wyschogrod follows the post-structuralists in rejecting the straightforwardly modernist model of a representation/fact or word/thing match, as if objects were independently sitting out there waiting to be picked off by rightly aimed representations, or as if facts straightforwardly settle debates about competing representations,[17] but she does not want to dismiss the objectivity Megill advocates. It is a question of priorities: not of ethics versus non-ethics, but of competing ethical priorities.

3.

Let us see if we can get to the bottom of this debate by starting off with Megill's idea that "history's 'responsibility toward the dead' is *built on top of* the process of reconstructing the past." While Wyschogrod is right enough to insist upon our responsibility to the dead, Megill thinks, such ethical valuation must wait its turn on the queue, where this responsibility comes after we have first settled the cognitive facts. First there must be an empirical, cognitive determination of an objective fact of the matter; then there is an ethical valuation. This model would seem to have the advantage of common sense and it certainly has the advantage of two hundred years of epistemology (in the seventeenth and eighteenth centuries) behind it. But it has not stood up well under the fire of criticism, both continental and Anglo-American, in the twentieth century, which is the standpoint adopted by Wyschogrod and her heterological historian.

In many ways Megill has adopted the position that Husserl held, and which Heidegger criticized in *Being and Time* and in *The History of the Concept of Time*.[18] His very language reminds us of Husserl's distinction between the founding and the founded. Husserl himself was critical of the atomistic theories of perception handed down by empiricism that reduce concrete perceptual experience to a cluster of atomic sensations bundled together by psychological rules like association. Against this view, Husserl held that we experience not subjective splashes of sense data, but concrete things. Rather than having subjective greenish sensations, we "perceive" concretely given green plants or houses, say, in intentional acts directed at objects that are transcendent to the inner stream of consciousness itself. But Husserl continued to uphold a fundamentally empiricist (or objectivist) distinction between a foundational perceptual stratum and what is built up on top of it, between a "founding" spatiotemporal object and the ethical values that are "founded" on it. At the core of the given for Husserl is a pre-ethical and purely cognitive base upon which the act of valuation is subsequently layered. It should be noted that Husserl did not think there were in fact two different intentional acts—that was Brentano's position, which Husserl criticized. Husserl held only that the perceptual act was composed of a logically separable and prior noematic core that served as the common and founding basis of several different acts (the same object could be perceived, remembered, desired, imagined, etc.).[19]

In the 1920s, the young Heidegger criticized this position as still another dogma of empiricism lacking in phenomenological credentials. Heidegger in effect said that "perception" was as much a fiction as was the "sensation" criticized by Husserl. In just the way that Husserl argued we perceive concretely given things, and do not experience subjective sense data, Heidegger said that what is given are the concrete things of use, which he called "*Zuhandensein*," not value-free objects, which he called "*Vorhandensein*." The latter are abstractions that are constructed after the fact by reflection; they are never given. The reason for this is that things are always already given—as a hammer or a light switch, say—to a living and active agent whom Heidegger called "*Dasein*," a being that is always already doing things, not just looking at them. For Heidegger, whatever is given is given "as" such and such, in such and such a concrete context of the needs of life. Things do not "appear" as pure "objects" for a purely "neutral" "consciousness," unless we contrive to have them do so. One could hear a "pure noise," as opposed to someone's voice in the next room, only by way of purposely suspending or toning down the intensity of "being-in-the-world," resulting in such an abstract and after the fact construction.[20]

Husserl thought it was possible to "neutralize" consciousness and its presuppositions in order to get at the essence of experience, and that, in the interest of an objective and presuppositionless science, the only kind Husserl thought possible, it was crucially necessary to do so. Heidegger thought that such a neutrality modification was not possible—inasmuch as *Dasein* is always and already thrown into the world, thrust from the start into a language and a set of historical-cultural presuppositions—and that such neutrality could not in any case claim presuppositionlessness on its side. On the contrary, it involved a massive metaphysical presupposition of its own, namely, it presupposed that the being of this thing called consciousness (it sounded better in German: the *Sein* of *Bewusstsein*) was such that it was or could *be* self-neutralizing. Pure consciousness for Heidegger is not a presupposition that steered clear of metaphysics, but rather an unexamined piece of modernist and dualist metaphysics, making the massive assumption of the possibility of a worldless and solitary self-conscious subject (Cartesianism).[21] The question for Heidegger was not to set out in search of some sort of pure cognition or pure knowing that stood clear of metaphysical presuppositions about being, but to get being (to get one's basic presuppositions) right in the first place. On this point Heidegger was an Aristotelian, not a Cartesian-Husserlian. He was arguing that knowledge is a function of being, that the mode of cognition (*modus cognoscendi*) follows upon the mode of being (*modus essendi*), that one knows as one is. But the being of *Dasein* is essentially worldly, temporal and historical, having been "thrown" into a historical world of inherited beliefs and practices, and this sets the terms or parameters of understanding, or what Heidegger called our "projective horizons."

Seen in these terms, Levinas's *Totality and Infinity*—and Levinas is the central background figure in Wyschogrod's work, in *An Ethics of Remembering* and in general—may be viewed as yet a further, albeit dissident, contribution, a fundamental course correction, of this progressive search for the ever more concrete subject, which for Levinas is the fully ethical subject. Levinas is a critic of what he calls the "intellectualist thesis," which he describes as "representational thought." He is referring to Husserl's thesis that to a value-free

> intention called theoretical, basis of the I, would be added volitions, desires, and sentiments, so as to transform thought into life. The strictly intellectualist thesis subordinates life to representation. It maintains that in order to will it is first necessary to represent to oneself what one will . . . But how would the tension and care of a life arise from impassive representation . . . Representation is conditioned. Its transcendental pretension is constantly belied by the life that is already implanted in the being representation claims to constitute.[22]

But Levinas is no less a critic of Heidegger. He insists that *Dasein* too is an abstraction—a user of tools who dies but whose "sensibility," whose bodily birth and sensuous embodiment, are never properly described, whence Levinas's famous sally that "*Dasein* in Heidegger is never hungry"[23]—which must be replaced by the truly concrete subject. This concreteness Levinas locates in one who is "always already" (*immer schon-heit* is a basic category in *Being and Time*) *ethical*, that is, addressed by the face of the other, implicated in an ethical relation with the other, and all the other others, and this from the start. It is a violence to imagine the other is constituted as another ego just like I am (Husserl) or to imagine that the other is given within a horizon of being that makes her appearance possible (Heidegger). The other comes to us from on high, from out of herself (*kath'hautos*), on her own terms (*à partir de soi*). In Levinas's terms, fundamental ontology is not fundamental; the truly fundamental subject is ethical, not (what Heidegger calls) ontological. Ethics is first philosophy. The ethical relation to the other is first, last and constant.

Now it is of the utmost importance to see that this Heideggerian and post-Heideggerian perspective does not throw the idea of "objectivity" to the four winds; it simply forces one to reconceptualize objectivity in a new and less modernist way, one that Heidegger describes in *Being and Time* as "hermeneutical"—a move that put this word on the map of contemporary continental philosophy. For Heidegger, objects are constituted as objects by being projected upon certain horizons of objectivity, which Heidegger called "basic concepts" (*Grundbegriffe*); objects are picked out as objects by being framed in a certain way (as pure extension, as mathematically measurable, as deeds documented in ancient records, etc.).[24] Data are a function of the frameworks that pick them out. Movement occurs in science in either of two ways: when there is an incremental confirmation or disconfirmation of data within the existing framework, or when fundamental shifts occur within the *Grundbegriffe* themselves—like those brought about by Copernicus in astronomy, Luther in theology, or Einstein in physics—in which a new framework forces the old one off the table. Notice that at such moments of crisis or critical shifts, the new frameworks are actually short on data but long on promise; still, they are preferred to the old frameworks, which are long on data but have run out of promise. The process is by no means restricted to the natural sciences. Such fundamental shifts are as likely to be found in theology and history as they are in mathematics or physics. Heidegger did not think that the natural science/human science divide, thematized most famously by Dilthey, mattered in principle. Heidegger was more interested in the divide between the particular or "ontic" sciences that turn on their respective *Grundbegriffe* (studied in what he and Husserl called "regional ontologies") and the science in which this is all laid out, which he called "fundamental ontology."

That is obviously a very different way of thinking about "facts" than the one put forward in empiricism. Facts are far from arbitrary, but they do not have a prior, independent and coercive power on their own. As Quine said, "there are no facts of the matter," no uninterpreted facts,[25] because facts are a function of the interpretive framework that picks them out. Those frameworks in turn are neither higher-order facts, nor have they dropped from the sky. They are the historically conditioned ways concrete subjects have been motivated to frame things out. Things are never given in a value-free way, and science does not consist in assembling freestanding, value-free facts.[26] Rather, concretely living beings, driven by their several needs and desires, set out in search of a way of framing or projecting things that is a function of what Heidegger called their "care," or what we (with Kant) might call our "interests." In that sense, the only way to be fully disinterested is to be dead.

While Heidegger gives the idea of objectivity a hermeneutical rendering, Levinas treats it as a specifically ethical obligation. In communication I rise up from my immersion in my personal world and assume my place in the interpersonal world, which I share with the other. Communication and the production of truth are part of my interpersonal life, part of the general requirements of "justice," my obligation not only to the other one immediately before me, who requires everything of me, but also to all the other others, who also require everything of me. A rational world is a world full of others. Justice precedes truth and indeed makes truth possible by requiring it. That is, in the movement of justice as it is conceived by Levinas, I offer the world to the other, who accepts and confirms it, even as I expose myself to the other who has something to say that I have not heard. That is a Levinasian way of adopting Husserl's notion of objectivity as intersubjective agreement and inscribing it within an ethical context: the "objective" world is our world, a public and intersubjectively constituted world, in which we reason together as a part of the justice we owe one another. *Objectivity* is taken not in the sense of mind-independent realism, but in the sense of intersubjective agreement, and intersubjective agreement is inscribed in ethical space.[27]

The Levinasian idea that justice precedes truth, and the Heideggerian idea of the hermeneutical situation are, in my view, the background standpoints from which Wyschogrod is constructing the notion of the "heterological historian." From Heidegger she has borrowed certain methodological priorities, and from Levinas her substantive view of the ethical. The heterological historian is a Levinasian subject, always already addressed by the call of the other—past, present, and future—but specifically laid claim to by the solicitations of the dead. She is a concretely existing subject of infinite responsibility to the silenced voices of the past, which can be ignored or denied, but never be neutralized, since even denial presupposes the address. That is why Wyschogrod cites Lyotard's "hyperbolic" claim that "Satan is God's best servant," for in disobeying God so saliently, Satan thereby recognizes God's authority.[28]

In what remains I want to defend the idea of the heterological historian against Megill's criticisms by invoking first the more Heideggerian point and then the Levinasian one.

4.

On the precise methodological issue of the place of "facts," of the "purely epistemological" stratum, the heterological historian depends upon the hermeneutical framework opened up by Heidegger in *Being and Time*. It is just this hermeneutical turn in Wyschogrod that Megill resists, a rejection Megill himself makes explicit. Megill agrees in part with Wyschogrod's Heideggerian assertion that the historian always interprets something "as" something. But he argues that *prior* to this interpretive movement there must be something "argumentative," that is, some purely cognitive, epistemological, fact-finding relation to things,[29] which is the historian's defining professional obligation. That, I think, is the heart of the issue between them.

The right response to Megill's position in this matter is twofold. First, as Heidegger says, it is a misunderstanding of understanding to think that the projective horizon upon which understanding depends—in this case an ethical preunderstanding of or preorientation to the murdered—blocks or distorts our access to things. On the contrary, such perspectives give us access to things in the first place, both because without them we would have no angle from which to approach things and because without them our interest would not have been drawn to these things to begin with. They provide our point of view and enable, even as they limit, access. It is not a question of getting rid of these projections, or horizons of understanding, but of finding felicitous and fruitful ones. Without our "care"—our existential interests, our ethical passions, our hopes, our memories—we would not care about things, neither insofar as they are immediately useful to us in some way (practical interests), nor as objects of purely speculative or scientific interest, the way mathematicians love theorems with no evident application and collectors love ancient artifacts from which they expect no useful advantage. Without these projective understandings, we would have neither motive nor means to pursue our interests (care).

So when, in the course of claiming that we have to get the facts right before making the evaluation of the fact *as* an ethically significant event, Megill adds parenthetically, "(e.g., certain instances of violence in the years 1939–45),"[30] the expression "the years 1939–45" leaps off the page at us. Every historian who works in the wake of "the years 1939–45" is always already held captive by the events of those years, which form an irreducible part of her living memory and hence of the horizon of her historical interests. It is a conceptual artifact, a construction after the fact, to imagine a neutral epistemological subject surveying the scenes of history, disinterestedly combing the facts, and then noticing and being led to pause over "certain instances of violence in the years 1939–45," from which purely descriptive operations certain prescriptions inevitably flow, however discreetly.

The historian has been *turned in advance* to these scenes, and to countless others, "always and already" turned there in "memory," and even in her unconscious, turned to scenes which belong not to her "past" (*Vergangenheit*), as Heidegger says, not as if they were "over," but to what we have been (*Gewesenheit*), what we (still) are, the full story of which—the story of what we will have been always already turned to in advance—having not yet been told. We have been turned in advance to this war (and the long history of wars), to the Holocaust (and to every holocaust), that for better or worse have made us who we are. We are turned to the dead, *aux morts*, if one can say that in French, the way Levinas says we are always already turned *à dieu*, turned *to* God/the dead, turned *by* God/the dead. By the same token, women today are turned in advance to the voices of the women of the past: Where have they all gone? What happened to them? What were they doing? We know they were there and we care about them in advance, even though, precisely because the historical record shows so little trace of them, we must set out in advance to find them and give them voice. Or the sexually different? Or the slaves? Or the "mad"? The list goes on, and tomorrow the list will be longer or at least different.

But, secondly, *everything* that Megill calls for in the way of a professional ethic of objectivity, of methodological controls, rules of evidence, investigative integrity, "dispassionate" research, unbiased fact-finding, has its place. It has its place *here*, at this point, in and as the eye of the heterological historian is already turned to the Holocaust, or as Derrida says, to "all the Auschwitzes,"[31] where Auschwitz is a proper name, a placeholder for a singular nameless cataclysm, and a placeholder for other names of other nameless and equally singular cataclysms. Here, where we have been carried by the momentum of the deepest concerns of our being, it is important to get the facts right and not to be led astray by personal views, however well intentioned. Objectivity is an ethical value, an ethics of its own, as Megill rightly insists, and as Levinas himself also insists. Wyschogrod would be the last to deny that. But it is a question of ascertaining the place of this value. For Wyschogrod, as I understand *An Ethics of Remembering*, this is a particular ethical value that belongs to the wider spectrum or repertoire of a larger, "interested" and value-oriented subject, even as for Levinas truth is one of the requirements of justice. The structure of that subject, its being-interested, is always already oriented toward and led to seize upon certain themes, events, stories, which *now*, at the point of research and documentation, have to be sifted through "dispassionately." But there are no "pure" objects; that is a misunderstanding of understanding and of objectivity. Objectivity is a feature of a scientific field—a "field of interest"—that has been carved out and preconstituted by living interested subjects, fields aflame with human stories, to which we have been drawn *in advance*. Here, having been led to this point of interest, is the place for the methodological techniques of "history" to step on stage and take over where personal "memory" has first of all led us.[32]

Like Megill, I think that the question of the status of scientific objectivity would be helped along if we could come up with a good descriptive model for it. Rather than implicating oneself in far-flung and, in my view, indefensible theoretical assumptions about pure disinterested subjects and pure objects, it would be far better—as Megill for the most part actually does—to insist pragmatically upon "rules of evidence" and to keep a safe distance from such theoretical constructions as well as from Colling-wood's rhetoric of truth and certainty.[33] We would do better to stick to a word like "evidence" and save the word "truth" for commencement addresses. "Historians," like all scientists, are to be guided by the shifting weight of "evidence," and in their highest moments of methodological rigor, they are least inclined to say that such and such is "true," and most inclined to say that such is where the weight of evidence presently rests. It is only in the hotel bar of an evening, after the conference papers of the day are over and the methodological controls have been lifted, that we might let slip the word "truth."

Even the language of the objective historian as "dispassionate" needs to be parsed, lest it imply a Kantian pure reason trying to rise above its "pathological" inclinations, which itself reminds us of the Platonic philosopher practicing death. As living embodied beings, we are always already "attuned" to the world, as Heidegger says, always already "mooded" (*bestimmt*). To be dispassionate is, for a bodily being, to have a particular passion, a dispassionate *disposition*, and it is sometimes necessary to check one disposition with another, to check the heat of outrage or indignation with another disposition, like being "calm, cool and collected." Heidegger says, "[W]hen we master a mood, we do so by way of a counter-mood; we are never free of moods."[34] Under another description, the dispassionate researcher is a passionate searcher for information who is willing to let the chips fall where they may—and she feels very strongly about this! If objectivity is an ethical value, then that is something she feels strongly about, and it makes her very cross when she runs into people practicing history with an axe to grind.

In pursuit of a good analogy or model for scientific objectivity, Megill recommends we think of the objective historian as a "judge" (another Kantian image) who can rise above the adversarial claims of the lawyerly advocates of competing interests. The reason the debates in the United States Senate about judicial nominees can get so heated is that *everybody* knows how biased judges can be.

The safest model is to stick closely with Megill's insistence on "rules of evidence," and to treat these rules on an analogy with the rules of a game. Drop the questionable theoretical assumptions about the neutrality of consciousness, drop the background rhetoric about a "metaphysics of truth," and be content to treat the historian—or any "*Wissenschaftler*" in the German sense, anyone in the natural or social sciences or humanities—as someone playing a game. If you want to play the game, abide by the rules—otherwise the results will not count. You can write all the propaganda you can get published, put all the crazy ideological junk you want on your Web site, write as many book reviews for Amazon.com as you please, but if you want to achieve results that are going to "count" as "historical" and be taken seriously as "history writing," then keep the rules of the profession, document what you say, and produce the evidence according to the rules of historical evidence. "Objective" results are results produced by keeping the rules. That's enough; drop the rest. That's what "objective" *means*. But the reason why one is playing one game rather than another, American football instead of European soccer, chess rather than blackjack, researching human cloning rather than ancient Roman coins, writing the history of the Holocaust rather than the history of needlework, has to do with cultural-historical contexts, personal passions and overriding ethical priorities. But whatever the game, keep the rules. Do not inflate this analogy, either, because athletes these days are notorious for using performance-enhancing drugs, in which case their records should not "count."

Finally, to return to the question of what should be put "on top of" what, to use Megill's very Husserlian image, I would respectfully turn Megill's assertion around and say that the process of a careful reconstruction of the past is built on top of, or it belongs within the context of, "history's 'responsibility toward the dead,'" which is the very position of the heterological historian defended by Wyschogrod. Historical writing, as Wyschogrod says, is "always already implicated in a prediscursive ethics before it is a conveying of facts."[35] Cognitive precision is required to clear a field whose significance has first of all been seized upon and carved out by the ethical, or heterological, subject.

Objectivity is not an illusory but a local phenomenon. Objectivity is a second-order, higher-level stratum of objectifying constitution, and objectification is constituted by rule keeping. It occurs in local contexts as a higher order objectification of fields that have been constituted in the first place by living-breathing, passionate-interested, value-positing, multi-valenced, prediscursive, historically influenced . . . in short, "heterological" . . . subjects. Wyschogrod makes it clear that the heterological historian knows these rules as well as anyone else, and she knows that to ignore or break them would be her ruin as a professional historian. But the rules are not why she is in this game rather than another, and they do not give a deep account of what her professional life as an historian is finally about. She is there because she is haunted, because she hears voices, because she hears the call of the dead and has been called upon to respond, and because, like Derrida, she is dreaming of being a historian.

Memory and Violence, or Genealogies of Remembering

WERNER H. KELBER

That which can in no way be figured by the *historia rerum gestarum*, the cataclysm, a nihil whose sheer magnitude and unfigurable ethical force—a law prior to all law—resists emergence in word or image.
                                    Edith Wyschogrod, *An Ethics of Remembering*[1]

What we celebrate under the title of founding events are, essentially, acts of violence legitimated after the fact by a precarious state of right. What was glory for some was humiliation for others. To celebration on one side corresponds execration on the other. In this way, symbolic wounds calling for healing are stored in the archives of the collective memory.
                                    Paul Ricoeur, *Memory, History, Forgetting*[2]

Memory is a festering wound.
                                    Friedrich Nietzsche, *Ecce Homo*[3]

Three interrelated features may be said to characterize the work of Edith Wyschogrod. There is first an interdisciplinary drive to rise above institutionally sanctioned boundaries and to retrieve intellectual categories from their disciplinary captivity so as to reconfigure them in novel contexts. It is this desire and the ability to bring widely differing genres, discourses and traditionally separate intellectual orbits into productive coalitions that have increasingly distinguished her writings. This linking of philosophy and theology, psychoanalysis and science, literary criticism and linguistics, architecture and the arts, media studies and above all, ethics, is carried off with a high degree of learning and refinement. Undoubtedly, the intellectual agility she has mastered and the philosophical voice that has distinctly become her own are the product of prolonged reflection.

Second, from the beginning of her writing career to the present, her work is deeply informed, not to say haunted, by the death events of the twentieth century, those mass exterminations that were *sui generis*. A central topos underlying her philosophical work is the conviction that the very magnitude of the organized mass murder of peoples that epitomizes the necropolis of the twentieth century has, or ought to have, altered all our philosophical, psychological, religious and ethical assumptions about and perspectives on the human condition. Undoubtedly, the challenge she poses runs up against autonomous intellectual agendas and their entrenched disciplinary *Eigengesetzlichkeit*.

Third, in following Emmanuel Levinas, she has made the ethics of alterity a pillar of her own philosophy. Driven by the ethical passion for the Other and a corollary respect for difference, more perhaps than by virtue of intrinsically linguistic, literary rationales, she shares postmodernism's anxiety about totalizing imperatives and the imposition of sameness in religion, politics, science, culture—everywhere. Time and again, her thought has explicated the self not as a monadic, self-contained subject and not as an integrally rational and cognitive self, but rather as a corporeal, social self who finds identity in the face of the Other. Undoubtedly, the concept of self that her work calls into question is one founded on the myth of individual autochthony and one that in the modern world is increasingly defined by economic production and consumption.

In *An Ethics of Remembering*, which marks the culmination of her ethical/philosophical work, Wyschogrod has pondered with her customary acuteness and sympathetic generosity the role of the contemporary historian and the moral responsibilities and quandaries (s)he faces, both in a general epistemological sense, and specifically in view of a history disfigured by institutionalized mass murder.

As far as the grounds of knowledge are concerned, there is the general issue all historians are confronted with, namely, the irrecoverable nature of the past. Is it not a truism that the past cannot be brought back in all its lived realities? More than that, is it not accurate to state that the past seems lost beyond retrieval? Given this claim, how can one speak for the past, let alone retrieve it? What is it that we are doing when we bring the past into present articulation so as to carry it forward into the future? Then there is the well-known demise of representational epistemology, the theory of knowledge which stipulates that language can make the world transparent in terms of factual correctness. To put this issue in terms coined by Ricoeur, does not "the fundamental vulnerability of memory" result from "the relation between the absence of the thing remembered and its presence in the mode of representation"?[4] Given this demise of a positivistic epistemology, how can linguistic articulation do justice to what Wyschogrod refers to as the *historia rerum gestarum*? How does one move from ineffability to language, and should or could one aim at a mode of language that transcends the representational impulse? In a slightly different vein, is there something still to be said in favor of the polarity of fact versus fiction? Or, if we come to understand representation as necessarily constructed and fictional, how does the inevitability of fictional representation square with the urgency of telling the truth about the past? Can fiction be distinguished from lie? What does it mean and what does it take to tell the truth about the past?

Today's historians, moreover, find themselves consciously living and operating at a medium transit from print to electronics, an experience that heightens sensibilities toward modes and materialities of communication and their complicity in our construction of the past. Looking back upon previous media stages—the age of the voice, the ocular age of the scribal visualization of language, and the age of the mechanical reproduction—historians find themselves caught in the web of an electronically manipulated communications culture that reduces knowledge to information and information to numbers "in conformity with the Pythagorean principle that the world is made of numbers."[5] How are the digitization processes in the current culture of globalizing electronic technologies and commodity distribution systems impacting both the commitment to and the representation of the past? How do films, photographs, and television change both the modes of transmission and the perception of past events, and hence our narratives of them?

As the title of Wyschogrod's major philosophical work indicates, the historian's treatment of the past is inextricably linked with memory and remembering, remembered images and memory places, mnemonics and commemoration, and predominantly with an ethics of remembering—all topoi that were perceived to be central to civilizing developments in Western culture, and lately have risen to the status of paradigmatic significance in the humanities and some of the social sciences. If one holds with Aristotle that "all remembering implies lapse of time" [*dio meta chronou pasa mnēmē*],[6] remembering is inescapably involved in reflections on and constructions of temporality, indeed enveloped in temporality. If one aspires to the dream of recovering the past, one has to confront the need to configure temporality, the diachronicity of lived time. And in reclaiming past events, does one interpret time as a continuous homogeneous flow or in punctiform fashion, to mention but one pair of alternatives?

Those who have made it their particular objective to write about the death events, who passionately wish to retain knowledge of human-contrived mass murder, are faced with exquisitely difficult challenges. The linguistic and philosophical issue of the demise of representational epistemology aside, how can the unrepresentable cataclysms of history ever be re-presented? The paradox is stark and searing: what cannot be shown and hardly articulated is precisely what, on ethical grounds, ought be shown and said. Is mass annihilation to be mediated through the organizing effects of narrative, or the intellectualizing efforts of philosophy, or the aestheticizing impact of artifacts, or the moralizing deliberations of ethics, or the anesthetizing effects of solipsistic meditation? Ethically, can and should the historian be "both the narrator of events and litigant for the powerless"?[7] In short, how can the historian manifest her/his "eros for the dead,"[8] this responsibility toward those who have been rendered mute? How can this "passion for the dead others who are voiceless"[9] be transposed in language? What stance does the reporter take and from what place does (s)he speak? Is there a position "within the cataclysm,"[10] and if so, will one gain a hearing, an understanding even, by speaking from within, if this is possible? Is one to rely on witnesses, and, in the face of diverse and discordant affirmations, whose testimony is to be trusted? How do oral testimonies of survivors differ from memoirs committed to writing? "Covenanted to the dead,"[11] as the historian is, how can (s)he fulfill her/his covenantal promise truthfully and with a passion for rectitude?

For the survivors, death, far from bringing closure, marks the inaugurating occasion for a process of rememorizations. Put differently: for those not (yet) consumed by extinction, death has every appearance of being a traumatic yet memorially productive experience. Unsurprisingly, therefore, human efforts to revisit the violence of the past and to work through the trauma of death traditionally enlist the works of memory. Whether it is by dint of historiography, narrative, art, or psychoanalysis that we seek to repossess the past and call back its dead, memorial methods and practices invariably infiltrate our historical, fictional, artistic and psychoanalytic endeavors. A sharp conceptual distinction, therefore, between narrative, history, art, and psychoanalysis vis-à-vis memory is not necessarily warranted. Driven by the desire to connect with the dead, memory comes into its own, as it were, acting out the role it seems destined to play in the face of death. Hence Wyschogrod's strong claim on behalf of the role of memory regarding the ethical responsibilities of the historian to address and bring to consciousness the mass extermination of peoples.

Highlighting memory and memorial responses to the cataclysms and their victims, Wyschogrod pondered a series of concepts of memorial practices, ranging from mnemotechnical and archival to neurological, all the way to computational models. What memorial practices does the historian appropriate and how does (s)he implement them? If so-called facticity and what is memorially recalled are not homologous, what is it that is being remembered? To what extent do present experiences infiltrate our recollections of the past? What are the processes of remembering and those of forgetting? Precisely how are remembering and forgetting correlated? When is forgetting epistemologically meaningful, therapeutic even, and when is it dishonorable, immoral? Is the content of what is forgotten irretrievably lost, or is memory—to use the broadly conventional spatial model—conceivable as a chamber whose *magna vis* and intricate vastness moved Augustine to rhapsodic excitation in the tenth book of his *Confessions*? Or, still abiding by the spatial model, should memory be thought of as a crypt, a reservoir of dead images, or as an impenetrable labyrinth, a blur of indistinguishable sensations? Remembering the dead, especially those victimized by state-ordered decrees, or killed as a result of crass casualness, can be agonizingly painful. Hence, if one is to remember the wounds of and the outrages inflicted upon the Other, can one occupy a station where one "neither ignores nor is overwhelmed by the cataclysm"?[12] Can one try to bring sense to the senseless without advocacy? And as far as the issue of emotions is concerned, dare we duplicate affect in remembering the pained torments of the victims? May one rely on the ambiguities of metaphor or on the anesthetizing effects of understatement, or do "the claims of alterity demand nothing less than a crying out, a shriek of protest"?[13]

In this piece which is to honor the work of Edith Wyschogrod, the point is not, and cannot be, to take up and respond to each of the issues raised in *An Ethics of Remembering*. The very least of our objectives is—to use an intellectually irresponsible phrase—to bring closure to questions, many of which defy the possibility of satisfactorily descriptive and analytic answers. Indeed, the construction of closure would betray the victims of twentieth-century traumas, the incalculability of the horrors they faced and the unmitigated darkness of a "night" in the face of which all human responses seem insubstantial. Instead, what this piece intends is to take into serious account the issues raised in Wyschogrod's work by allowing them to form a prism of intelligibility, a spectrum of sensibilities, acting as a generative more than a regulative force, so as to facilitate a newly refracted reading of a foundational genre of texts.

Remembering as Remedy and Poison

The texts under consideration are the Passion narratives, writings that are foundational to Christian identity and canonical with regard to their scriptural status in Christianity. In this piece, closer attention is given to the story in Mark than to the other three narratives. What is often referred to as their reception history is marked by what we will call a dramatic double complicity. On the one hand, these narratives have operated as generators of a deeply felt piety and faith and as mentors for musical and artistic representations of great dramatic power and aesthetic brilliance. On the other hand, these Passion texts and their pictorial, choral, and instrumental representations have motivated perpetrators of terror, persecution, and bloodshed. Sometimes hostilities have been generated as a result of bluntly polemical interpretations and provocative exposition in preaching. Sometimes seemingly minor artistic characteristics and subtle verbal insinuations have instilled or reinforced feelings of antipathy. More often than not, however, responses have been the products of a history of happenings and heartfelt experiences of happenings, of genealogies of remembering that had and have deep investments in the past.

To illustrate this memorially empowered response mechanism, one may think less of overtly aggressive interpretations and representations, and more of the impact of acknowledged pieces of art: Johann Sebastian Bach's *Passion According to St. Matthew*; Matthias Grünewald's *Isenheim Altar* in the Musée d'Unterlinden in Colmar, France; Salvador Dalí's *Crucifixion*; and El Greco's *Christ Carrying the Cross*, to name but a few of the most prominent exemplars. By Western reckoning at least, these are artistic commemorations of unquestionable magnificence. It may justly be said that they do not convey anti-Jewish sentiments in as overt a fashion as, for example, the medieval Passion Plays that culminated, both in terms of performative style and moral insensitivity, in the Oberammergau dramatizations. Nor are they as subtly complicit in anti-Jewish sentiments as Mel Gibson's *The Passion of the Christ*. But whatever the degree of anti-Jewish sentiments that these commemorative masterpieces may or may not convey, they inevitably come to be heard and viewed within webs of cultural, religious, and political remembering that mobilize a range of responses. Always in remembering, people's own present experiences and, more deeply, their history of remembering, affect the desire to preserve the past and infiltrate remembrances of it. Depending on one's particular memorial experiences, symbols that are central and unifying to some can bring up rather different, indeed oppositional memories for others, generating a remembering of one against the Other. The cross, for example, a central symbol of redemption in Christianity, and the dramatized center of the Passion narratives, can in Jewish recollection be viewed as a symbol that has haunted Jews throughout the ages. Mr. Naftali Lavie has eloquently expressed Jewish memories and sensibilities from the experiences of his Polish childhood:

> I still remember the fears that haunted us as children, as we tried to escape the presence of the cross. In our heavily Christian communities, Catholic funeral processions were always led by a young boy holding a long metal scepter with a cross on top. Behind the children the priest would march, reading the prayers. Any Christian passer-by meeting the procession would remove his hat, bend his knees and bow to the cross.
>
> Jewish adults knew how to handle this situation, sometimes seeking shelter in doorways to avoid confronting the cross. Children were less experienced, and were occasionally beaten when the procession passed by and they did not bend their knees before the cross.
>
> The cross continued to pursue us during the horrible period of World War II. On Sundays and Christian holidays, Jews would lock themselves in their houses in the ghetto. We took care not to get involved with the Catholic guards who watched us when they returned from church services. We don't know what the priests preached to their flock, but by the look of anger on the faces of the God-fearing oppressors, and even more so, by the ease with which they beat us, we did not get the feeling that they were told to have pity on us.[14]

Mr. Lavie's experience illustrates the profoundly ambiguous status of the cross in Jewish-Christian memorial history and explicates why it is that even the commemorative Passion masterpieces may receive an equivocal reception. What for one faith conjures up memories of self-giving sacrifice on behalf of the Other, for the other faith may bring back memories of brutalizing actions taken against its own. In part at least, the dual reception is due to viewers' and auditors' personal and collective genealogies of memories.

Importantly, however, this double complicity, far from being a symptom confined to the reception history of the canonical Passion texts, extends far back to these very texts themselves. To the extent that both redemption and rejection—celebration and execration, to invoke the epigraph to this piece from Ricoeur—are in various degrees already inscribed in these inaugurating texts, the double history of their remembering is but an extension of initial narrative impulses. Something of a fateful coherence and fatal continuity exists between the inaugural narratives and a subsequent history of representing and remembering them. The lines of demarcation between the master narratives and their memorial representations are all the more blurred if, as will be shown below, the Passion texts themselves are products of remembering. Remembering the killing of the charismatic leader, these stories, in the most general sense, strive to make sense of what happened, and they manifestly do so in the interest of present circumstances. This is why all of them, we shall see, are infiltrated by present experiences. The differentiation, therefore, between the canonical Passion texts on one hand and their oral, literary, and artistic reception histories on the other, masks their memorial commonality, i.e., the fact that they all participate in a commonly shared history of memorializing activities. To be sure, from the perspective of canonicity, the four Passion stories are the master narratives that are secondarily reinterpreted in a subsequent reception history. No doubt, as Jan Assmann has reminded us, canonicity breathes enhanced normativity (*gesteigerte Verbindlichkeit*)[15] into texts, enabling them to conquer and control variance (*Bändigung der Varianz*).[16] But in extension of Assmann, it will have to be conceded that the postcanonical history invariably shows that even canonical texts, no matter how unbending their authority was meant to be, are ultimately never fully controllable. From the perspective of memory, however, the distinction between canonical and postcanonical textual identity is of little consequence, if not misleading. Memorially speaking, the Passion narratives are memory texts themselves that endeavored to commemorate the death of the fallen leader, and in turn generated memorially empowered verbal and artistic responses.

Mark

It is necessary here to rehearse and analyze a summation of features in the canonical narratives that contributed to the duplicitous history of remembering. In the case of the Markan Passion narrative, the high priest and Pilate function in parallel fashion in the twin trials (Mark 14:55–65; 15:2–15). Both ask Jesus about his messianic identity (14:61; 15:2), both encounter Jesus' silence (14:61; 15:5), and both receive a qualifying or indirect answer (14:62; 15:2). But this is where the similarities end. The high priest and his priestly establishment seem determined to gain Jesus' conviction so as to put him to death (14:55). They persuade the crowds to plead for his execution and to have a man of (probably revolutionary violence) released in his place. Pilate, on the other hand, is a more complex figure. Although he sees through the high priestly motivation (15:10), he yields to the pressure placed upon him by the crowds, has the man of violence released, and turns Jesus over to his executioners (15:15). Still, he does so contrary to his own better judgment to release Jesus (15:6–9), and remains unconvinced of Jesus' culpability (15:14). He "wonders" (15:5) while Jesus is alive, and following Crucifixion and death he "wonders" (15:44) whether Jesus was already dead. Subsequently Pilate grants the request of "a respected member of the council" (15:43), who dared approach him [*tolmēsas eisēlthen*], to honor Jesus with a dignified burial (15:42–46). Thus while Jesus' own high priest and the priestly establishment press indictment and conviction, Pilate, representative of the colonial foreign power, mistrusts the priestly motivation (15:10) and seeks to save the life of Jesus.

This particular plot development reaches its culmination in the "testimony" of the Roman centurion. Observing the manner of Jesus' dying and the circumstances surrounding his death, he makes what amounts to a confession: "Truly, this man was God's Son" (15:39). In the overall plot construction, two features add special weight to this testimony. One, the "Son of God" designation carries the blessing of the Markan narrator. Programmatically located by the narrator (in some manuscripts) in 1:1, and announced by the heavenly voice both at baptism (1:11) and transfiguration (9:7), it is, apart from the high priest's interrogation (14:61), invoked only by the unclean spirits (5:7; 3:11) who speak the "truth" out of ignorance. Two, the centurion's "testimony" constitutes not merely the "correct" confession, but the only "correct" confession made by a human being in the Gospel. In character with the Markan plot logic, the disciples who should have made this confession failed to make it. They abandoned Jesus at the outset of his last and fateful journey into Jerusalem, while the man in charge of the execution paradoxically pronounced the "confession" that should have been theirs to make.

The rhetorical impact of this narration is to incline Christian hearers/readers sympathetically toward Pilate and still more so toward the centurion over and against the high priest. While the narrator unmistakably speaks for and takes the place of the victim, (s)he also sides with the Roman authorities against the high priestly establishment on the issue of moral and judicial responsibility. This pro-Roman proclivity injected an element of forgetfulness, distortion even, into Christian memory, the repercussions of which will be felt throughout the Jewish-Christian memorial history of the Passion texts.

Matthew

In regard to the Passion text in Matthew, few biblical declarations have left more bloodstained traces in the history of Jewish and Christian remembering than all the people's response to Pilate: "His [Jesus'] blood be on us and on our children" (Matt. 27:25). As a consequence of Christian rememorization, this verse, fraught with a sense of vagueness from the outset, became deeply tainted as it contributed to the shedding of Jewish blood by Christians throughout the centuries.

In the Matthean context, the identity of "the people as a whole" [*pas ho laos*] who invoked judgment upon themselves introduces a fateful element of ambiguity. While in the Septuagint *laos* predominantly signifies *people* in the sense of *nation*, the statistically prevalent sense in the New Testament, including Matthew's text, connotes *crowd* or *population* (Matt. 4:23; 26:5; 27:64). It is, therefore, entirely reasonable to identify all the people who declare themselves ready and willing to accept the consequences of Jesus' death with the Jerusalem crowd(s) (*ochlos* or *ochloi*) (27:15, 20, 24) that were assembled before Pilate's judgment seat, and not with the covenantal people through the centuries. This localized reading seems all the more warranted because Matthew exhibits a notable preoccupation with the fate of Jerusalem, "the city of the great King" [*polis . . . tou megalou basileōs*] (5:35).

In Matthew, anxiety over the destruction of the holy city is more saliently inscribed in the narrative surface than in Mark. In the parable of the marriage feast (22:1–10) the king responds to the unwillingness of the invited guests to attend his son's wedding with anger: "He sent his troops, [and] destroyed those murderers, and burned their city" (22:7). In remarkably realistic terms, the parable connotes the destruction of Jerusalem as punishment for the people's disobedience. Furthermore, the seven notorious anti-Pharisaic woes (23:13–31), the Matthean Jesus' most direct attack on the Jewish leaders of his day, culminate in the warning that the blood of the innocent righteous ones shed on earth will come to haunt the people: "Truly I say to you, all this will come upon this generation" [*epi tēn genean tautēn*] (23:36). This anticipation of the impending doom to be inflicted "upon this generation" is immediately followed by Jesus' lament over Jerusalem (23:37–39) and his subsequent prediction of the destruction of the city's temple (24:1–2). Unquestionably, Matthew, like many Jews after 70 C.E., viewed the fall of Jerusalem as the temporal punishment for the sins of his people. Looking back upon the physical and metaphysical disaster of the temple's destruction, he writes in the conviction that Jesus' ominous prediction has come to fateful fruition in his generation.

With regard to Matthew's text, a broad-based scholarly opinion holds that the experience of a post-70 conflict between a Pharisaic, rabbinic form of Judaism and Matthew's dissident messianic Judaism has deeply infiltrated the narrative.[17] While the dispute between these two representatives of Judaism may well have had roots in events prior to 70 C.E., it reached a new level of intensity in the aftermath of the catastrophic conflagration of the temple. That catastrophe forced the issue of Jewish identity with exceptional intensity, setting national-religious interests and ideologies against each other: "Thus the Gospel of Matthew should be read along with other Jewish postdestruction literature, such as the apocalyptic works of 2 Baruch, 4 Ezra, and Apocalypse of Abraham, early strata of the Mishnah, and Josephus."[18] It suggests that Matthew, from his perspective, is critically involved "in a struggle for the future of Judaism."[19] Locked in an intra-Jewish conflict of identity, he advocates a messianically motivated observance of the Torah, indeed a Torah radicalization combined with a rigorous sense of righteousness in opposition to rabbinic, Pharisaic Torah observance. In this context, the Gospel's vituperative language is largely designed to delegitimize Pharisaically guided Judaism, and to legitimize its own brand of messianically inspired Torah observance. In Matthew's time, the future of post-war Judaism was still an open question, but within a short time "Matthew lost the battle over Judaism."[20]

The Matthean antagonism toward Pharisaism is entirely comprehensible as an intra-Jewish conflict. After all, the dissenting community of Qumran was likewise involved in a conflict with the Pharisees.[21] But when Christianity began to position itself as the absolute religion in the Western and Eastern hemisphere, its custodians of memory were driven by the desire to legitimate their increasingly universal Christian claims vis-à-vis what was now judged to be the old, superseded religion. The result was a Christian reconfiguration in universalist terms; Matthew's conflict between a Pharisaic, rabbinic and a dissident, messianic type of Judaism was metamorphosed into an irreconcilable estrangement between Christianity and Judaism.

In this new historical context, the intra-Jewish configuration that was mirrored in the Matthean narrative fell into oblivion. With the temple conflagration receding into an ever more distant past, its demise ceased to be understood as a pivotal watershed that had been perceived as temporal punishment for the sins of the people. To all intents and purposes, Matthew's Jerusalem localization and the momentous religious import of the fall of the temple were eclipsed in conformity with Christianity's universal claims and ambitions. Matthew's localized setting of the people of Jerusalem was now reimagined in terms of a people who had spoken on behalf of Jews everywhere and at all times, and their response to Pilate was thought to have imposed an everlasting punishment upon Judaism as a whole. Given the nexus of new power constellations, with Christians comprising the majority and Jews in the extreme minority, the former arrogated to themselves the role of vengeful executioners of a people who, in their view, had been branded with an eternal curse. In this manner, memory's desire to redescribe the Matthean Passion story with a view toward vindicating the Christian position of universal power paved the way for demonizing fantasies and murderous actions.

Luke

More than any other canonical Gospel, Luke has foregrounded the demise of Jerusalem and its temple. His narrative refers to the military siege and destruction of the city in historically graphic terms: Jerusalem is "surrounded by armies" (Luke 21:20); the "enemies will set up ramparts around you and surround you, and hem you in on every side, and crush you to the ground" (19:43–44). The city will be "trampled on by the Gentiles" (21:24), and people "will fall by the edge of the sword" (21:24). But in spite of Luke's historical awareness of Rome's overwhelming military power and the tragic affliction of the population of Jerusalem, his Gospel issues neither complaint nor criticism concerning Roman brutalities, and refrains from holding Roman military and political authorities responsible for the people's suffering. What is lamented is Jerusalem, not the Romans. The fault, Luke argues, lies with the city and its citizens, who habitually killed prophetic messengers (13:34) and missed the appropriate time (*kairos*) of God's visitation (19:44).

Notably, Luke abides by the Markan pattern of absorbing the destruction of city and temple into the context of the story of Jesus, instead of relocating the catastrophe, as would appear historically logical, into his own second volume. Like Matthew and, we shall see, Mark, Luke constructs links between Jesus and the fate of the city. Over and above the lament over Jerusalem (13:34–35), narrated in Matthew (23:37–39) but not in Mark, and Jesus' prediction of the destruction of the temple (Luke 21:6; Mark 13:2; Matt. 24:2), Luke alone introduces two more lament scenes: Jesus weeping over Jerusalem (19:41–44) and grieving over the daughters of Jerusalem (23:27–31). Both scenes are located in the Passion narrative, one at Jesus' entry into the city and one on the way to Crucifixion, thereby closely connecting his fate with that of the city—both being doomed. Undoubtedly, Luke is in possession of detailed knowledge about the demise of Jerusalem and the mass extermination of its people, yet his narrative logic is not driven as much by passion for the dead as by a conventional, religious rationale: the sins of the people were the root cause of their demise.

Luke's traditional theme of the culpability of the people interacts with the theme of the *apologia Romana*, creating a theological reasoning that was to become programmatic in Christian memory. As narrated by Luke, the twin issues of Roman taxation and Jewish messiahship are linked together in bringing Jesus to trial. When brought before Pilate, the charge against him is that "we found this man perverting our nation, forbidding us to pay taxes to the emperor, and saying that he himself is the Messiah, a king" (23:2). Kingship, messianism, revolution and refusal of Roman taxation constitute the core of the indictment, a potent political charge that is designed to secure the death sentence. Luke, although not unaware of Pilate's gross insensitivity toward ethnic and religious particularities (13:1), nevertheless goes further than either Mark or Matthew toward promoting the Roman governor into a model Christian. Pilate responds not once, but three times: there was no basis for the charges (23:4), Jesus was not guilty (23:14), and there is, therefore, no judicial basis for issuing the death sentence (23:22). This is the first time in Christian memory that the formal charge of political culpability has been brought against Jesus—only to be dismissed, and dismissed by the principal Roman authority in charge of the case. Henceforth, the *apologia Romana* is firmly entrenched in Christian memory.

After Pilate has pronounced Jesus innocent, Luke will not have the latter tortured by Roman soldiers. In Mark, Pilate has Jesus flogged (15:15) before he turns him over to the soldiers who in turn mock and humiliate him (15:16–20). Hence, prior to his execution, the Markan Jesus twice undergoes physical and mental suffering on the instruction of Roman authorities and by Roman hands. In Luke, however, Roman soldiers verbally abuse Jesus while he suffers on the cross (23:36), but neither they nor Pilate will subject him to physical or mental degradation prior to his execution. Instead, Luke's narrative projects the physical abuse scene back into the courtyard of the high priest, where "the men who were holding him" subject him to mocking and physical mistreatment (22:62–65). This is a harbinger of things to come in Christian commemoration: the culpability for Jesus' suffering and death is increasingly transferred from Roman to Jewish authorities, and eventually to the Jewish people at large. Luke's *apologia Romana* reaches its peak with the centurion, the Roman official in charge of the execution, who, when viewing Jesus' death, pronounces him righteous or, legally speaking, innocent [*ontēs ho anthrōpos houtos dikaios ēn*] (23:47). As far as Luke is concerned, therefore, Jesus' death was a judicial error forced upon the Romans by the Jewish crowds in Jerusalem.

In seeking to make a case for the compatibility of the new religion with Rome, Luke is aware that he needs to address the controversial issue of Jesus' political culpability. Crucifixion by the Romans made Zealotic criminality eminently plausible. He concedes that the charge of revolutionary culpability was indeed an issue and the principal reason for the hearing before Pilate. But Luke's *apologia* is so contrived a construction that it strained not only historical plausibility, but narrative logic as well. Whereas the people view Jesus as a political revolutionary and want to see him executed, Pilate, the man in charge of imperial law and order, does not. On the other hand, the people demand the release of a political revolutionary, Barabbas, who, Luke emphasizes, "had been put in prison for an insurrection that had taken place in the city, and for murder" (23:19). Thus Luke's Pilate not only sentences a man whom he considers innocent of the charge of messianic, Zealotic culpability, but he lends support to insurrectionism by giving in to the people's pressure in ordering the release of Barabbas, a known Zealotic insurrectionist.

In view of Luke's sympathy toward Gentile culture and Roman power, the ending of his two-volume work gives us a clue to his narrative perspective. After Paul, a Roman citizen by birth (Acts 22:25–29; 23:27), arrives in Rome to appeal to the Roman emperor (25:10–12), he spends two years in the capital proclaiming the Gospel without interference on the part of the authorities (28:16–30). Viewed from the angle of narrative construction, this is a revealing ending because Luke's second volume entails, as all narrative does, some degree of plotting backward from its anticipated ending. This interior retrospectivity[22] implies that both Luke's Gospel and Acts are constructed with a view toward, and from the viewpoint of, the city of Rome that Paul was to reach at the end of Acts. In different words, Luke designed his two volumes from the perspective of a Christianity that had to be sensitive to its existence and survival in the capital.

John

When Clement of Alexandria espoused the idea that the author of the fourth canonical Gospel, encouraged by his friends and prompted by the Spirit, "composed a spiritual gospel" [*pneumatikon poiēsai euaggelikon*], the early Church father intended to draw a distinction between the Johannine narrative and the other three canonical Gospels. Whereas the Synoptics had grasped the "corporeal things" [*ta sōmatika*], the Gospel of John had come into existence under the special guidance of the Spirit.[23] There is no denying that the fourth Gospel entertains a high estimation of the Spirit, if only because—unlike any other canonical or noncanonical Gospel—John had developed the figure of the Paraclete, who sustains the presence of the Spirit in the absence of Jesus. Clement and the tradition he relied upon had rightly sensed the spiritual, indeed metaphysical, underpinnings of the Gospel.

There is, however, a growing awareness of an aspect seemingly at odds with the Gospel's spirituality: its profound anti-Jewishness. Even Raymond Brown, a mainstream interpreter of the Gospel, concedes that "in setting up a contrast between Christian and Jew, John may well be the strongest among the Gospels."[24] Not infrequently, Christian exegesis has been inclined to claim that the animosity John exhibits toward the Jews is antithetical to its spirituality and irreconcilable with its theological profundity. Should it not be possible to isolate and excise the unspiritual elements in the interest of highlighting the Gospel's spiritual and ethical grandeur? Tempting as this proposition might be, it seems that John's spirituality and its anti-Jewish animus are tragically intertwined features. Antipathy toward the Jews and philosophical ambition are concurrent phenomena in this Gospel. This is another way of saying that the Gospel's anti-Jewish sentiments, far from being a spurious offshoot of its spiritual core, are an essential component of its metaphysical agenda.[25]

Reaching back to the beginning of beginnings, to a state outside of time and prior to creation, the Johannine prologue lodges the Logos in foundational primordiality [*en archē*] (1:1). In what appears to be a strikingly logocentric gesture, the Gospel shows forth its metaphysical ambition. Yet it is a metaphysical ambition that is complicated from the outset. The noteworthy feature of the metaphysical Logos is not its absolute transcendence and undifferentiated identity, but a status of ambiguity. In being both "with God" [*pros ton theon*] (1:1) and "God" [*theos ēn*] (1:1), the Logos, in almost classical fashion, manifests difference in identity. Inscribed into the logic of identity is the irrepressible nature of difference. From the beginning, therefore, John's Gospel creates a dilemma for the Logos; this has a critical bearing on the subsequent narrative and its readers.

As the Logos embarks upon his earthly career, he chooses the status of incarnation, which enlarges his difference from divinity. But inasmuch as he differs, he simultaneously seeks to retain his identity from above. As John's Gospel time and again asserts, the Logos who enters into the flesh does so for the purpose of manifesting his glory. The Jesus who submits to spatiotemporal conditions never tires of pleading his unity with the heavenly Father. In principle, therefore, the Logos, once descended into the status of humanity, acts out a problematic that had been inscribed *en archē*. But the transfer to earth has magnified the dilemma into one of above versus below, glory versus flesh, and transcendence versus contingency. The status of incarnate Logos, initially described as being God who was with God, is now more accurately defined as divinely incarnate—seeking to retain the glory while naturalized in the flesh.

How does John's Gospel take up this central dilemma, deal with it, negotiate it, attempt to resolve it? Its principal hermeneutical tool seems to be a linguistic duality, a twofold structuring of language that is enacted in both narrative and discourse sections. Upon entering into the condition of the flesh, the Logos speaks words that are both in conformity with worldly intelligibility and in excess of it. This is the linguistic trait of the double entendres that characterize Johannine language, including a whole semiology of symbols and signifying features. It serves to dramatize a differential quality of communication, giving rise to tensions between apparent and intended meanings, and eliciting ascending moves from corporeality to transcendence. In the ebb and flow of the narrative, John's metaphoric language seeks to make room for the literal while at the same time encouraging transcendence in pursuit of spiritual aspirations. In short, insofar as both narrative and discourses embolden hearers/readers to let themselves be "lifted up" from literalness to spirituality, they operate in the interest of the Gospel's metaphysical agenda.

In the perspective of most contemporary practitioners of the narratological approach to the Gospel, John's double entendres and the inevitable misunderstandings engage hearers/readers in a process of education. Through symbolization and consequent misunderstandings, it is suggested, the narrative enables them "to ascend again and again to the higher plateau of meaning"[26] so as to rise from the naïveté of literalness to genuine enlightenment. In this way, the recurrence of misunderstandings which arise primarily over the ambiguities of language seem calculated to usher hearers/readers into the circle of privileged insiders.

Lest we grow overly confident in assuming that linguistic duality, irony and the whole scheme of signification—as if by fiat of language—"sweetens and spices the fellowship between reader and narrator,"[27] we need reminding that ironic double talk can serve as a tool of marginalization and as a means of exclusion. In the philosophical tradition, it was Kierkegaard who viewed irony less as a catalyst of illumination and more as an instrument of destruction. For him, the Socratic execution of the pedagogy of irony was "exclusively negative" in carrying out a "destructive activity": "Thus irony is the brand, the two-edged sword, which he

[Socrates] wielded over Hellas like a destroying angel."[28] Even if Kierkegaard's interpretation of irony seems far-fetched, it may serve to make us mindful of irony's potential in acting not necessarily as a benign educator, but as perpetrator of negativity, of cruelty even.

Where there are insiders, there also are those who are cast to the outside. As the Johannine Gospel dramatizes its persistently dichotomous plot, the Jews are the ultimate victims. Their exclusion is coexistent with the metaphysical aspirations of the narrative. Whether the protagonist strives to carry the burden of the flesh while manifesting glory, or the discourses address audiences from below while seeking to communicate a truth from above, or the narrative opens the space of signifying differences in gesturing toward the metaphysical signified, the narratological, linguistic, and theological enactment of this Johannine agenda coexists with the marginalization, indeed the demonization (8:44) of the Jews. The more metaphor and irony are doing their divisive work, the more are characters in the narrative marginalized, above all the Jews.

In anticipating the Crucifixion, the Jews are barred from the *Aufhebung*, this central event of lifting the whole plot of double entendres onto a new level of synthesis. Three times the Johannine Jesus speaks in mysteriously metaphorical language about his death in terms of being "lifted up" [*hypsōthēnai*; *hypsōsēte*; *hypsōtō*] (3:14; 8:28; 12:32). At the third and last time, the veil of obscurity is slightly drawn aside and a hint is given of the double meaning of *Aufhebung*, conceding access to the transcending ascent that is to coincide with the moment of fatal destruction (12:33). To the crowd, however, the dual signification of being "lifted up" remains unintelligible. Since the Messiah is to remain forever on earth, his presence is unambiguously terrestrial, and the thought of his death, let alone the paradoxical sublation of his death on the cross, is irreconcilable with his identity (12:34).

As in Matthew, so has also in John the experience of an intra-Jewish conflict between a synagogal community (possibly subject to the Jamnia Academy) and John's dissident messianic community deeply infiltrated the narrative.[29] And, as was the case with Matthew, that conflict has to be dated in the post-war years following the physical and metaphysical trauma of the temple's destruction, a period marked by intense struggle over religious, ethnic and cultural identities. At issue in John is neither the Torah nor the Gentiles, but commitment to the messiahship of Jesus, the role of Moses (especially his identity as Prophet Messiah based on Deut. 18:15, 18), and the status of signs (miracles) in relation to messiahship. Unlike Matthew, John polemicizes not primarily against the Pharisees as a distinct group within Judaism, but against "the Jews" collectively.

Seventy times the hearers/readers are alerted to the designation of "the Jews" in John's Gospel (compared to five or six occurrences in the three Synoptics altogether). Moreover, the Johannine use of *aposynagōgos poiein/genesthai* (9:22; 12:42; 16:2), a hapax legomenon with no known use prior to or outside of the fourth Gospel, reflects the historical experience of an expulsion from the synagogue. Hence, what commenced as a local, intra-Jewish conflict appears to have deteriorated into a schism, a separation into two communities espousing different and opposing religious identities.

To be sure, the Gospel's language of double entendre is meant to place both characters in the narrative and hearers/readers of the narrative on the royal road to unity with the Father. But again, it is precisely this linguistic duplicity that plays havoc with the welfare of the Other. In this intricately metaphorical and ambitiously metaphysical narrative, "the Jews" by and large remain stuck on the literal level, unable to lift themselves up to the spiritual level. Undoubtedly, the difficulties inscribed in John's metaphysical agenda affect all characters in the narrative and its hearers/readers as well. But no one faces greater obstacles than "the Jews" because the metaphorical plot dynamics are primarily played out against them. In this sense the Gospel has created the precondition for the fateful Christian supersessionism which asserted that Judaism was in carnal servitude to the letter, taking "signs of spiritual things for the things themselves."[30]

In sum, we see the four canonical Passion texts redescribing a past event by variously resorting to present experiences. The past is pressed into the service of the present, just as the horizon of present experience serves as frame of reference for the narration of a past event. In this respect, the Passion texts operate precisely according to the norms of cultural memory as defined by Jan Assmann (who is indebted to Maurice Halbwachs): "Therefore memory [*Gedächtnis*] proceeds reconstructively. The past cannot be preserved intact in memory. As the present progresses forward, the past is continuously reorganized in the changing social frameworks [*Bezugsrahmen*] of that present."[31] What this suggests is that neither the canonical Passion narratives nor their subsequent history of verbal and artistic representation can preserve the past as "pure" past. In all instances, the past is preserved as a remembered past, and this remembering takes place within social frames of present references. These *Bezugsrahmen*—or, to use Halbwachs's term, *cadres sociaux*—which control and organize remembering are subject to continuous alterations because of ever-changing present circumstances.[32] It is noteworthy that the dramatic element of double complicity, this remembering as remedy and poison, and in particular the feature of marginalization, antagonism, and demonization, enters the Passion texts primarily via the continually changing social frames of present references, reflecting increasingly tense relations between a Jewish and an emergent Christian identity. As a result, the language of these Christian foundational narratives increasingly runs the risk of evoking an identity of the Other as a target for violence. As we saw, once invaded by duplicity that is spurred by present experiences, the Passion texts in turn inspire an interpretive remembering which likewise continues to be impacted by people's personal and collective memories. In this way, the commemorative Passion narratives and their subsequent memorial representations constitute a single, duplicitous mnemohistory over the long haul of the genealogies of remembering—for better and for worse.

Remembering Violence

Until the recent arrival of literary narratological criticism, interpretations of the Passion texts, and of the Gospels at large, were the prerogative of historical criticism. Among the key features that typify the strictly historical approach, the following may be cited: excavation of an assumed pre-Markan Passion narrative; reconstruction of a compositional history postulating one or two pre-Markan stages in the tradition; explication of ideational shifts in the compositional history of Mark's narrative from a Jewish toward a more Gentile-oriented text, from a martyrological narration to a theological conception, or from a historically grounded account to legendary embellishments; definition of the generic identity of the Markan Passion narrative; investigation of the literary relations among the three Synoptic Passion texts, and between the Passion in Mark and the Gospel of Peter; examination of discrepancies between Synoptic and Johannine chronologies; determination of the chronology of Jesus' death (day, month, and year); comparison of the Last Supper traditions in Paul and the Synoptic narratives; judicial issues raised by the trial (the legal competence of the Sanhedrin, the high priest, and the Roman procurator respectively); and the issue concerning the historicity of the law (or convention) of amnesty.

Pursuing the strictly historical, documentary approach, scholarship endeavored to gain control over the text by way of compositional stratification, literary classification, and historical clarification. Once the text was thus fully categorized, the conditions for understanding were assumed to have been met. Within the confines of the historical paradigm, this procedure seems entirely reasonable. We see here the triumph of the model of truth as literary, generic and historical correctness. And yet, the epistemological search for authentic textuality and originality, for historicity and chronology, fails to connect with the commemorative and psychodynamic impulses that feed the narrative. At a minimum, it falls short of probing the deeper springs that motivate and nourish the narratives of death, and at a maximum it embodies category mistakes.

In apprehending the Passion narratives as commemorative texts, interpretation proceeds from a focus on trauma, ever mindful of the founding event as an act of gross violence. Such is the monstrosity of that event that it must have posed severe challenges to all modes of narration: one cannot verbally communicate the unvarnished, unedited terror in its factual rawness. Little wonder that Roman authors, while virtually unanimous that crucifixion was horrific business, exercised reticence in writing about it. "Crucifixion was widespread and frequent, above all in Roman times, but the cultured literary world wanted to have nothing to do with it, and as a rule kept quiet about it."[33] Caesar, Lucretius, Virgil, Statius, the younger Pliny, Aulus Gellius, Horace, Tacitus, and many others were either silent or exceedingly restrained in giving any account of the Roman death penalty. Nor is it possible to find principled objections to crucifixion in Roman sources. There is hardly any mention of it in inscriptions. "This means, however, that the relative scarcity of references to crucifixions in antiquity, and their fortuitousness, are less a historical problem than an aesthetic one, connected with the sociology of literature."[34] Cognizant of the constraints on narrative, the memory approach presses questions about the limits of representation and the transference of trauma onto the arena of language.

Perhaps no event in early Christian history has made greater demands on memory than Jesus' death. How is memory to deal with this massively disruptive trauma of execution by crucifixion? How is this "exhibitionist act of political violence"[35] made accessible to hearers/readers by writing it up, or better, by writing about it? Apart from death's ritualization in the Last Supper, can this founding event of violence be commemorated in any narrative form? One strategy of memory is the fusion of (recollections of) the past with (recollections in) the present. We have observed this habitual procedure throughout the genealogies of Passion rememberings, and we have detailed its efficaciousness *ad bonam et ad malam partem*. By drawing on the past from the perspective of the present, one retains not the past itself, but a recreated, freshly remembered past. One principal memory strategy, therefore, is to refuse to let past history ever fully define those who remember.

In what follows, three more memory strategies will be elaborated that are operative in Mark's Passion narrative. One feature concerns the construction of a "memory place" that provides a safely familiar habitat for what seems utterly unrepresentable. A second feature deals with the retrieval of scriptural references as interpretive "keys" in the formation of the narrative. The third feature seeks to offset the traumas of history and its disrupting effects by devising causal connections and a sense of normative coherence. What all three strategies—"memory place," interpretive "keying," and explanatory rationalization—have in common is a mode of encoding "the festering wound [*die eiternde Wunde*]," to use Nietzsche's poignant expression, in older, familiar patterns and in a network of newly constructed causalities so as to make violence both comprehensible and in a sense bearable.

Concerning "memory places," the scholarly realization of a commonplace pattern underlying the Markan Passion text has been a matter of growing awareness via the studies of Lothar Ruppert, George Nickelsburg, Burton Mack, and Arthur Dewey.[36] In the 1970s Ruppert published a series of books that offered a comprehensive survey of the motif of the offended, assaulted, and persecuted righteous one(s). Covering nearly a millennium of Jewish scribal productivity, ranging from the Hebrew Bible and the Septuagint, across Hellenistic-Jewish, Qumran and apocalyptic literatures, he observed and traced a number of trajectories of the motif of the *passio iusti* or *iustorum* through the centuries. While Ruppert's work remained strangely inconclusive in its limited focus on isolated occurrences of the motif in their respective semantic fields, it has nonetheless succeeded in uncovering a widely dispersed and tradition-honored complex of standard features associated with the sufferings of the righteous one(s). Nickelsburg was far less reticent in drawing firm and bold consequences. Confining his investigation to a smaller number of comparative texts, he argued that the motif of "the rescue and vindication of a persecuted innocent person or persons"[37] had been emplotted in the Markan Passion text. Moreover, what for Ruppert was a motif, for Nickelsburg was a genre, in fact a "literary genre" that, owing to its discrepancy with Markan redaction, was "best explained by the hypothesis that [it] . . . derive[s] from a pre-Markan Passion narrative."[38] Assuredly, this represents thinking in the register of the documentary paradigm, which is prone to solve the issue of commonplace patterns by reference to a hidden text behind the text. Mack, while generally—although not in all details—agreeing with Nickelsburg's assessment of the existence of the motif in Mark, refrained from linking it with a distinct stage in the assumed pre-Markan history of the Passion because "there is no evidence for a passion narrative before Mark."[39] Not fully aware of the wide-ranging dispersion of the motif as demonstrated by Ruppert, he chose to associate the motif exclusively with wisdom. This wisdom motif of the persecuted righteous one, Mack reasoned, served Mark as a "basic narrative design" on which he constructed the merger of the Hellenistic Christ myth and traditions stemming from the Jesus movement.[40] Here we see how a potentially promising approach is forced back into the Bultmannian model of the genesis of Mark's Gospel, a model for which there is little evidence.

We owe to Dewey the beginnings of a thoroughgoing rethinking of basic assumptions about the Passion texts. His achievement has been to link the commonplace pattern in the Markan Passion narrative with memory. Inspired by Mary Carruthers's studies on memory in medieval culture,[41] he proposed that the construction, or more precisely *inventio*, of a commonplace pattern in the narrative commemoration of Jesus' death was precisely the kind of device one could expect from memory's operations. "The work of memory was not to re-present, not to reduplicate, but to construct, to deliver a place for images" that could serve as a habitat for the trauma. In short, memory's principal objective was "to 'invent' a locus for his [Jesus'] death."[42] Rhetorically speaking, the *inventio* did not mean the invention of something new, but rather the (re)discovery of topoi or a set of familiar, perhaps even tradition-honored, categories that could provide an organizational framework for the founding event of violence. For Dewey, therefore, memory supplies the rationale for the existence of the commonplace pattern of the *passio iusti* in Mark—a repertoire of features that were widely known, socially accessible, and hence suitable for the mediation of a trauma. In this way, Nickelsburg's literary genre and Mack's wisdom story have been transposed into a "memory bed" which was to bring the unthinkable event of violence into accord with a familiar, almost normative pattern. In other words, the commonplace pattern of the *passio iusti* "normalizes" Jesus' death.

Dewey has placed scholarly deliberations about the Markan Passion text on a new footing. Indeed, his work provides a corrective to our own thinking on memory. Earlier, we observed that the commemoration of Jesus' death labors under the predicament of representation: how can the virtually incommunicable founding event of violence be represented in verbal narrative form? This may well be the problem memory has to contend with in the case of the initial trauma, but it does not get us to the core of memory's design. The representational theory of knowledge may still be too closely tied in with modernity's linguistic, literary, and historical sensibilities. For memory's objective, it turns out, is not primarily the literary representation of reality in the sense of the issue Auerbach has raised,[43] nor primarily the problematic of narrating trauma within the confining boundaries of historiography. Memory's primary impulse was not representative, mimetic or iterative, but rather heuristic, inventive and constructive. To that end, it devised a narrative sepulcher of Jesus' death by tapping into the cultural reservoir in search of topoi capable of localizing and humanizing what was deemed unspeakable as well as indescribable.

Concerning interpretive "keying," it is well known that large segments of Mark's Passion narrative are suffused with and even constructed on citations, paraphrases, and imagery from Hebrew scripture. Primarily psalms of lamentation (22; 31; 41; 49; 69), but Isaiah 53, Zechariah 13, and Daniel 7 were also complicit in the composition of that text. Among principal Markan motifs that are composed on the basis of scriptural resources are the following: conspiracy to kill, betrayal by friends, desertion of followers, grief unto death, false witnesses, false accusers, silence before accusers, Son of Man confession, mocking by adversaries, dividing of garments, derision of onlookers, cry of dereliction, and vinegar for thirst. The prevailing exegetical tendencies to explain the phenomenon have been midrash and apologetics. Strictly speaking, however, the diffusion of and allusion to scriptural references across the Passion text bears no resemblance to midrash's moral, homiletical, and allegorical explication of scriptural stories that had become clouded by the passage of time. Nor does the observed phenomenon conform to the pesher technique, which features citation of text followed by formal interpretation. As for the Passion apologetic, widely employed in both forthright and subliminal fashion, it views the scriptural references as proof texts, sometimes assumed to have been derived from a collection of "Old Testament" testimonies. Their designed purpose was to "prove" that the Passion was the realization of scripturally grounded prophecies. In that case, the evidence was pressed into the schematization of promise and fulfillment. It is by far the preferred mode of explication. Even Frank Kermode, literary critic par excellence, declared that Psalm 22 "is clearly a source, or, if you prefer, a prophecy or promise of incidents in the historical Passion Narrative."[44] That the doctrinal pattern of promise and fulfillment, while clearly operative in Matthew and Luke, it is not applicable to Mark, is a cautionary lesson that has been taught us by Alfred Suhl. In an impressive work exclusively devoted to the function of scriptural citations and references in Mark, he argued that scripture in that gospel was a "traditional entity [*Grösse*]"[45] generally perceived to be revelation operating as source of inspiration and interpretation. The specific reason for Mark to refrain from the doctrinal schematization was that time in that Gospel was not yet sufficiently stretched into a temporal duration to allow for differentiation in terms of promise and fulfillment.

Regarding the so-called scriptural citations, two features merit attention. To begin with, almost none of the passages under consideration are marked by a citation formula. They are for the most part not identified as "scriptural," and for this reason do not alert hearers/readers to their origination in scripture. It is the modern specialist who can lift these passages from their narrative context and classify them by chapter and verse in reference to the printed translation of the Hebrew Bible. Nor do they function as "proof texts" in the sense of announcing the consummation of a prior text assumed to be harboring an anticipatory potential, unless one reads these passages under the smothering embrace of Mark's powerful successors, Matthew and Luke. In Mark, the so-called scriptural passages are entirely enmeshed in narrative, constituting "narrative germs"[46] that are not distinguishable as scriptural sources.

Secondly, all the "scriptural" passages lend support to and enhance the commonplace structure of the *passio iusti*. They are, we must now say, an integral part of memory's observed construction of the commonplace framework that underlies the Passion text. Rather than viewing them as "scriptural citations" or "proof texts," one should see in them the work of *inventio*, memory's search of topoi for the normative framework of the commemoration of Jesus' death. Both compositionally and thematically, therefore, the issue of the commonplace pattern and the so-called scriptural passages are one and the same phenomenon. Here we have arrived at the primary enigma of the memorial phenomenon: its extensive appropriation of traditional topoi and its constructive skills in the formation of the Passion text. In it we recognize the technique of what Kirk, relying on Barry Schwartz,[47] has termed interpretive "keying" whereby familiar, even archetypal language is reclaimed to serve as the key to understanding the excesses of violence within older, established frames. In the case of Mark's Passion text, the ample use of traditional topoi has converted Jesus into a socially and memorially accessible *Erinnerungsfigur*.[48]

Concerning the explanatory powers of memory, finally, one recalls the etymological rationale of re-membering and re-collecting, which evokes the notion of a retrieval of dispersed members and their reintegration into a new contextuality. A major theme of the Markan Passion text is the temple motif, or, as it is more appropriately called, the anti-temple motif. It is clearly not part of the *passio iusti* commonplace pattern. One may see in it a reminiscence of a historical temple "incident" which, however, is amplified by the intervention of present (Markan) circumstances and recollections. Memory's constructive achievement is evident in the connection of the anti-temple motif with the death of Jesus, thereby providing a narrative rationale for hitherto unconnected traumas of history.

In Mark's Passion, Jesus enters Jerusalem three times, on three successive days. In each instance, his entry into the city amounts to an entry into the temple (11:11, 15, 27). At his first entry he undertakes a survey of the temple, then leaves for the place from which he had departed (11:11). The second entry is conventionally associated with the so-called "cleansing" of the temple. However, Mark's plot frames the temple incident (11:15–19) with the story of the cursing of the fig tree (11:12–14, 20–22), suggesting more serious implications than a mere "cleansing." Mark's well-known framing device establishes a connection between the framing stories concerning the fig tree and the framed story concerning the temple. Accordingly, the fig tree stands for the temple and the dead tree symbolizes the temple. The third journey into the city takes Jesus once again into the temple (11:27) making it (12:35, 41) the locale for controversial teachings directed toward the guardians of the temple and the guarantors of tradition. Notably, none of the three temple visits is associated with prayer and worship. Having symbolically identified the temple with the dead fig tree and dissociated himself from all authorities associated with the temple, Jesus exits the temple for the last time (13:1), never to return to it, and promptly announces its physical destruction (13:2). This announcement marks a preliminary culmination of his persistent anti-temple activity.

Additionally, the narrative establishes a close connection between Jesus' anti-temple mission and the plot on his life. The initial death plot (resuming the programmatic announcement in 3:16) is reported in reaction to Jesus' symbolic cursing of the fig tree (11:18). The plan to kill him is reiterated by the temple authorities when he identifies himself with the rejected cornerstone (12:12). Following Jesus' announcement of the destruction of the temple (and subsequent communication regarding a coming time of war and bloodshed) the death plot is made known for the third time (14:1). Within the broader structure of the Passion text, therefore, a link is made between the death of the temple and the death of Jesus.

Not surprisingly, the issue of the temple surfaces in the trial and at the hour of death. In the hearing before the high priestly assembly, Jesus' pronouncement concerning the temple is introduced as evidence against him. The charge is that he was heard saying: "I will destroy this temple made with hands" (14:58), an accusation repeated by the passersby at the Crucifixion (15:29). But the witnesses are immediately refuted as giving false and inconsistent testimony, and the passersby are discredited as adversaries. In the context of the narrative logic, Jesus is the opponent of the temple who symbolically enacted and announced its downfall, but not the agent of its destruction. The final culmination of the anti-temple motif is reached with the rending of the temple curtain at the moment of death (15:38). The interpretation of the incident is controversial. Either the veil is in front of the Holy of Holies and its tearing asunder facilitates universal access, or the tearing from top to bottom symbolizes the destruction of the temple. Three observations incline the interpretation toward the latter meaning.[49] In Josephus and the Septuagint, *naos*, the term used by Mark in 15:38, is never used to designate the Holy of Holies. In Mark, *naos* is also used both by the false witnesses (14:58) and the mocking passersby (15:29) in reference to the temple building. In the narrative context, the rending of the curtain brings the anti-temple motif to the point of culmination. At this point the narrator has synchronized the death of the temple and the death of Jesus.

So densely is the temple motif integrated into the narrative realism, and so persuasive is its reality effect, that interpreters rarely step back to reflect on Mark's constructive achievement. Yet Mark is the first Christian who faced up to the two principal traumas suffered by first-century Christians: the death of Jesus and the destruction of the temple. His principle mechanism in dealing with the traumas was to construct a linkage between them. Jesus anticipated, even precipitated the temple conflagration, and in part it was in the process of his mission against the temple that he was destroyed himself.

Epilogue

Mark's Passion text came to be written under the aegis of a twofold death. The challenge was not to face death as the great equalizer who levels all destinies, but to confront the historical specificity of two traumas: the death of the Just one and the death of the holy city. There is lurking beneath the narrative surface a sense of poignant absence. In the most general sense, therefore, the narrative is the work of mourning, seeking to mediate conciliation with the twofold loss.

More precisely, the Passion narrative is the work of memory. Inciting the powers of memory, the twofold trauma proved to be a memorially productive experience. Remembering in this context is best understood not as repetition, and not strictly as updating, but as a new realization of the past. The narrated past was thereby constructed as a remembered past or, put differently, the past was memorialized to facilitate remembering so as to better serve both present and future.

A principal strategy in coping with the aporias of representation was the construction of a normative pattern made up of commonplaces that pertained to the sufferings of the Just one. This "memory place" is not a locus in the topographical sense but something in the nature of a grid of relevant topoi. It is clearly a place of memory and not of history, although it is endowed with the remarkable capacity to generate an immense genealogy of rememberings.

One can understand the history of the Passion text, a memory text itself, and the subsequent history of continuous rememberings as mnemohistory. But mnemohistory, while empowered by memory, denotes not simply a history of memory in the abstract, but rather an intricate interweaving of memory with history. It is history that breeds memories of the past that are nourished by present history and in turn interact with present history and generate more memories. History begets memories, which beget more history and more memories. In this sense, the concept of mnemohistory occupies the position formerly held by tradition.

Throughout mnemohistory, present historical experience is an active coproducer in the formation of memories. As Christianity sought accommodation with the Roman imperial power structure, and relations between Jews and Christians grew more tense, memories of the Passion texts accentuated certain aspects at the expense of others. The specificity of anti-temple motif was increasingly subsumed under the emergent theme of the anti-Jewish polemic. Instead of serving as an antidote to violence, the memories of the victim of violence ushered in further violence. Tragically, reviving the memory of the Just One has often imperiled the lives of a multitude.

The Historian and the Messianic "Now"

Reading Edith Wyschogrod's An Ethics of Remembering

BETTINA BERGO

To Edith, one of the most generous of interlocutors and a cosmopolitical thinker.

Introduction

In his *Ursprung des deutschen Trauerspiels*, Walter Benjamin[1] turned to one of the most forgettable moments of European history—the German baroque of the seventeenth century—to unearth the work of writers who, by all accounts, rested happily in their oblivion. The *Trauerspiel* is in no way classical tragedy; it is a mourning play in which a spectacle is made of the buildup of ruin upon ruin, culminating in an apotheosis of abjection. These plays, derisively referred to as *Sturm und Drang* (storm and stress), piled corpses upon corpses in what was no gesture of remembering. Like an anticipation of the image industry of the twentieth century, the baroque drama provided the site of dark scenes that profiled skeletons and death heads, all of this to considerable popular entertainment. Or so we understood it until Benjamin. In conscious contradistinction to Nietzsche's *Birth of Tragedy* opposition of the Dionysiac and the Apollonian, Benjamin performed, on seventeenth century drama, a paradoxical gesture of remembering that wrested from the trivial its unanticipated, universal signification.

Heartfelt thanks to Gabriel Malenfant (University of Iceland) for his help, his suggestions, his criticism, and his unending patience.

The work of the *Trauerspiel* is done through the technique of allegory. In allegory, the misery of the world, the bathos of failed human loves and dreams, becomes part of a signifying moment that points toward the (all too human) necessity of redemption. In so doing, these abject elements themselves become internally transformed. The entire process is rather like the transformation of the morpheme from ideogram to the alphabetic phoneme. Unlike the ideogram, the linguistics of Benjamin's *Port-Royal* taught us that the phonetic word was like a window through which one glimpsed meaning, even as the *technē* (the word itself) vanished in its materiality. Thus, too, the *Trauerspiel*, its actors, scenes, and devices: starting from the material of "cataclysm," the *Trauerspiel*, to use Wyschogrod's word, came to point beyond its *own mise en scène* toward responsibility as the unperceived correlate through which a certain hope came to light, however fragile—or even absurd—it might be.

Throughout his brief, complex life, Walter Benjamin worked toward an ethical mnemonics. It is an open question whether, had he survived his 1940 flight into the Pyrénées and escaped the Nazis by traveling through Spain, he would have conceived an ethics of remembering from the shards of the ruins of the twentieth century. Suffice it to say that his was what we might call a postmodern relationship to that piling of ruin upon ruin (as witnessed by his "Angel of History") which was still being touted as progress. The question for me here is also that toward which Edith Wyschogrod is working: can one think a history of ruins—life-altering ruins—under the figure of ethics, or, better, as Adorno put it, under that of redemption? Wyschogrod will pose the question otherwise: can we think cataclysms like Auschwitz at all? What Idea is implicit in a project of reflection of that kind? Finally, can we navigate such thinking between descriptive images—which, through their incessant multiplication, risk making the historic "event" into a fetish—and moral discourse, which slides toward passion and plaint, often distant from the density of the event itself?[2] Only a superficial reading would insist that Benjamin's project was the opposite of Wyschogrod's. In his recovery of the most ostensibly trivial of art forms, he understood the stormy imagery, took its meaning from its ability to point beyond itself toward something unthematizable—a certain redemption. This outer side of redemption, in turn, had a dialectical effect on the words and images of the play, transforming the most insignificant ones from within, such that they signified more than was promised by their facticity. For Wyschogrod, the question of thinking catastrophe entails a related regressive movement, through which we learn why it is that the past stands before us as our future, why it is that a certain "redemption" may pervade remembering.

For Benjamin, as for us, the difficulty of thinking the accumulation of ruins under the figure of redemption lies in the near impossibility of imagining redemption as still somehow meaningful. In the midst of the temporal and epistemic totalizations produced by twentieth-century knowledge framing (time is global, linear, efficient; we can know everything, calculate everything; the aleatory is subject to rationalization by being transformed into a constant), the only redemption imaginable would take the form of interruptions, of protest or witnessing that would lead us far afield from history's other requisite: doing justice to the past, its situations and its actors. After all, it is the witness who proves least reliable when it comes to reconstructing the facts. If thinking the ruins, which we have increasingly agreed to see as piling up rather than ascending in some social teleology—under a figure of redemption means working out the practical dimension of an ethics of remembering, then we have to ask what it is about that practice that needs clarification. This is part of Wyschogrod's task when she examines the new technologies by which the past is inscribed and figured in art and film.

Indeed, this is also what makes Benjamin's contribution to the study of allegory precious. Understanding the way in which a figure, by the destroying or devaluing the reality to which it points, opens an imaginary space for another world or another site (alternately alienating us through deterritorialization or creating hope, thanks to a critique of identity and belonging),[3] one understands the plasticity of the imagination[4] and its power to institute the different in the midst of cultural formations that may entertain us but have largely lost their power to do much else; this might be something like opening a space for dreaming. Now, thinking critically about surpassed forms with an eye toward discerning the ex-centric in them required of Benjamin a particular relationship with the past that, he would later say, consisted in apprehending an uncanny "appointment" [*Verabredung*] between us and the present and the non-time of the closed past. As he put it in his "Theses on History" (sketched in the 1920s, reworked in 1940):

> The past carries a familiar index with it, through which it is referred toward redemption [*auf die Erlösung verwiesen wird*]. Does not a breath of wind struggle against us, a breath that once surrounded the earlier ones [*um die Früheren*]? Is there not in voices, to which we could have loaned our ears, an echo henceforth silenced? Have the women, with whom we circulate, not sisters, who no longer recognize them? If it is this way, then there consists a secret appointment [*eine geheime Verabredung*] between past generations, [*Geschlechtern*] and our own.[5]

For Benjamin, doing justice to the secret appointment we have with the dead and even their secret breath meant "reading through" that history, wresting from it the resources through which an evanescent hope could be restored. Is this not Levinas's hope as he condemns the history of great texts in his preface to *Totality and Infinity*?[6] History is violence and war, he says. Being has but one face, and it is worse than Heraclitus's change; the lost breath of history is recaptured only in the gesture that seems antithetical to remembering: a particular responsibility here and now. It is here that Wyschogrod poses our extraordinary, almost irreverent question—what might a heterological (Levinasian) historiography look like?

If "reading through" is the necessary first step to being present at the secret appointment between lost generations, its fulfillment may well come to light in the form of a "weak messianic force." Benjamin wrote: "Then to us as to every generation that came before us, is conferred a *weak* messianic force, to which the past has a claim. It is not cheap to dispatch [*abzufertigen*] this claim."[7] A weak force and a certain responsibility that grows out of it: this is the Benjaminian-Levinasian leitmotif that runs through Wyschogrod's writing.

One other capacity is required of the heterological historian in her work of preservation: "reading under." This may just be an awkward way to express a different search, one that excavates underlying structures that pass in the popular imagination from generation to generation. "Reading under" produces a historiography as contentious as it is generous. It was the enterprise of Carlo Ginzburg, among others. In his *Ecstasies: Deciphering the Witches' Sabbath*,[8] Ginzburg traces the persistence of nature religions through the testimony of those indicted for sorcery by the sixteenth century Inquisition. It was Ginzburg's quixotic task to read beneath the explicit words of the trial testimonies, in search of traces of meaning that might form a continuum with ancient themes—again, of rebirth and redemption—that structured "millennia . . . of myths, fables, rites and ecstasies."[9] In that respect, Ginzburg is studying the persistence of a dionysianism well past the emergence of Greek tragedy, into the political tragedy of the pyres of the Inquisition. Combining structuralism and the *Annales* historian's concern with lost documents that constitute the microhistory of cultures, Ginzburg distilled the truth of abjected groups from the discursive "hegemony" serving the *culture savante* and perpetually rehashed by academics.

The witches' Sabbath was mastered by intellectual culture, which transformed it into sorcery by applying the schemata of the dominant culture, that of Catholic theologians. If popular culture is the culture of subaltern classes and *culture savante* is that of dominant classes, then the conflicts between these two cultures are conflicts between the dominant and the dominated. If, on the other hand, popular culture is a fundamentally different culture . . . then we must know more about this culture, whose traces are attested by ethnographic research . . .[10]

Whatever we make of the ecstatic dimension of religious and aesthetic expression, it doubtless performs the function of a vector whereby redemption as hope is presaged by an embodied *sortie de soi*. Like a theater of transcendence, ecstasy invents a voyage toward the end of time or space from which a fundamental lesson (often, about justice) is gleaned. Of course, reading traces beneath history—under the signs of Kant, Nietzsche, and Benjamin, in search of forces and fragments—entails a hermeneutic circle. How can we avoid retrojecting the phantasm of a larger meaning, putatively rising out of a lost religion, when we speak, if not of a Jungian collective unconscious, then certainly of an ethnographic collective unconscious? We cannot avoid this, short of elaborating an impossible key to decoding the symbols and discourses of which only fragments remain. For this, Ginzburg has been amply criticized—as much by empirical historians as by structuralists.[11]

Our desire for a criterion by which to distinguish first a superficial practical level, immediately apparent in social formations, from a deeper symbolic level, pursues a certain ideal. All we have by which to make this distinction are recurrent traces, the histories of sacred narratives and practices, and the rules provided us by structuralism's study of kinship relations and myths. The skeptical historian who wants to know how Ginzburg can account for a persistence of shamanism or nature religions beneath the witches' sabbath is asking for proof. Beneath this proof lies a different striving, however: something like an Idea that assures that ostensible evil will hide what is resistance to manifest persecution, as well as a quest for transcendence. The motivation behind his call for proof is close to Wyschogrod's aspirations to understand the kind of idea necessary to think cataclysm and the nothingness it produces. This is to my mind a Levinasian theme and reveals the surreptitious appointment between Levinas's thought and the historian's task.

Having shown in the second chapter of *An Ethics of Remembering* that the discursive practices that make up history writing proceed in a temporal and event-weaving hermeneutic that is not unlike fiction writing, even if the events that serve as the referents of history *versus* those of fiction are different,[12] Wyschogrod sets out the principles of a philosophical history.

She follows Kant in this in three ways. First, she determines how an idea that surpasses the understanding can function analogously to the negative sublime in the mature Kant. Second, she reminds us that the Categorical Imperative proceeds on an "indispensable complement," the will of the other.[13] Third, she rethinks, using Levinas, the context in which the regulative ideal hidden within the sublime is brought forth.[14]

Wyschogrod reminds us that regulative ideals, like freedom, God, or the immortality of the soul, are never understood for themselves, but only by analogy. We understand God not as he is in himself, but "as he is in relation to us, by *analogy*." This is not a categorical understanding; no category needs to be schematized with time to open to this sort of thinking. It is rather a thinking of relations: "We are related to God as clock to clockmaker. It is the relations that are analogous and not the relata."[15] The Idea of Reason becomes a norm for thinking the history of the unthinkable in two respects. First, it becomes a norm because understanding a historical catastrophe tames the event and denatures it: "Common sense appears to dictate that mass annihilation belongs to the sphere of the calculable: so many persons killed in the Bosnian conflict, so many in Rwanda, Burundi, or the Sudan . . . [we suppose that] *l'esprit de géométrie* will suffice."[16] However, if we attempt to think these events precisely as singularities, then, according to Kant's logic, "a rule is needed that makes the presentation of the cataclysm as such possible."[17] It seems conceivable to think catastrophes on the basis of analogy, though the *relata* held together under the analogy would continue to shift. Secondly, Wyschogrod's search for the form of the rule is her philosophical gesture—one which Ginzburg apparently did not make, and which Benjamin named "a *weak* messianic force," our fragile rendezvous with disappeared generations. The Idea of Reason, in regrouping the particulars, allows us to step beyond the aporia created by the deconstruction of the historical and literary narratives, that aporia in which truth and fact are dissolved in a multi-perspectival explosion of metaphors and figures. While recognizing, with Hayden White, that beneath historical enterprises is a moralizing impetus, the Idea of Reason allows us to bring together events with sufficient coherence that they could serve three ends: a politics of interpretation;[18] a fragile coherence from which to derive what Kant called a "presentation" [*Darstellung*] that is ideal and ethical; finally, the setting forth of something like a weak messianic force or a principle of hope. Wyschogrod searches for this idea in Kant's practical reason, only to relinquish this source in favor of an equally disappointing examination of his "conceptless" dynamic sublime. Ultimately, she will turn to Levinas for a radical rereading of the sublime. Let us see how she examines practical reason.

Searching Kant's practical reason, Wyschogrod asks whether the rule that would enable the presentation of the cataclysm should be moral: is it like a subjective maxim that could be universalized? This search proves impracticable as it demands what empirical historians wanted of Ginzburg: that there be a logic *prior* to the logic of historical events, a universal key to understanding a diachronic meaning that then founds the significance of synchronic events. "The question of whether there can be an Ethics that precedes the categorical imperative repeats the logical structure of the Augustinian query, 'Can there be a time before time?' and its answer: 'Time prior to time is unthinkable.' An Ethics prior to the ethics of imperatives cannot be thought. Yet there is an 'indispensable complement' to imperatives, the will of the other."

Wyschogrod argues that for Kant, nevertheless, the will of the other fails as an ethical ground on two counts. It fails because Kant's moral logic is caught between the pole of duty and the pole of moral feeling, so that the other or his will should be a matter of affecting a subject in a particular way. An example of this is of course "love," understood as "an intimate relation." There, my will is affected by virtue of the other and the emotions I feel toward her. Even if an intimate relation can inflect my hypothetical maxims, it should not have any impact on the rational perspicuity of my universalizable maxims. Nevertheless, Wyschogrod insists that "the sheer pressure of alterity, of a will not my own . . . impels me to form my maxims by responding to this alien will." It may do this to such an extent that the pressure of the other (in the event of our face-to-face encounter) would explode Kant's free self-legislation of practical reason if the affectivity that it engendered entered into conflict with the legislating will. "Alterity can only weigh in as a sheer demand," but as she points out, "Kant leaves unthought the implications of this extraordinary intrusion of alterity."[19]

And yet it seems to pervade Kant's third *Critique*, provided we establish parallels between the latter and his practical philosophy. For Kant's description of our failed intuition of the infinite inevitably orients our concept of nature toward a suprasensible substrate. This movement, not without violence, proves not to be the work or effect of the phenomenon we intuit, but rather, something that lies within ourselves. Kant calls it a disposition and a power.[20] If we leave the notion of an innate power aside for a moment, and acknowledge the parallel between the outcome of our failed intuition of the infinite and Kant's distinction between a price and dignity in the *Foundations of a Metaphysics of Morals*, then we see that both share a peculiar quality: they are nonrelatively great, they elude measure and evaluation. Understood in light of the "indispensable complement"—whether it be the will of the other or the natural prod to our imagination—it ceases to matter what that immanent power is. Instead, a dynamic relationality emerges, in which the feeling of our inability to reach an intuition, much less to find an idea that could give us a law of representation, seems primary. I am not trying to objectify the sublime spectacle, whose sublimity, we know, is situated in reason's own vocation to pass beyond the sensible. I am taking up Wyschogrod's reminder of the complement provided to reason (and to the imagination) by the other person or the sublime object or event. It was very much Kant's intent that the affectivity aroused by the sublime correlate with, even take precedence to, the norm presiding over moral action. It would take precedence over the practical postulates of the immortality of the soul and the existence of God. It is no accident that out of the Kantian system, Hermann Cohen—intellectual ancestor of Levinas—derived his concept of correlation from the study of the Kantian reason and imagination (one function of his return to Judaism).

In abandoning the resource of practical reason as her source for a regulative idea, Wyschogrod gestures toward Levinas as the necessary supplement to Kantian moral autonomy. It would seem that the heteronomous "complement" is insufficient for creating an ethics beyond the bounds of reason alone. So it seems, at least in Wyschogrod's investigation, that histories of ethics—or ethical contestations of reason—since Kant, have certainly proceeded from the conviction that reason's regulative ideas do not suffice to assuring other-directed ethical conduct. Wyschogrod's supplementary reading of Levinas opens questions as well. I will return to this.

In a paradoxical discussion of the unfortunate history of the twentieth-century appropriation of the sublime that combines its critique with a recovery by Levinas of an un-Kantian interpretation of the sublime, Wyschogrod carries out her search for a concept by which to think annihilation. This would suggest that the resources afforded by the sublime to thinking are irreplaceable in our time. As we noted earlier, the function of the mathematical sublime is to establish a bridge between the aesthetic and moral vocations of reason. This bridging is possible through a recognition that reason effects concerning its own "fictional" capacities. For example, confronting the immensity of the pyramids of Egypt, Kant quotes a comment made by Savary about obtaining the "full emotional effect from their magnitude."

> One must neither get too close to them nor stay too far away. For
> if one stays too far away, then the apprehended parts (the stones on
> top of one another) are presented only obscurely, and hence their

presentation has no effect on the subject's aesthetic judgment; and if one gets too close, then the eye needs some time to complete the apprehension from the base to the peak, but during that time some of the earlier parts are invariably extinguished in the imagination before it has apprehended the later ones, and hence the comprehension is never complete.[21]

At stake here is striking an equilibrium between the distance at which the parts are lost and with them the aesthetic effect, and the proximity at which each block may be discerned, in which case the impact of the magnitude creates the aesthetic effect as the imagination loses hold on the sequence of its apprehensions: the first, second, third to the nth stone. In the wake of the untotalizable experience that reason would assemble under an idea, the feeling produced is that of satisfaction. It is as though the "imagination reaches its maximum, strives to expand that maximum," and fails. The pleasure is aroused by our admiration for this process of expansion and the imagination's inability to contain an infinite otherness. Reason recognizes, in that failure, that it has a supersensuous vocation that nevertheless remains caught in the universal formal structure of "subjectivity" evinced by Kant.

Now, the resistance to totalization is likewise a matter of the incalculable and of the sheer violence of a natural event like a thunderstorm. It never inheres in a face or a catastrophe that threatens our lives. Thus in a sense, the critique of Kant's aesthetics—that it is constructed from the perspective of a spectator—is fair. Recent attempts to restore to the natural event its due as "donation" redress this unilaterality. Before the neo-Kantians, nothing like a focus on intersubjectivity could be found in Kant's transcendental project, much less a sublime that might be tied into historical events whose destructive potential would have been difficult to imagine. What Wyschogrod will attempt is the enlargement of striving—beyond Kant's rational ideas—to which the experience of our imagination's inadequacy leads us.[22] The understanding, which sought to give the imagination concepts of unity, succession, even number, fails to fulfill this function in the case of great magnitudes even as imagination shoots up in pursuit of the "infinitely" high. Nevertheless, reason "makes us unavoidably think of the infinite (in common reason's judgment, *as given in its entirety* (in its totality)."[23] We should not think that this is a totality that is dialectically achieved or even closed. Reason does not stop there with its presentation of a totality: "to be able even to think the infinite as *a whole* indicates a mental power that surpasses any standard of sense."[24] Gradually, reason understands this in its immanence as failure and sign.

It recognizes that the feeling of elevation and admiration comes from its own activity, which suggests its structural capacity to surpass both imagination and understanding taken separately: "Hence the feeling of the sublime in nature is respect for our own vocation."[25]

Whether we are frightened or exalted by it, the sublime pulls us forward, recognizing firstly that it is in us and that "even the greatest power of sensibility is inadequate."[26] But this inadequacy does not set us against rational ideas; rather, it makes us "strive toward them,"[27] law-like. Totalization as an effort of the imagination, outstripping the concepts' capacities of presentation, is the necessary bridge to understanding ourselves as given structurally to thinking beyond the Kantianization of pure, or practical, concepts—much less intuition. And this drive to totalization, certainly a fragile bridge between ethical and aesthetic judgment, is more necessary *as our creation* than it is normative in the mode of later Idealism (Hegel's).

Today, however, the task would have to be to think this effort at totalization without making it depend on awe, majesty, or political sentimentality. As Wyschogrod reminds us, the unfortunate destiny of the Kantian sublime has become, in the twentieth century, "the medicine that would cure the meaninglessness of objective history but could conceivably inject into both event and historical narrative the poison of fascism."[28] We know the use that Nazi ideology made of the mathematical sublime (among others, in its architecture, which galvanized those who had variously assembled into participants in a movement). If it were the case, however, that a kind of "subliminal" sublime performed a different function, then the resources of the sublime might not be so predetermined or historically corrupted. For Wyschogrod, this is precisely what Levinas's notion of the "there-is" [*il y a*] does.

We might have thought that a certain conception of the sublime was surreptitiously announced in Heidegger's thinking of the event (*Ereignis*). For example, when he writes in 1936 that "lighting and concealing, making out the essencing of truth must therefore be taken neither as an empty passing of something or as an event of 'knowledge'. The lighting and concealing are displacing-in-placing [captivating] the event itself."[29] In short, the event as displacing and captivation is redolent of a tension between the understanding and the imagination, just as the lighting and concealing brings to mind the "agitation" Kant finds in the subject confronted with the sublime, before it fixes this sublime in the intimation of reason's suprasensible vocation. That may well be the case. The architectonic imagery of Being in the *Beiträge* is widespread, naturalist, sometimes bordering on the mystical, e.g., "Being is the trembling of this divinity, the trembling as the spreading out of the temporal-play-space."[30] But the emphasis that Levinas places on the abyssal quality of Being, as the *il y a*, is to rip the core of the self out of itself in a logic of loss that parallels the loss of self we experience in facing the human being. If these two logics can be set side by side, then the Levinasian dual recasting of the Kantian sublime and of Heidegger's *Seyn* is *formally* related to the event that constitutes us as ethically interested selves. Is that enough to allow us to use the sublime as our approach to a weakly unified concept of annihilation and cataclysm? Yes, if, from this, some sense of our *geheime Verabredung* with absent persons and generations is thereby felt. It is certainly more satisfactory, today, than either the sign Kant proposes as suggestive of the historical progress made by the Idea of Reason (enthusiasm on the part of the observers of the French Revolution) or even the adaptation that Jean-François Lyotard proposes for that sign today (despair on the part of observers of contemporary political events). In the first place, Kant argued that the enthusiasm of the spectators of the French Revolution implied that, without thereby becoming partisans, they could recognize in that event the spread of freedom and the advancement of humankind. A mere sign, this enthusiasm, but hardly plausible today. By contrast, Lyotard suggests that the only sign possible today for the spread of anything like a consciousness of humans' supersensual vocation would have to be something like "a vigorous melancholy."[31]

Wyschogrod is attempting to provide us with resources—notably, grounded in Levinas's thought—with which to write a history that remains conscious of its responsibility to the dead and the murdered, *and* cognizant of the hermeneutical critique to the effect that all history "moralizes" and "fictionalizes" its object, by virtue of what Paul Ricoeur called its "intrigue" [*mythos*].[32] This entails more than just "emplotment"; it determines the structure of the "plot" beyond the simple model of adequation between events and story. I cannot address the question of whether the resources Levinas gives for historiography could ever satisfy historians. In fact, the question is ill conceived; no formal conditions of possibility contribute to defining the role of pragmatic normative standards in projects like the writing of history. What they do is provide what we could call a positive and negative regulative ideal. The positive "ideal" amounts to the continuous understanding of a responsibility that is tensed between what is to come and what we live and are entrusted with now. The negative "ideal" is that critiques of historical practices and totalizing institutions always come from one or many hitherto "invisible" others—from those witnesses or victims of the wrongs that, as Levinas insists, "God" alone sees. In that sense, Levinas provides us with what Adorno called the challenge of contemplating things historical "as they would present themselves from the standpoint of redemption." Moreover, Levinas does so within a formal structure that has everything of Buber's psychology in its immediacy (Thou-saying) and yet avoids the compelling but perplexing mysteries of Walter Benjamin's "secret rendezvous with the past.[33]

For this reason, I want to pass, now, to Wyschogrod's treatment of time in history, holding constantly in mind the notion of messianic time which we find in Levinas, but also in Benjamin, Scholem, and Adorno. I will begin this with a citation from Jean-Luc Nancy's "The Judeo-Christian." In this citation we see, in all its discomfort and *Unheimlichkeit*, the compression of the messianic into a present that can no longer be properly called religious or secular. This compression may explain why it is possible to note parallels between the thought of Heidegger and Franz Rosenzweig, Heidegger and Derrida, Derrida and Levinas.

> What is changing, in the instituting configuration of the West, is that man is no longer the mortal who stands before the immortal. He is becoming the dying one in a dying that doubles or lines the whole time of his life. The divine withdraws from its dwelling sites—whether these be the peaks of Mount Olympus or of Sinai—and from every type of temple. It becomes, in so withdrawing, the perpetual imminence of dying. Death, as the natural end of a mode of existence, is itself finite: dying becomes the theme of existence according to the always suspended imminence of *parousia*.[34]

Nancy draws the additional consequence from Nietzsche's realization of the manifold deaths of God (and even those gods that occupied sacred "dwelling sites"), that the evacuation of immortality causes mortality to expand into a gamut of modes of being and temporal stages threatened or eroded by decay. The subject is threatened by the disappearance of the master signifier, and God, become the mortal (under threat of disappearing even if he is reduced to being the last prophet, whether Dionysus or Zarathustra), slides towards Nancy's *mourant*, the dying one. It is not a matter of awareness that we die at every moment of our lives—or some other anthropological platitude. It is rather that at every moment the recognition is possible that in our finitude, our efforts are pervertible because they are overtaken by the anonymity of natural and human events, themselves neither precisely finite nor infinite, given their interconnectedness and their frequent invisibility. Levinas already recognized the parallelism between the limit that death places on my will to know and the power to halt embodied by the human face that impacts my will to consume or to master. However, Levinas was acutely aware of the continuous—and strange—threat that the anonymity noted above—an anonymity without gods but with considerable power—entailed for a life, even considered outside of the perversion of futility. What his awareness requires of the heterological historian is that she look in historic moments, as also in contemporary existence, for moments of concentration and limited transcendence, whereby mortality opens onto an ever-deferred "not yet" (not-yet-but-soon) whose call is responsibility—on whatever scale. Nancy calls this the "always suspended imminence of *parousia*." And perhaps that is also what Adorno meant by viewing history from the standpoint of redemption. The question that opens, in light of this, is how to understand this vision, which was already formally present in Heidegger in the 1930s as the "arrival of an event." How to understand it after the self-destruction of soteriologies—and the assertion of the "interminable" character of other *therapeia*? It is not clear, even with Levinas, that we are past the dilemma that Jaspers resolved by insisting that philosophical knowledge be understood as yet another form of faith without revelation. However, the critical idea remains operative for the historian even if the content of Benjamin's *geheime Verabredung* stands as caught between mysticism and skepticism. With the critical task, of course, begins the question.

Parousia comes into Wyschogrod's discussion in connection with the responsible act—for the historian as for any person—of remembering. To that end, Wyschogrod moves through Benjamin's second Thesis on History concerning the fragile but secret rendezvous with the past to an intensive discussion of theories of time. She concludes that the recapture of the past as truth event(s) remains a task whose epistemic impossibility does not touch its normativity. This normativity is intensified as history and other questioning discourses are evacuated by the accelerating time of information exchange in late capitalism. Even with the reduction of sentences to a cry, an incipiently ethical act is inaugurated, and must be pursued. Wyschogrod writes:

> The "I" uttered by the historian refers directly and cannot be transposed into the descriptive phrase "the woman who writes about history" . . . instead, she is likely to maintain silence, a silence that affirms but does not refer to her as the bearer of discourse. Yet, the unspoken indexical "I" inscribes itself in her narrative. Noting the ethical character of indexicals, Robert Nozick remarks, "reflexive [self-aware][35] indexicality is the birthmark of ethics."[36]

As a *degré zéro*, then, bearing witness in whatever person (whether in-scribed by an "I," or as addressed to "you") is minimally assured its repe-tition in time. With that, the reconstruction of the past receives the indexical birthmark of ethics as responsibility for a critical account of that past. Yet its fragility has something daimonic to it. Benjamin's air in-breathed by a predecessor, which may well be the air I too breathe, may also be the air of a score of tormentors and those who scoff at responsibil-ity. That is why this fragility and agnosticism about the past entail the further complication that, precisely in light of its over-determination, that past is "always already infiltrated by futurity."[37] Multiply determined in function of its context, Wyschogrod argues that whether we are realists or antirealists about time, the past is, as Heidegger saw, closed; it is *Gewesenheit.*

"Like the 'no longer' of the painter [who has stopped painting accord-ing to the foregoing description], the past of their "amours" [Swann and Odette in Proust] is never finished . . . but constantly present as always already before them"[38]—constantly present, but as a complex of events, and closed. If the present is magnetized by the future, then the past, while closed and perfect, remains with us, whether as primary remembrance or as haunting—and in this sense, the past can be simultaneously finished and futural, historical, daimonic, or messianic. That is why the existential-ist readers of messianic thought—from Benjamin to Rosenzweig to Levi-nas—understood that the past has its absoluteness but cannot be absolved in itself or in regard to our choices. The past is "always already ahead of" us; thus we can and cannot change it. When we understand the tripartite temporality of the present, we understand, too, that action and belief are simultaneously punctiform and tentacular events. This is why when Jean-Luc Nancy studies the rather emaciated Epistle of James, he argues that it was conceived as a corrective to Paul's insistent intellectualization of mes-sianic time and faith. Nancy displaces Paul's history of the founding event of the Messiah's passage through history onto what Nancy calls "not a thinness [of detail or systematicity], but . . . a retreat of theology, or a theology itself in retreat, that is, a withdrawal of any representation of contents in favor of an active information by faith—of that alone which activates the contents."[39] What activates these contents is a movement of affectivity, perhaps an intensification thereof, in any case, one that is threatened by forgetfulness or by resistance to cognitive positing, like the face-to-face encounter described by Levinas. This revision of Paul's messi-anic time by James recalls a Jewish dynamization of Paul as translated by Luther: we have to keep in mind that Benjamin, thinking through his

"Theses on history," was reading Luther's translation of the Pauline letters. In so doing, Benjamin, like James, provides a continuous critical corrective to the danger of hypostatizing messianic time.

In her extensive discussions of theories of time—phenomenological time, time in analytic philosophy, time in post-Hegelian thought—the challenge Wyschogrod takes up remains close to that of Benjamin. It is the call to act—*not* the question "to what end?"—that counts, knowing that the present is complex because it disappears "into a past that can never be re-entered"[40] and it functions with the *Nachträglichkeit* that reveals past meaning and senses inevitabilities in the future. Thus, claims such as "the French Revolution preceded the Russian Revolution"[41] are invariably true, but truncated to the point of naïveté. Even if claims like "John Major is the Prime Minister of Great Britain" are true only at a given moment, they are pregnant with past and future and the future will reconstruct them even as it surpasses them quantitatively in Benjamin's buildup of new disasters.

A meager surpassing, indeed. On the basis of this quantitative buildup, which is often the pileup of ruin upon ruin that is touted for progress— "the narrative historian can reply that . . . time's passing supports the position that she holds from the start: historical narratives are *ficciones*, neither point-for-point mirroring of events nor sheer fabrication . . . epistemic fluidity [proves] intrinsic to statements about matters of fact."[42] But this epistemic fluidity concerns acting before it is ever a matter of epistemology. If we expunge our naïveté about the present as univocal, then the futural haunting of the past and the hermeneutic *Nachträglichkeit* proper to the future teach us that the time of the historian must be understood as a point containing vectors *and* as a kind of persistent miasma, like the social imaginary that Castoriadis describes. Does this solve the question of the meaning of time for the historian? A simple solution was never Wyschogrod's project. Her project more resembles James's conception of faith: it provides a decisive correction to tendencies to lose oneself in formalist or ontological debates about how and why things happened. Her questions are as follows: How do we compose these *ficciones* such that they allow the dead to bear witness? How do we bring events that cut across our history, changing everything about the future (until the future then changes them), under a concept that neither reduces them nor forces them into a telic dialectic? How do we hold fast to a complex thinking of history, given the volatilization of time in an age where the reign of the image, of montage, of virtual reality, and the bytefication of knowledge as "information" is irreversible? How, finally, to strike a balance between constructivism, historical closure, and the under-standing that the future is the new past? Extended to us, then, is the question that preoccupied Hannah Arendt: how does the historian, as everyday spectator and intellectual, remain an actor; and is there a way beyond personal example to incite us to responsible action in the name of the *geheime Verabredung* and despite the pileup of memories whose lesson is that the intellectual alters precious little?

If it is a refreshing overview of the critical philosopher's history, Wyschogrod's work is above all a struggle with the meaning of "messianic time" in the present, as the passage we cannot recover and as the now of our awareness of it. Messianic time is the recognition that our present is overfilled with the past and magnetized by the future; is it still the convic-tion of the possibility of action *in the retreat of every theology, secular or otherwise*? If so, then it seems that Wyschogrod has also taken up where Levinas left off. But we have to remember Horkheimer's remark that "to salvage unconditioned meaning without God [without a third party or some radical externality that perceives] is an idle task."[43] It is always possi-ble to read such a claim as a condemnation of any new attempt at mes-sianism or as a warning against the resurgence of fanaticism. Certainly, Levinas's attempt to reinstitute a temporality beyond unitary succession or even the coup by the historical Actor (who no longer carries the ruse of reason with him), either failed, or contracted into the mythic narrative of the time of generations. In 1961, his *Totality and Infinity* proposed, with an ostensible pragmaticism, that change was the exclusive prerogative of the arrival of a new generation: the son can forgive the sons of fathers who offended or destroyed his own father. Is it the son's role to pardon the offending fathers as well? And how deep is the responsibility implicit in Benjamin's *geheime Verabredung*? There are, it seems, two "messianic" answers to this question. The more hyperbolic of the two depends on forgetfulness vis-à-vis the past, while the second answer is limited to the present in its punctual particularity. I am not certain which one Wyscho-grod would ultimately sanction. Yet, there are clearly times where Levinas suggests that, in the "vigilance of the messianic consciousness," a trans-temporal forgiveness is necessary *and* possible. At least, in spirit.

> The dream of a happy eternity, which subsists in man along with his happiness, is not a simple aberration. Truth requires both an in-finite time and a time it will be able to seal, a completed time, the completion of time is not death, but messianic time . . . secured against the revenge of evil whose return the infinite time does not prohibit. Is this eternity a new structure of time, or an extreme vigi-lance of the messianic consciousness?[44]

If Levinas concludes that that question "exceeds the bounds of his book [*Totality and Infinity*]"[45] because with the responsibility born in the time of the family (wherein the father enacts a concrete election of the son), ethics stands outside objective history and *may* permit its critique, but *may also* perpetuate the risk of an inclosing narcissism, then we cannot simply follow him and say that the question exceeds the bounds of our condition. Hence, the challenge to historians comes from the tenuous responsibility arising from the face to face encounter. Tenuous and eccentric, we have seen that it opens to a temporality called *messianic*, and thus to the aporias of the ethical structuralism unfolded by thinkers like Carlo Ginzburg. The question did not exceed the bounds of Wyschogrod's *An Ethics of Remembering*, but the gesture to which she invites us exceeds the bounds of the book's two covers.

Saints and the Heterological Historian

PETER OCHS

Introduction

In *An Ethics of Remembering*,[1] Edith Wyschogrod draws from out of the sensibilities of postmodernism a means for the historian to attend, after all, to the voice of the suffering other in history. Her remarkable argument may leave one question unanswered: how, in the end, do we learn from what she calls "the heterological historian" how to respond to the needs of this otherwise forgotten voice? I believe this apparent omission may be more adequately identified as a sign of modesty, of two sorts. I will suggest that, if we press the logic of her argument in ways she does not, then either Wyschogrod or God (however named) appears ultimately responsible for training her book's readers in the practice of heterological history.

The first lesson I will draw from Wyschogrod's book is that whatever the heterological historian has to teach us about the suffering other will come as a result of the changes of behavior that (according to our reading) the voice of this other elicits in the heterological historian herself. The second lesson is that, if the heterological historian has to learn how to hear and be transformed by this voice, then she would have to learn this from Wyschogrod herself, or from anyone who authors a book with the thesis of *An Ethics of Remembering*. The implication of both these lessons is that Wyschogrod (or a comparable author) would teach by way of the changes in her behavior that are elicited by the voice of the suffering other. The third lesson is that, if we ask how Wyschogrod may have learned how to hear and be transformed by this other, then we will find ourselves in a quandary. If the suffering other (or her voice) were herself the teacher, then either all historians would already be heterological historians, or the suffering other would be his/her own redeemer. If Wyschogrod needed no teacher, then she, and perhaps a few other comparable authors, would alone be our teachers. This remains a logical possibility, but if so, it is odd that *An Ethics of Remembering* did not include a chapter on sages. If Wyschogrod had claimed that Levinas or some other sage were her teacher, then turning to Levinas's work would lead us in either of two directions. We might identify R. Chouchani as his teacher and conclude that to learn to be a heterological historian is to take one's place in a chain of teacher-sages that extends indefinitely far into the past and, potentially, into the future. Or, we might distinguish between the Other and any other and conclude that the Other refers not to any sufferer whose voice calls us, but to that unique other, sufferer or not, whose voice calls us with unparalleled force to hear the voices who call us and instructs us on how to hear.

My thesis is that the logic of *An Ethics of Remembering* recommends the last two options and recommends our maintaining both of them, with their ambiguity and double-codedness. To learn to be a heterological historian is to enter and participate in a long chain of teacher-sages, and it is to encounter an Other perhaps known to them as well. The two ways of learning are distinct, but with overlapping features. According to Wyschogrod's equally remarkable *Saints and Postmodernism,* this dual or double-coded learning has a parallel in what she calls "learning from saints."[2] I suggest, in fact, that learning to be a heterological historian makes most sense if it is a species of learning to be saintly.

According to *Saints and Postmodernism,* this is the kind of learning recommended by the Matthean injunction to "leave self behind and follow me." To learn from saints is to attend to their behaviors the way they tend to the cries of suffering others: leaving their own self-concerns behind and following those cries, attending to whatever the others need by attending to them in such a way that their habitual ways of responding are thereby reshaped.[3] This may be one way to understand what Levinas means by "being hostage to the other." It is all about service, not just as a matter of will, but also as a matter of what is brought forward by the will: the stuff of knowing, responding, doing, seeing, interpreting that we bring to the actions we intend. It is not just to *do* for others but to be re-done for the sake of others. Lest we go down some of the hyperbolic paths of some Levinas readers, this last phrase cannot mean to be "thoroughly re-done"; it is, instead, a dramatic way of saying that we must learn from others what we need to bring to them. In these terms, to learn from saints is to attend so attentively to the way that they attend to the world that we simply fall out of the habit of attending, self-reflectively, to ourselves. Put non-hyperbolically, this does not necessarily mean shedding all material belongings and donning saffron robes and a beggar's bowl, nor abandoning literal self-awareness to such an extent that we forget to wash or dress or parse our sentences. But it may mean imitating a hint of that literal behavior in the way that we give up self-worry and self-repetition as the setting for our moving out toward others.

But from where do saints learn this behavior? And how can they teach it? Asking the same question of saints that I asked of the heterological historian introduces the source of my overall thesis about the heterological historian: the observation that, according to the logic of these two books of Wyschogrod's, the heterological historian must ultimately be taught by saints, and the chain of teacher-sages that instructs the heterological historian must include saints. While the linkage may appear odd at first, I believe it discloses features of Wyschogrod's work that may otherwise remain veiled. She displays the first feature clearly: learning from saints means learning from hagiographic histories of saints, so that what we know of saints depends, after all, on the work of historians. The second feature—that only a certain kind of historian can compose a hagiography, in the sense of a narrative that not only offers historiographic discourse about saints, but also helps the interested reader learn saintliness—is not explicit. According to our analysis of learning to be a heterological historian, this must be a historian who narrates saintly lives the way Wyschogrod narrates the heterological historian's work. This is a historian who reads a saintly life the way the heterological historian hears the voice of the suffering other: attending to the alterity of that life—being held hostage to it, one might say—and being transformed by it. The third feature is puzzling, or at least double-coded: that the hagiographer must therefore be someone who is somewhere in the process of learning saintliness. The feature is double-coded, since writing history is saying something the reader understands, while learning saintliness is learning not to say but to attend. The last feature both completes and continues the puzzle: that the hagiographer may, at the very least, be a cousin to the heterological historian. Like the heterological historian, the hagiographer writes about a life whose character interrupts the discourse of writing and transforms the writer—and, potentially, the reader. But unlike the heterological historian, the hagiographer does not necessarily attend to a voice of suffering per se, but to the actions of one who attends to suffering. This difference may indicate that we are dealing here with two related but distinct kinds of writer, or it may indicate that the two writers are in fact interdependent. If we take Wyschogrod's "saint" to be the one whose life teaches us what it means to hear the other's voice, then the saint may be (or at least illustrate) the teacher of the heterological historian. This is one whose life not only heals others who suffer, but also attracts others who seek instruction, compelling them to observe, perhaps to write what they observe, perhaps to leave self behind and follow or imitate. Among these are writers who seek through their writing to discover what it means to imitate saints and, thereby, to hear the voice of the suffering other. The hagiographer may be one of the heterological historian's teachers: the one who introduces her to those who hear the sufferer's voice and, thereby, opens her to a new model of history writing. This is not to write about saints but to write history as a way of attending to others the way saints do; it is to write history in a saintly manner. Perhaps the heterological historian is, or is in the process of learning to be, a saintly historian.

My thesis comes to its conclusion by applying to this latter sentence the double-coded lesson I drew earlier from *An Ethics of Remembering*: learning to be a heterological historian is both/either to participate in a long chain of teacher-sages and/or to encounter an Other perhaps known to them as well. *Per hypothesis*, say we reportray Wyschogrod's saints as those whose encounter with an Other enables or accompanies their attending to the cries of suffering others. If so, we might then reportray the heterological historian as a historian for whom the lives of saints compel attention to the voices of both the other in history and the Other in history writing. In this case, one earlier example or perhaps prototype of heterological history is the work of the Deuteronomic historian, or the Torah as a whole, or the Tanakh, or also the Gospels and New Testament and the Qur'an—if these are read not as hagiographies (*about* saintly lives), but as saintly histories or writings through which the voice of the suffering other is heard or through which the reader is compelled to listen to it. For Wyschogrod, these scriptural histories would not, of course, be singular examples of heterological history—for her historian may emerge within any religious tradition or nonreligious tradition. But introducing these scriptural examples into discussion displays yet another form of Wyschogrod's service: that it enables secular postmodernists to hear voices of the scriptural other as well as enabling religious thinkers, including scripturally grounded ones, to hear voices of the postmodern other.

Learning Saintliness in More Detail

The introduction has introduced my entire thesis about saints and heterological historians. All that is left is to fill in some details, beginning here with details about learning saintliness and then turning to consider how these details may help open up more details about learning to be a hetero-logical historian. While all of *Saints and Postmodernism* is a lesson about learning saintliness, three elemental claims of Wyschogrod suffice to guide our discussion:

> *Saints are singular*s.
>
> As narrated in hagiographic literature, *their lives are wholly devoted to caring for the Other.*
>
> As narrated in that literature, *saints' lives are lived in* imitatio dei *or in imitation of the life of an Other who is wholly devoted to its other and of which we, who read this literature, have evidence only by way of the saintly lives it narrates.*

Wyschogrod's study of saints may be read as a way to introduce the cate-gory of singularity into postmodern theory. It is thereby her means of restoring human agency and normativity within the bounds of postmod-ern criticism. Wyschogrod makes clear at the outset that the rules that validate saints' lives are immanent to them; "legitimated by neither the theological nor the prudential structures of their epoch,"[4] these "validat-ing rules" and the hagiography that promotes them need not raise post-modern anxieties about master narratives or foundationalist discourses, nor late-modern anxieties about heteronomy, or about enslaving the self to the gaze of the other. These rules are, moreover, immanent to the saints' bodily lives: "Thrown into saintly experience are not only the en-semble of perceptual, tactile and kinesthetic structures that constitute ev-eryday bodily experience but the viscera and bones, in short the saint's entire body."[5] We need not fear, therefore, that saintliness enslaves the body to the ideals and concepts of the self. Nor need we fear spiritualiza-tion, since the actions of the saints' bodies are wholly responsive to the lives of others in the singularity of their historical, sociopolitical settings. Disclosed through hagiographic literature, the lives of saints are texts in which corporeal behavior is integrated into the politics and sociality of particular times and places.

Reading saints' lives as types of singularity, Wyschogrod takes pains to disassociate her account of saintly lives from two other models of altruism. The first is Nicolas Rescher's commonsense understanding of altruism, which she classifies as a "theory of moral sentiments." She argues that, like Heidegger's *Mitsein*, Rescher's "sentiment of sympathy" presupposes a sense of "the Other's prior destitution."[6] Since destitution can be mea-sured only against one's prior sense of the fullness of being, she concludes that both Rescher's and Heidegger's accounts of sympathy retain late modernist presumptions about the unquestionable givenness of being. For them, the Other is not wholly other, but conditioned by my sympathy. The second model is Julia Kristeva's ecstatic phenomenology of the abject: a liminal being who "is radically excluded and draws me towards the place where meaning collapses."[7] Wyschogrod observes that, in these terms, "the saint can be viewed as an abject loathsome to herself/himself but taken up into the compensatory love of God." But "this interpretation would reduce the role of alterity, the appeal of the other's destitution in saintly life, to an endless quest for overcoming abjection."[8] For Wyschogrod, Kristeva and Rescher form a contrast pair and, in that sense, share in the same late-modern logic. Where Rescher subjects the Other too much to the moral and political economy of my desire, Kristeva subjects the Other too much to the apolitical aesthetic of my self-loathing. The result is "Kristeva's Docetism, her failure to treat the Other as a creature of flesh and blood" and, with it, a surprisingly Marcionite totalism that pits Christian, "aesthetic quietism" against Jewish legalism and materialism.[9]

The implication is that saintliness cannot be represented as a common-sense virtue and, in that sense, cannot be represented as a hypostatized object of moral desire *or* as the abject negation of that desire. The logical lesson is that singularity cannot be identified with either generality or individuality (as the logical contradictory of generality). In the wonderful term Wyschogrod adopts from Merleau-Ponty, singulars display "carnal generality"[10] "in the sense of a *general thing* midway between the spatio-temporal individual and the idea, a sort of incarnate principle that brings a style of being wherever there is a fragment of being. The flesh is in this sense an 'element of being.' "[11] So defined, "carnal generality" appears to correspond to what Charles Peirce called "vagueness" or "indefiniteness" or "real possibility," and "singularity" to what he called "Thirdness," the character of things in the world (and living symbols and laws and beings potentially not in the world).[12] As "the subject of hagiographic narrative," the saint may be defined as

> one whose adult life in its entirety is devoted to the alleviation of sorrow (the psychological suffering) and pain (the physical suffering) that afflicts other persons without distinction of rank or group or, alternatively, that afflicts sentient beings, whatever the cost to the saint in pain or sorrow. On this view, theistic belief may but need not be a component of the saint's belief system.[13]

In these terms, the saint desires something that has moral consequences, but, unlike commonsense morality, the desire is not *for* the sake of morality per se, nor is the object finite. In this sense, the desire displays abjection, but not for the sake of abjection; enacting this desire may have ecstatic consequences, but it is not enacted for the sake of such ecstasis. The desire is simply and wholly for the Other and the other.

How then does one learn to be saintly? For Wyschogrod, "neither saintly practice nor saintly power is, for the most part, transmitted in standard normative discourse," but it can be transmitted through "non-verbal pedagogy."[14] This not to say that what she calls "saintly pedagogy" excludes speech and language, but that its object cannot be reduced to what is represented in discourse. It is pedagogy in action and affect, and, by way of narrative or observation, this is pedagogy that raises up in the student a desire to live and care for the Other. Although she does not offer much detail on the matter, I assume she understands this to be learning by apprenticeship: imitating another's actions, bit by bit, so that habits of action arise that *other* observers might judge to be saintly. The judgment comes only after the fact; like the Gospel of Matthew says of a prophet's actions, saintly actions are "known only by their fruit." On this, Wyschogrod is quite clear. She argues, *pace* Kristeva, Guattari and Deleuze, that, yes, saintliness is something that can spoken of and learned, but *pace* Rescher, something that cannot be identified prior to any action. There is a saintly *character*—a tendency to act in certain ways—but we cannot know before the fact what actions will follow from it. Christian accounts of *imitatio Christi* offer the clearest illustration: "A background belief of virtually all Christian hagiography is that saints live their lives in the light of Christ's life. *Imitatio Christi* is the apothegm that illuminates saintly contemplation and the command that guides saintly conduct."[15] The challenge is that, since "human nature . . . cannot conform itself to divine perfection," Christ's conduct cannot be clearly represented. And the same, according to Wyschogrod, applies to Buddhist accounts and all other accounts of saintliness; both saintly lives and efforts to imitate them are "doubly coded."[16]

A ubiquitous feature of her theory, "double-coding" refers in this case to the *coincidentia oppositorum* of the saint's self-emptying—a renunciation of power—and the saint's enacting this renunciation in a field of material relations, somatic and sociopolitical. This is another way of identifying the carnal generality of saintliness (at once nonindividual *and* nongeneral) and its normative yet nonconceptual and imitable yet nonrepresentable character. Most of the hagiographic literatures, we may note, are theistic, which means that for them the *coincidentia oppositorum* is captured within the name and reality of God. Wyschogrod is one of very few writers who identify this theistic model without reduction while, at the same time, identifying nontheistic parallels. We may add that the latter achieve their greater generality at the cost of more elaborate explanation. For the theistic literatures, God names the person whom saints may imitate but not represent, whose character is disclosed only through his/her actions and effects. For the nontheistic literatures, saintly action is known only through the earthly contradictions of its double-coded effects: the action that is uniquely active and abject, imitable yet nonpresent.

Wyschogrod appears, then, to offer a doubly coded response to our question about how to learn saintliness, and the double-coding works on several levels. To learn from saints is to be apprenticed to their hagiography; then again, this apprenticeship cannot be completed, since what the teacher does can both be imitated and not imitated. Put in theistic terms, to learn from the saint one must "leave self behind and follow God." To learn from God is both possible—since God's actions and words are offered for us to imitate—and not possible, both because we cannot complete an infinite task and because we cannot be sure we have got even any part of it right (each part of the infinite is an image of the infinite). Then again, the lesson to be learned is about wholly desiring the well-being of the other. In one sense this can be learned, since to seek to learn from God is itself to desire the good of this Other; in another sense, it cannot, since we will not know if indeed we have learned it. But this ambiguity should not discourage us. To admire saints is not to admire godliness or infinity per se (for that is the character of God, not saints) but the poignant beauty of a human being striving after and touched by the infinitely receding Other. However difficult to realize, this beauty belongs to our own kind. To desire any part of saintliness is to desire a life of ambiguity. But what seeds that desire in any one of us? If we are drawn by it, what gives us courage to persist despite the pain of losing what we may lose in pursuit of it and despite the discomforts of ambiguity?

Since Wyschogrod offers a relational and dynamic account, rather than a somatic one, I assume she would place the "what seeds" and "what gives" in some relation to Other/other rather than in something of "my" habits of action or emotive dispositions. An example is what she reports, affirmatively, about Levinas's account of proximity.

It is not the said, the language of ontology, that is the ultimate source of signification, but the Saying that signifies prior to language and being, to essence and nomination . . . [T]he question persists: "How does one arrive at Saying?" Levinas's first response is "through proximity": by which he means something "quite distinct from every other relationship . . . [one] conceived as a responsibility for the other; it might be called humanity, or subjectivity, or self." These expressions cannot be taken in their ordinary signification. Far from the term humanity signifying a generalized sympathy, or subjectivity and self-signifying ego or will, Levinas intends these terms to point to a divestiture of the assertive properties generally attributed to them . . . [T]he subject of proximity approaches the Other by "deposing or de-situating the self ."[17]

In these terms, I assume Wyschogrod would identify the questions "what seeds?" and "what gives?" with the question "how does one arrive at Saying?" I expect her answer to be Levinas's answer: proximity. In *An Ethics of Remembering*, she identifies proximity with "a shift in orientation, a turning away from apprehension of the world and toward the reception of the other."[18] If I were to reiterate my question—"But what seeds, encourages, supports this shift?"—I assume she would reiterate her response: "whatever turns the saint toward the Other." I hear this response as both/ either theistic (proximity to God seeds and maintains what only God can seed and maintain) and/or formalist and ascetic (self-divestiture cannot include any positive account of self-activity, whether somatic, emotive, or psychological). Or perhaps the response simply restricts itself to matters of sociality, bracketing any issues of self-activity. In any case, I cannot overcome some astonishment at such responses. I would want to hear about more intermediate matters, whether of angels, prayer, halacha, or habits of the heart. If proximity marks relations among singulars, and if singulars display "carnal generality," then I would want to hear more about the carnal, as well as the general and nongeneral.

Learning Heterology

According to my thesis, the historian learns heterology by turning to the lives of saints in history, that is, by taking an interest in, reading, and then writing hagiographies. Here, we understand hagiographies to be historical narratives that are at once discursive and performative: narrating the lives of saints in a way that stimulates the reader to imitate such lives. This means narrating saints' lives *as* events of interruption that also elicit interruption: interruptions, that is, in the everyday life of self, society, and polity, and for the sake of caring for the suffering other, which caring, we discover, is at once and also for the sake of the Other. Hagiography is heterological history once removed; the latter emerges to the degree that historiography itself embodies saintliness.

In this section, I suggest how this thesis arises out of a particular reading of Wyschogrod's work. For each stage, I read one aspect of her work and then comment on its contribution to my thesis.

1. A Philosopher for the Other

Over the years, I have on several occasions asked Wyschogrod to write an essay responding to some collection of lectures or papers I wanted to put together—one of those "Final Essays by a Great Thinker" that give a collection both a wider reputation and a deeper wisdom. On most occasions she said yes, despite her seriously over-packed schedule. And each time she said yes, she read and responded to the individual essays with a care and hearing that I would now recognize under the sign of *heterologist*. To take the earliest example: in 1993, she introduced and concluded a collection of five essays meant to illustrate "Trends in Postmodern Jewish Philosophy."[19] Receiving us in our own, philosophic-and-Jewish terms, she also heard those terms as voicing various historically situated discomforts, particularly our discomfort with the modernist canons of reasoning that still appeared to dominant our fields. Sympathetic to our concerns, she identified these canons as "concealed narratives that lay claim to totalizing power, to being all-encompassing frameworks into which the contingencies of aberrant experience and social and linguistic context are stretched to fit and must be interpreted as such."[20] She then identified three ways in which our postmodern Jewish thought challenged these canons: (1) transforming "ethics from an emphasis upon theory to a concern with alterity, or the other human being"; (2) "a shift from the effort to depict the world to dissolution of the boundary between world and text"; (3) "a turning away from analyzing the meaning of being to tracing the signs of radical negation, the breaks, rifts, or fissures in language and being."[21] While consistent with postmodern theory, she argued that these challenges turned "in no small measure both to recent Jewish experience and to traditional Jewish modes of interpretation."[22] She then drew our concerns and proposals to their implicit edge: that for us, the text precedes and gives birth to the world; that this notion is foreign to classical Western and modern philosophy; but that this notion already has a home in classical rabbinic Judaism and should come to have a home in postmodern philosophy as well, Western as well as Jewish. In this way, she both affirmed and also challenged the theme *we* thought gathered a collection together. She situated our efforts in broader historical contexts, praised us for having shifted our gaze to issues of malaise or suffering, but then also very gently pushed us to shift even more to the anguish of even more occluded voices within our own gathering as well as in the traditions we sought to repair.[23]

The manner in which Wyschogrod offered these essays introduced me to her own double-coded writing offered not only as discourse (for example, on the theme of "the other"), but also as part of a broader performance of attending to the other's voice. In the terms of this essay, I was introduced to Wyschogrod as heterological philosopher. But that also means philosopher as heterological historian, since the heterological philosopher hears philosophic speech as embodied in others' voices, and those voices as embodied in historically situated persons who comment on the writings of other historically situated persons. This is what I observed in the contents of each of Wyschogrod's contributions to those collections.[24]

2. A Heterologist for the Modern Other

Perhaps the most striking feature of Wyschogrod's responses is that her postmodernism appears consistently as a consequence, rather than as an a priori condition, of her attentiveness to the Other's voice. She therefore refuses to hypostatize the intellectual project of modernity as the logical contradictory to her own postmodernism, as if the postmodern were not also part of the modern project. The modern project means a turn from tradition-based narratives to the self-consciously individual authorship of some thinker situated somewhere in historical space and time. The modernism that oppresses us reflects only a subproject of modernity: an effort, among other things, to accept the individual standpoint of the author but remove its *rational* achievements from historical space-time and treat them as if they spoke, on behalf of "reason," for all time and thus "universally." But this oppressive effort is not to be hypostatized as some idea set that is to be corrected by another "postmodern" idea set. Instead, Wyschogrod portrays it as a refusal or incapacity to hear the voice of the other, and the conceptual apparatus of her postmodern criticism emerges only as a tracing of what happens to the conceptual framework of modernism as, step by step, it is brought to hear this voice. She therefore refuses to accept the various forms of postmodern theory as conceptual resting places; they mark only the various encampments of the modern project in its gradual exodus from modernism. This refusal, and the persistent attention to the other that it displays, is also a conspicuous characteristic of the heterological historian in *An Ethics of Remembering*.

3. Sharing in the Historiographic Subproject of the Modern Project

As Wyschogrod offers it, postmodernism does not designate any theoretical position or "having" per se, but rather a certain movement toward the Other. Marked by its particular point of origin in the modern project, this postmodernism is not a species of formalism, but traces a particular movement from the conceptual apparatus and practices of the modern project toward the Other. She emerges within this project not only as a heterological philosopher, but also as one who urges the historian to become the heterological historian. Heterological history also belongs to the modern project of historiography and shares its conceptual apparatus and critical concerns—including reasonable worries about the moral, political, scientific, social, and/or rational failings of some identifiable aspects of a given author's inheritance. But the heterological historian is distinguished, among other modern historians, by her concerns about the practice of history, observing that, when it attends exclusively to this or that voice of the suffering other, critical inquiry can itself occlude or repress other voices. The heterological historian therefore emerges as the identity of the modern historian who has turned toward the other in history.

This turning is not without its own challenges, however, since the heterological historian inherits not only the conceptual tools of modern historiography, but also its inherent tensions. Foremost among these is a set of conflicting tendencies: on the one hand, to uncover complexity, detail, and ambiguity; on the other hand, to achieve cognitive clarity and coherence. In the modernist camp, the heterological historian observes a tendency to resolve the conflict in favor of coherence, for example by replacing thick narratives of the past with a few bite-sized lessons or uncomplicated principles, or by occluding the voices of a multiplicity of others in service to the voice of some particular one. At the same time, she observes two countertendencies in the postmodernist camp. One is to resolve the conflict in favor of ambiguity, as illustrated by Roland Barthes's proclamation of the death of the referent, or by what she considers to be Hayden White's overly binary contrast between objective history and narrative.[25] Another, more extreme choice is the one that may call most directly for *An Ethics of Remembering*: to abandon the modern historiographic project altogether, since it will inevitably reduce the complexity of history beyond recognition and thereby falsify the past.[26]

The achievement of the heterological historian is to neither deny nor submit to the conflicting tendencies she inherits, but to receive into her work a third element that transforms the conflict into something else, a single but double-coded practice.

4. At the Ground of a Double-coded History
Is the Face of Another

While Wyschogrod writes at times of the heterological historian's "trans-forming" modern inquiry, I believe a more passively active verb fits her argument better. When modern inquiry is turned to face the Other, then its inner conflicts are *transformed* into the double-coded character of het-erological inquiry. The "agent" of transformation is no single subjectivity, but rather this relationship between the heterological historian and the Other, a relation of what Levinas calls "proximity."[27]

> What is it that must precede the conveying of history? Must there not be the declaration of a double-passion, an eros for the past, and an ardor for the others in whose name there is a felt urgency to speak? To convey that which was in a light of this passion is to be-come an historian. Because the past is irrecoverable . . . she cannot hope that her passion will be reciprocated. To be a historian then is to accept the destiny of the spurned lover . . . The historian's re-sponsibility is mandated by another who is absent, cannot speak for herself.[28]

Like the double-codedness of saintliness, the double-codedness of hetero-logical history turns on the simultaneity of positive activity and self-emp-tying, in this case, writing history (rather than abandoning the written word in the face of the other) while also receiving and displaying what undoes writing (rather than writing the other out of history). But this double code is also another name for the proximity of writer to Other, a proximity that would not be imaginable if it did not occur. We do not yet see, however, what prompts Wyschogrod to call the historian to turn in such a way that she might fall into this proximity.

5. Shoah, or Holocaust, as the Context of Turning—But Only
Saints and Heterologists as Teachers

According to this fifth stage of reading, Wyschogrod suffers the event of the Shoah (Holocaust) as the defining context of her turning. If so, then it is doubly difficult to draw inferences from this suffering. If the Shoah is suffered as utterly effacing the voice and body of the Other, then how is the heterologcal historian brought thereby into such proximity to the Other that her share in modern inquiry is utterly transformed? Is this not a faceless Other, a facing into naught? Pondering her words, I am led in this section to a series of inferences that she may not intend. In the follow-ing, I list one inference at a time, citing relevant words of Wyschogrod's and suggesting how I have read or misread these words to arrive at the inference.

(a) *Shoah is the context of learning heterology.* The Shoah has been a defining and dividing theme in all of Wyschogrod's writings, most focally *Spirit in Ashes*,[29] and it is the primary point of reference in *An Ethics of Remembering*. If we are introduced to the heterological historian "reading Kant," she is reading Kant against the challenge of "mass annihilation": "the cataclysm is the non-place from which the heterological historian writes,"[30] and this is the epoch of cataclysm.

(b) *But we cannot speak of "learning heterology" from what one faces in the naught of Shoah; learning means desiring and acquiring a new habit of action, and there is no desire or model or representation of action to be received from this naught.* I want to read her literally and infer that "the non-place from which the heterological historian writes" is a context of writing, not a source of direct instruction. If learning heterology is double-coded, then it is not only abjection, but also imitation. But there is nothing to imitate in the non-events of this non-place.

> In *Writing of the Disaster*, Maurice Blanchot tries to think negation as the destruction of the traditional metaphysical interpretations of being, time, and history . . . at the same time he envisages the disaster as the actuality of the twentieth-century's cataclysmic events which for him is concentrated in the Holocaust. Defining disaster, Blanchot writes, "I call disaster that which does not have the ultimate for its limit: it bears the ultimate away in the disaster." Because the disaster is a sweeping away of all limit, there is neither self nor event to describe . . . properly speaking there is no experience of the disaster, not only because the I that undergoes experience has been carried away but because of the disaster's mode of self-temporalization. The disaster recurs in perpetuity not as something positive but as a non-event . . . the time of the disaster is a time that always already was and a time that will be in the mode of not being it.[31]

If the Other is a singularity, characterized by carnal generality, shall we infer that cataclysm refers to the defacement of Other, the utter devastation that divests her of any voice?[32] If so, shall we infer that nothing can be learned about this Other from the cataclysm?

(c) *We may, however, speak of "unlearning," since the de-facement one addresses in the Shoah should indeed rupture the modern inquirer's confidence in her own activity.* "Have not events when read through the cataclysm, the inversion of the Hegelian absolute, lost their meaning as history in that they no longer belong to the order of temporalization inhabited by the historical subject?"[33] Turning to the non-event of the Shoah disembarrasses the modern inquirer from confidence in her capacity to behold, let alone come to the aid of the Other. At the same time, this unlearning engages the subject in her own singularity, even if for the sake of self-loss: "If the heterological historian's promise to tell the truth is to be meaningful, she must invent ways to disrupt specularity, not by ignoring or evading its cultural omnipresence but by creating a specific form of negation that is intrinsically related to it."[34] In this citation, we see the heterological historian already having entered her practice and seeking ways to bring others to it by way of disruption.

> The heterological historian realizes that the historical artifact that she has created is inherently incomplete: there is always some condition that threatens her narrative, calls it into question. What differentiates her deconstructive account from that of the objective historian who subjects herself only to the principle of corrigibility is the heterologist's recognition that her narrative requires the supplement of the cataclysm.[35]

"The [disruptive] supplement of the cataclysm" introduces the modern historian to what will become practice of the heterological historian. It is a disruption, per se, in the historian's conceptual autonomy, namely her presuming the universality of the historian's clear and distinct judgments. Thus, of the modern whose power to judge comes "under the sign of Kant," Wyschogrod writes that a "discursive space for alterity" will not open up as some mere "diffraction within universality."[36] No discursive space can receive the cataclysm; the disruption is only an unlearning.

(d) *But are there two identities of the Other, one that accompanies unlearning, one learning?* At the same time, Wyschogrod appears to move directly from cataclysm to "the intrusion of alterity that obligates me"[37] to my being "at the disposal of the other."[38] This is the move that gives me pause, for it may suggest that the unlearning is itself a learning-to-be-obliged to the other, as if the alterity of cataclysm—the defacement of the Other—were ipso facto the alterity of an Other. Can we move so directly between the apparent generality of cataclysm as a type to the singularity of some Other? For that matter, could we, beforehand, have moved so directly from the singularity of Shoah-as-Wyschogrod-receives-it to the generality of cataclysm as type?

Perhaps Wyschogrod does not offer this as some mere "move in general," but as the modern historian's singular movement from conceptual universality to the postmodern unlearning that marks cataclysm, and then to the heterologist's recognition of the singularity of the Other. If so, my only question would be about the latter step. Is the Other's negativity isomorphic with the negativity of cataclysm? Too much isomorphism here would threaten the singularity of each. But perhaps Wyschogrod has only traced a single step in the modern historian's conversion. Here, the cataclysm has introduced alterity into the historian's inquiry, and she identifies all interruption with the negativity of Other. We cannot yet speak of proximity. But, if and when proximity follows, then another step is possible: to see, within the "embrace" of this Other, the Other's singular negativity. This negativity is double-coded so that, embracing it, the historian finds herself not only self-dispossessed in the infinity of the Other, but also re-enlisted in her own carnal singularity as this-one-in-proximity-to-this-Other. Only when she is re-enlisted in this way would the historian inquire again after the Other in history, without despair (self-abjection) or optimism (trusting in her discourse). And only then would we call her a heterological historian.

(e) *Proximity alone conditions the possibility of learning.* If the heterological historian's turning to the suffering Other is a source only of unlearning, shall we say that her learning begins when she encounters a second identity of the Other-in-proximity? If so, then learning exceeds what the heterological historian can will, since proximity comes only as it will—by grace, as theologians say. Proximity engages the heterological historian in the carnal generality of a singularity. To speak of the "conditions" of such a singularity would be to suppose, errantly, that its generality can be abstracted from out of its carnality. There is generality, and the event of proximity therefore gives rise to reasoning, but a reasoning that emerges only by way of the event and not before. The event cannot therefore be reduced to the terms either of modernism, which seeks to remove the general from its carnality, or postmodernism, which presumes the triumph of carnality, as if generality could not be entertained after the event and as if, therefore, nothing could be learned from the event, no recognizable habits of conduct acquired.

In these terms, learning to be a heterological historian turns first on the grace of proximity, and then on some initial claim to generality for and after proximity. But what claim could stand against the Other's alterity?

(f) *Learning in and after proximity begins with a wager, and a wager displays a face of the One and not the Other, but One for the Other.*

The question is not one of the reality or unreality of the past but rather of its hyperreality. The past is always already hyperreal, volatized, awaiting only the technological instantiation it has now received . . . that which opens up through negation, the past, appears to offer itself to my grasp, but *the only way the past can return is as word or image*.[39]

Wyschogrod's words suggest that the suffering Other whose voice is not heard cannot be heard until the heterological historian risks proposing some word or image for her. The proposal is neither mere fiction nor a direct percept, but a wager (in Pascal's sense) or an abduction (in Charles Peirce's sense): a mark that may (or may not) prove instrumental in setting a context for this other's relation of proximity to the heterological historian. If so, then the Other-in-proximity-to-the-heterological-historian represents an identity we may distinguish from the Other-whose-voice-is-unheard, just as we may distinguish the unhearing historian from the heterological historian who seeks to hear, and her in turn from the heterological-historian-in-proximity-to-the-Other.

There is thus at least a three-pronged relation of heterological historian to Other, since the heterological historian offers a word or image of the Other only for the sake of some third party, her reader. In these terms, the relations of the heterological historian to the Other unheard and to the Other in proximity bear resemblance to the distinction Kant draws between *Gegenstand* and *Objekt*. However much Wyschogrod may distance her account of cataclysm from Kant's account of the sublime, the Other who might be heard by way of word or image does not to that extent belong to the cataclysm, but has also entered a modern project of inquiry. She has entered as interrupter, but no longer infinitely so; once the heterological historian turns to her, the Other's infinite emptiness sacrifices its own infinity, as it were, accepting this finite relation. The Other lends herself to the heterological historian as suffering teacher.

I previously expressed the hope that Wyschogrod would separate Other as sufferer from Other as teacher, and here I have just referred to a moment in which the Other appears as teacher. But this is shorthand for yet another relationship. Attending to the Other's voice, the heterological historian remains Wyschogrod's student; the image and word she offers up for and about the Other come from somewhere—first from her writing. This suggests that the second identity of the Other, once "heard," is not only bi- and tri-, but at least quadri-relational. It is the Other-(for) the heterological historian-(for) her reader-(by way of) Wyschogrod's words. Once engaged in this relationship, the heterological historian may be said to "follow after Wyschogrod"; the heterological historian has "left behind" her former selfhood not for the sake of infinite self-abjection, but for the sake of a new selfhood-in-relation, to Wyschogrod, to Other, to reader.

(g) *Wager becomes learning through the test of time and extended relations.* Reflecting on this process (for example, by writing about Wyschogrod), the heterological historian may also wager/propose/draw another set of images or words: this time, about Wyschogrod. This would not be for Wyschogrod's sake, but for the sake of what else the heterological historian may become. If the heterological historian speaks of the Other by way of Wyschogrod's words, then she may wager that Wyschogrod's writing displays some parallel set of relations, for example, of Other-(for)Wyschogrod-(for)Wyschogrod's reader-(by way of) _____'s words. The blank would be filled by Wyschogrod's teacher. We need not name this One, but we get hints of such a teacher's identity when she cites Levinas (and a few others) somewhat in the way that we are citing her. We might then make a parallel wager about Levinas's writing (in relation to R. Chouchani or whomever). The result, you might imagine, may be some indefinite chain of identities, such as Other-(for)Wyschogrod-(for)Wyschogrod's reader-(by way of) Levinas's words-(by way of) C's words-(by way of) . . . N's words.

I will suggest or wager that this latter chain represents a transhistorical identity within which each of the double-coded identities of the Other are both afforded a distinct place and brought into intimate relation, one to the other: Other (as the first item in such a chain, an unheard voice "heard" by way of this chain) and One (as the last item in such a chain, the inquirer-become-heterologist-by-way-of-this-Other). The heterological historian imitates the One for the sake of the Other and, in relation to the Other, may even serve as One to some others. Drawing such a chain offers a means of making wagers about the identities of the heterological historian's teacher and, thereby, of responding to our questions about how one learns to be a heterological historian. It suggests how both suffering Other and caring One may share in the heterological historian's education while respecting the (finite or creaturely) modesty of the One and the (finite or creaturely) silence of the Other.

But there is also a danger in drawing such a chain, and this danger may have a lot to do with Wyschogrod's simultaneous participation in and critique of both the modern project and its postmodern subproject. Besides helping her understand her sources and paths of learning, such a chain might also tempt the heterologist to premature conclusions about how to hear and draw near the Other. Concluding that the chain defines her "tradition of knowing the Other" per se, she may wager that "getting to know the Other more deeply" means getting to know this chain more deeply, and she may begin to substitute reading-the-tradition for turning-always-openly to hear voices of the Other. In her reading, the modern project is a critique of tradition, and this is in part a critique of any inquirer's temptation to substitute a learning tradition for encountering the Other. According to her postmodern critique, modernists are modern inquirers who fall unwittingly into the same temptation by adopting modern inquiry as itself a tradition for knowing the Other—only this time, the Other's voices are silenced behind a barrier of conceptual constructions, rather than received literatures and practices. In *Saints and Postmodernism* and *An Ethics of Remembering*, Wyschogrod introduces heterology as a means of repairing yet another version of the modern temptation. This is the postmodernist effort to reduce the failings of modernists and traditionalists alike to the single error of closure: believing that meaning or signification or truth or value can be possessed at all. The temptation here is to promote yet another substitute for actual voices of the Other: this time, a practice of indefinite criticism and a commitment to the ideal and idea of alterity. If not even a finite closure can be risked, no voice can be heard.

Wyschogrod's heterological critique of postmodernist temptations brings us full circle, back to the chain of identities as a way of imagining the proximity of One to the Other. The danger of drawing such a chain may be no different than the danger of offering up any word or image of the Other. In either case, they are fallible drawings, wagers, abductions that are judged by their usefulness in eliciting other drawings. Not to risk them is to risk not hearing the Other's voices. Not to remember that they are wagers, guesses, is to risk hearing the other's voice other than as it is offered. Wyschogrod's call to the historian is a call to turn toward the other and a call to take the risk of guessing, wagering. To learn how to do this is both to read and follow Wyschogrod, imitate (non-identically) and re-perform. Along the way, that will most likely mean to read and follow some of her teachers as well, but also to follow other teachers, depending on where a given reader locates writings or narratives of Ones who care for the Other in the midst of each given project of inquiry. And it means following others' voices as they appear. Their places and contexts will be unpredictable. The consequences of hearing them will be unpredictable. This unpredictability should be protection enough against the dangers of wagering about the Other.

PART IV

Response

An Exercise in Upbuilding

EDITH WYSCHOGROD

In this extraordinary collection of essays, I encounter myself in a Kierke-gaardian sense as "the single individual," the one by whom the work itself "wishes to be received as if it had arisen in [the] heart" of the self whom it addresses. I read each essay as a discourse in *upbuilding*, as Kierkegaard understood the term, so that the writer whose name is affixed to the essay is one who generously accepts responsibility for its every word. Neither a sermon nor a treatise that is designed to increase abstract knowledge, the discourse that is upbuilding drives the addressee between alternatives and solicits one thus driven to exist with passion. It is all too easy for her/him to avoid the realization that, "tossed between eternity [as] a winged horse infinitely fast and time [as] a worn-out jade, the existing individual is the driver."[1] These texts should not be dubbed *edifying*, an adjective once been used for them, since *edification* suggests a disapproving finger-wagging correction of errors committed. They ought rather be seen as *ophyggellig*, the Danish adjective that should be rendered as *upbuilding*, a term suggesting depth as well as height. If, as Kierkegaard maintains, "one wished to erect a tower that reached the sky . . . [and] it lacked a foundation it would not actually be built up."[2]

I shall take these works not only as openly edifying, but also as appeals to don and doff the personae proffered by the author. To read in this way is to accept the solicitation to "build up" by becoming the self depicted by the other's discourse, a self that is not a mask or one who is dissembling, but one whose existential possibilities are thought to be one's ownmost possibilities by a discerning reader. It is as such that I hope to respond.

Still, am I not trapped in a dilemma, that of undecidability, to which Derrida points? Far from positing the claim that one is paralyzed when confronted with meaningful alternatives, Derrida maintains that in order for there to be decision, there must be undecidability. "If we know what to do, if I knew in terms of knowledge what I have to do before the decision, then the decision would not be a decision. It would simply be the application of a rule, the consequence of a premise." When two solutions present themselves as equally justifiable, I must assume responsibility for my choice without appeal to knowledge claims and thus, in a Kierkegaardian sense, undergo the anguish attendant upon deciding. Derrida does not deny the necessity for knowledge that prepares for decision, but he asserts that the decision transcends claims to knowledge.[3]

In his account of *aut/aut*, either/or, Kierkegaard describes choice not as a moment of reasoned deliberation about specifiable alternatives, but as a moment of existential involvement in the options at hand. If stages, or what I here call personae, are markers of identity, then even if they resemble one another in their affective intensities, a disjunctive logic such as Kierkegaard's either/or or *aut/aut* is not a moment of reasoned deliberation but an affective involvement in the available choices. That which is chosen has, for Kierkegaard, the most profound relation to the one who is choosing. But if I am involved in a choice of whence and whither, where I'm coming from and where I mean to go, then encountering the ethical presents a quintessential moment of choice. If the ethical is indissolubly bound up with choice, can it ever be transcended? Kierkegaard reflects upon a paradox in the ethical itself. What would it mean in the present context to be right? If I am persuaded that I have done right by the interpreter of my thinking by rejecting her or his view and persisting in my original position, but my interpreter goes her/his own way or does otherwise, then by not having changed her/him, I have failed. I have done wrong by the other. But doing wrong is itself edifying. By calling me to attention, doing wrong gives a lesson in upbuilding. It is just here that Kierkegaard's account of being in the wrong can bring to the fore the price that can be paid for upbuilding. The more often I am in the wrong, the more upbuilding.

If the personae I attribute to my interlocutors constitute an exercise in upbuilding, do they not, when taken together, form a narrative, and specifically a work of fiction? And are not such works artworks in the Levinasian sense, works of bewitchment by images "that go from being to being by skipping over the intervals of the meanwhile"? The writer of fictions (the composite of my interlocutors) speaks by "allusions, by suggestion, by equivocations . . . as though he moved in a world of shadows, as though he lacked the force to arouse realities, as though he could not go to them without wavering, as though he spills half the water he is bringing us."[4] It is the function of criticism, Levinas avers, to speak frankly and in candor, through concepts that choose and limit. I should like to argue that the attitude attributed to literature by Levinas applies to what Milan Kundera calls the "lyrical attitude" that is characteristic of youth when the writer focuses upon her/himself. Kundera contends that "the lyrical chrysalis" must be torn away in order in order for the novel to be born. The birth of the novelist should be envisaged as "a *conversion story*: Saul becoming Paul; the novelist being born from the ruins of his lyrical world."[5] The work is neither a didactic tale, a fable in the Aesopian sense, nor a lyrical outburst of affect. As Kierkegaard already knew and Flaubert is credited with saying, the artist to protect the personae of his oeuvre " 'must make posterity believe he never lived.' "[6] Such a work enables the reader to discern in her/himself what she/he might otherwise have missed.

In assuming a persona, in attempting to see what I have missed, am I not entering into conversation with my interlocutors, a complex interaction aimed at communication in which my word has reached the other and that of the other has reached me? Does such an exchange not imply a mutuality of understanding? Gadamer, who seems to hold this approach, concedes that understanding is always "understanding differently (*andersverstehen*)." What changes when the other's words reach me is not a fixed identity. "To understand means that one is capable of stepping into the place of the other in order to say what one has there understood and what one has to say in response."[7] Agreement is not necessarily the outcome of this perspective. It does however entail being able to "stand for the other" and represent the matter through her/his eyes. Have I not then, as Levinas might conclude, undermined the alterity of the other? If the other's word to me results in my commitment to maintaining the continuity of the new condition, I have at least formally entered the terrain of the ethical as Kierkegaard understood it. Is the upbuilding discourse not a challenge to maintain one's position but also to undo it? Does failing to read the challenge in the text of the other not abandon the tension of the Kierkegaardian either/or, of the lure of the possible?

I would concur with Ricoeur that the possible must be understood in terms of action, "of being able," as he would have it. But its actualization, I would hold, is always open to undoing, so that possibility is to be understood as an ongoing sequence of possibles. The interpretation of a text I am always in the process of becoming opens and closes off the chain of possibles and, in so doing, constructs a narrative of who I am. As such, I am also the one whose possibles I was, one who is her past. As Ricoeur maintains, "Now we may tell *different* stories about ourselves. So, we have to learn to vary the stories that we are telling about ourselves . . . We have to enter this process of exchange. We are caught in the stories of others, so we are protagonists in the stories we are told by others and we have to assume for ourselves the stories that the others tell about us."[8]

But if I am to assume various personae, must I not be able to see myself, as Ricoeur would have it, as another? Since some of my interlocutors identify my persona as that of an "ethical thinker," without entering into the complexities of recent analyses of personal identity, I am constrained to ask "Who am I?" If I am seen as an ethical thinker, is my identity to be construed as marked by what is often ascribed to the ethical: reliability, constancy of belief and action, what is traditionally designated as "character"? Although in actual existence character expresses itself in multiple ways, in abstract terms for Ricoeur, character consists of a composite of identity markers that permit the reidentification of the human individual as being the same. This view is in conformity with Kierkegaard's depiction of the ethical as conformity to the universal expressing itself as duty. Seeking a less ossified view of the self than what is intrinsic to the received view of character, Ricoeur attempts to develop an account of selfhood that allows for continuity and consistency without stifling change by distinguishing a hard and fast view of self as substance from a more flexible account of self as melding the Latin *idem*, whose basic characteristic is permanence in time, as opposed to *ipse*, which implies no unchanging core of personality, but which allows for continuity. In *Oneself as Another*, he contends that

> *ipse* identity involves a dialectic complementary to that of selfhood and sameness, namely the dialectic of self and other . . . From the outset, the selfhood of oneself implies otherness to such an intimate degree that one cannot be thought of without the other, that instead one passes into the other . . . To [the] "as" [of the title of this book] I should like to attach a strong meaning, not only that of a comparison (oneself as similar to another) but indeed that of an implication (oneself inasmuch as being other).[9]

In respecting the differences among my interlocutors, I shall eschew the constancies or *Eigenschaften* of *idem* and turn instead to the *ipse* of difference and temporal passage by donning and doffing multiple personae.

Thinking the Ethical: *Gedacht oder Geglaubt*

I am profoundly grateful to Mark C. Taylor, who is one of those who designate me as "an ethical thinker" whose work goes beyond the bounds of ethics as currently conceived. Recent ethical philosophy, he maintains, is often a-contextual and fails to explore the possibility of ethics; he notes that I feel impelled to consider what ethics becomes when it takes up into itself the story of its own ontological errancy, a critical term that, in Taylor's own work, refers to a sauntering without shelter. I feel impelled to question what happens to ethics when shards of the metaphysical history through which it has passed, in a return of the suppressed, percolate at the surface of its claims. Such claims bring out, as Nietzsche and later Derrida would have it, the fact of their worn-outness, " 'like coins which have lost their pictures and now matter as metal and no longer as coins.' "[10]

I have interpreted this perspective as a moment of negation, "an ethic of ethics" contingent upon the otherness of the other person and, in concurrence with Levinas, see the other not as a phenomenon but as language, a proscription against violence. Taylor sees that I have been propelled in this direction by the genocidal catastrophes of the twentieth and twenty-first centuries, which cannot yet must be thought. An ethic of alterity is also challenged by the deterministic implications of genetic research upon conceptions of altruism as a moral stance. As Dominique Janicaud has pointed out, the impact of the marriage of science and technology, of tele-technoscience, has become a model for thinking. Bearing these caveats in mind, Taylor asks perceptively whether such a nonnomological ethics is not nihilistic and what is more, whether dispensing with moral certitude does not undermine the absolutist logic of the death-event. I would ultimately distinguish, as Levinas does, between the ethical as a primordial responsiveness to the call of the other, to the "extreme exposure and sensitivity of one subject to the other," and morality as "a series of rules relating to social behavior and civic duty" that is founded on responsibility to the other.[11] Thus I am not liberated from the onus of the ennui of ethical theory to which Bernard Lewis engagingly points, in that theoretical disputes are indispensable. If so, I cannot endorse Derrida's view that the temporal aporias, the metaphysics of presence, preclude agreed-upon meaning, that language cannot be communication. As Gadamer remarks, the Tower of Babel does not refer exclusively to a multiplicity of language but "encompasses in its meaning the strangeness that arises between one human being and another, always creating new confusion. But precisely in this fact lies the possibility of overcoming confusion. For language is conversation."[12]

Taylor also notes that I read the death event as interpreting persons as mathematized homogeneous units so that they are indistinguishable from one another, as well as transposing the real into images that eventuate in a "pandemic hyperreality"; thus, the death event enacts itself in two forms of ideality. In response, he maintains, I am trying to return to the real by way of an ethics of otherness. He has indeed captured one of the motives of my account.

The Ethical and Transcendence: *Geglaubt*

Having followed Merold Westphal's powerful criticisms of ontotheology in his own work with great interest, I am not surprised that he has profoundly understood my turn from abstraction to hagiographic discourse, to the exemplary life of another who provides a locus for manifesting ethical existence rather than stating ethical claims. Moral theory, he notes, persuades those who inhabit the same realm of discourse. The force of his presentation lies in his doing what I have claimed needs to be done: appealing to a compelling narrative, Philip Hallie's *Lest Innocent Blood Be Shed*, a recounting of the rescue of five thousand Jews by the French villagers of Le Chambon at great risk to themselves. Westphal makes the powerful point that if theory can be compelling as it is for Kant, it is because good will already inheres in the natural understanding. We need only make reason attend closely to that which is antecedent to it, an attitude different from that of intellectual clarity. What is required, Westphal reminds us, is remembering what is right and wrong at decisive moments.

Especially compelling is Westphal's appeal to Kierkegaard's Climacus, a turn that constitutes an authorial layering—Westphal, Kierkegaard, Climacus, and myself—an upbuilding move that reinforces my claim that the essays in this volume can be taken as lessons in upbuilding. Kierkegaard reminds us that an objective uncertainty inwardly appropriated is truth and that truth thus construed is faith. In his reminder, Westphal perceptively exhumes the theological roots of my seemingly secular account of sainthood as a life devoted to the alleviation of psychological and physical pain. Yet he also maintains that my refusal to acknowledge the religious roots of sainthood lies in my identification of religion with mysticism. To be sure, my reservations lie in the ways in which the term *mysticism* is seen to refer to states of ecstasy that would occlude the ability to act on behalf of others. I may, however, be less wary than Westphal thinks in this regard. In a conversation with John Caputo, I refer to the eros of transcendence as *le désir de Dieu*, a desire whose ambiguity I gloss as my desire for God and God's own desire.[13] What is more, Westphal points out, goodness as a subject of narration may save others from despair by showing how goodness comes about. The addressee of Westphal's story of self-sacrifice by a woman in Chambon must ask herself, if tested, whether she would empty her suitcase, disbursing what she possesses to those who need it rather than self-interestedly clinging to it, and whether giving would mitigate the despair she might happen to feel. Would she apprehend the emptied suitcase as a rainbow, an incursion of transcendence that she must render into narrative discourse?

I am deeply grateful to Graham Ward who, like Taylor and Westphal, has grasped the centrality of what I see as the ethical question of our age: the death-event, and the death-worlds intrinsic to it, enclaves of extraordinary privation and suffering in which persons are confined. Ward, as a Christian theologian, claims that he speaks otherwise, from a place that is not mine. Yet in affirming a certain Abrahamic theological lineage, we speak together. As he writes here, in "being stretched out towards a future hope," we live for "a promise that is not received . . . to confess that [each of us is] a stranger and a pilgrim on the earth, to set out not knowing where [each] will end up, for a place which will be received only retrospectively." Thus we are, in Gadamer's sense, a conversation, "a living exchange of question and answer and by extending reciprocity, allowing conversation to take place."[14]

I am also grateful to Ward for his upbuilding gloss of the meaning of the words "stranger" and "wanderer," in terms of an irony that my claim to a Kierkegaardian stance demands. Ward alludes to my account of an old African American man encountered on a street in New York who refused my offer to help him to a hospital and asked instead that I remember his name, Billy Joe; this is a move, as he points out, "from anonymity to self-identification and attestation." Cannot the impossibility of naming God to which Derrida points not apply to one who is destitute, whose amplitude is, so to speak, negative, that of destitution itself? Pointing to the doubleness of saving and losing, Derrida maintains, "It was necessary to save the name, to save everything but the name (*sauf le nom*) as if it was necessary to lose the name in order to save what bears the name."[15] Can one, as Derrida suggests, forget it by calling it? Having heard the command and promised obedience, I shall take that risk and continue to advocate that historians pronounce the names of the dead others.

Ward remains critical of an ethics of alterity, of fetishizing the other and thereby diminishing affinities that can eventuate in cooperative engagement. Levinas concedes that because there are more than two, we must pass from the perspective of ethics to that of the whole or totality, and in that context specify *who* the others are in the interest of establishing common juridical positions so that conflicting claims can be adjudicated. Ward argues further that most versions of Christianity are in opposition to Levinas's rejection of a kenotic theology in that God becomes human in Jesus. Levinas's view remains antikenotic even if divine entry into human existence is evident in numerous passages in the Hebrew Bible. Does God not walk and talk in the garden and descend to speak with Moses? To be sure, there is no immanentization of transcendence in the readings of those who, with Maimonides, parse these narratives as necessary anthropomorphisms written in the interest of the simpleminded. I would, with Levinas, locate the kenotic in the surplus of meaning intrinsic to the human face but also and, contra-Levinas, in the overwhelming power of nature or, in more recent terms, in cosmic magnitude. I have maintained that God is "dazzling in his excessiveness," an overflowing to which one must be receptive. This excessiveness is not to be identified with the idea of the infinite which is not for Levinas a content, but a direction, "a toward God."[16]

Thomas Altizer designates my work as that of an ethical thinker, but one who is covertly theological yet manages to avoid the aridity of current theological ethics. Altizer reads my ethics as an apocalyptic ethics in tension with a primordial ethics with which I had heretofore been identified. The latter is grounded in the otherness of the other person who as other must remain undisclosed, and also in a formless and an-anarchic past that cannot be brought into plenary presence. As an apocalyptic thinker, I speak, he contends, under the aegis of biblically grounded prophecy, a revolution whose goal is the creation of an absolute future. By bringing these antinomies to light, as well as highlighting the ecumenicity of my perspective, Altizer places my thinking within the ambit of Pauline theology and Paul's fissured Christian ethics. As further confirmation, Paul is said to have experienced the collapse of a historical world that he could only know as a nihilistic world, a situation comparable to our own. But—and this is the crucial point—such an apocalyptic ending is inseparable from the advent of a new world, a Pauline stance carried forward in Hegel, Nietzsche and Heidegger. Altizer discerns in the paucity of references to God in my account of death a certain theological lineage. In eliciting "the groundlessness of all established ethics" as well as positing "the vacuity of our ethical categories," have I not, in making this Nietzschean move, joined Altizer as a death-of-God theologian? I have spoken of the incursion of transcendence with the advent of the other as freeing and absolving one from a purely immanental time scheme of everyday existence. What I have alluded to as an absolutely archaic time is one of requirement and obligation. Moreover, if the time of transcendence is that of a past that cannot become present as an eschatological time, how does a future that cannot become present differ from the archaic past? Do Genesis and messianism come together? Altizer maintains, as does Levinas, that "their respective and contrary identities now appear to be passing into one another, thereby dissolving . . . the individual identities of beginning and end."[17]

Paul as apostle can make bedfellows of strangers, pairing new and radically disparate thinkers. A brief comparison of Altizer and Alain Badiou may bring out the ways in which Tom may be right with respect to my apocalyptic dimension. Thus Alan Badiou, who imposes daunting complex technical demands upon his readers into which I shall not try to enter, argues that mathematics (whose quintessential expression for him is set theory) is ontology. In a passage paraphrasing Paul and oddly Altizerian in its vision of destruction, Badiou writes, "God has chosen the things that are not in order to bring to nought those that are."[18] For Paul, "in contrast to the philosopher, [who] knows eternal truths; the prophet knows the univocal sense of what will come . . . The apostle who declares an unheard of possibility, [the resurrection] dependent upon an evental grace," properly speaking, knows nothing.[19] What is meant by an event? Badiou declares that "[it] is not a miracle but is extracted from a situation always related back to a singular multiplicity, its state its language."[20] As such, "it is a fragment of being related to its site, defined as part of a situation all of whose elements are at the edge of a void."[21] One commentator also notes that "using the language of counting, if the aggregate elements each count as one, the event is supernumerary—it exceeds the count."[22] Void and excess, thus described, could not be more Altizerian. In the same vein, Badiou distinguishes knowledge from truth in that the former refers to facts and opinions in the usual commonsense fashion, whereas truth, although not in opposition to knowledge, "as a generic subset, is a gap or break in the encyclopedic organization of knowledge" that constitutes its specific void. "A truth is a truth about the whole situation, not about this or that."[23]

I have gone into some detail in regard to Altizer's and Badiou's affinities to bring out that a key factor that ties together their views of Paul is a stress upon the emergence of novelty in relation to a void. It would seem, however, that in considering this affinity, one must bear in mind Kierkegaard's distinction between the brilliant genius, who knows what is accessible to the privileged few, and the apostolic path of passion that is open to all. For Badiou truth is inseparable from an esoteric mathematical specialty that is its *sine qua non*. What links Altizer's Paulinianism to mine and separates him from Badiou is the pathos that attaches to death and, for me, to the death of the other. For Badiou mathematics has put an end to pathos, to suffering as intrinsic to situation. Ontotheological expressions of the One are precluded by mathematically configured multiplicities and concomitantly the infinite is secularized. For Altizer and me, passion is indispensable for renewal. We share the tension that obtains between the primordial and the apocalyptic, but not the manner in which novelty emerges from the apocalyptic.

The philosopher, for Adriaan Peperzak, is one who inhabits and has been formed by a world prior to reflecting upon it. For him, philosophy is the owl of Minerva that flies by night to borrow Hegel's metaphor in that it supervenes upon historical existence. One might add that it retraces itself by navigating through its own history. At the same time, does it not renew itself? What is more, God has been the subject and the horizon of speculative philosophy and has been understood in multiple ways, each of which was ultimately undone by God's unencompassable infinity. Modernity's craving for autonomy based on the rule of reason, in essence justifiable, Peperzak concedes, was a protest against the tie to an absolute seen as undermining human autonomy and as an authoritarian impoverishment of human existence. Although we cannot establish that the name of God has a referent about which or whom true propositions can be uttered, the yearning for God does not disappear. Must God not always already be in some way in consciousness as an absence, Peperzak asks? I have argued that this absence that is other than the consciousness it inhabits creates an insatiable desire that is neither sexual nor cognitive in its intent, but is a desire for something more, an excessiveness that eludes the grasp of consciousness. My Levinasian position is in consonance in this respect with that of Peperzak.

He is also in agreement with my further claim that the encounter with the face of the other human being is in the track or trace of transcendence and, I would add, as such in the track or spoor of humankind. My relation to the human other is not a relation to the infinite. In this regard, Peperzak makes an important distinction: my responsibility to the other is absolute but not infinite, since that term is reserved for God alone. In conformity with this distinction and with Levinas, I would maintain that divine extravagance is conveyed in the term *the infinite*. To be sure, God lays claim to the self to heed the suffering of the other, but the infinite is rather, as Levinas has suggested, a direction, a "toward God."

Practices of Influence

The essays to which I shall now turn, those of Hollywood, Wolfson, and Gibbs, offer disclosures that proceed in the languages of erotic communication. In the context of corporeality, the issue framing its erotics cannot be parsed without turning to the question of gender. It is hard to imagine a more graphic way (or, better yet, a more graphematic way, since it is

Derrida of whom she writes) of attesting the ineradicability of gender than Amy Hollywood's tracking its errancy in Derrida's account of Freud's daughter Anna in relation to the father. Anna reads a statement, speculatively attributed by Yerushalmi to her father, that serves as an entering wedge into the question of whether psychoanalysis is to be considered universal, scientifically verifiable knowledge, or whether it is a "Jewish science," thereby opening the highly charged particularist/universal issue. Has Derrida, in reading their genealogical relation, archivally opened the way for reading Anna as more than a "surface" for the relation of son to father, and if so how is "Jewishness" to be understood? Derrida's critique of historian Yerushalmi's reading rests on the latter's desire to efface the name of the daughter and to replace it with his own as the "son," the true heir of Freud. As Hollywood points out, Derrida's analysis goes on to show that for Yerushalmi only the son can be Jewish since, for Derrida, it is the corporeal trace of circumcision that is the mark of Jewishness and the determinant of who controls the archive. The virtualization of writing would diminish the corporeality of the inscribed trace, but its dimming down of difference might fail to benefit women. Is there a site from which the daughter can, as Derrida asks, speak in her own name and not only with the voice of the father?

Hollywood movingly asks whether Derrida can loosen his grip on us or we on him "to empty a space for other words." Are there sites from within the tradition from which the woman speaks in her own name? What Derrida's account never considers are the implications of the rabbinic view that it is maternal descent that determines Jewish identity. Woman is the vehicle of biological lineage, a position that, it goes without saying, presents great difficulties to which attention has frequently been called. Still, woman remains a prior condition for the exercise of power. In the case of intermarriage between a Jewish mother and non-Jewish father, a daughter born to this union is Jewish. She in turn may marry a non-Jew, who on the rabbinic account may lead the offspring (who, via his mother, is Jewish) away from the practices of Judaism, thereby turning the child to apostasy and sin (Deut. 7:3–4). Thus here is an inerasable graphematics of *différance.* It is only on the prior ground of the relation to the mother that the male's speech acquires theological significance.

To be sure, Derrida's view is enforced by the paternal manifestations of the perquisites of power in regard to social roles in the traditional framework. Priesthood is inherited through the male, even if Jewish lineage is determined through the female. In every case where there is a union deemed legitimate, the child follows the priestly role of the father, whereas in a case where the union is not licit (e.g., a marriage between a

Jew and a gentile) the child merely acquires the status of the mother. In sum, Jewish identity is determined by maternal lineage, whereas honorific status is the legacy of the father (M. Kiddushin 3:12). In attempting to surmount traditional constraints, Levinas has drawn upon received views of the role of women as icons of hospitality, as making the home habitable, as well as upon paradigmatic figures of Sarah and Esther, whose actions merit acclaim because they defy their assigned roles. Can the attributes of the good wife (Prov. 31:10–31), the paradigms of conjugal trustworthiness, and oikonomically productive activities speak otherwise than in subservience? Does woman not "see that her business goes well"? Does she not "disburse goods to the poor"? Admire her not for her "charm and beauty"; rather "Praise her for all she has accomplished; let her achievements bring her honor at the city gates" (Prov. 31:31). What might Derrida have exhumed from this site?

Elliot Wolfson's magisterial reading of kenosis and time in the writings of Abraham Abulafia falls within the parameters of the Neoplatonic tradition that I have maintained continues to recur in significant ways. To be sure, Wolfson's work tracks important conceptual additions, such as the role of the Active Intellect derived from Maimonides. The ontological stasis and unity of the One of Plotinian neopaganism are no longer the focus of contemplation, but have been supplanted by the divine name as it is written in the Hebrew Bible, *yod he vav he*. In a terse formulation as cited by Elliot in his article, Abulafia writes, "God, blessed be he, blessed be his name, is not a body or a faculty in a body, and he never materializes." And much to the point, "the truth is in his names. Every speech in the Torah in which God spoke to Moses or the prophets is not like our speech but rather like what the prophet hears," Abulafia maintains. What is crucial is that there is nothing comparable to the wisdom that is to be derived from the composite of the letters of the name, for "his names are the truth of his Torah."

In a remarkable parallel to Abulafia's view of the name, Derrida, using Angelus Silesius's attempt to refer to what the name presumes to name that is beyond itself, writes: "The nameable beyond the name, the unnameable nameable . . . as if it was necessary both to save the name and everything except the name (*sauf le nom*)."[24] In this characteristically Derridean passage, unnameability betrays the inadequation of language. It can be argued that despite Levinas's express rejection of unitive mysticism that Abulafia is a "kabbalist of rupture" who sees a way to God in the breaking of the divine name rather than in its restoration, a point that is repeated in Levinas's account of an Infinite that cannot shut itself up in a word but must unsay itself and also unsays this undoing.[25] It is not difficult to detect traces of a Judaic legacy that both is and is not antinomian that wends its way into their accounts of language, one to which I have in many ways attached my own thinking.

What I found especially compelling in relation to my own recent thought is Wolfson's explication of Abulafia's account of how the soul is separated from the body through acts of self-purification, not via ablution or self-mortification "but the vocalization of different combinations that follow in a rapid pace and effect the trancelike state into which the adept temporarily succumbs" (32). For Abulafia, one of several standpoints from which mystical union may be viewed is for one "to be incorporated within the textual embodiment of the word of God." Astonishingly, numerological equivalents based upon the number value of the letters of the names in the text, the back and forth migration from numbers to letters, hold the secret of creation.

The graphematics of Elliot's detailed account provides the numerological and alphabetic lineage that, despite the deconstruction of interiority, I attribute to a new conceptual landscape in which a dematerialized subject has emerged. Genes, a mathematized string of ancestral molecules, have replaced the dematerialized Plotinian soul. I have turned to Iamblichus, who considers the soul as an intertwining of mathematical figure and number. Radicalizing the claim that "that the soul exists in ratios common with all mathematics," he maintains "the definition of the souls contains in itself the sum total of mathematical reality,"[26] a primacy of the mathematical I have already alluded to in regard to Badiou's claim that mathematics is ontology. Wolfson's elaborate analysis of Abulafia's interpretation of the significations of the name provides a rich historical backdrop in support my claim that the impulse to dematerialize, to find irreducible "simples" whose interactions constitute the essence of a process, does not disappear. What is upbuilding is not only confirmation of the persistence of Pythagoras's claim that the world is made of numbers, but the challenge to seek beyond existing countervalent models of the lived body to discover new modes of configuring the flesh.

That the provocation of the Tetragrammaton is intrinsic to what has been referred to as the provocation of Levinas is brought out in Robert Gibbs's discussion of Levinas's interpretation of the name of God. To call upon God is to utter the name without indicating a referent, yet, insofar as we call upon God, we speak a name and, in so doing, betray God. The name in Hebrew is never uttered, but only written. In rabbinic discourse the term for God is a proper name, but it is transposable only into other proper names, so that the structure of deignation disintegrates beneath the sheer weight of multiple names. What is more, inexpungable tensions inhere in naming the name, as Gibbs shows in his analysis of Levinas's depiction of the problem. On the one hand, shifting to the written name does not change the proscription regarding the withdrawal of the name in that it is not to be effaced. Yet does not writing itself constitute an entering wedge into the effacement or withdrawal of the specificity of the name, in that a certain universality or breadth of meaning attaches to a word that is written? The written text is also subject to the hermeneutical variations of its interpreters. In sum, writing is, as Gibbs shows, "a risk that transcendence runs in the name of God." At the same time, shockingly, are there not effacements of a text that are biblically commanded? Can that which is prohibited be ordered?

I should like to expand on Gibbs's account by turning to the familiar account of the destruction of the golden calf, according to which Moses takes the calf that the Israelites had made, burns it, grinds it to powder, scatters it on the water, and compels the people to drink it (Exod. 32:20). By ingesting the ash, the Israelites conceal and internalize that which had been forbidden, but which will return spectrally as language. How, it may be asked, can ash be transformed into language? Rashi, in his classical interpretation, links this narrative to a narrative cited by Gibbs: the *Sotah*, the ritual for the woman accused of adultery, who is forced to drink a mixture of holy water, dust from the tabernacle, and the written text of curses she has been compelled to utter. Her innocence is established if the text of the curses is effaced. What is crucial is that in the transformation of the ashes of the calf into text, that which is written remains and the idol rearises spectrally within the word, whereas in the case of the *Sotah*, if the text is to exonerate, it does so in its effacement. Does not this tension of discourse that proscribes effacement while also facilitating it persist as a desideratum in the virtualization of language, the transformation of bytes into words, words into bytes, a process that offers inexpugnable retention and at the same time promises the possibility of total erasure?

Channeling History

Several essays in this collection are devoted to my account of the historian's task, of how the subject matter of history is to be configured and of the perquisites that are to belong to the historian who undertakes it—a historian who must be "both the narrator of events and litigant for the powerless." In *The Ethics of Remembering*, I attempt to explore the historian's task, the configuring the subject matter of history and the site where the historian as history channel is to situate herself. Prior to her filling out the contours of the proposition, "thus it was," the narrative of what has transpired, the historian is to be stationed in an ethical terrain of the suffering other whose voice has been occluded or obliterated.

In Peter Ochs's complex and closely reasoned interpretation of my construct, that of the persona of the heterological historian, he concludes that in her pedagogical role, she herself morphs into an embodiment of alterity. In Ochs's Peircean riff, whose strategy is that of "musement" (a term Peirce uses to refer to "a kind of pure play of the mind" whose progress is guided by the concentrated observation of the ones who "muse"[27]), Ochs attempts to draw out the quandaries that arise when one asks how the formation of the heterological historian is to be understood. Bringing together my description of the heterological historian and what may seem to be the unrelated claim underlying my contention that hagiographic discourse, narratives of saintly lives, provides a paradigm for the moral life as such, Ochs maintains that the two are linked. Ultimately, the heterological historian must be taught by saints and her work must be considered in light of its own existential appropriation of saintliness, although Ochs concedes that I do not abandon an appeal to evidence. This position manifests a certain double-codedness: existential transformation on the one hand and, on the other, the transmitting of what can be understood. The singularity of an individual life functions as a bodily general thing, a "carnal general."

I cannot enter into the many significant issues raised by Ochs but shall focus upon two matters first, that *from which* responsibility can be learned and those *from whom* one learns, a kind of magisterium of philosophical and religious contemporaries and forebears. First, Ochs recognizes that the Shoah is a defining context of my account of the heterological historian. As the ultimate undoing of the other, a *nihil*, it cannot be interrogated, he reasons. It can only be a site of nonlearning. Can unlearning instill obligation? When put in this way, I must ask whether the *nihil* is not a question of radical subtraction, of the absence of others who once were there and, as such, a general problem for historians. Sartre's well-known account of the emergence of the other in the other's absence (of the waiter in the café who was but is not present, yet in his absence is there more compellingly[28]) suggests a proximity that may be irrecoverable in its bodily *Leibhaftigkeit* but inerasable as a reproach. In the case of the Shoah, those who had been arise not in the mode of presence but in the mode of the future anterior, a proximity in absence, a past that arises proscriptively as a warning that all may be undone. The historian must live within the paradoxical bounds of the claim that the victims of the Shoah are specifiable, identifiable by time and place, yet their proscriptive power calls all to responsibility.

In regard to the formation of the heterological historian, Ochs depicts a pedagogical chain both genealogical and contemporary, in which continuity and slippage alternate. He argues that, in my role as the author of an ethics of remembering, I am the student of the suffering other. The heterological historian, who is the student of my writing, is in turn taught by me and also by the Other who has taught me. What is more, Ochs argues that I have been instructed by philosophical predecessors and contemporaries and by religious tradition. The most experientially grounded account of the process of transmission that enables me to learn that which I might become or, in Peircean language, to abduct what is and is not possible, I learned viscerally as an adolescent through the practices of modern dance. In studying with a teacher whose style was derived from that of the renegade Isadora Duncan, I learned not by verbal instruction but largely by following the bodily movements of the teacher, movements that functioned as imperatives, a silent speech that solicited approval or reproof as I attempted to make the movements after her that she in turn had learned from and unlearned from the masters of modern dance. Was there not a lineage that could be traced to the Terpsichorean traditions of ancient Athens? To be commanded is to follow but also to make new.

In writing about the heterological historian, do Ochs and the thinker so crucial to his own work, Charles Sanders Peirce, not also become my teachers? This is a situation I am not unhappy to acknowledge, in that a common-sense pragmatism is enriched and corrected by scriptural rules and compassionate readings. Thus Ochs writes, "The divine word does not, therefore, legislate human construct directly, but only by way of modifications of the rule of common sense, as mediated through a community's traditions of biblical interpretation. Over time, the rule of common sense therefore bears the imprint of a history of such modifications."[29]

The role of the chain of filiation so aptly analyzed by Ochs is fleshed out by Werner Kelber in the context of the transmission of the Passion narratives of the New Testament, especially that of the Gospel of Mark. Kelber's work attests in rich detail how narratives intended as commemorative "constitute a single, duplicitous mnemohistory." In their double-coding, the texts display what Kelber calls a double duplicity, that of a faith and piety that has, on the one hand, generated works of extraordinary aesthetic power and, on the other, siphoned off this power into acts of bloodshed and persecution. Thus the iconic power of the cross, he points out, has generated compelling works of Western culture such as

Grünewald's *Isenheim Altar*, but also the anti-Jewish sentiments of the medieval Passion plays.

Kelber's extraordinary control of the transmission history of the New Testament enables him to establish that the double complicity is discernible in the canonical Gospels from their inception. Thus the imbroglios entangling the faction of Pilate and that of the high priest unfold in Mark to favor Pilate, who mistrusts the priests and attempts to spare the life of Jesus. Kelber explicates with the same care the ways in which the tension between Pharisaic Judaism and the messianic Christian faction is played out in relation to the destruction of Jerusalem and how this conflict is later expressed in the universalist claims of Christianity. In Luke, as in Mark, the sins of the people are alleged to be responsible for the fall of the city. In his account, Kelber posits the subsequent narrative construction of the Gospels as a kind of post hoc constitution of the origin. In considering the Gospel of John, Kelber turns to recent interpretive strategies that replicate earlier tensions. For example, he considers a number of strategies, such as the quest for hidden text that presumably would illuminate its meaning but sees what is alleged to be remembered not as mimetic, as reduplicating that which was, but as constructive. Kelber's account alerts the interpreter to the manner in which the scriptural lineages of the text, its internal citations, are themselves also constructs. The narrative is not a place of history but one of memory. For Kelber, one cannot say, "thus it was," that an assertion is matched by a specifiable referent, but rather "thus it has been remembered," thereby acknowledging the constructed character of the "it." Still, are there not better and worse narratives? Does not Kelber's meticulous hermeneutics of memory enable us to exhume factional interests so that one can appeal to the caveat intrinsic to abduction or counterfactuality? One must consider what could not have been.

I am deeply grateful to John D. Caputo for his straight talk about the vexing issue that continues to arise in connection with the task of the historian: should the historian not try to tell the truth, and is doing otherwise not a moral failure? Allan Megill, in his review of *An Ethics of Remembering,* as Caputo points out, warns of the dangers intrinsic to preexisting ideological commitments that guide the lines of historical research. However worthy the cause, is there not the danger of distorting that which was the case, and does advocacy not lead to corruption? Assumption of responsibility for the dead, Megill argues, should follow upon rather than precede a dispassionate examination of the record. My claim is that even if, *per hypothesi,* a value-free creation of the historical record were possible, this record of the facts could not generate moral norms, since the creation of the record itself presupposes an anterior set of values.

Caputo points out that Heidegger has shown that agency belongs to a being who is already installed in a world, in a concrete context, and that the notion of a purely cognitive consciousness is a dogma of modern empiricism. Our way of being in the world, Caputo reminds us, is primordially one always already determined by *Stimmung* or mood, and not as a cognitive relation to objects. The impossibility of a centerless and featureless perspective is perhaps graphically captured in Thomas Nagel's phrase, "the view from nowhere." Nagel argues not for the reconciliation of subjective and objective perspectives, but rather for learning to live with the discomfort of their difference.[30]

But the question remains as to whether objectivity is not itself a value, whether there are not rules of evidence, rules of the game, that when followed provide good reason for preferring one narrative over another? Although there is no definitive answer to this question, I would argue that to construct a historical narrative, it is necessary for the historian to grasp historical occurrences not only in terms of that which was but also by considering that which could *not* have been. Thus historical narratives are doubly disclosive. As I have written elsewhere: "what the historian narrates is that which occurred surrounded by a penumbra of negated possibles each of which is expressed in the modal form: 'X was possible but X did not occur.'"[31] This procedure undoes the predicative and iterative schema that provide the usual conditions of discourse, thereby allowing only those narratives that pass muster to be transmitted.

Refusing to interpret historical narratives grounded in catastrophe nihilistically, Bettina Bergo finds a redemptive dimension in my view of the catastrophe's mode of temporalization. The past that is remembered stands before us as the future pointing towards something that was but is not yet, something unthematizable, an otherness to which we are answerable, a "messianic now." This is a view she also finds in the work of Walter Benjamin. I would ask Bergo whether an eschatological hope could provide the condition that would engender a utopian politics. She maintains that Kant's principle of practical reason cannot provide the underpinnings for such a politics, since it is caught between the poles of duty and moral affect. As I have maintained, appealing to his concept of the dynamic sublime does not provide an escape. When the sublime as a powerful affect is tamed and configured as the beautiful, it is again under the aegis of reason. When untamed, "the tempestuousness of the sublime and its apprehension through a feeling of enthusiasm [may] lead to the aestheticization of politics as expressed in fascism."[32]

I am grateful for Bergo's reference to Benjamin's allusion of the piling up of ruins, in that ruins can morph into what I call artifactual existents, implements or tools as depicted by pragmatist John Dewey. Abstract as regards the conception of their function and concrete in their material manipulability, tools embody a certain ideality but are made in the interest of an end that is absent and a world that may but has not yet come into existence. Like tools, ruins demonstrate our ability to distinguish their immediate existence from their future usefulness in attesting that which was. The detritus of antecedent life, its ruins, its shards in addition to its writings, are given not only as a system of signs to be deciphered, but as having been embedded in an environing Lebenswelt. Artifactual existents represent a set of actual and possible relations establishing a bond between that which was and that which will be. Consider that as "we gaze at the ruins of Ankhor or the relatively sound Sainte Chapelle each is already fissured by time. Even restoration . . . attests to the depredations of time . . . Each of these instances becomes a simulation of itself in Benjamin's sense of reproduction, but now one that lacks an original. Yet it is time's power negated and the negation of this negation, or denegation as Derrida calls it, that opens the way for an aesthetics of recovery of a past that is present and absent."[33] It is this recovery that is the responsibility of the historian.

Notes

Introduction
Eric Boynton and Martin Kavka

1. Edith Wyschogrod, "Religion as Life and Text: Postmodern Re-figurations," in *The Craft of Religious Studies*, ed. Jon Stone (New York: St. Martin's Press, 1998), 241.

2. See note 8 below.

3. See note 16 below.

4. Wyschogrod, *Crossover Queries: Dwelling with Negatives, Embodying Philosophy's Others* (New York: Fordham University Press, 2006), 2.

5. Wyschogrod, "Religion as Life," 241.

6. Ibid., 242.

7. See *Oxford English Dictionary*, s.v. "stead, v." I.c and ff. http://diction ary.oed.com/cgi/entry/50236596 (accessed March 3, 2007).

8. Wyschogrod, "Sport, Death, and the Elemental," in *The Phenomenon of Death: Faces of Mortality*, ed. Wyschogrod (New York: Harper & Row, 1973), 173.

9. Ibid., 196.

10. Wyschogrod, "Doing Before Hearing: On the Primacy of Touch," in *Textes pour Emmanuel Levinas*, ed. François Laruelle (Paris: Jean-Michel Place, 1980), 185. Part of this essay was revised and expanded in "Empathy and Sympathy as Tactile Encounter," originally published in *The Journal of Medicine and Philosophy* 6 (1981): 23–41, and now reprinted in *Crossover Queries*, 157–72. For another phenomenological analysis of Aristotle's and other ancients' writings on touch, see Jean-Louis Chrétien, *The Call and the Response*, trans. Anne A. Davenport (New York: Fordham University Press, 2004), 83–130.

11. Wyschogrod, "Doing Before Hearing," 194.

12. Ibid., 192.

13. Wyschogrod, *Spirit in Ashes: Hegel, Heidegger, and Man-made Mass Death* (New Haven, Conn.: Yale University Press, 1985), 216.

14. Elie Wiesel, *The Gates of the Forest* (New York: Holt, Rinehart, and Winston, 1966).

15. Wyschogrod, "Hasidism, Hellenism, Holocaust," in *Interpreting Judaism in a Postmodern Age*, ed. Steven Kepnes (New York: NYU Press, 1996), 308.

16. Wyschogrod, *Saints and Postmodernism: Revisioning Moral Philosophy* (Chicago: University of Chicago Press, 1990), 54–58.

17. See Franz Rosenzweig, *The Star of Redemption*, trans. Barbara Galli (Madison: University of Wisconsin Press, 2000), 144–45, where Rosenzweig argues that the multiplicity of created things introduces flux into created life: "The thing does not possess stability as long as it is there quite alone. It is conscious of its singularity, of its individuality, only in the multiplicity of things. The thing can be shown only in connection with other things . . . as specific thing, it has no essence of its own, it does not exist in itself."

18. Wyschogrod, *An Ethics of Remembering: History, Heterology, and the Nameless Others* (Chicago: University of Chicago Press, 1998), xi.

19. Ibid.

20. Ibid., 66.

21. Wyschogrod, "From Neo-Platonism to Souls in Silico: Quests for Immortality," in *Crossover Queries*, 202.

22. Ibid., 201.

23. Wyschogrod, *Saints and Postmodernism*, 36–39.

24. Emmanuel Levinas, *Totality and Infinity: An Essay on Exteriority* (Pittsburgh: Duquesne University Press, 1969), 172.

25. Van A. Harvey, *The Historian and the Believer* (New York: Macmillan, 1966).

26. Wyschogrod, *An Ethics of Remembering*, xiii.

27. Gilles Deleuze and Félix Guattari, *What Is Philosophy?* trans. Hugh Tomlinson and Graham Burchell (New York: Columbia University Press, 1994), 81.

28. Søren Kierkegaard, *Works of Love*, trans. Howard and Edna Hong (New York: Harper & Row, 1962), 201.

29. M. Jamie Ferreira, *Love's Grateful Striving* (Oxford: Oxford University Press, 2001), 141–42.

30. Ibid., 140.

31. See Deleuze and Guattari, *What Is Philosophy?*, 73.

The Uncertainty Principle
Mark C. Taylor

1. Emmanuel Levinas, *Otherwise than Being, or Beyond Essence*, trans. Alphonso Lingis (Dordrecht: Kluwer Academic Publishers, 1991), 15.

2. Edith Wyschogrod, *Saints and Postmodernism: Revisioning Moral Philosophy* (Chicago: University of Chicago Press, 1990), xiii–xiv.

3. Edith Wyschogrod, "The Warring Logics of Genocide," in *Crossover Queries: Dwelling With Negatives, Embodying Philosophy's Others* (New York: Fordham University Press, 2006), 222.

4. Maurice Blanchot, *The Writing of the Disaster*, trans. Ann Smock (Lincoln: University of Nebraska Press, 1986).

5. Edith Wyschogrod, *An Ethics of Remembering: History, Heterology, and the Nameless Others* (Chicago: University of Chicago Press, 1998), 14.

6. Wyschogrod, *Saints and Postmodernism*, xiii.

7. Ibid., 244.

8. Wyschogrod, *Spirit in Ashes: Hegel, Heidegger, and Man-made Mass Death* (New Haven, Conn.: Yale University Press, 1985), x, 15.

9. G. W. F. Hegel, *Phenomenology of Spirit*, trans. A. V. Miller (New York: Oxford University Press, 1977), 355, par. 581 (italics and brackets in the original).

10. Quoted in *Spirit in Ashes*, 92 (italics in the original).

11. Martin Heidegger, *Identity and Difference* (New York: Harper & Row, 1969).

12. Jacques Derrida, "The Pit and the Pyramid: Introduction to Hegel's Semiology," in *Margins of Philosophy*, trans. Alan Bass (Chicago: University of Chicago Press, 1982), 108.

13. Martin Heidegger, *The Question Concerning Technology and Other Essays*, trans. William Lovitt (New York: Harper Torchbooks, 1977), 23, 26.

14. Wyschogrod, *Spirit in Ashes*, 26–27.

15. Ibid., 36.

16. Wyschogrod, "The Warring Logics of Genocide," 234.

17. Ibid., 230.

18. It is important to note that there are ways to interpret the *il y a* that do not collapse differences into "formless being." Levinas's account of *il y a* and *le dire* in *Otherwise than Being, or Beyond Essence* approaches Heidegger's analysis of the *es gibt* through which being is given. The *es gibt* is not formless being, but is the event through which being as such emerges. When understood in this way, Heidegger's *es gibt* and Levinas's *il y a* anticipate Derrida's *différance*. For an elaboration of this reading of Levinas, see Mark C. Taylor, *Altarity* (Chicago: University of Chicago Press, 1987), 185–216.

19. Wyschogrod, *An Ethics of Remembering*, 65.

20. Jean Baudrillard, *Symbolic Exchange and Death*, trans. Ian Grant (London: Sage Publications, 1993), 13, 88.

21. Baudrillard, *The Evil Demon of Images*, (Sydney: Power Institute of Fine Arts, 1987), 23.

22. Ibid., 24–25.

23. Wyschogrod, *An Ethics of Remembering*, 110–11.

24. Ibid., 112.

25. For a more extensive analysis of the multiple religious and aesthetic dimensions of disfiguring, see Mark C. Taylor, *Disfiguring: Art, Architecture, Religion* (Chicago: University of Chicago Press, 1992).

26. Wyschogrod, "The Warring Logics of Genocide," 232.

27. Wyschogrod, *Saints and Postmodernism*, xxi.

28. Ibid., xv.

29. Alterity, of course, entails relation, but it is a relation predicated on exteriority and difference rather than a quasi-interiority and similarity. As connectivity increases, subjectivity becomes nodular. For a consideration of this issue, see Mark C. Taylor, *The Moment of Complexity: Emerging Network Culture* (Chicago: University of Chicago Press, 2001), 195–232.

30. See Maurice Blanchot, *The Unavowable Community*, trans. Pierre Joris (Barrytown: Station Hill Press, 1988) and Alphonso Lingis, *The Community of Those Who Have Nothing in Common* (Bloomington: Indiana University Press, 1994).

The Impossible Possibility of Ethics
Thomas J. J. Altizer

1. Edith Wyschogrod, *Saints and Postmodernism: Revisioning Moral Philosophy* (Chicago: University of Chicago Press, 1990).

2. Wyschogrod, *Spirit in Ashes: Hegel, Heidegger, and Man-made Mass Death* (New Haven, Conn.: Yale University Press, 1985).

3. Friedrich Nietzsche, *The Antichrist*, in *The Portable Nietzsche*, ed. and trans. Walter Kaufmann (New York: Viking, 1954), 586.

4. Edith Wyschogrod, *An Ethics of Remembering: History, Heterology, and the Nameless Others* (Chicago: University of Chicago Press, 1998).

The Empty Suitcase as Rainbow
Merold Westphal

1. Edith Wyschogrod, *Saints and Postmodernism: Revisioning Moral Philosophy* (Chicago: University of Chicago Press, 1990), xvi.

2. Ibid., xxv.

3. Ibid.

4. Philip P. Hallie, *Lest Innocent Blood Be Shed* (New York: HarperPerennial, 1994), 274.

5. Ibid., 273. Hallie, the philosopher, is not entirely precise on epistemic matters. He writes, "Ethics is an interpretation men lay upon the facts, but men can agree on that interpretation" (23). But he also writes, with reference to the belief "that it is better to help than to hurt," that "people like us may violate or compromise that belief in our actions and feelings, but we will never let anybody argue us out of believing it. It is not a matter of opinion for us; it is a fact" (xviii).

6. Hence the following prayer: "Heavenly Father, in you we live and move and have our being: We humbly pray you so to guide and govern us by your Holy Spirit, that in all the cares and occupations of our life we may *not forget* you, but may *remember* that we are ever walking in your sight; through Jesus Christ our Lord. *Amen.*" *The Book of Common Prayer* (New York: Seabury Press, 1979), 100 (emphasis added). Cf. Ecclesiastes 12:1, "Remember your creator in

the days of your youth . . ." Stimulating discussions of remembering and forgetting can be found in Jean-Yves Lacoste, *Experience and the Absolute*, trans. Mark Raftery-Skeban (New York: Fordham University Press, 2004) and Jean-Louis Chrétien, *The Unforgettable and the Unhoped For*, trans. Jeffrey Bloechl (New York: Fordham University Press, 2002).

7. Immanuel Kant, *Grounding for the Metaphysics of Morals*, trans. James W. Ellington (Indianapolis: Hackett, 1981), 20, Ak. 407. Kant is talking about doing the right thing for the wrong motive, but might just as easily have been talking about rationalizing behavior we know to be wrong.

8. Elie Wiesel, foreword to *The Courage to Care: Rescuers of Jews During the Holocaust*, ed. Carol Rittner, RSM, and Sondra Myers (New York: New York University Press, 1986), x. I am indebted to Katie Kirby for calling this volume to my attention.

9. Matt. 13:3–9; Mark 4:3–9; Luke 8:4–8. The parable is explained in subsequent verses.

10. Kant, *Grounding*, 9, Ak. 397.

11. Ibid., 16, Ak. 404. See also ibid., 16, Ak. 405: "Consequently, even wisdom—which consists more in doing and not doing than in knowing—needs science, not in order to learn from it, but in order that wisdom's precepts may gain acceptance and permanence."

12. See also Emmanuel Levinas, "From Consciousness to Wakefulness" and "Philosophy and Awakening," both in *Discovering Existence with Husserl*, trans. Richard A. Cohen and Michael B. Smith (Evanston: Northwestern University Press, 1998).

13. Kant, *Grounding*, 3, Ak. 390.

14. Ibid., 16, Ak. 405.

15. Ibid., 17, Ak. 405.

16. Wyschogrod, *Saints and Postmodernism*, xxiii.

17. See Richard Foster, *Celebration of Discipline: The Path to Spiritual Growth* (San Francisco: Harper & Row, 1978). Foster divides his discussion into three parts: the inward disciplines of private self-formation before God, the outward disciplines that concern the shape of one's life in the world of others, and the corporate disciplines that make spiritual disciplines more (but not less) than merely personal. Cf. Dietrich Bonhoeffer, *Life Together* (New York: Harper & Row, 1954).

18. Alasdair MacIntyre, *After Virtue* (Notre Dame: University of Notre Dame Press, 1981), 181–203.

19. Plato, *Euthydemus* 303a; *Republic* 608a.

20. Plato, *Laws* 741ae.

21. Marcel's account of disposability as this deliberate vulnerability is relevant here. See *Creative Fidelity*, trans. Robert Rosthal (New York: Fordham University Press, 2002), chapters 1–4.

22. Søren Kierkegaard, *Concluding Unscientific Postscript to Philosophical Fragments*, trans. Howard V. Hong and Edna H. Hong (Princeton, N.J.:

Princeton University Press, 1992), I: 203. In the next paragraph, Climacus adds, "But the definition of truth stated above is a paraphrasing of faith. Without risk, no faith. Faith is the contradiction between the infinite passion of inwardness and the objective uncertainty." No doubt there is a correlation between this infinite passion and the infinite responsibility spoken of by both Levinas and Kierkegaard—in *Works of Love*, trans. Howard V. Hong and Edna H. Hong (Princeton, N.J.: Princeton University Press, 1995).

23. Wyschogrod, *Saints and Postmodernism*, p. xxiii.

24. Jean-Luc Marion, *God Without Being*, trans. Thomas A. Carlson (Chicago: University of Chicago Press, 1991), 19–22, 110.

25. Wyschogrod, *Saints and Postmodernism*, xiv, xxiii (emphasis added).

26. Ibid., 34.

27. Ibid., 35.

28. Ibid., 34–39.

29. One might say the same about Karl Marx.

30. Thus Robert McAfee Brown warns that even in the face of radical altruism inspired by religious faith, we should not draw hasty conclusions: "First, there are too many people whose actions on behalf of those in danger spring from other motivations for us to claim that their actions are the result of religious commitment. Second, the overall track record of religious people is abysmally weak" (Brown, "They Could Do No Other," in *The Courage to Care*, 144–45).

31. The combination of the two would be in accord with Jesus' summary of the law and the prophets in terms of the two commandments: to love God with all one's heart and to love one's neighbor as oneself (Matt. 22:34–40).

32. I have in mind a confluence of the vertical and horizontal that is *formally* akin to Weber's notion of innerworldly asceticism in which deeply held religious beliefs decisively influence worldly behavior.

33. Deut. 19:10 (RSV). Not only is Hallie's title drawn from this text, but his narrative is shaped by it.

34. See note 21 above.

35. I don't mean here the religious that has already been reduced to the ethical. For example, Hallie writes, "Our awareness of the preciousness of human life makes our own lives joyously precious to ourselves . . . For me, that awareness is my awareness of God." For him, the God referred to in the Shema ("Hear, oh Israel, the Lord our God, the Lord is One") is "the object of our undivided attention to the lucid mystery of being alive for others and for ourselves." By contrast, the Buddhist recitation

> I go to the Buddha for refuge
> I go to the Dharma for refuge
> I go to the Sangha for refuge

signifies three elements constitutive to the religious as I intend it, often referred to, not too helpfully, as "organized" religion. First there is a super-or-trans-natural metaphysical point of reference; second, there is a doctrine derived from normative, scriptural texts; then there is a structured religious community derived from and in the service of the first two elements. Buddhist apophaticism will deconstruct all three refuges, lest the faithful cling to them, but the *Abgrund* to which it points grows out of this threefold *Grund*. Even Zen masters must be certified.

36. Hallie, xxi.

37. Ibid., 62.

38. Ibid., 34, 265.

39. Martin Buber, *I and Thou*, trans. Walter Kaufmann (New York: Charles Scribner's Sons, 1970), 126–43. The *"causa-sui* project," as described by Ernest Becker, is another version of the "false drive for self-affirmation." See Becker, *The Denial of Death* (New York: Free Press, 1973).

40. Hallie, 58–60.

41. Ibid., 222.

42. Ibid., 83.

43. Ibid., 34 (emphasis added). For Trocmé embodied forgiveness meant self-sacrifice. In 1955 he would write, "The person of any one man is so important in the eyes of God, so central to the whole of His creation, that the unique, perfect being, Jesus, (a) sacrificed his earthly life for that one man in the street, and (b) sacrificed his perfection in order to save that single man. Salvation has been accomplished without any regard to the moral value of the saved man." See Hallie, 160.

44. Ibid., 161. In Kierkegaardian language, we can say that Trocmé and his followers moved from Religiousness B to Religiousness C, in which Jesus is no longer just the Paradox to be believed but the Prototype, Paradigm, Pattern to be imitated. See my "Kierkegaard's Teleological Suspension of Religiousness B," in *Foundations of Kierkegaard's Vision of Community*, ed. George B. Connell and C. Stephen Evans (Atlantic Highlands, N.J.: Humanities Press, 1992).

45. See Brown, 146.

46. Hallie, 46, 92, 107, 146, 159, 161.

47. Ibid., 7.

48. Ibid., 129.

49. "Influenced" would be right, so far as it goes, but the term is too weak here. It is worth noting that "inspiration" is one concept in that semantic spaghetti bowl with which Levinas tries to say what he means by substitution; see *Otherwise Than Being, or Beyond Essence*, trans. Alphonso Lingis (Boston: Kluwer Academic Publishers, 1991), 114, and *Alterity and Transcendence*, trans. Michael B. Smith (New York: Columbia University Press, 1999), 35. For Levinas, "inspiration" signifies the influence of the Other on me, by virtue of which I am able to welcome, even to the point of substitution. In our context the term signifies the influence of the example of another Other that enables that welcome, that substitution. Levinas also discusses inspiration in its more theological home, in connection with the concepts of scripture and revelation. See "On the Jewish Reading of Scriptures" and "Revelation in the Jewish Tradition," both in *Beyond the Verse: Talmudic Readings and Lectures*, trans. Gary D. Mole (Bloomington: Indiana University Press, 1994), 101–15 and 129–50.

50. Hallie's is not the hagiography of pure and sinless holiness. He presents his characters with their warts in full view.

51. Wyschogrod, *Saints and Postmodernism*, xxiii.

52. Hallie, 161 (emphasis added).

53. Wiesel, *The Courage to Care*, 100.

54. As if mindful of Kierkegaard's critique of the preaching he takes to be prevalent in "Christendom," Hallie writes, "A sermon in a Huguenot parish is not a performance that is supposed to be esthetically enjoyed by auditors, and then ignored or praised . . . Behind a Huguenot sermon is the history of a besieged minority trying to keep its moral and religious vitality against great adversity. The sermons of the pastor are one of the main sources of this vitality" (171–72).

55. Hallie, 27, 110, 170.

56. Ibid., 85.

57. Compare Hallie's account of Trocmé's preaching with that of the guest preacher from Switzerland. Ibid., 101, 109, 170.

58. Ibid., 17, 172–73.

59. Ibid., 17.

60. Ibid., 55.

61. Karl Barth, *Church Dogmatics*, vol. 1, part I, *The Doctrine of the Word of God*, trans. G. T. Thompson (Edinburgh: T & T Clark, 1936), §4.

62. "And the Word became flesh and lived among us . . ." John 1:14.

63. "Long ago God spoke to our ancestors in many and various ways by the prophets, but in these last days he has spoken to us by a Son . . ." Heb. 1:1–2.

64. See, for example, the emphasis in the *Lotus Sutra* on hearing, believing, reciting, and preaching the sutra.

65. Perhaps the practice of silence, long since associated with a certain kind of saintly life, needs to be recovered as a necessary condition of hearing the voice of God.

66. Hallie, 20–21.

67. Ibid., 127.

68. Ibid., 154.

69. Ibid., 233. Robert McAfee Brown reports similar reactions among the Danes, who at great risk helped 95 percent of Denmark's Jews to survive the Holocaust; see Brown, 142–44.

70. I am drawing here on *Works of Love*.

71. Beyond the Kantian picture of doing one's duty in the face of only contrary inclinations.

72. Hallie, 21 (emphasis added).

73. Ibid., 284 (emphasis added).

74. Ibid.

75. Ibid., 180.

76. A little more than a month later they were released, against all odds and for no apparent reason. They returned to their dangerous work. Those left behind in the French prison camp "were deported to concentration camps in Poland and salt mines in Silesia. Almost all of them died at hard labor or in the gas chambers of a death camp." See Hallie, 44.

77. Hallie, xv.

78. Philosophers should shake free from Socrates on this point, as Hallie's book itself testifies. For nothing in the story tells us that the lives saved by the Chambonnais were examined lives or that their preciousness required this.

79. Hallie, 8, 12.

80. Ibid., 7.

81. Or perhaps from cynicism, the most popular current form of despair.

82. Hallie, xvii–xviii.

Hosting the Stranger and the Pilgrim: A Christian Theological Reflection
Graham Ward

1. "The Human Cost of Fortress Europe," *Amnesty* 132 (July/August 2005), 18–19.

2. See Jacques Derrida, "At This Very Moment in This Work Here I Am," trans. Ruben Berezdivin, in *Re-Reading Levinas*, eds. Robert Bernasconi and Simon Critchley (Bloomington: Indiana University Press, 1991), 11–48.

3. Edith Wyschogrod, *An Ethics of Remembering: History, Heterology and the Nameless Others* (Chicago: University of Chicago Press, 1998), 144.

4. I could reserve the word *violence* for only those situations in which destruction is without redemption. But, while not sharing Hegel's optimism, I am far from sure we can isolate the purely destructive. Time situates and contextualizes, and all disruption, displacement, interruption are modes of de-creating. As such they are modes of violence. There is no immediate access to what John Milbank, in his *Theology and Social Theory* (Oxford: Blackwell, 1990) has called "an ontology of peace." The grace that enables access is by faith and truly gratuitous (though not, for that, arbitrary). I employ "negative violence" to describe a violation that in wounding paralyzes ongoing relation, and distinguish this mode of violence from that which accompanies critique or deconstruction, which has a telos beyond its immediate effect in the continuation of relation.

5. Mahmoud Darwish, *Victims of a Map*, ed. and trans. Abdullah al-Udhari (London: al-Saqi Books, 1984), 30–31.

6. Wyschogrod, *An Ethics of Remembering*, 5.

7. Ibid., 157 (emphasis mine).

8. See Søren Kierkegaard, *The Sickness Unto Death*, trans. Walter Lowrie, in *A Kierkegaard Anthology*, ed. Robert Bretall (Princeton, N.J.: Princeton University Press, 1973), 339–71.

9. See Kierkegaard, *The Concept of Anxiety*, ed. and trans. Reidar Thomte and Albert B. Anderson (Princeton, N.J.: Princeton University Press, 1980).

10. Emmanuel Levinas, "Who Is One-Self?" in *New Talmudic Readings*, trans. Richard Cohen (Pittsburgh, Pa.: Duquesne University Press, 1999), 113.

11. Jacques Derrida with Anne Dufourmantelle, *Of Hospitality*, trans. Rachel Bowlby (Stanford: Stanford University Press, 2000), 153.

12. See Levinas, "Who Is One-Self?" for an account of "Abraham's glorious humility" (118). Levinas is giving an interpretation of a Talmudic reading of Abraham's acknowledgement before God, "me, ashes and dust"; an acknowledgement that comes at the end of chapter 18, when the three men have left for Sodom and Abraham wrestles with God for the salvation of any righteous in the city. For Levinas, what is glimpsed as glorious in this humility is an "[o]ntology open to the responsibility for the other" (126). "It is the 'as-for-oneself' which discovers itself 'as-for-the-other,' a presentiment of holiness" (122). We will return to Levinas's reading of the other later.

13. See Jacques Derrida, *The Politics of Friendship*, trans. George Collins (London: Verso, 1997) and *Of Hospitality* for discussions of the ambivalence of *hostis* as both host and enemy.

14. Edward Said, "Reflections on Exile," in *Reflections on Exile and Other Literary and Cultural Essays* (London: Granta Publications, 2001), 183.

15. The compiler of *Genesis* structurally relates this story with the reception of the two angels in the city of Sodom (in chapter 19). At the end of the chapter the three men look towards Sodom as if they themselves have been sent by God there to oversee its destruction. The angels, though well received by Lot, are treated shamefully by the "men of the city," who wish to have anal intercourse with them. The act of such intercourse builds a relation between the resident and the alien, a relation of domination. The "men of the city" cannot tolerate the otherness of the stranger. They lack Abraham's humility. Their arrogance as city builders and dwellers is repaid with destruction.

16. *Of Hospitality*, 55. Neither, with Abraham, do we enter the paradoxical problematics of practising hospitality *out of duty* (83).

17. See Graham Ward, *Christ and Culture* (Oxford: Blackwell, 2005), 199ff.

18. There is an interesting collection of essays concerning kenosis and postmodern thought: *Letting Go: Rethinking Kenosis*, ed. Onno Zijlstra (Bern: Peter Lang, 2002).

19. Wyschogrod, *An Ethics of Remembering*, 219.

20. Ibid., 148.

21. Ibid., 240.

22. Emmanuel Levinas, "Meaning And Sense," in *Collected Philosophical Papers*, trans. Alphonso Lingis (The Hague: Martinus Nijhoff, 1987), 91.

23. Ibid., 92.

24. Kierkegaard, *Sickness unto Death*, 351–57.

25. Levinas, "Means of Identification," in *Difficult Freedom*, trans. Seán Hand (London: Athlone, 1990), 51.

26. Paul Claudel, "La Sensation du Divin," in *Nos sens et Dieu: Etude Carmelitaine XXXIII* (Bruges, 1954), 97.

27. Levinas, "God and Philosophy," in *Collected Philosophical Papers,* 169.

28. *Contra Arianos* I:42.

29. Wyschogrod, *An Ethics of Remembering,* 241.

30. Ludwig Wittgenstein, *Philosophical Investigations,* trans. G. E. M. Anscombe (Malden, Mass. and Oxford: Blackwell, 1953), 190.

31. Wyschogrod, *An Ethics of Remembering.,* 240.

32. Levinas, "Meaning And Sense," 92.

33. Ibid.

34. Ibid., 94, 97.

35. Ibid., 94.

36. Jean-Louis Chrétien, *La voix nue: phénoménologie de la promesse* (Paris: Minuit, 1990); *L'appel et la response* (Paris: Minuit, 1992), trans. Anne A. Davenport as *The Call and the Response* (New York: Fordham University Press, 2004); and *L'arche de la parole* (Paris: PUF, 1998), trans. Andrew Brown as *The Ark of Speech* (London and New York: Routledge, 2004).

37. I would add that the theological differences should not be minimized, and Chrétien's own standpoint within Roman Catholicism cannot be underestimated. But what interest me here are the phenomenological investigations each undertakes into the call of the other and the diachrony of the saying in the said.

38. Chrétien, *The Ark of Speech,* 12.

39. Ibid., 10.

40. Chrétien, *The Call and the Response,* 19.

41. Chrétien, "The Wounded Word," in Dominique Janicaud et al., *Phenomenology and the "Theological Turn": The French Debate,* trans. Jeffrey L. Kosky and Thomas A. Carlson (New York: Fordham University Press, 2000), 170.

42. Chrétien, *The Ark of Speech,* 111.

43. Edward Said, "Reflections on Exile," 183.

"God," Gods, God
Adriaan T. Peperzak

1. Edith Wyschogrod, *Crossover Queries: Dwelling with Negatives, Embodying Philosophy's Others* (New York: Fordham University Press, 2006), 5.

2. For a critique of Heidegger's critique of Western ontotheology, see my *Philosophy between Faith and Theology* (Notre Dame, Ind.: University of Notre Dame Press, 2005), 85–102. The label *metaphysics* is less helpful for characterizing the philosophical past, because its meaning is even more ambiguous than that of *ontotheology,* and many writers who use it dismiss what they call *metaphysics* without showing familiarity with any classics of metaphysics by Plato, Aristotle, Plotinus, Thomas, Scotus, Eckhart, Cusanus, Kant, Hegel, or Schelling.

3. God's infinity (which coincides with an absolutely noncomposite simplicity) should, of course, be confused neither with a mathematical kind of endless repetitiousness, which—as "bad infinity"—is a most finite form of finitude, nor with Hegel's own infinity, which coincides with the encompassing concept of totality.

4. For the history of *the infinite*, see, for example, Leo Sweeney, *Divine Infinity in Greek and Medieval Thought* (New York: Peter Lang, 1992) and Anne A. Davenport, *Measure of a Different Greatness: The Intensive Infinite, 1250–1650* (Leiden: Brill, 1999).

5. I capitalize "Desire" to distinguish it from the multiplicity of *epithumiai*, *pathē*, inclinations, *Neigungen*, and *drives* that fight with one another for influence on the motivation of particular decisions, moods, emotions, and types of behavior.

6. This expression (*ho zētoumenos*) is used by Gregory of Nyssa as a name for God in his *Life of Moses*.

7. To what extent the existence of God can be validly *postulated*, for example by Kant in the *Dialectic* of his second *Critique*, should be answered in a separate examination, which I will not develop here. Its result would confirm that the gap that separates the finite terms of the premises from the Infinite of the projected conclusion cannot be bridged except by a leap in the name of some sort of immediate, pre-logical, and always already given link.

8. Cf. Matthew 22:36–40, 25:31–46; Galatians 5:14; 1 John 4:7,12, 20–21.

The Name of God in Levinas's Philosophy
Robert Gibbs

1. Edith Wyschogrod, to whom this essay is devoted, has written and taught in just this vocation. Her own pioneering and extraordinary attention to this call to think and to unsay has both instructed us and displayed a precise sense of what writing can hold open. Moving beyond the place of interpreting Levinas (although she opened up the field for English-speaking philosophers), she continues to explore new areas, crossing disciplinary boundaries. Her work testifies and so inspires me, and many others, to respond to the call.

2. Emmanuel Levinas, *Autrement qu'être ou au-delà de l'essence* (Dordrecht: Martinus Nijhoff, 1974), 206; Emmanuel Levinas, *Otherwise than Being, or Beyond Essence* (The Hague: Martinus Nijhoff, 1981), 162. All translations in this essay are my own.

3. Levinas, "Le Nom de Dieu d'après quelques textes talmudiques," in *L'au-delà du verset: lectures et discours talmudiques* (Paris: Minuit, 1982), 143–57; Levinas, "The Name of God According to a Few Talmudic Texts," trans. Gary D. Mole in *Beyond the Verse* (Bloomington: Indiana University Press, 1994), 116–28.

4. Levinas, *Totalité et l'infini* (The Hague: Martinus Nijhoff, 1961), 50; Levinas, *Totality and Infinity*, trans. Alphonso Lingis (Pittsburgh: Duquesne University Press, 1969), 77.

5. Levinas, *Totalité et l'infini*, 269; Levinas, *Totality and Infinity*, 293.

6. Levinas, *Totalité et l'infini*, 51; Levinas, *Totality and Infinity*, 78–79.

7. Levinas, *Autrement qu'être*, 190; Levinas, *Otherwise than Being*, 149.

8. Levinas, *Autrement qu'être*, 188; Levinas, *Otherwise than Being*, 147.

9. See Robert Gibbs, *Correlations in Rosenzweig and Levinas* (Princeton: Princeton University Press: 1992), 229–54, and *Why Ethics? Signs of Responsibilities* (Princeton: Princeton University Press: 2000), 131–224.

10. Levinas, *Autrement qu'être*, 201–02; Levinas, *Otherwise than Being*, 158.

11. See Gibbs, *Why Ethics?* 66–113.

12. Levinas, *Autrement qu'être*, 217; Levinas, *Otherwise than Being*, 171.

13. Levinas, *Autrement qu'être*, 193; Levinas, *Otherwise than Being*, 151.

14. Levinas, *Autrement qu'être*, 199; Levinas, *Otherwise than Being*, 156.

15. Levinas, *Au-delà du verset*, 147; Levinas, *Beyond the Verse*, 119.

16. B. Berakhot 12a.

17. Levinas, *Au-delà du verset*, 150–51; Levinas, *Beyond the Verse*, 122.

18. See Hayyim ben Isaac Volozhiner, *Nefesh ha-Hayyim*, II:1, and *Midrash Tehillim* 16: 8.

19. Levinas, *Au-delà du verset*, 149; Levinas, *Beyond the Verse*, 121. See Derrida's citation and interpretation of this passage in "En ce moment même dans cet ouvrage me voici," in *Textes pour Emmanuel Levinas*, ed. François Laruelle (Paris: Jean-Michel Place, 1980), 57–58; "At This Very Moment in This Work Here I Am," trans. Ruben Berezdivin, in *Re-Reading Levinas*, eds. Robert Bernasconi and Simon Critchley (Bloomington: Indiana University Press, 1991), 45.

20. Levinas, *Au-delà du verset*, 153; Levinas, *Beyond the Verse*, 124.

21. B. Shevuot 35b; B. Shabbat 127a.

22. Levinas, *Au-delà du verset*, 154; Levinas, *Beyond the Verse*, 125.

23. 23. Levinas, *Au-delà du verset*, 155ff.; Levinas, *Beyond the Verse*, 126ff.

Kenotic Overflow and Temporal Transcendence: Angelic Embodiment and the Alterity of Time in Abraham Abulafia
Elliot R. Wolfson

1. Elliot R. Wolfson, "From Sealed Book to Open Text: Time, Memory, and Narrativity in Kabbalistic Hermeneutics," in *Interpreting Judaism in a Postmodern Age*, ed. Steven Kepnes (New York: New York University Press, 1995), 145–178; Wolfson, "The Cut that Binds: Time, Memory, and the Ascetic Impulse," in *God's Voice from the Void: Old and New Studies in Bratslav Hasidism*, ed. Shaul Magid (Albany: State University of New York Press, 2002), 103–154; Wolfson, *Alef, Mem, Tau: Kabbalistic Musings on Time, Truth, and Death* (Berkeley: University of California Press, 2006). For a philosophical account of hermeneutics and the phenomenon of time reversibility, see Wolfson, *Language, Eros, Being: Kabbalistic Hermeneutics and Poetic Imagination* (New York: Fordham University Press, 2005), xv–xxxi.

2. Friedrich Nietzsche, "The Convalescent," in *Thus Spoke Zarathustra: A Book for All and None*, trans. Walter Kaufmann (New York: Modern Library, 1995), III:13, 217–218: "In every Now, being begins; round every Here rolls the sphere There. The center is everywhere. Bent is the path of eternity." See also "On The Vision And The Riddle," III:2, 158. After describing the meeting of two paths of eternity in the gateway of the moment, one that stretches backward

and the other that extends forward, Nietzsche has the dwarf proclaim, "All that is straight lies . . . All truth is crooked; time itself is a circle." Significantly, the image of the circle is juxtaposed to the notion of crookedness. A crooked circle is a curve, a break in a cyclical pattern of repetition. See note 7 below. My interpretation of Nietzsche is indebted to the nuanced analysis in Edith Wyschogrod, *An Ethics of Remembering: History, Heterology, and the Nameless Others* (Chicago: University of Chicago Press, 1998), 155–159.

3. See Wolfson, *Alef, Mem, Tau*, 174, and a select number of sources cited at 217n118, a list to which many more could have been added.

4. See, for instance, Joseph Gikatilla, *Ginnat Egoz* (Jerusalem, 1989), 26–27: "And what you must contemplate is that this name [YHWH] stands without any change, and just as he does not change, so the name that is unique to him does not change, and his name, blessed be he, attests to the secret of his existence and the truth of his being, before the world was created, in the existence of the world. And after the existence of the world, as it says 'the Lord reigns' (Ps. 10:16), 'the Lord reigned' (Ps. 93:1), 'the Lord will reign' (Exod. 15:18), thus you [discern that] 'reigns' (*melekh*) is the present (*howeh*), 'reigned' is the past (*we-hayah*), and 'will reign' is the future (*we-yihyeh*). And concerning the three-fold occurrence in this verse of YHWH, YHWH, YHWH, their secret is present, past, and future (*howeh we-hayah we-yihyeh*), corresponding to 'reigns' (*melekh*), 'reigned' (*malakh*), and 'will reign' (*yimlokh*). Thus, you [discern] that his name attests that he was before time, in time, and after time, for he does not change from his essence, blessed be he." See also ibid., 60–61, 163, 221–222. On the unique role assigned to the Tetragrammaton as the only name that can instruct one about the existence and essence of the divine, see Joseph Gikatilla, *Hassagot le-Sefer Moreh Nevukhim*, in Isaac Abarbanel, *Ketavim al Maḥshevet Yisra'el*, vol. 3 (Jerusalem, 1967), 23d. See also *Midrash Simeon ha-Ṣaddiq* in *Qabbalat ha-Ge'onim* (Jerusalem, 2006), 19. Concerning the provenance of this text, see Mark Verman, *The Books of Contemplation: Medieval Jewish Mystical Sources* (Albany: State University of New York Press, 1992), 79, 211–212.

5. Wolfson, *Alef, Mem, Tau*, 76–78. The view I attribute to kabbalists resonates with the temporalization of the eternal affirmed by some nineteenth-century German Romantic philosophers. See Arthur O. Lovejoy, *The Great Chain of Being: A Study of the History of an Idea* (Cambridge, Mass.: Harvard University Press, 1936), 317–326, and my own brief discussion of Schelling in *Alef, Mem, Tau*, 34–42.

6. Wyschogrod, *An Ethics of Remembering*, 147.

7. Recall the language of Nietzsche, *Thus Spoke Zarathustra*, III:2, 158: "Behold . . . this moment! From this gateway, Moment, a long, eternal lane leads backward: behind us lies an eternity. Must not whatever can walk have walked on this lane before? . . . And are not all things knotted together so firmly that this moment draws after it all that is to come? Therefore—itself too? For whatever can walk—in this long lane out there too, it must walk once more" (emphasis in original).

8. Gilles Deleuze, "Active and Reactive," trans. Richard Cohen, in *The New Nietzsche: Contemporary Styles of Interpretation*, ed. David B. Allison (New York: Delta Books, 1977), 86.

9. Gilles Deleuze, *Difference and Repetition*, trans. Paul Patton (New York: Columbia University Press, 1994), 242–243.

10. Gilles Deleuze, *Pure Immanence: Essays on a Life*, trans. Anne Boyman (New York: Zone Books, 2001), 87 (emphasis in original).

11. For an earlier expression of this motif, see Wolfson, "Divine Suffering and the Hermeneutics of Reading: Philosophical Reflections on Lurianic Mythology," in *Suffering Religion*, eds. Robert Gibbs and Elliot R. Wolfson (London: Routledge, 2002), 115–116.

12. Here I list a sampling of the studies on Abulafia and his school of mystical thought and practice, but let me preface the list by saying I am citing only a portion of the published research of Moshe Idel on this topic, though in subsequent notes, interested readers will find reference to other works of his: Gershom Scholem, *Major Trends in Jewish Mysticism* (New York: Schocken Books, 1956), 119–155; Scholem, *The Kabbalah of Sefer ha-Temunah and Abraham Abulafia*, ed. Joseph Ben-Shlomo (Jerusalem: Akkademon, 1965) (Hebrew); Scholem, *Kabbalah* (Jerusalem: Keter, 1974), 53–55, 180–181; Moshe Idel, *The Mystical Experience in Abraham Abulafia* (Albany: State University of New York Press, 1988); Idel, *Studies in Ecstatic Kabbalah* (Albany: State University of New York Press, 1988); Idel, *Kabbalah: New Perspectives* (New Haven, Conn.: Yale University Press, 1988), 61–67, 97–103; Idel, *Language, Torah, and Hermeneutics in Abraham Abulafia* (Albany: State University of New York Press, 1989); Idel, "The Contribution of Abraham Abulafia's Kabbalah to the Understanding of Jewish Mysticism," in *Gershom Scholem's Major Trends in Jewish Mysticism 50 Years After*, eds. Joseph Dan and Peter Schäfer (Tübingen: J. C. B. Mohr, 1993), 117–143; Idel, "Abulafia's Secrets of the Guide: A Linguistic Turn," in *Perspectives on Jewish Thought and Mysticism*, eds. Alfred Ivry, Elliot R. Wolfson, and Allan Arkush (Amsterdam: Harwood Academic Publishers, 1998), 289–329; Idel, *Absorbing Perfections: Kabbalah and Interpretation* (New Haven, Conn.: Yale University Press, 2002), 314–351; Idel, "The Kabbalistic Interpretation of the Secret of ʿArayot in Early Kabbalah," *Kabbalah: Journal for the Study of Jewish Mystical Texts* 12 (2004): 89–199 (Hebrew); Wolfson, *Abraham Abulafia—Kabbalist and Prophet: Hermeneutics, Theosophy, and Theurgy* (Los Angeles: Cherub Press, 2000); Ron Kiener, "From *Baʿal ha-Zohar* to Prophet to Ecstatic: The Vicissitudes of Abulafia in Contemporary Scholarship," in *Gershom Scholem's Major Trends in Jewish Mysticism 50 Years After*, 145–159; Meirav Karmeli, "Men of the Ladder: The Explication of R. Abraham Abulafia to the Section 'Wa-yeṣe' in Genesis in Comparison with Other Thinkers" (master of arts thesis, Hebrew University, [2002]) (Hebrew); Harvey J. Hames, "The Resurgence of Mysticism in the Kingdom of Aragon in the Thirteenth Century: Abraham Abulafia and His Place in Contemporary Society," (master of philosophy thesis, Cambridge University, [1992]); Hames, "From Calabria Cometh the Law, and

the Word of the Lord from Sicily: The Holy Land in the Thought of Joachim of Fiore and Abraham Abulafia," *Mediterranean Historical Review* 20 (2005): 187–199; Hames, *Like Angels on Jacob's Ladder: Abraham Abulafia, the Franciscans and Joachismism* (Albany: State University of New York Press, 2007).

13. Moshe Idel, "Some Concepts of Time and History in Kabbalah," in *Jewish History and Jewish Memory: Essays in Honor of Yosef Hayim Yerushalmi*, eds. Elisheva Carlebach, John M. Efron, and David N. Myers (Hanover, Md.: Brandeis University Press, 1998), 170–176; Idel, "'The Time of the End': Apocalypticism and Its Spiritualization in Abraham Abulafia's Eschatology," in *Apocalyptic Time*, ed. Albert I. Baumgarten (Leiden: Brill, 2000), 155–185.

14. See Wolfson, *Abraham Abulafia*, 152–154, and the relevant studies of Scholem and Idel cited at 153–154nn158–161.

15. Idel, *Studies*, 144n22, suggests that Abulafia's use of the term *derekh* betrays the influence of the word *tariqa* as it is employed in the Sufi lexicon. See note 138 below.

16. Scholem, *Major Trends*, 136–138; Idel, *Mystical Experience*, 14–24; Idel, *Language*, 101–109. For a more elaborate account of the textual and historical background to this taxonomic understanding of kabbalah, see Idel, "Defining Kabbalah: The Kabbalah of the Divine Names," in *Mystics of the Book: Topics, Themes, and Typologies*, ed. Robert A. Herrera (New York: Peter Lang, 1993), 97–122.

17. Abraham Abulafia, *Ḥayyei ha-Olam ha-Ba*, 2nd. ed. (Jerusalem, 1999), 73.

18. Moses Maimonides, *The Guide of the Perplexed*, trans. Shlomo Pines (Chicago: University of Chicago Press, 1963), II:12, 279.

19. Abulafia, *Ḥayyei ha-Olam ha-Ba*, 56.

20. Abulafia, *Or ha-Sekhel* (Jerusalem, 2001), 115–116. Concerning this terminology in Abulafia, see Idel, *Mystical Experience*, 130–131.

21. Judah Halevi, *Sefer ha-Kuzari*, trans. Yehuda Even Shmuel (Tel-Aviv: Dvir Publishing, 1972), IV:15, 172, and see the brief but incisive characterization in Harry A. Wolfson, *Studies in the History of Philosophy and Religion*, eds. Isadore Twersky and George H. Williams (Cambridge, Mass.: Harvard University Press, 1977), 2:141.

22. It should be noted that the equation of Torah and the Tetragrammaton affirmed by Abulafia and his disciples is accepted as well by kabbalists that have been placed into the school of theosophic kabbalah according to the reigning typological taxonomy adopted by contemporary scholars of Jewish mysticism. This is one of several main principles shared by the different trends of medieval kabbalah, a sharing that at least problematizes to some degree the sharp distinctions made between so-called theosophic and ecstatic kabbalists.

23. Abulafia, *Mafteaḥ ha-Ḥokhmot* (Jerusalem, 2001), 60.

24. Idel, *Language*, 12–14, 16–27, 143, 145n55, 146n71; Wolfson, *Abraham Abulafia*, 58–59, 62–64. The derivative status of all languages from Hebrew

is expressed by the numerical equation of the expressions *shiv'im leshonot* ("seventy languages") and *ṣeruf ha-otiyyot* ("permutation of the letters"). See Idel, *Language*, 142n47. Abulafia's distinction between the conventional status of all languages and the exceptional status of Hebrew as the natural language is affirmed as well by Gikatilla, *Hassagot*, 20a–b.

25. Wolfson, *Language, Eros, Being*, 197–202.

26. *Sefer Yeṣirah* (Jerusalem: Yeshivat Kol Yehuda, 1990), 2:2. According to the surmise of A. Peter Hayman, *Sefer Yeṣira: Edition, Translation and Text-critical Commentary* (Tübingen: Mohr Siebeck, 2004), 53 and 102–103, these words do not belong to the earliest layer of the text. In my judgment, to speak of *Sefer Yeṣirah* in these terms has little meaning, since it is not possible to reconstruct the earliest layers of the text given the material that is extant. Indeed, I would go further and say that there is no such thing as the earliest layer; the text took shape over a course of many years and up to a certain point (around the time that commentaries begin to be written and the text is stabilized to some degree in its different recensions) there is no credible way to distinguish "original" layers and supplemental accretions. See Hayman's own observations in "The 'Original Text': A Scholarly Illusion?" in *Words Remembered, Texts Renewed: Essays in Honour of John F. A. Sawyer*, eds. Jon Davies, Graham Harvey and Wilfred G. E. Watson (Sheffield: Sheffield Academic Press, 1995), 434–449.

27. Abulafia, *Oṣar Eden Ganuz* (Jerusalem, 2000), 66.

28. Scholem, *Major Trends*, 131; Idel, *Mystical Experience*, 134–137.

29. In *Oṣar Eden Ganuz*, 344, Abulafia applies the dictum transmitted in the name of R. Ishmael, which he refers to as a *qabbalah*, concerning knowledge of the measurement of the Creator (*shi'uro shel yoṣer bere'shit*) to gnosis of the Tetragrammaton. To be sure, already in the ancient *Shi'ur Qomah* fragments, two strands of tradition are woven together such that inconceivable physical dimensions and incomprehensible magical names are attributed to the limbs of the divine. However, Abulafia has reinterpreted the tradition by denying the former entirely and collapsing the very idea of corporeal proportions in his notion of the magnitude of the name. Underlying this strategy is the alternative conception of linguistic embodiment. See Wolfson, *Language, Eros, Being*, 190–260, and esp. 236–242 where other Abulafian material is engaged.

30. For instance, see Abulafia, *Imrei Shefer* (Jerusalem, 1999), 190: "Know that *alef* is one, and it is the matter of all the *sefirot* in thought, but *yod*, which is ten, is their end. Therefore, they called it *shekhinah*, which is the end of thought. But *yod*, which is the matter of the twenty-two letters, and also *alef*, is their end, for it is the great body [*ha-guf ha-gadol*] that is in all of their forms."

31. Abulafia, *Ḥayyei ha-Olam ha-Ba*, 159.

32. Abulafia, *Sefer ha-Ḥesheq* (Jerusalem, 2002), 10.

33. For a discussion of the phenomenon of receiving God's name according to the prophetic kabbalah, set against the background of the philosophical notion of the continuous chain of being, see Idel, *Enchanted Chains: Techniques and Rituals in Jewish Mysticism* (Los Angeles: Cherub Press, 2005), 76–109.

34. Idel, *Mystical Experience*, 124–134; Idel, *Studies*, 1–31.

35. Abulafia, *Ḥayyei ha-Olam ha-Ba*, 79.

36. On the identification of the Active Intellect and the Holy Spirit, see Halevi, *Kuzari* I:87, 28.

37. Abulafia, *Or ha-Sekhel*, 114.

38. Abulafia, *Imrei Shefer*, 104–105. See ibid., 106–17, where the rabbinic idiom "speculum that shines" [*aspaqlaryah ha-me'irah*] is applied to the ten *sefirot*, that is, the ten separate intellects, which are like a mirror (*mar'ah*) in which one sees the forms of all reality.

39. Scholem, *Major Trends*, 139–140; Idel, *Mystical Experience*, 116–119.

40. The confusion of ontic boundary between angel and God is a much older motif that I have long thought serves as one of the most archaic elements of Jewish esotericism, an idea that has much relevance to assessing the points of convergence and divergence in the mystical currents of the three Abrahamic faiths, Judaism, Christianity, and Islam, a point I share with Henry Corbin. For references to my work on the matter of the glorious angel or angelic glory, and citation of other relevant scholarly treatments, see Wolfson, *Language, Eros, Being*, 430–431n354, 543n421. In that context, I neglected to mention the study by Daniel Abrams, "The Boundaries of Divine Ontology: The Inclusion and Exclusion of Metatron in the Godhead," *Harvard Theological Review* 87 (1994): 291–321.

41. Abulafia, *Oṣar Eden Ganuz*, 139.

42. The role of the Active Intellect as the medium underlies Abulafia's insistence that the Torah is the intermediary, an identification based on the numerical equivalence of the words *torah* (400 + 6 + 200 + 5 = 611) and *emṣaʿit* (1 + 40 + 90 + 70 + 10 + 400 = 611). See Idel, *Language*, 37–38.

43. In this connection, it is of interest to note Abulafia's remark in *Imrei Shefer*, 85, that the description of wisdom as God's "confidant" [*amon*] in Proverbs 8:30 refers to one "who is human [*ben adam*] from one side and an angel [*mal'akh*] from the other."

44. For discussion of this aspect of Abulafia's understanding of prophecy, see Idel, *Mystical Experience*, 89–90, 100–104. With respect to the matter of the angelic body beheld in the prophetic vision, there is an interesting affinity between Abulafia's kabbalah and Islamic mysticism, especially Shīʿite esotericism as presented by Henry Corbin. See Wolfson, *Language, Eros, Being*, 239.

45. Abulafia, *Ḥayyei ha-Olam ha-Ba*, 49.

46. Abraham Abulafia, *Sefer ha-Malmad* (Jerusalem, 2002), 18.

47. Idel, *Studies*, 9–10. It is worth recalling here the statement of Maimonides, *Guide*, I:62, 152, that divine science (*ḥokhmat ha-elohut*), i.e., metaphysics, which he also identifies as the rabbinic "account of the chariot" [*maʿaseh merkavah*], consists of "the apprehension of the Active Intellect." See Shlomo Pines, "The Limitations of Human Knowledge according to Al-Farabi, ibn Bajja, and Maimonides," in *Studies in Medieval Jewish History and Literature*, ed. Isadore Twersky (Cambridge, Mass.: Harvard University Press, 1979), 90–91; Alexander

Altmann, *Von der mittelalterlichen zur modernen Aufklärung: Studien zur jüdischen Geistesgeschichte* (Tübingen: J. C. B. Mohr, 1987), 118–119; Herbert A. Davidson, "Maimonides on Metaphysical Knowledge," *Maimonidean Studies* 3 (1992–93): 92–98.

48. Abulafia, *Sefer ha-Ḥesheq*, 8.

49. See especially the words of Maimonides, *Guide*, II:6, 264–265: "Thereby we have stated plainly to him who understands and cognizes intellectually that the imaginative faculty is likewise called an *angel* and that the intellect is called a *cherub* . . . We have already spoken of the fact that every form in which an *angel* is seen, exists *in the vision of prophecy*" (emphasis in original). On the identification in Maimonides of the angelic form seen and/or heard in prophecy as either the Active Intellect or the imaginative faculty, an imprecision that doubtlessly influenced Abulafia, see Howard Kreisel, *Prophecy: The History of an Idea in Medieval Jewish Philosophy* (Dordrecht: Kluwer Academic Publishers, 2001), 236–237.

50. The positive valorization of imagination can be seen, for instance, in Abulafia's explanation in *Sitrei Torah*, 21, of the "image" and "likeness" with which Adam was created according to the biblical account (Gen. 1:26): "Thus it has been explained that the matter of the image [*ṣelem*] is the form of intellect [*ṣurat sekhel*], and the matter of the likeness [*demut*] is the image of knowledge [*dimyon daʿat*], for it is known that intellect and imagination are the image and likeness." To grasp the import of the last sentence, one must bear in mind that the expressions *ha-sekhel we-ha-dimyon yeduʿim* and *ṣelem u-demut* both numerically equal 616.

51. Abulafia, *Oṣar Eden Ganuz*, 121, cited in Idel, *Language*, 21, 56–57, and see Idel, *Studies*, 35–39.

52. Abulafia, *Oṣar Eden Ganuz*, 83.

53. Here, as elsewhere in my work, I am thinking in the footsteps of Henry Corbin. For a more extensive discussion of the incarnational element of Corbin's thinking, with reference to other places in my own work where this influence is detectable, see Wolfson, "Imago Templi and the Meeting of the Two Seas: Liturgical Time-Space and the Feminine Imaginary in Zoharic Kabbalah," *Res: Anthropology and Aesthetics* 51 (2007): 121–125.

54. On this threefold classification in Abulafia, see the passages from *Mafteah ha-Shemot* and *Sefer ha-Meliṣ* cited and analyzed in Idel, *Studies*, 38–39. See also *Sefer ha-Malmad*, 18, where Abulafia speaks of the "matter of prophecy" in the threefold manner of the "creation of the human body," the "creation of Satan," and the "creation of the angel."

55. Abulafia, *Imrei Shefer*, 26.

56. Idel, *Mystical Experience*, 96–97; Idel, "Kabbalistic Interpretation," 161n507.

57. Abulafia, *Sefer ha-Malmad*, 3.

58. Ibid., 44. This passage is cited and analyzed by Idel, "Some Concepts," 174.

59. Abulafia repeatedly uses the image of the warp and woof (*sheti wa-erev*) to characterize form and matter. For instance, see *Or ha-Sekhel*, 94; In a number of contexts, the expression *sheti wa-erev* is transposed into *berit esaw*, that is, the "covenant of Esau." See *Perush Sefer Yeṣirah Almoni mi-Yesodo shel Rabbi Avraham Abula'fiyah*, ed. Israel Weinstock (Jerusalem: Mosad ha-Rav Kook, 1984), 29; *Oṣar Eden Ganuz*, 9, 286.

60. I am here deliberately avoiding the question of the precise definition of humanity in Abulafia's writings. The matter is complex, as, in some passages, he affirms a more philosophical approach akin to that of Maimonides and thereby views the rational faculty as the distinctive mark of *homo sapiens* regardless of the ethnic or religious backgrounds of particular human beings. There is, however, another perspective attested in his teaching, an identification of the true human with Israel, an ethnocentric position that accords better with the esoteric and/or mystical material that influenced him. According to the latter perspective, it is not only the case that the tradition about the name and the possibility of attaining prophecy implied thereby is unique to the Jewish nation (see, for example, *Imrei Shefer*, 195–196), but the latter alone seem capable of being transformed angelically by means of the experience of conjunction. For a preliminary discussion of this issue, see Wolfson, *Venturing Beyond: Law and Morality in Kabbalistic Mysticism* (Oxford: Oxford University Press, 2006), 58–73. A gesture towards a more universalistic orientation can be located in Abulafia's surmise in *Mafteaḥ ha-Shemot* that in the future all three Abrahamic religions will know the supreme name of God. See Idel, *Studies*, 50. The messianic vision is anticipated to some degree by Abulafia's claim that the seventy languages are all contained within Hebrew, a view that attenuates to some extent the seemingly insurmountable distinction he makes between Hebrew as the natural language and all other languages as conventional. On this point, see Idel, *Studies*, 50n24, and see especially the passage from *Ner Elohim* cited by Idel, *Language*, 19. See also Abulafia's remark in *Ḥayyei ha-Nefesh* (Jerusalem, 2001), 10: "There is no doubt that in every language secrets from this matter can be found, for the final intention of human existence is to reach perfection, and the ultimate of all perfections is knowledge of God, blessed be he, and on this is dependent the life of the world-to-come."

61. Abulafia, *Perush Sefer Yeṣirah*, 29.

62. On the collaboration between intellect and imagination, the angel and Satan, see the text from *Oṣar Eden Ganuz* cited by Idel, *Language*, 19.

63. Wolfson, *Abraham Abulafia*, 167–168n197.

64. Abraham Abulafia, *Ish Adam*, in *Maṣref ha-Sekhel* (Jerusalem, 2001), 44, and see Wolfson, *Abraham Abulafia*, 220n125.

65. Abulafia, *Oṣar Eden Ganuz*, 344. On the numerical equivalence of the words *qarov* and *raḥoq*, see Baruch Togarmi, *Maftehot ha-Qabbalah*, in Scholem, *Kabbalah of Sefer ha-Temunah*, 236.

66. Abraham Abulafia, *Sitrei Torah* (Jerusalem, 2002), 149–151. For an alternative translation and analysis of this passage, see Idel, *Mystical Experience*, 96–97.

67. This is the reading in the printed edition and it is supported by MS Paris, Bibliothèque Nationale héb. 774, fol. 159b. The transcription of this manuscript version in Idel, *Mystical Experience*, 96, "*koaḥ ha-meʿorer*," should be corrected. The text has been properly transcribed in the Hebrew edition of Idel's *The Mystical Experience in Abraham Abulafia* (Jerusalem: Magnes Press, 1988), 78. On the use of the term *koaḥ ha-mitʿorer*, see also *Sitrei Torah*, 138.

68. Abulafia, *Sitrei Torah*, 150.

69. Ibid.

70. Ibid.

71. For a similar phenomenological reading of the concept of *et* in zoharic kabbalah as the interval that demarcates concomitantly the unification and separation of opposites, see Wolfson, *Alef, Mem, Tau*, 98–107.

72. Abulafia, *Sitrei Torah*, 150.

73. Ibid.

74. See the important passage from Togarmi's *Maftehot ha-Qabbalah* transcribed in Scholem, *Kabbalah of Sefer ha-Temunah*, 234: "Thus, I have said to you above in explicating the scale of merit and the scale of guilt that the two of them are the word of the tongue [*millat lashon*] and the letters of the foreskin [*otiyyot maʿor*], that is, between the two of them there are four matters. With respect to the mouth, which is the tongue, the wise one said concerning it, 'Death and life are in the power of the tongue' (Prov. 18:21). And with respect to the phallus [*milah*], which is the covenant [*berit*], there is the obligatory intercourse [*beʿilat miṣwah*], [connected to] procreation [*periyyah u-reviyyah*], and there is the illicit intercourse [*beʿilat zenut*], and the two of them are the secret of Paradise [*gan eden*], that is 'the mouth or mouth' [*peh o peh*] . . . 'the phallus or the phallus' [*milah o milah*] . . . Adam and Eve [*adam we-ḥawah*] . . . the Jew and Gentile [*ha-yehudi we-ha-goy*] . . . and the two of them are hot and cold [*ḥam we-qar*], cold and hot [*qar we-ḥam*]. And with this the secret of the marking [*qaʿaqa*] [Lev. 19:28] will be known to you, for they are the mouth of the phallus [*peh milah*], the phallus of the mouth [*milah peh*], and the two of them are Shaddai YHWH." Explicating the parallelism between the covenant of the tongue and the covenant of the foreskin affirmed in *Sefer Yeṣirah*, Togarmi emphasizes that each one exemplifies a polarity: the former embraces death and life, and the latter the permissible and forbidden forms of cohabitation. The critical claim is Togarmi's further observation regarding the ultimate unity of these oppositional pairs, a point that is confirmed in the statement that the "two of them are the secret of Paradise." The identity of opposites is corroborated by the numerical equivalences of the expressions *gan eden* (3 + 50 + 70 + 4 + 50 = 177), *peh o peh* (80 + 5 + 1 + 6 + 80 + 5 = 177), *milah o milah* (40 + 10 + 30 + 5 + 1 + 6 + 40 + 10 + 30 + 5 = 177), as well as the numerical equivalences of *adam we-ḥawah* (1 + 4 + 40 + 6 + 8 + 6 + 5 = 70) and *ha-yehudi we-ha-goy* (5 + 10 + 5 + 6 + 4 + 10 + 6 + 5 + 3 + 6 + 10 = 70). The duplicity is also expressed as the pairing of hot and cold, *ḥam we-qar* or *qar we-ḥam*, each of which equals 354, which is the sum of the combination of *peh o peh* (= 177)

and *milah o milah* (= 177). Finally, this insight is related to the shared numero-logical value of the expression *qaʿaqa* (100 + 70 + 100 + 70 = 340), a word especially suitable to denote duality, inasmuch as it is composed of the doubling of the two letters *qof* and *ayin*, and the sum of *peh milah* (80 + 5 + 40 + 10 + 30 + 5 = 170) and *milah peh* (40 + 50 + 30 + 5 + 80 + 50 = 170), which is also the value of the amalgamation of the two names, Shaddai (300 + 4 + 10 = 314) and YHWH (10 + 5 + 6 + 5 = 26). Togarmi alludes to the same principle in another passage (*Kabbalah of Sefer ha-Temunah*, 235) by noting that the "profane language" [*leshon ha-ḥol*] and "sacred language" [*leshon ha-qodesh*] as well as the "language of blood" [*leshon ha-dam*] and the "language of faith" [*leshon ha-dat*] are all in the "power of the supernal world" [*bi-reshut ha-olam ha-elyon*]. For a reverberation of Togarmi's chain of associations, see Abulafia, *Oṣar Eden Ganuz*, 110.

75. *Sefer Yeṣirah*, 1:7; Hayman, *Sefer Yeṣira*, 74–76.

76. Abulafia, *Oṣar Eden Ganuz*, 20.

77. See Ithamar Gruenwald, "Some Critical Notes on the First Part of *Sēfer Yeẓirā*," *Revue des études juives* 132 (1973): 492; Wolfson, *Abraham Abulafia*, 143–144.

78. *Sefer Yeṣirah*, 3:2; Hayman, *Sefer Yeṣira*, 110–112.

79. Abulafia, *Oṣar Eden Ganuz*, 111.

80. Idel, *Language*, 61–63, discusses the notion of "trial" in Abulafia's thought, and specifically as it is related exegetically to the narrative of the binding of Isaac, in terms of the intellect overpowering the imagination, the overpowering of the good inclination over the evil inclination.

81. Abulafia, *Sitrei Torah*, 151.

82. This is the figurative understanding of the exodus of Egypt offered by Abulafia. See Idel, *Language*, 69.

83. Carl G. Jung, *Mysterium Coniunctionis: An Inquiry Into the Separation and Synthesis of Psychic Opposites in Alchemy*, trans. R. F. C. Hull (Princeton, N.J.: Princeton University Press, 1970), 16–17, 79, 93, 97, 101, 184–185, 187, 295, 304, 340, 490–491, 506–507, 510; Jung, *Alchemical Studies*, trans. R. F. C. Hull (Princeton, N.J.: Princeton University Press, 1970), 217–220. Affinities between Mercury (the Roman analogue to Hermes) and Metatron, including the roles of mediator and scribe, have been noted by Nathaniel Deutsch, *Guardians of the Gate: Angelic Vice Regency in Late Antiquity* (Leiden: Brill, 1999), 164–167. On the ascription of the images of scribe and mediator to the figures of Enoch and Metatron, including references to Mesopotamian sources whence the later traditions may have evolved, see Andrei A. Orlov, *The Enoch-Metatron Tradition* (Tübingen: Mohr Siebeck, 2005), 34–37, 50–70, 97–101, 104–112, 184–188, 203–207.

84. See, for example, Abraham Abulafia, *Ḥotam ha-Hafṭarah*, in *Maṣref ha-Sekhel*, 112: "On account of this he is the angel of the moon, and the name that is unique to him in truth is 'Metatron, the archon of the face,' and [the designa-tion] 'Mordecai the Jew' is attributed to him. Therefore, we say [B. Megillah 7b]

arur haman ['cursed be Haman'] and *barukh mordekhai* ['blessed be Mordecai']."
To articulate the two-faced nature of Metatron, Abulafia utilizes the rabbinic directive that on Purim one should drink to the point of no longer discerning the difference between the wicked Haman and the righteous Mordecai (the collapse of opposites is based on the numerical equivalence of the expressions *arur haman* [1 + 200 + 6 + 200 +5 +40 + 50 = 502] and *barukh mordekhai* [2 +200+ 6 + 20 + 40 + 200 + 4 + 20 + 10 = 502]). See also *Imrei Shefer*, 62: "It is known that the letter *yod*, which is the first of the name, is numerically ten [*asarah*], and it is known that when you invert [the letters of *asarah*] you have the wicked one [*ha-rasha*] who surrounds the righteous . . . and the secret of the ten [*asarah*] is the evil inclination [*yeṣer ha-ra*] [*asarah* and *yeṣer ha-ra* both equal 575], and he governs the lower world. In the beginning of his being he was matter without form, and when he received form there arose from him a being that is called 'man' [*ish*], and the *yod* is within the fire [*esh*], and every form [*ṣurah*] is fire [*esh*] [*ṣurah* and *esh* both equal 301], and thus 'the form' is 'the woman' [*ha-ṣurah* and *ha-ishah* both equal 306]." On the dual nature of Metatron, see citation and analysis of some other relevant sources in Wolfson, *Abraham Abulafia*, 172–173n213.

85. See the passage cited above in note 28.

86. Abulafia, *Or ha-Sekhel*, 94. See Wolfson, *Abraham Abulafia*, 143–145.

87. Abulafia, *Oṣar Eden Ganuz*, 243, and see other sources (including a passage from Togarmi's *Maftehot ha-Qabbalah*) cited and discussed in Wolfson, *Abraham Abulafia*, 143–144n135.

88. Abulafia, *Ḥayyei ha-Olam ha-Ba*, 152.

89. Regarding these technical terms, see Wolfson, *Abraham Abulafia*, 59n167.

90. Abulafia, *Sitrei Torah*, 132. For full citation, see reference to my work in note 89.

91. Abulafia, *Imrei Shefer*, 44.

92. Ibid., 44–45.

93. Abulafia, *Ḥayyei ha-Nefesh*, 73.

94. In *Oṣar Eden Ganuz*, 256, Abulafia similarly explains that the name *purim* is derived from the "name of the lot [*shem ha-pur*] that is explicit [*ha-meforash*] in the secret of the explicit name [*be-sod shem ha-meforash*] that is known, face [*panim*] and back [*aḥor*], the intermediary [*emṣaʿi*] in the world." Compare Togarmi, *Maftehot ha-Qabbalah*, 237: "The tongue and the phallus [*ha-lashon we-ha-milah*] [5 + 30 + 300 + 6 + 50 + 6 + 5 + 40 + 10 + 30 + 5 = 487], right and left [*yamin u-semoʾl*] [10 + 40 + 10 + 50 + 6 + 300 + 40 + 1 + 30 = 487], and the secret of 'the nature, front and back' [*ha-ṭeva panim wa-aḥor*] [5 + 9 + 2 + 70 + 80 + 50 + 10 + 40 + 6 + 1 + 8 + 6 + 200 = 487], and thus it says concerning him 'Open my eyes (Ps. 119:18), Shaddai' [*gal einai shaddai*] [3 + 30 + 70 + 10 + 50 + 10 + 300 + 4 + 10 = 487]." On the mystery of time associated with Purim, see also *Sefer ha-Meliṣ*, in *Maṣref ha-Sekhel*, 30; *Sitrei Torah*, 133; *Mafteaḥ ha-Sefirot* (Jerusalem, 2001), 87.

95. See Abulafia, *Imrei Shefer*, 44: "In the secret of the name *purim*, which are days of celebration and joy that were engendered by male and female, Mordecai and Esther." The twin character of Purim is accentuated further in *Ḥotam ha-Hafṭarah*, in *Maṣref ha-Sekhel*, 112, where Abulafia draws a link between this holiday and the revelation of Sinai, which occurs in the third month of the year whose astrological sign is that of Gemini.

96. Abulafia, *Sitrei Torah*, 132. On the image of the scales of merit and guilt, see also *Ḥayyei ha-Olam ha-Ba*, 145.

97. See note 55 above.

98. Abulafia, *Sefer ha-Ḥesheq*, 18.

99. Abulafia, *Ḥayyei ha-Olam ha-Ba*, 187.

100. I have accepted the reading in the printed text (see note 99 for reference), which is attested as well in some manuscripts, for example, MS Moscow, Guenzberg 133, fol. 80b. The reading in other manuscripts, such as MS Oxford, Bodleian Library, 1582, fol. 74a, is *levusho mel'akhto*, "his garment is his work," which seems to me to be a scribal error.

101. Maimonides, *Guide*, II:6, 265.

102. *Genesis Rabbah*, eds. Julius Theodor and Chanoch Albeck (Jerusalem: Wahrmann Books, 1965), 50:2, 517.

103. Concerning this treatise, see the recent study by Harvey J. Hames, "Three that is One or One that is Three: On the Dating of Abraham Abulafia's 'Sefer ha-Ot,'" *Revue des études juives* 165 (2006): 179–189.

104. Abulafia, *Imrei Shefer*, 44, writes, "Know from this secret of explicit name [*sod ha-shem ha-meforash*], and know that it is engraved and sealed on the heart of each man from the human species [*ḥaquq we-ḥatum be-lev kol ish meishei ha-min ha-enoshi*]."

105. See Idel, *Mystical Experience*, 97.

106. Adolph Jellinek, "Sefer ha-'t: Apokalypse des Pseudo-Propheten und Pseudo-Messias Abraham Abulafia," in *Jubelschrift zum Siebzigsten Geburtstage des Prof. Dr. H. Graetz* (Breslau: S. Schottlaender, 1887), 81. For a more recent edition, see Abraham Abulafia, *Sefer ha-Ot* (Jerusalem, 2001), 30. Idel, *Language*, 97, already cited and analyzed the passages from *Sefer ha-Ot* in conjunction with the text from *Sitrei Torah*. See Idel, *Language*, 113.

107. Jellinek, "Sefer ha-'t," 81; Abulafia, *Sefer ha-Ot*, 32. The images of blood and ink are employed repeatedly by Abulafia. Some of the relevant references are cited by Idel, *Mystical Experience*, 157–158n138.

108. Jellinek, "Sefer ha-'t," 82; Abulafia, *Sefer ha-Ot*, 33. Compare *Sefer ha-Meliṣ* in *Maṣref ha-Sekhel*, 29: "What was for others a drug of death [*sam ha-mawet*], which is the Tree of Knowledge, was for Raziel an elixir of life [*sam ha-ayyim*], and he did not stumble with respect to it like the others."

109. Abulafia, *Imrei Shefer*, 80.

110. B. Berakhot 2b; B. Shabbat 34b.

111. Abulafia, *Sefer ha-Malmad*, 21.

112. See the text from Abulafia's *Perush Sefer Yeṣirah*, MS Paris, Bibliothèque Nationale héb. 768, fol. 9a, cited by Idel, *Language*, 41. For a published version

of the text, see *Perush Sefer Yeṣirah*, 24, and see below at note 163, where the passage is translated.

113. On the representation of the time cycle in terms of diurnal and nocturnal rotation, see the extended discussion in Abulafia, *Sefer ha-Ḥesheq*, 7–8.

114. Abulafia, *Oṣar Eden Ganuz*, 90. See ibid., 56, and compare *Perush Sefer Yeṣirah*, 32: "And when you attach the serpent to Adam and Eve, you find that man is a satan just as satan is a man [*ha-adam saṭan eḥad ka'asher ha-saṭan adam eḥad*]." The passage is cited by Idel, *Studies*, 37, from MS Paris, Bibliothèque Nationale héb. 768, fol. 11a. See also *Ḥayyei ha-Olam ha-Ba*, 141: "every man is satan, every satan a man [*kol adam saṭan kol saṭan adam*."

115. It should be noted that in his writings Abulafia repeats the identification of Satan as the evil inclination and the angel of death reported in the name of Simeon ben Laqish in B. Baba Batra 16a, and repeated by Maimonides, *Guide*, III:22, 489–490. See, for example, *Oṣar Eden Ganuz*, 56, 291; *Sitrei Torah*, 139; *Imrei Shefer*, 27; Idel, *Studies*, 38.

116. See note 84 above.

117. Wolfson, *Venturing Beyond*, 62–63, and particularly the passage from *Mafteaḥ ha-Shemot* cited on 62n195.

118. Idel, *Studies*, 45–61; Idel, *Messianic Mystics*, 62, 97–99.

119. On the vision of the human form and prophecy in Abulafian kabbalah, see Idel, *Mystical Experience*, 95–100.

120. Idel, *Studies*, 51–52. On the correlation of the Tree of Knowledge and the Tree of Life with Cain and Abel, see Abulafia, *Imrei Shefer*, 65.

121. Abulafia, *Ner Elohim* (Jerusalem, 2002), 85–86.

122. Scholem, *Major Trends*, 138–142; Idel, *Mystical Experience*, 88–91, 124–134; Scholem, *Studies*, 7–11; Wolfson, *Language, Eros, Being*, 236–242.

123. The matter of mystical union in Abulafia has been well discussed in the scholarly literature. The most detailed exposition can be found in the essay by Idel, "Abraham Abulafia and *Unio Mystica*," published in his *Studies*, 1–31, and reprinted in *Studies in Medieval Jewish History and Literature*, vol. 3, ed. Isadore Twersky and Jay M. Harris (Cambridge, Mass.: Harvard University Press, 2000), 147–178.

124. Many of the central images in Abulafia's writings are anticipated in a passage from Togarmi's *Maftehot ha-Qabbalah* transcribed in Scholem, *Kabbalah of Sefer ha-Temunah*, 232. The conjunction of the intellect and soul is portrayed by the images of the kiss, which is related to the description of God conversing with Moses mouth-to-mouth, *peh el peh* (Num. 12:8) and to the coupling of the king and queen, *ziwwug ha-melekh we-ha-malkah* (the expressions *peh el peh* and *ha-melekh we-ha-malkah* both equal 201). The sensitive implications of this matter are underscored by Togarmi's comment that "it is not possible to write about this secret explicitly or to transmit it orally [*peh el peh*] until one first comprehends its principle, and afterwards it can be transmitted in a tradition to those who contemplate his name through the fear of him [based on Malachi 3:16]."

On the image of the kiss in Abulafia's ecstatic kabbalah, see Idel, *Mystical Experience*, 180–184; Michael Fishbane, *The Kiss of God: Spiritual and Mystical Death in Judaism* (Seattle: University of Washington Press, 1994), 39–44.

125. Idel, *Mystical Experience*, 179–227; Idel, "Sexual Metaphors and Praxis in the Kabbalah," in *The Jewish Family: Metaphor and Memory*, ed. David Kraemer (New York: Oxford University Press, 1989), 200–201; Idel, "Eros in der Kabbala: Zwischen gegenwärtiger physischer Realität und idealen metaphysischen Konstrukten," in *Kulturen des Eros*, eds. Detlev Clemens and Tilo Schabert (Munich: Wilhelm Fink Verlag, 2001), 85–90; Idel, *Kabbalah and Eros* (New Haven, Conn.: Yale University Press, 2005), 77–81, 94–95. While I accept the merit of distinguishing between the symbolic approach to the sexual in the theosophic kabbalah and the allegorical approach of the prophetic kabbalah, I am of the opinion that the distinction cannot be made in an absolute manner, as the symbolic orientation is itself indebted to an allegorical understanding that kabbalists likely derived from philosophical sources in order to formulate their notion of spiritual or intellectual eros, a noetic state of conjunction facilitated by ascetic renunciation. See Wolfson, *Abraham Abulafia*, 90–91; Wolfson, *Language, Eros, Being*, 345–346, 348–351.

126. Abulafia, *Ḥayyei ha-Olam ha-Ba*, 142.

127. In *Imrei Shefer*, 68, Abulafia writes that the letters that are contemplated (*otiyyot ha-neḥshavot*) are neither a body nor a faculty in the body.

128. Scholem, *Major Trends*, 135; Idel, *Mystical Experience*, 20; Idel, *Language*, 3–11; Wolfson, *Abraham Abulafia*, 56n159, 160n179.

129. Idel, *Enchanted Chains*, 97–98.

130. Maimonides, *Guide*, III:51. The scholarly treatment of this topic is extensive, and hence I will mention here only a select number of relevant studies: Marvin Fox, *Interpreting Maimonides: Studies in Methodology, Metaphysics, and Moral Philosophy* (Chicago: University of Chicago Press, 1990), 297–321; Ehud Benor, *Worship of the Heart: A Study in Maimonides' Philosophy of Religion* (Albany: State University of New York, 1995). I have discussed the topic in "*Via Negativa* in Maimonides and Its Impact on Thirteenth-Century Kabbalah," *Maimonidean Studies* 5 (2008): 363–412. It would be too difficult to sketch the various lines of my argument, but suffice it to note that I attempt to show that in the case of both Maimonides and the kabbalists, who evolved spiritually and intellectually in his shadow, the phenomenon of prayer has to be understood from the standpoint of a dialectic juxtaposition of the kataphatic and apophatic approaches to the possibility of God-language. There are, of course, significant differences, but they do share a common challenge.

131. Maimonides, *Guide*, I:59, 139. For an explication of the apophatic orientation of Maimonides framed in light of the critical verse from Psalms, see Diana Lobel, " 'Silence is Praise to You': Maimonides on Negative Theology, Looseness of Expression, and Religious Experience," *American Catholic Philosophical Quarterly* 76 (2002): 25–49. See also Kenneth Seeskin, "Sanctity and Silence: The Religious Significance of Maimonides' Negative Theology," *American Catholic Philosophical Quarterly* 76 (2002): 7–24; Seeskin, Metaphysics and

Its Transcendence," in *The Cambridge Companion to Maimonides*, ed. Kenneth Seeskin (New York: Cambridge University Press, 2005), 88–91.

132. Maimonides, *Guide*, I:59, 140.

133. Ibid., 139.

134. José Faur, *Homo Mysticus: A Guide to Maimonides's Guide for the Perplexed* (Syracuse: Syracuse University Press, 1999), 68–69. For a representative selection of other studies that deal with negative theology in Maimonides, see David Kaufmann, *Geschichte der Attributenlehre in der Jüdischen Religionsphilosophie des Mittelalters von Saadja bis Maimuni* (Gotha: F. A. Perthes, 1877), 428–470; Harry A. Wolfson, "Maimonides on Negative Attributes," in *Louis Ginzberg Jubilee Volume* (New York: American Academy for Jewish Research, 1945), 411–446, reprinted in Harry A. Wolfson, *Studies in the History of Philosophy and Religion*, eds. Isadore Twersky and George H. Williams (Cambridge, Mass.: Harvard University Press, 1977), 2:195–230; Joseph A. Buijs, "Comments on Maimonides' Negative Theology," *New Scholasticism* 49 (1975): 87–93; Buijs, "The Negative Theology of Maimonides and Aquinas," *Review of Metaphysics* 41 (1987/88): 723–738; David Burrell, *Knowing the Unknowable God: Ibn Sina, Maimonides, Aquinas* (Notre Dame: Notre Dame University Press, 1986); Maurice-Reuben Hayoun, *Maïmonide et la pensée juive* (Paris: Presses Universitaires de France, 1994), 197–212; Charles Manekin, "Belief, Certainty, and Divine Attributes in the *Guide of the Perplexed*," *Maimonidean Studies* 1 (1990): 117–141, esp. 130; Ehud Benor, "Meaning and Reference in Maimonides' Negative Theology," *Harvard Theological Review* 88 (1995): 339–360; Hilary Putnam, "On Negative Theology," *Faith and Philosophy* 14 (1997): 407–422; Faur, *Homo Mysticus*, 5–9, 20–52; Martin Kavka, *Jewish Messianism and the History of Philosophy* (Cambridge: Cambridge University Press, 2004), 70–84; Herbert A. Davidson, *Moses Maimonides: The Man and His Works* (Oxford: Oxford University Press, 2005), 360–365; Wolfson, "*Via Negativa*," and the references to Lobel and Seeskin cited above in note 131.

135. Maimonides, *Guide*, I:59, 139.

136. See Wolfson, "Beneath the Wings of the Great Eagle: Maimonides and Thirteenth-Century Kabbalah," in *Moses Maimonides (1138–1204): His Religious, Scientific, and Philosophical Wirkungsgeschichte in Different Cultural Contexts*, eds. Görge K. Hasselhoff and Otfried Fraisse (Würzburg: Ergon Verlag, 2004), 228, and reference to other scholars cited 228n79.

137. Wolfson, *Abraham Abulafia*, 87–90, 194–195, 216–220; Wolfson, *Venturing Beyond*, 63–69. It is worth mentioning in this context Abulafia's assertion in *Imrei Shefer*, 44, that the Tetragrammaton is "engraved and sealed in the heart of every man from the individuals of the human species in accord with the lot that falls upon him."

138. The connection between the Abulafian ideal of *hitbodedut* and the Sufi practice of *dhikr* was noted by Idel, *Studies*, 106–107. On the possible influence of Sufism on the prophetic kabbalah, see also Scholem, *Major Trends*, 147,

384n105; Scholem, *Kabbalah*, 54, 180; ʿObadyāh ben Abraham ben Moses Maimonides, *The Treatise of the Pool: Al-Maqāla al-Ḥawḍiyya*, ed. Paul Fenton (London: Octagon Press, 1981), 21–22; Idel, *Mystical Experience*, 14, 24, 46n59, 104; Idel, *Studies*, 43n30, 74–76, 79, 91–101, 105, 126, 144n22.

139. Idel, *Mystical Experience*, 40.

140. On Abulafia's use of the image of ascent to describe the spiritual journey that results in the attainment of prophecy, see Idel, *Mystical Experience*, 83, 156–157n128, and Idel, *Ascensions on High in Jewish Mysticism: Pillars, Lines, Ladders* (Budapest: Central European University Press, 2005), 38–40.

141. Idel, *Mystical Experience*, 132.

142. Abulafia, *Or ha-Sekhel*, 3: "I composed this treatise . . . and I called its name as the name of the First Cause [*ha-sibbah ha-ri'shonah*], which is the light of the intellect [*or ha-sekhel*]."

143. This is an admittedly difficult expression to translate. It should be noted that in a number of manuscripts (for example, MS Paris, Bibliothèque Nationale héb. 774, fol. 68a; MS Paris, Bibliothèque Nationale héb. 828, fol. 230a; MS Paris, Bibliothèque Nationale héb. 1092, 165b) the reading that has been preserved in *meyyaḥed min ha-meyyaḥed*, "to unify from the unifier."

144. Adolph Jellinek, *Auswahl kabbalistischer Mystik*, Erstes Heft (Leipzig: A. M. Colditz, 1853), 25.

145. See note 75 above.

146. Abulafia, *Imrei Shefer*, 42.

147. Idel, *Studies*, 12–14.

148. Concerning this terminology, see Philip Merlan, *Monopsychism, Mysticism, Metaconsciousness: Problems of the Soul in the Neoaristotelian and Neoplatonic Tradition* (The Hague: Martinus Nijhoff, 1963), and see my brief comments in *Language, Eros, Being*, 283–284.

149. Abulafia follows Maimonides on this point, but even with regard to this basic matter there is not perfect agreement between the two. The burden of the Jewish esoteric tradition concerning the names of God simply weighed too heavily on Abulafia's mind to accept without qualification the view of Maimonides that all names (with the exclusion of the Tetragrammaton) signify attributes of action as opposed to essential attributes, that is, attributes that are indicative of our way of speaking about God's providence in the world rather than asserting anything positive about the divine nature. For a typical statement of Abulafia that marks his deviation from Maimonides, see *Ḥayyei ha-Olam ha-Ba*, 128. After delineating the ten paths connected to the seventy-two letter name, which are specified in the tradition (*qabbalah*), he writes: "Know that there is nothing in all the sacred wisdom like this wisdom, for it is the holy of the holies, and it is the limit of all the paths that one can comprehend in the knowledge of God, and in the comprehension of his actions, and in the discernments of his ways and his attributes, for his names, may he be elevated, are matters very close to him, and they are the truths of his Torah." The concluding remark about the names and the Torah is precisely the spot where the paths of Maimonides and Abulafia differ, as the latter remained faithful to a tradition that the former could not justify

philosophically. For a more extensive discussion, see Wolfson, *Abraham Abulafia*, 152–177.

150. Abulafia, *Ḥayyei ha-Nefesh*, 60.

151. Abulafia, *Or ha-Sekhel*, 28–29, 41.

152. It is worth noting here the expression "one who governs" [*ha-manhig*] seems to be associated with Metatron, the archon of the face (*sar ha-panim*), near the conclusion of the short recension of *Sefer-ha-Iyyun*, a thirteenth-century kabbalistic text of a highly speculative nature, transcribed in Verman, *Books of Contemplation*, 36, and translated somewhat differently on 48. In the same context, Metatron is also depicted as the "end of the act of the supernal ones and the beginning of the foundation of the lower ones." Although not stated explicitly, the Maimonidean-Abulafian identification of Metatron as the Active Intellect and archon of the world well suits the view that may be extrapolated from this mystical composition.

153. Maimonides, *Guide*, II:6, 264. See Maimonides, *The Guide of the Perplexed*, ed. Michael Schwartz (Tel Aviv: Tel Aviv University Press, 2002), 280n23 (Hebrew), where the demiurgical characterization of the Active Intellect is traced to Abū Naṣr al-Fārābī, *On the Perfect State (Mabādi' ārā' ahl al-madīnat al-fāḍilah)*, ed. Richard Walzer (Oxford: Oxford University Press, 1985), 363n171.

154. B. Yevamot 16b; B. Sanhedrin 94a; B. Ḥullin 60a; *Exodus Rabbah* 17:4; Orlov, *Enoch-Metatron Tradition*, 127–130, 159–162. In *Pirqei Rabbi Eliezer* (Warsaw, 1852), ch. 27, 62a, Michael is identified as the "archon of the world" [*saro shel olam*].

155. Abulafia, *Oṣar Eden Ganuz*, 139; for a slightly different rendering of this passage, see Wolfson, *Abraham Abulafia*, 145. Compare the depiction of the tenth intellect in *Imrei Shefer*, 142, as the one that "governs everything" [*manhig et ha-kol*]. For background on this technical terminology and discussion of some of the sources that may have influenced Abulafia, see Wolfson, "God, the Intellect, and the Demiurge: On the Usage of the Word *Kol* in Abraham ibn Ezra," *Revue des études juives* 149 (1990): 77–111, and see the response to my essay by Howard Kreisel, "On the Term *Kol* in Abraham Ibn Ezra: A Reappraisal," *Revue des études juives* 153 (1994): 29–66.

156. Abulafia, *Imrei Shefer*, 121.

157. For a more extensive discussion of this matter, with appropriate reference to work of Scholem and Idel, see Wolfson, *Abraham Abulafia*, 94–177.

158. Idel, *Kabbalah and Eros*, 77–78, notes that the term *kenesset yisra'el* is a designation for the human intellect, and thus the allegorical explanation of the Song of Songs as the love dialogue between God and the community of Israel is transformed in the prophetic kabbalah of Abulafia into a description of the conjunction between the divine intellect and individual soul, personified respectively as male and female. See also Idel, "Sexual Metaphors," 200–201, and Idel, "Eros in der Kabbala," 86–88. I do not disagree with this assertion, but it must be pointed out that in some contexts the expression *kenesset yisra'el* is a proper

designation for the Active Intellect. With respect to this usage, Abulafia is appropriating the attribution of this name to *Malkhut* or *Shekhinah* in works that expound a theosophic symbolism. In Abulafia's mind, all of these designations should be ascribed to the Active Intellect, the object of human conjunction, an identification that is attested in other kabbalistic works from the thirteenth century.

159. On the symbol of the androgyne in Abulafian kabbalah as the conjunction of the human and divine intellects, see Idel, "Eros in der Kabbala," 85–90; Idel, *Kabbalah and Eros*, 77–81. On the numerical equation of the word *androginos* and the expression *zakhar u-neqevah*, see Idel, *Language*, 21.

160. Wolfson, *Language, Eros, Being*, 63–77.

161. See Wolfson, *Abraham Abulafia*, 119n66, where I cite a passage from Abulafia's *Shomer Miṣwah* in which the perfect soul is described as the "bride in which all is found" [*kallah asher ha-kol bah*], a locution that I proposed based on the theosophic depiction of Shekhinah as the "bride that is comprised in all" [*kallah ha-kelulah min ha-kol*], as we find, for example, in the commentary of Naḥmanides to Genesis 24:1.

162. The biblical model here is Moses who, out of his extreme humility, feared looking at God in the epiphany of the burning bush (Exod. 3:6), and, as a consequence, merited to behold the image of the Lord (Num. 12:9). See *Ḥayyei ha-Nefesh*, 65, and see also the passage from *Shomer Miṣwah* cited in Wolfson, *Abraham Abulafia*, 119n66. On the need for the mystic to veil the face in emulation of Moses, see the text from *Ḥayyei ha-Olam ha-Ba* discussed in Wolfson, *Abraham Abulafia*, 220n125.

163. Abulafia, *Perush Sefer Yeṣirah*, 24.

164. Idel, *Studies*, 10.

165. Abulafia, *Imrei Shefer*, 46.

166. Scholem, *Major Trends*, 141; Idel, *Mystical Experience*, 131–132; Wolfson, *Abraham Abulafia*, 87–88, 216–217n115.

167. Abulafia, *Sefer ha-Ḥesheq*, 30.

168. Scholem, *Major Trends*, 131–135; Wolfson, *Abraham Abulafia*, 54–55.

169. See Dov Schwartz, "The Neutralization of the Messianic Idea in Medieval Jewish Rationalism," *Hebrew Union College Annual* 64 (1993): 37–58 (Hebrew); Wolfson, *Abraham Abulafia*, 39n95, with specific reference to Abraham Ibn Ezra's understanding of the secret (*sod*) of conjunction (*devequt*), and 91, where I argue that the more spiritualized interpretation of the traditional eschatological term "world-to-come" is an approach shared by Abulafia and other masters of esoteric lore of his time who are classified by modern scholars (following the typological scheme proffered by Scholem and Idel) as "theosophic kabbalists."

170. Abraham Berger, "The Messianic Self-Consciousness of Abraham Abulafia: A Tentative Evaluation," in *Essays on Jewish Life and Thought Presented in Honor of Salo Wittmayer Baron*, ed. Joseph Blau (New York: Columbia University Press, 1959), 55–61; Idel, *Messianic Mystics* (New Haven, Conn.: Yale University Press, 1998), 58–100, 295–307; Idel, "'The Time of the End.'"

171. Scholem, *Major Trends*, 142, rightly points out that the "state of ecstasy as described by Abulafia . . . carries with it something like an anticipatory redemption." For elaboration of this facet of Abulafian kabbalah, see references in previous note.

172. On the priestly status of the messiah in Abulafia's writings, see Idel, *Messianic Mystics*, 94–97.

173. Abulafia, *Ḥayyei ha-Olam ha-Ba*, 67.

174. Idel, *Mystical Experience*, 116–119; Idel, *Messianic Mystics*, 65–77, and see especially the passages from Isaac of Acre cited and analyzed by Idel, *Messianic Mystics*, 303–306; Wolfson, *Language, Eros, Being*, 241.

175. Idel, *Language*, 34–41, 79–80, 163n33; Idel, *Absorbing Perfections*, 348–350.

176. On the use of the expression "word of God" by Abulafia to designate the Active Intellect, see Idel, *Language*, 33. See also Wolfson, *Abraham Abulafia*, 141, and on the identification of the visionary and the Torah in the supreme state of ecstasy, see Scholem, *Major Trends*, 141.

177. Abulafia, *Ḥayyei ha-Olam ha-Ba*, 129.

178. Ibid., 141.

179. Ibid., 137–139. See also Abraham Abulafia, *Gan Na'ul* (Jerusalem, 1999), 27: "And the secret of time [*zeman*] is *zy"n m"m nw"n*, and this is the supernal first matter [*ha-ḥomer ha-ri'shon ha-elyon*] and it is numerically [equal to the word] *nivra*, and this is its secret according to the form of the *sefirot*." The Abulafian influence is discernible in *Sefer ha-Peli'ah* (Przemysl, 1883), 75b: "And the secret of time [*we-sod ha-zeman*] you can elucidate and comprehend [by spelling out as] *zy"n m"m nw"n* [67 + 80 + 106 = 253], which is numerically *ha-ḥomer* [5 + 8 + 40 + 200 + 253] . . . and this is the first matter [*ha-ḥomer ha-ri'shon*], and it is the supernal one in relation to the first, *Keter Elyon* . . . and thus *ha-ḥomer* is numerically equal to *nivra* [50 + 2 + 200 + 1 = 253]."

180. See *Oṣar Eden Ganuz*, 353.

181. *Sefer Yeṣirah with Commentary by Dunash Ben Tamim*, ed. Menasche Grossberg (London: R. W. Rabbinowicz, 1902), 48.

182. Abraham Ibn Ezra, *Sefer Ṣaḥot* (Fürth: David Isaac Zürndorff, 1827), 13a; Ibn Ezra, *Sefer ha-Shem* (Fürth: David Isaac Zürndorff, 1834), 7a.

183. Halevi, *Sefer ha-Kuzari*, IV:3, 157.

184. See Gershom Scholem, *Origins of the Kabbalah*, trans. Allan Arkush, ed. R. J. Zwi Werblowsky (Princeton, N.J.: Princeton University Press, 1987), 337; Idel, *Mystical Experience*, 18, 22; Wolfson, *Abraham Abulafia*, 113n54.

185. Abulafia, *Ḥayyei ha-Nefesh*, 68.

186. Abulafia, *Oṣar Eden Ganuz*, 111: "And the secret of the median [*beintayim*] is *beit-kaf*, and their truth is the twenty-two [*kaf-beit*] letters whose secret is AHW"Y [1 + 5 + 6 + 10 = 22]." See Togarmi, *Maftehot ha-Qabbalah*, in Scholem, *Kabbalah of Sefer ha-Temunah*, 234. After establishing a connection based on the numerical equivalences of various denotations of "the all" [*ha-kol*], which I assume refers to Metatron or the Active Intellect, to wit, *zo't* (the feminine form of the pronoun "this"), *kol ha-merkavah elohim* ("the entire divine

chariot"), and *ziw shekhinah* ("splendor of the Presence"), which all equal 408, Togarmi writes: "And the secret with regard to him is known, and it is the unique name [*shem meyuḥad*], and with him are the powers, and it is *yo"d h"e wd"w h"e*, whose secret is the blood of male and female [*dam zakhar u-neqevah*], that is, *kaf-beit, beit-kaf* , or *ahw"y, ywh"a*." Togarmi does not mention the Torah in this text, but he does make a point of noting that the name AHW"Y equals twenty-two, the number of Hebrew letters, which are further related to the two-fold dimension of the Tetragrammaton symbolized by the masculine and feminine blood. The identification of the name and the Torah is affirmed by Togarmi, *Maftehot ha-Qabbalah*, in Scholem, *Kabbalah of Sefer ha-Temunah*, 238.

187. Idel, *Mystical Experience*, 86.

188. Abulafia, *Ḥayyei ha-Olam ha-Ba*, 63–64, 69, 162–167; *Oṣar Eden Ganuz*, 106, 242, 347, 381; *Sefer ha-Ḥesheq*, 8, 10, 14, 17, 18; *Imrei Shefer*, 181–182.

189. Abulafia, *Ḥayyei ha-Olam ha-Ba*, 64, 69; *Oṣar Eden Ganuz*, 242; *Sefer ha-Ḥesheq*, 8; *Imrei Shefer*, 181–182.

190. Abulafia, *Sitrei Torah*, 117.

191. Abulafia, *Sefer ha-Ḥesheq*, 29–30. On the attribution of the title *ḥakham medabber* to Metatron, see also *Maṣref ha-Sekhel*, 112, and *Ner Elohim*, 91.

192. The derivation of time from the Tetragrammaton is affirmed as well by Gikatilla, *Ginnat Egoz*, 289–290: "Know that the existence of all things is in the computation [*ḥeshbon*], and the existence of the computation is in him, blessed be he, and therefore it is called *ḥeshbon* from the expression *maḥshavah* [thought] . . . You should know that the secret of *ḥeshbon* [8 + 300 + 2 + 6 + 50 = 366] is *shem yhwh* [300 + 40 + 10 + 5 + 6 + 5 = 366], and thus you should contemplate this great principle, that the world is created and is governed by what was prepared at first in the power of the name YHWH, which is the secret of the computation [*sod ha-ḥeshbon*] . . . Since the world is governed by means of the computation, it is a clear and known matter that it is created, and time as well is in the class of created beings, for the reality of time is consequent to the reality of the sphere, and the reality of the sphere is consequent to the existence of movement, and the existence of movement is consequent to computation, and the existence of computation is in him, may he be blessed and exalted . . . Therefore, I say to you that the computation attests to the creation of the world, and it indicates that time is created, and hence you find this trustworthy witness whose secret is *ḥeshbon*, which is the secret of *shem yhwh*. If this is so, then the great name, may he be blessed and exalted, moves the entire world." On the linkage of the Tetragrammaton and the spatial dimension of the world, see ibid., 372–375, and compare Gikatilla, *Hassagot*, 28d, where the kabbalistic meaning of the attribution of *maqom* to God is said to be based on the numerical equivalence of that word (182) and the sum derived from squaring each of the letters of the Tetragrammaton ($10 \times 10 + 5 \times 5 + 6 \times 6 + 5 \times 5 = 182$). The numerology of *ḥeshbon* and *shem yhwh* is employed by Togarmi in his *Maftehot ha-Qabbalah*; see Scholem, *Kabbalah of Sefer ha-Temunah*, 234, and the

translation of the text in Wolfson, *Abraham Abulafia*, 142n132. For Togarmi, and for Gikatilla as well, the term *ḥeshbon* has both numerological and linguistic implications, as it relates to the mathematical value of letters as well as to their permutation; both connotations are aspects of the mystical import of the divine name. See the beginning from *Maftehot ha-Qabbalah* transcribed in Scholem, *Kabbalah of Sefer ha-Temunah*, 229. The play on words between *ḥeshbon* and *maḥshavah* appears in the writings of Abulafia as well. See *Or ha-Sekhel*, 46; *Imrei Shefer*, 46; *Oṣar Eden Ganuz*, 38. See also *Ner Elohim*, 59. On Gikatilla's relationship to Togarmi and Abulafia, see Shlomo Blickstein, "Between Philosophy and Mysticism: A Study of the Philosophical-Qabbalistic Writings of Joseph Giqatila (1248–C. 1322)," (PhD dissertation, Jewish Theological Seminary of America, [1983]), 109–115.

193. See, for instance, Abulafia, *Or ha-Sekhel*, 71: "The world is attributed to time, and time is attributed to the world."

194. The possible influence of Abulafia may be detected in the identity of time (*zeman*), place (*maqom*), and the Torah in the *Raza di-Meheimanuta* of Menaḥem Mendel of Shklov, *Kitvei ha-GRM″M*, (Jerusalem, 2001), 1:49. The philosophical point is made on the basis of adding the sum of the word *zeman* spelled out as *zy″n m″m nw″n* ($67 + 80 + 106 = 253$) to the word *maqom* spelled out as *m″m qw″fw″w m″m* ($80 + 186 + 12 + 80 = 358$), which equals 611, the numerology of the word *torah* ($twrh = 400 + 6 + 200 + 5$). In the printed text, the numerology of *maqom* is incorrect, as the latter *waw* is spelled out as *wy″w*. I have amended the text based on the correct numerology that appears in Menaḥem Mendel of Shklov, *Be'ur Mishnah Ḥasidim, Kitvei ha-GRM″*, 183. See also Menaḥem Mendel of Shklov, *Be'urei ha-Zohar*, in *Kitvei ha-GRM″M*, 2:106, and *Temunat ha-Otiyyot, Kitvei ha-GRM″M*, 278.

195. The text could also be vocalized as *bin ha-maqom*, which would be translated as "comprehend the place." Although I do not think it likely, perhaps Abulafia used the idiom *ha-maqom* in the rabbinic sense as a circumlocution for *God*. If that surmise is correct, then there is a parallelism drawn between the words *qomah*, *olam*, and *maqom*, which might suggest the idea that the physical world is the corporeal stature of the divine. Such an allegorical interpretation of the ancient Jewish esoteric speculation is attested in medieval philosophical sources, epitomized perhaps in the *Iggeret al Shi'ur Qomah* composed by the fourteenth-century Moses Narboni. See Alexander Altmann, *Studies in Religious Philosophy and Mysticism* (Ithaca: Cornell University Press, 1969), 180–209, esp. 202–205.

196. Abulafia, *Ḥayyei ha-Olam haBa*, 92.

197. Needless to say, numerous scholars have attempted to articulate the "true" view of Maimonides on creation. Providing an exhaustive list is well-nigh impossible. See Tamar M. Rudavsky, *Time Matters: Time, Creation, and Cosmology in Medieval Jewish Philosophy* (Albany: State University of New York Press, 2000), 30–38, and reference to other scholarly assessments listed on 201–202n32. For a more recent summary of the various perspectives, see Davidson, *Moses Maimonides*, 365–370. Also relevant here is the study by Lenn E. Goodman, "Maimonidean Naturalism," in *Maimonides and the Sciences*, eds. Robert

S. Cohen and Hillel Levine (Dordrecht: Kluwer Academic Publishers, 2000), 57–85.

198. Abulafia, *Sefer ha-Ḥesheq*, 37.

199. Ibid., 70. Regarding the origin of the numerology in Abulafia's writings and its reverberations in later philosophical sources, see Idel, *"Deus Sive Natura—The Metamorphosis of a Dictum From Maimonides to Spinoza,"* in *Maimonides and the Sciences*, 87–110, esp. 90–93.

200. Abulafia, *Sefer ha-Malmad*, 3.

201. Abulafia, *Ḥayyei ha-Olam ha-Ba*, 140.

202. Abulafia, *Ḥayyei ha-Nefesh*, 72.

203. Abulafia, *Or ha-Sekhel*, 29. See ibid., 106, for the diagram of the tenfold circle as an object of meditation, and discussion in Idel, *Mystical Experience*, 109–116.

204. On the threefold status of the name, which is connected with several images including that of the temporal designation *hayah, howeh*, and *yihyeh*, see *Imrei Shefer*, 53. For a more extended discussion of the "threefold unity" [*shillush ha-yiḥud*] or the "unity of the threefold" [*yiḥud ha-shillush*] in Abulafia, see Wolfson, *Abraham Abulafia*, 131–133n101.

205. Abulafia, *Oṣar Eden Ganuz*, 110.

206. Abulafia, *Sefer ha-Ḥesheq*, 67.

207. An allusion to the view articulated by Abulafia may be found in the following passage from Togarmi's *Maftot ha-Qabbalah*, transcribed in Scholem, *Kabbalah of Sefer ha-Temunah*, 233: "Three lovers [*ohavim*], 'he is, he was, and he will be' [*howeh we-hayah we-yihyeh*], and this is one matter [*zeh davar eḥad*], and it is the universal wisdom [*ha-ḥokhmah ha-kelalit*], the all [*ha-kol*], and this is the three mothers, that is, one in the entourage above, the vessel [*keli*] that is in the *alef, mem, shin* [i.e., the letters designated as 'mothers' according to the taxonomy in the *Sefer Yeṣirah* 2:3]." Implicit in Togarmi's comment is the belief that the numerical equivalence of the expressions *howeh we-hayah we-yihyeh* ($5 + 6 + 5 + 6 + 5 + 10 + 5 + 6 + 10 + 5 + 10 + 5 = 78$) and *ha-ḥokhmah* ($5 + 8 + 20 + 40 + 5 = 78$) signifies that the three temporal states are manifestations of the divine wisdom, which constitute the one reality that is the all (*ha-kol*), a vessel (*keli*) for the three matrix letters, *alef, mem*, and *shin*, an alternate semiotic demarcation of the three aspects of time contained in the Tetragrammaton. In another passage from *Maftehot ha-Qabbalah*, p. 234, Togarmi cites and interprets the description in *Sefer Yeṣirah* 2:3 of the three mothers in the image of the scale; the *alef* is the balance between the *mem* and *shin*, the scale of guilt and the scale of merit.

208. B. Sanhedrin 97a.

209. I have accepted the emendation of printed text from *ka-mawet* (the reading preserved in MS New York, Jewish Theological Seminary of America, Mic. 1801, fol. 33b) to *ba-mawet*, since this change is necessary to attain the correct sum of 522. I assume, therefore, that in this instance the manuscript witness is a scribal error.

210. Compare Abulafia, *Imrei Shefer*, 34: "Time is entirely enumerated [*ha-zeman kullo nispar*], and it is called 'the scribe' [*ha-sofer*], for it is the one who writes [*ha-kotev*], and it is the scribe [*ha-lavlar*], the scripter [*sofer*], for it writes the letters one by one." Abulafia is obviously drawing on the tradition that Metatron is the celestial scribe. See Wolfson, *Through a Speculum*, 259 and reference cited in n300. See note 83 above. Given Abulafia's portrayal of Metatron as the personification of time, it makes sense that he would describe the latter as well in scribal terms.

211. For discussion of this motif and references to other scholarly treatments, see Idel, "Enoch is Metatron," *Immanuel: A Bulletin of Religious Thought and Research in Israel* 24/25 (1990): 220–239, and the extensive analysis in Orlov, *Enoch-Metatron Tradition*. For an assessment of Idel's methodology as it pertains to this theme, see Lawrence Kaplan, "Adam, Enoch, and Metatron Revisited: A Critical Analysis of Idel's Method of Reconstruction," *Kabbalah: Journal for the Study of Jewish Mystical Texts* 6 (2001): 73–119.

Tribute to Derrida
Amy Hollywood
1. H. D., *Tribute to Freud* (New York: New Directions, 1984), 18.
2. Yosef Hayim Yerushalmi, *Freud's Moses: Judaism Terminable and Interminable* (New Haven, Conn.: Yale University Press, 1991), 99.
3. Ibid. Note the analogy between this abrupt ending and the untraditional final chapter of Yerushalmi's own book, in which he engages in a monologue directed to Sigmund Freud.
4. Ibid., 100, quoting Anna Freud, "Inaugural Lecture for the Sigmund Freud Chair at the Hebrew University, Jerusalem," *International Journal of Psycho-Analysis* 59 (1978): 148. Ellipses added by Yerushalmi.
5. Yerushalmi, 100.
6. Ibid., 77. Yerushalmi here cites Sigmund Freud, "An Autobiographical Study," in *Standard Edition of the Complete Psychological Works of Sigmund Freud*, ed. and trans. James Strachey in collaboration with Anna Freud, assisted by Alix Strachey and Alan Tyson (London: Hogarth, 1959), 20:8.
7. Yerushalmi, 100.
8. Jacques Derrida, *Archive Fever: A Freudian Impression*, trans. Eric Prenowitz (Chicago: University of Chicago Press, 1995), 43–44.
9. Ibid., 44.
10. In addition, whereas the daughter, *if* she ever speaks, only does so *as* the father, Yerushalmi argues that the son can speak *both* in his own voice *and* that of the father. In his reading of the relationship between Sigmund and Jakob Freud, Yerushalmi argues for a "deferred obedience" to the father, in which the son both follows and diverges from the father. Sigmund returns to the Bible as Jakob requested, but accepts its historical truth, not its material truth. Similarly, Yerushalmi recognizes the reasons for Sigmund Freud's insistence that psychoanalysis not be identified with Judaism, even as Yerushalmi argues that (in Derrida's formulation) "psychoanalysis should in the future have been a Jewish science." (See

Derrida, *Archive Fever*, 44.) This elliptical relationship to the father is denied to Anna Freud, who becomes a transparent surface through which the son relates to the father. Yet in demanding this transparency, Yerushalmi also denies his own claimed divergence from the father. In his case, however, this is meant to invest Yerushalmi fully with the father's authority.

11. Despite the fact that Yerushalmi often used "Jewishness" and "Judaism" interchangeably, Derrida demonstrates that Yerushalmi clearly marks a distinction between the two. Judaism, as Yerushalmi's subtitle marks, may be terminable, but it is Jewishness that is interminable. (See Yerushalmi, 90.) In Derrida's words, "it can survive Judaism." There is, Derrida explains, for Yerushalmi a "determining and irreducible essence of Jewishness" that "should not be mistaken as merging with Judaism, or with religion, or even with the belief in God" (Derrida, *Archive Fever*, 72). The gap between Judaism and Jewishness, moreover, is paralleled—perhaps even enacted—in that between messianicity and messianism. On the latter distinction in their different relationships to both the future and the archive, see ibid., 36 and 64–65.

12. Ibid., 26. As Elliot Wolfson shows, moreover, the two readings are linked within at least some midrashic and kabbalistic texts; the interpretation of scripture and the vision of God it enables can be carried out and undergone only by one who has been circumcised. The mark of circumcision opens the body to see God—in scripture or through visions—quite literally, it would seem, through the penis. See Elliot R. Wolfson, *Through a Speculum that Shines: Vision and Imagination in Medieval Jewish Mysticism* (Princeton, N.J.: Princeton University Press, 1994), 257ff. and Wolfson, "Circumcision, Vision of God, and Textual Interpretation: From Midrashic Trope to Mystical Symbol," *History of Religions* 27 (1987): 189–215.

13. Derrida, *Archive Fever*, 45–46.

14. Ibid., 48–49.

15. This may be behind Derrida's reading of Jakob Freud's inscription within Sigmund Freud's bible in terms of circumcision, rather than in terms of learning Hebrew (as it is read by Yerushalmi). On the role that food prohibitions can play in determining one's bodily relationship to Judaism and/or Jewishness, see Sarah Kofman, *Rue Ordener, Rue Labat*, trans. Ann Smock (Lincoln and London: University of Nebraska Press, 1996), esp. 13 and 42ff.

16. In *Memoirs of the Blind*, Derrida suggests that Freud's view of circumcision was limited (not to mention a little boring). To read circumcision as castration, and hence the circumcised Jew as threatening insofar as he figures the possibility of castration, is to miss the reality of phallic mastery marked on and by the penis. Playing on the ambiguity of the word *bandé*, *Memoirs* repeatedly insists that blinding—by bandaging the eyes—is coterminous with erection (*bandé*). Blinding and circumcision don't castrate but, on the contrary, in marking the penis (and its vulnerability) make it the signifier of mastery. The penis is inscribed as phallic through circumcision—it constitutes men as those who can read and be read (as in the *Zohar*). See Jacques Derrida, *Memoirs of the Blind*,

trans. Pascale-Anne Brault and Michael Naas (Chicago: University of Chicago Press, 1993).

17. The logic of both Yerushalmi's and Derrida's texts suggests it is impossible to be Jewish and a woman. Yet of course there are Jewish women. The problem is how the tradition figures women as Jewish—there is no mark of the covenant so crucial as circumcision, no similarly corporeal sign that inscribes Jewish women's bodies within interpretative and authoritative traditions. The question then becomes whether new modes of relationship between Jewish fathers and Jewish daughters can be discovered without eschewing the material mark of circumcision, by which Jewish filiation is handed down from father to son.

18. Derrida, *Archive Fever*, 4.

19. Note that the conference at which *Archive Fever* was first read was organized by Elisabeth Roudinesco, the most important historian of psychoanalysis in France.

20. Edith Wyschogrod, *An Ethics of Remembering: History, Heterology, and the Nameless Others* (Chicago: University of Chicago Press, 1998), 174–85, esp. 180; Wyschogrod, "Blind Man Seeing: From Chiasm To Hyperreality," in *Crossover Queries: Dwelling with Negatives, Embodying Philosophy's Others* (New York: Fordham University Press, 2006), 112–24.

21. Derrida wonders what the archives of psychoanalysis would have looked like if e-mail had been available to Freud and his circles, insisting that the form of the archive and its contents are inseparable. See Derrida, *Archive Fever*, 16–17.

22. Ibid., 12: "[I]f there is no archive without consignation in an *external place* which assures the possibility of memorialization, of reproduction, or of re-impression, then we must also remember that repetition itself, the logic of repetition, indeed the repetition compulsion, remains, according to Freud, indissociable from the death drive. And thus from destruction. Consequence: right on that which permits and conditions archivization, we will never find anything other than that which exposes to destruction, and in truth menaces with destruction, introducing, *a priori*, forgetfulness and the archiviolithic into the heart of the monument. Into the 'by heart' itself. The archive always works, and *a priori*, against itself."

23. See, for example, Wyschogrod, *An Ethics of Remembering*, 237.

24. Butler is interested in exploring whether the figure of Antigone presents the possibility of thinking new possibilities of kinship "after Oedipus," particularly in light of the actual radical reconfigurations of parenting and kinship relations being enacted today. This might be tied to Derrida's reference to what Freud got wrong about paternity and maternity, particularly his assumption that maternity is a sensible given, whereas determining paternity requires rational inference. As the apparently most material connections between human beings demand rethinking in light of current technologies, we can see that particularity and materiality aren't *negated*, but require reconfiguration in perhaps more inclusive, less silencing and repressive, ways. See Judith Butler, *Antigone's Claim* (New York: Columbia University Press, 2000), 19ff., 30, 66–67; Derrida, *Archive Fever*, 47–48.

Butler's discussion deals explicitly with Hegel and, more pertinently for this essay, with Lacan. She asks how closely the symbolic and the social and/or language and kinship should be tied together, suggesting that Lacan makes a particular social construction of kinship the universal (although contingent) condition of the symbolic and language. Against this, she—like, I think, Derrida and another, more radical reading of Lacan—suggests that we can and should dissociate kinship grounded in the paternal and language (with its move toward oneness). Or is the more radical claim being made by Derrida that we can decenter the very move toward oneness that grounds language and the patriarchal archive? This is also the debate running throughout my reading of Irigaray's relationship to Lacan. See my "Divine Woman/Divine Women: The Return of the Sacred in Bataille, Lacan, and Irigaray," in *The Question of Christian Philosophy Today*, ed. Francis J. Ambrosio (New York: Fordham University Press, 1999), 224–46, and *Sensible Ecstasy: Mysticism, Sexual Difference, and the Demands of History* (Chicago: University of Chicago Press, 2002), esp. 173–273.

25. I am thinking here of Michael Warner's worry with regard to Butler and certain deployments of queer theory that if the normative and the queer are seen as always inevitably engendering and implicated with each other, the reality of "queer counterpublics" is elided, and with it "the world-making activity of queer life that neither takes queerness to be inevitable nor understands itself from the false vantage of 'society'" (Warner, *The Trouble with Normal: Sex, Politics and the Ethics of Queer Life* [Cambridge, Mass.: Harvard University Press, 2000], 147). So for example, within Judaism, food is also often a key marker of inclusion, one that doesn't necessarily reinforce gender hierarchies and exclusions the way that circumcision does, although it does still and necessarily involve an exclusionary gesture.

26. Derrida, *Archive Fever*, 95.

27. Ibid.

28. The move from reading relations between Judaism and Christianity in terms of fratricide rather than patricide also marks a movement from nineteenth-century figurations to post–World War II figurations of their relationship. My thanks to Susannah Heschel for this point.

29. Again, my thanks to Susannah Heschel for this point.

Hearing the Voices of the Dead: Wyschogrod, Megill, and the Heterological Historian

John D. Caputo

1. "*Confessions* and 'Circumfession': A Roundtable with Jacques Derrida," in *Augustine and Postmodernism: Confessions and Circumfession*, eds. John D. Caputo and Michael Scanlon (Bloomington: Indiana University Press, 2005), 31–32.

2. Edith Wyschogrod, *An Ethics of Remembering: History, Heterology and the Nameless Others* (Chicago: University of Chicago Press, 1998), xi.

3. Ibid., 13.

4. See Edith Wyschogrod, *Spirit in Ashes: Hegel, Heidegger and Man-made Mass Death* (New Haven, Conn.: Yale University Press, 1985).

5. Wyschogrod, *An Ethics of Remembering*, 3.

6. Ibid., 4.

7. Allan Megill, "Some Aspects of the Ethics of History-Writing: Reflections on Edith Wyschogrod's *An Ethics of Remembering*," in *The Ethics of History*, eds. David Carr, Thomas R. Flynn and Rudolf A. Makkreel (Evanston: Northwestern University Press, 2004), 45–75, quotation on 51.

8. Ibid., 51, 55–56.

9. Ibid., 48.

10. Ibid., 66.

11. Ibid., 52–53 (emphasis in original).

12. Wyschogrod, *An Ethics of Remembering*, 22.

13. Megill, 65.

14. Wyschogrod, *An Ethics of Remembering*, 23, 39.

15. Ibid., 24–26.

16. In Allan Megill, *Prophets of Extremity: Nietzsche, Heidegger, Foucault, Derrida* (Berkeley: University of California Press, 1987), Megill attempts a likewise critical but judicious commentary on these figures who, he says, call the normal canons of rationality into question—and therefore make it difficult to comment on their work—but who do so with a "therapeutic" aim, namely, to provide an opening in the rush of ordinary life to reinvent and reenvisage ourselves.

17. Wyschogrod, *An Ethics of Remembering*, 26–27.

18. Martin Heidegger, *Being and Time*, trans. John Macquarrie and Edward Robinson (New York: Harper & Row, 1962); *History of the Concept of Time: Prolegomena*, trans. Theodore Kisiel (Bloomington: Indiana University Press, 1985) .

19. See Edmund Husserl, *Ideas Pertaining to a Pure Phenomenology and to a Phenomenological Philosophy*, First Book, trans. Fred Kersten (The Hague: Martinus Nijhoff, 1983), §§39–46, 99, 109, 121.

20. Heidegger, *Being and Time*, §§16, 34.

21. Heidegger, *History of the Concept of Time*, §§10–12.

22. Emmanuel Levinas, *Totality and Infinity: An Essay on Exteriority*, trans. Alphonso Lingis (Pittsburgh: Duquesne University Press, 1969), 168–69.

23. Ibid., 134.

24. Heidegger, *Being and Time*, §§3, 69(b).

25. W. V. O. Quine, "Facts of the Matter," in *Essays on the Philosophy of W. V. Quine*, eds. R. Shahan and C. Swoyer (Norman: University of Oklahoma Press, 1979).

26. See Hugh Lacey, *Is Science Value Free? Values and Scientific Understanding* (London: Routledge, 1999).

27. Levinas, 168–75, 209–14.

28. Wyschogrod, *An Ethics of Remembering*, 10.

29. Megill, "Some Aspects," 60.

30. Ibid.

31. See the exchange between Derrida and Jean-François Lyotard at Cerisy after Lyotard's paper "Phrasing 'After Auschwitz,'" in *Les fins de l'homme: à partir du travail de Jacques Derrida* (Paris: Galilée, 1981), 311–13; trans. by Georges Van Den Abbeele in *The Lyotard Reader*, ed. Andrew Benjamin (Oxford: Blackwell, 1989), 386–89.

32. Of course I have no intention of denying a process of one thing leading to another, and of uncovering things of which one had no premonition, and of the gradual transformation and reworking of fields. Being willing to follow a road that leads I know not where is an essential part of research. I am not denying that. I am just trying to contextualize it.

33. Megill, "Some Aspects," 67–70.

34. Heidegger, *Being and Time*, §29, 175.

35. Wyschogrod, *An Ethics of Remembering*, 3.

Memory and Violence, or Genealogies of Remembering
Werner H. Kelber

1. Edith Wyschogrod, *An Ethics of Remembering: History, Heterology, and the Nameless Others* (Chicago: University of Chicago Press, 1998), 66.

2. Paul Ricoeur, *Memory, History, Forgetting*, trans. Kathleen Blamey and David Pellauer (Chicago: University of Chicago Press, 2004), 79.

3. Friedrich Nietzsche, *The Anti-Christ, Ecce Homo, Twilight of the Idols, and Other Writings*, trans. Judith Norman, ed. Aaron Ridley (Cambridge: Cambridge University Press, 2005), 80.

4. Ricoeur, 57–58.

5. Wyschogrod, 16.

6. Aristotle, *On Memory and Recollection*, 449b28–29.

7. Wyschogrod, 248.

8. Ibid., xiii.

9. Ibid., 38.

10. Ibid., 70.

11. Ibid., 10.

12. Ibid., 213.

13. Ibid., 178.

14. Naftali Lavie, "Auschwitz: A Fitting Site for a Christian Cross," *Jerusalem Post*, September 19, 1989.

15. Jan Assmann, *Religion und Gedächtnis* (Munich: C. H. Beck, 2000), 82. See also Assmann, *Das kulturelle Gedächtnis: Schrift, Erinnerung und politische Identität in frühen Hochkulturen* (Munich: C. H. Beck, 1992), 103–29.

16. Assmann, *Das kulturelle Gedächtnis*, 123–24.

17. See Anthony J. Saldarini, "The Gospel of Matthew and Jewish-Christian Conflict," in *Social History of the Matthean Community: Cross-Disciplinary Approaches*, ed. David L. Balch (Minneapolis, Minn.: Fortress, 1991), 38–61; Reinhart Hummel, *Die Auseinandersetzung zwischen Kirche und Judentum in*

Matthäusevangelium (Munich: Chr. Kasiser, 1966), 26–33; Peter F. Ellis, *Matthew: His Mind and His Message* (Collegeville, Minn.: Liturgical Press, 1974), 3–6.

18. Saldarini, 39.

19. Ibid., 43.

20. Ibid., 60.

21. See Martin S. Jaffee, *Torah in the Mouth: Writing and Oral Tradition in Palestinian Judaism 200 BCE–400 CE* (Oxford: Oxford University Press, 2001), 39–61.

22. See Walter Ong, *Interfaces of the Word: Studies in the Evolution of Consciousness and Culture* (Ithaca, N.Y.: Cornell University Press, 1977), esp. 240ff.

23. Eusebius the Caesarean, *The Ecclesiastical History,* 6.14.5–10.

24. Raymond E. Brown, *The Gospel According to John (i-xii)* (Garden City, N.Y.: Doubleday & Co., 1966), lxx. Space does not permit discussion of an intra-Johannine conflict reflected in the narrative. See D. Bruce Woll, *Johannine Christianity in Conflict: Authority, Rank, and Succession in the First Farewell Discourse* (Atlanta, Ga.: Scholars, 1981); Werner H. Kelber, "The Authority of the Word in St. John's Gospel: Charismatic Speech, Narrative Text, and Logocentric Metaphysics," *Oral Tradition* 2:1 (1987), 108–31; Tom Thatcher, *Why John Wrote a Gospel: Jesus—Memory—History* (Louisville, Ky.: Westminster John Knox, 2006).

25. See Werner H. Kelber, "Metaphysics and Marginality in John," in *What Is John?: Readers and Readings of the Fourth Gospel,* ed. Fernando F. Segovia (Atlanta, Ga.: Scholars, 1996), 129–54.

26. R. Alan Culpepper, *Anatomy of the Fourth Gospel: A Study in Literary Design* (Philadelphia: Fortress, 1983), 199.

27. Ibid., 180.

28. Søren Kierkegaard, *The Concept of Irony,* trans. L. M. Capel (New York: Harper & Row, 1966), 232, 234, 236.

29. See J. Louis Martyn, *History and Theology in the Fourth Gospel,* 2nd ed. (Nashville, Tenn.: Abindgon, 1979).

30. Augustine of Hippo, *De doctrina Christiana,* III:6.

31. Assmann, *Das kulturelle Gedächtnis,* 41–42.

32. Maurice Halbwachs, *Les cadres sociaux de la mémoire* (Paris: PUF, 1952), trans. Lewis A. Coser as "The Social Frameworks of Memory," in *On Collective Memory,* ed. Coser (Chicago: University of Chicago Press, 1992), 37–189.

33. Martin Hengel, *Crucifixion in the Ancient World and the Folly of the Message of the Cross,* trans. John Bowden (Philadelphia: Fortress, 1977), 38.

34. Ibid, p. 38.

35. Alan Kirk, "The Memory of Violence and the Death of Jesus in Q," in *Memory, Tradition, and Text: Uses of the Past in Early Christianity,* eds. Kirk and Tom Thatcher (Atlanta, Ga.: Society of Biblical Literature, 2005), [191–206] 192.

36. Lothar Ruppert, *Der leidende Gerechte: Eine motivgeschichtliche Untersuchung zum Alten Testament und zwischentestamentlichen Judentum* (Würzburg:

Echter, 1972); Ruppert, *Jesus als der leidende Gerechte?* (Stuttgart: KBW, 1972); Ruppert, *Der leidende Gerechte und seine Feinde: Eine Wortfelduntersuchung* (Würzburg: Echter, 1973); George Nickelsburg, "The Genre and Function of the Markan Passion Narrative," *Harvard Theological Review* 73 (1980): 153–84; Burton L. Mack, *A Myth of Innocence: Mark and Christian Origins* (Philadelphia: Fortress, 1988); Arthur J. Dewey, "The Locus for Death: Social Memory and the Passion Narratives," in *Memory, Tradition, and Text: Uses of the Past in Early Christianity*, eds. Kirk and Tom Thatcher (Atlanta, Ga.: Society of Biblical Literature, 2005), 119–28.

37. Nickelsburg, 156.

38. Ibid., 163, 183.

39. Mack, 268.

40. Ibid., 268, 276.

41. Mary Carruthers, *The Book of Memory: A Study in Medieval Culture* (Cambridge: Cambridge University Press, 1990); Carruthers, *The Craft of Thought: Meditation, Rhetoric, and the Making of Images, 400–1200* (Cambridge: Cambridge University Press, 1998).

42. Dewey, 126, 127.

43. See Erich Auerbach, *Mimesis: The Representation of Reality in Western Literature*, trans. Willard R. Trask (Princeton: Princeton University Press, 1953).

44. Frank Kermode, *The Genesis of Secrecy: On the Interpretation of Narrative* (Cambridge, Mass.: Harvard University Press, 1979), 106.

45. Alfred Suhl, *Die Funktion der alttestamentlichen Zitate und Anspielungen in Markusevangelium* (Gütersloh: Gerd Mohn, 1965), 166.

46. Kermode, 88.

47. Kirk, 194; Barry Schwartz, *Abraham Lincoln and the Forge of National Memory* (Chicago: University of Chicago Press, 2000).

48. Assmann, *Das kulturelle Gedächtnis*, 200–02.

49. John R. Donahue, *Are You the Christ?: The Trial Narrative in the Gospel of Mark* (Missoula, Mont.: Society of Biblical Literature, 1973), 201–3.

The Historian and the Messianic "Now": Reading Edith Wyschogrod's *An Ethics of Remembering*

Bettina Bergo

1. See Walter Benjamin, *The Origin of German Tragic Drama*, trans. John Osborne (London: Verso, 1985).

2. See Edith Wyschogrod, *An Ethics of Remembering: History, Heterology, and the Nameless Others* (Chicago: University of Chicago Press, 1998), 238.

3. Ibid., 237.

4. See, for example, Immanuel Kant, *Critique of Judgment*, trans. Werner S. Pluhar (Indianapolis: Hackett Publishing Company, 1987), 116–35, Ak. 253–75. In regard to the sublime, for example, where the imagination "finds nothing beyond the sensible that could support it," it proceeds to reflect on its own way of thinking, experiencing its ideas as superior to sensibility and withal

a certain hope. Thus Kant says: "Though an exhibition of the infinite can as such never be more than merely negative, it still expends the soul." The best example of this—or the most ethical—comes out of Judaism: "The most sublime passage in the Jewish Law is the commandment: Thou shalt not make onto the any graven image, or nay likeness of any thing that is in heaven or on Earth . . . this commandment alone can explain the enthusiasm that the Jewish people . . . felt for its religion . . . The same holds also for our presentation of the moral law . . . for once the senses no longer see anything before them, while yet the unmistakable and indelible idea of morality remains, one would sooner need to temper the momentum of an unbounded imagination . . . than to support these ideas with images and childish devices" (135).

5. Walter Benjamin, "Über den Begriff der Geschichte," in *Gesammelte Schriften I.2*, eds. Rolf Tiedemann and Hermann Schweppenhäuser (Frankfurt am Main: Zuhrkamp Verlag, 1980), 694, my translation. (See also "On the Concept of History," trans. Harry Zohn, in *Selected Writings: 1938–1940*, eds. Howard Eiland and Michael W. Jennings [Cambridge, Mass.: Belknap/Harvard, 2003], 390.) This is how Benjamin understands a "*weak* messianic force [schwache *messianische Kraft*]."

6. Emmanuel Levinas, *Totality and Infinity: An Essay on Exteriority*, trans. Alphonso Lingis (Pittsburgh: Duquesne University Press, 1969).

7. Benjamin, "Über den Begriff der Geschichte."

8. Carlo Ginzburg, *Ecstasies: Deciphering the Witches' Sabbath*, trans. Raymond Rosenthal (Chicago: University of Chicago Press, 1989).

9. See Giovanni Busino, "Causalisme, symétrie et réflexivité. Une lecture des travaux des Carlo Ginzburg" in *L'acteur et ses raisons*, eds. Jean Baechler et al. (Paris: PUF, 2000), 25–42, esp. 40.

10. Ibid., 41.

11. As Giovanni Busino, whose discourse is usually too confident for what it purports to say, argues (38): "Ginzburg's methodology is imprecise. It offers us no criterion allowing us to distinguish what is dominant, or subordinate, in a composite social formation. It does not even say what the criteria are by which we could define a social composition. Ginzburg tells us only that the Sabbath is constituted by two strata. At the surface, there is satanism, the cult of Satan, the pact with the devil. Below, there is shamanism, the voyage into the beyond . . . [and] this second stratum is the organic substructure of the phenomenon because its primordial beneficent signification (the Shaman is the warrior of the good) is transformed into a horrifying maleficent ceremonial, both harmful and occult. But this transmutation comes to pass . . . without even extra-logical mechanisms to produce it."

12. Wyschogrod, 31.

13. Ibid., 48.

14. Ibid., 59.

15. Ibid., 44–45.

16. Ibid., 45.

17. Ibid., 46.

18. Ibid., 63.

19. All quotations in this and the previous paragraph are from Wyschogrod, 48.

20. Immanuel Kant, *Critique of Judgment*, trans. Werner S. Pluhar (Indianapolis: Hackett Publishing, 1987), 111; Ak. 255. Kant writes: "The infinite, however, is absolutely large . . . Compared with it, everything else . . . is small. But . . . to be able even to think the infinite as *a whole* indicates a mental power that surpasses any standard of sense . . . a power that is supersensible."

21. Ibid., 108; Ak. 252.

22. Ibid., 115; Ak. 258.

23. Ibid., 111; Ak. 254.

24. Ibid., 111; Ak. 254.

25. Ibid., 114; Ak. 257.

26. Ibid., 115; Ak. 258.

27. Ibid.

28. Wyschogrod, 64.

29. Martin Heidegger, *Beiträge zur Philosophie* (*Vom Ereignis*) [*Gesamtausgabe* 65] (Frankfurt am Main: Vittorio Klostermann, 1989), 236. Translation mine. (See also *Contributions to Philosophy* (*From Enowning*), trans. Parvis Emad and Kenneth Maly [Bloomington: Indiana University Press, 1999], 167.) The German reads, "Lichtung und Verbergung, die Wesung der Wahrheit ausmachend, dürfen daher nie als leerer Verlauf und als Gegenstand der 'Erkenntnis,' als eines Vorstellens, genommen werden. Lichtung und Verbergung sind entrückend-berückend das Ereignis selbst."

30. Ibid., 244. (See also *Contributions to Philosophy*, 173.)

31. Jean-François Lyotard, *The Differend: Phrases in Dispute*, trans. Georges Van Den Abbeele (Minneapolis: University of Minnesota Press, 1988), 179. Also see Wyschogrod, 59–62.

32. See "Emplotment: A Reading of Aristotle's *Poetics*," in *Time and Narrative*, vol. 1, trans. Kathleen McLaughlin and David Pellauer (Chicago: University of Chicago Press, 1984), 31–51.

33. See Theodor Adorno, *Minima Moralia: Reflections from Damaged Life*, trans. E. F. N. Jephcott (London: Verso, 1978), 247. Benjamin, "Über den Begriff der Geschichte," 694.

34. Jean-Luc Nancy, "The Judeo-Christian," trans. Bettina Bergo and Michael B. Smith, in *Judeities: Questions for Jacques Derrida*, eds. Bettina Bergo, Joseph Cohen, and Raphael Zagury-Orly (New York: Fordham University Press, 2007), 232.

35. Square brackets are Wyschogrod's.

36. Wyschogrod, 170–71.

37. Ibid., 173.

38. Ibid., 158.

39. Nancy, 220.

40. Wyschogrod, 172.

41. Ibid., 160.

42. Ibid., 162.

43. Max Horkheimer, *Critique of Instrumental Reason*, trans. Matthew J. O'Connell et al. (New York: Seabury Press, 1974), 47.

44. Levinas, 284–85.

45. Ibid., 285.

Saints and the Heterological Historian
Peter Ochs

1. Edith Wyschogrod, *An Ethics of Remembering: History, Heterology, and the Nameless Others* (Chicago and London: University of Chicago Press, 1998).

2. Edith Wyschogrod, *Saints and Postmodernism: Revisioning Moral Philosophy* (Chicago: University of Chicago Press, 1990). For comparable treatments of saints within Christian theology, see Stanley Hauerwas, "The Necessity of Witness," in *With the Grain of the Universe: The Church's Witness and Natural Theology* (Grand Rapids, Mich.: Brazos Press, 2004), chap. 8, and David Ford, "Love as Vocation: Thérèse of Lisieux" and "Polyphonic Living: Dietrich Bonhoeffer," in *Self and Salvation: Being Transformed* (Cambridge: Cambridge University Press, 1999), chaps. 9–10.

3. See the trope of "cry" in David Ford, *Christian Wisdom: Learning to Live in the Spirit* (Cambridge: Cambridge University Press, 2007).

4. Wyschogrod, *Saints and Postmodernism*, 13.

5. Ibid., 17.

6. Ibid., 242.

7. Ibid., 246, citing Julia Kristeva, *Powers of Horror* (New York: Columbia University Press, 1982), 2.

8. Ibid., 246–47.

9. Ibid, 251. Note the parallels with Marcionite tendencies in Radical Orthodoxy.

10. "Language is founded upon the phenomenon of the mirror, ego-alter ego, or of the echo, in other words of a carnal generality: what warms me warms him." Maurice Merleau-Ponty, *The Prose of the World*, trans. John O'Neill (Evanston, Ill.: Northwestern University Press, 1973*)*, 20n.

11. Maurice Merleau-Ponty, *The Visible and the Invisible*, trans. Alphonso Lingis (Evanston, Ill.: Northwestern University Press, 1968), 130. Cited in Wyschogrod, *Saints and Postmodernism*, 51.

12. "*Abduction* is the process of forming an explanatory hypothesis. It is the only logical operation which introduces any new idea . . . Abduction merely suggests that something *may* be. Its only justification is that from its suggestion deduction can draw a prediction which can be tested by induction, and that, if we were are ever to learn anything or to understand phenomena at all, it must be by abduction that this is to be brought about." Charles Sanders Peirce, "The

Nature of Meaning," (1903), in *The Essential Peirce: Selected Philosophical Writings*, ed. the Peirce Edition Project (Bloomington: Indiana University Press, 1998), 216.

13. Wyschogrod, *Saints and Postmodernism*, 34.

14. Ibid., 47.

15. Ibid., 13.

16. Saints' lives should not be imagined as emanating from some specific religious community, but as found throughout a broad spectrum of belief systems and institutional practices. A saintly life is defined as one in which compassion for the Other, irrespective of cost to the saint, is the primary trait. Such lives unfold in tension with institutional frameworks that may nevertheless later absorb them. Not only do saints contest the practices and beliefs of institutions, but in a more subtle way they contest the order of narrativity itself. Their lives exhibit two types of negation: negating the self and negating something absent in the life of the Other.

17. Edith Wyschogrod, "From Ethics to Language: The Imperative of the Other," *Semiotica* 97, 1/2, 1993: 168–69. Quotations from Levinas in this passage are from *Otherwise than Being*, trans. Alphonso Lingis (The Hague: Martinus Nijhoff, 1981), 46 and 48.

18. Wyschogrod, *An Ethics of Remembering*, 9, paraphrasing Emmanuel Levinas, "Language and Proximity," in *Collected Philosophical Papers*, trans. Alphonso Lingis (The Hague: Martinus Nijhoff, 1987), 116.

19. This was published as "A Symposium on Jewish Postmodernism," in *Soundings* 76:1 (Spring 1993), 129–96. The contributors were Edith Wyschogrod, Peter Ochs, José Faur, Robert Gibbs, and Jacob Meskin.

20. 20. Wyschogrod, "Trends In Postmodern Jewish Philosophy," *Soundings* 76:1 (Spring 1993), 129.

21. Ibid., 130.

22. Ibid.

23. Wyschogrod's caution was sharpened in "Trends in Postmodern Jewish Philosophy: Contexts of a Conversation" (not to be confused with the essay cited in note 20), her response to the conversation between Robert Gibbs, Steven Kepnes, and Peter Ochs in *Reasoning After Revelation: Dialogues in Postmodern Jewish Philosophy* (Boulder, Colo.: Westview, 1998), 130: "I am moved but also troubled by the way in which the appeal to hermeneutical endeavor by the dialogue's participants is seen to exalt and redeem. Can a post-Holocaust return to the text be productive of joy (even if not unalloyed) any more than the vanished world of Hasidism that Buber tried to recreate? More disturbing is the absence of appeal to that internal Jewish Other who is excluded from learning for whatever reason, the *am ha'aretz* (man of the soil, or unlearned man), and the woman . . ."

24. In addition to the essays cited in notes 20 and 23, see also "Reading the Covenant: Some Postmodern Reflections," in *Reviewing the Covenant: Eugene B. Borowitz and the Postmodern Renewal of Jewish Theology*, ed. Peter Ochs with Eugene B. Borowitz (Albany, N.Y.: SUNY Press, 2000), 60–68.

25. Roland Barthes, "The Discourse of History," in *Comparative Criticism: A Yearbook*, ed. E.S. Shaffer (Cambridge: Cambridge University Press, 1981), 16–18, cited in Wyschogrod, *An Ethics of Remembering*, 20. Hayden White, *The Content of the Form* (Baltimore, Md.: Johns Hopkins University Press, 1987), cited in Wyschogrod, *An Ethics of Remembering*, 20 and 63.

26. Wyschogrod argues (*An Ethics of Remembering*, 2) that "this description of recovering the past, of its re-signing, has been called into question by the critiques of post-structuralists and analytic philosophers alike on the grounds that the relation of the language to both time and the referent have been misunderstood. Yet both [of them] . . . often fail to notice that their presumably new theories are often unrecognized repetitions of concepts previously explored in the thought of those whose concepts they believe they have transcended . . . [Instead,] I explore the claim that the promise to tell the truth about the past should continue to provide the warranty for the historian's assertions that re-signing, linguistic appropriation of that which was, need not disappear but is to be transformed."

27. See note 18 above, and also Wyschogrod, *An Ethics of Remembering*, 10: "The other is a theme neither of historical analysis nor description but functions as an ethical placeholder in historical discourse, as a texturally invisible demand placed upon the historian that she fulfill the promise of truthfulness."

28. Wyschogrod, *An Ethics of Remembering*, xi–xii.

29. Edith Wyschogrod, *Spirit in Ashes: Hegel, Heidegger and Man-made Mass Death* (New Haven, Conn.: Yale University Press, 1985).

30. Wyschogrod, *An Ethics of Remembering*, 41.

31. Ibid., 140, citing Maurice Blanchot, *The Writing of the Disaster*, trans. Ann Smock (Lincoln: University of Nebraska Press, 1986), 28.

32. Wyschogrod likens this silencing of the Other to what Lyotard calls the *differend*: "Lyotard has redescribed the silence of the victims in terms of an inequality of power among speakers, a situation he names a 'differend': 'I would like to call a differend between two parties the case where the plaintiff is divested of the means to argue and becomes for that reason the victim.'" Wyschogrod, *An Ethics of Remembering*, 23, citing Jean-François Lyotard, *The Differend: Phrases in Dispute*, trans. Georges Van Den Abeele (Minneapolis: University of Minnesota Press, 1988), 9.

33. Wyschogrod, *An Ethics of Remembering*, 131.

34. Ibid., 71.

35. Ibid., 144.

36. Ibid., 48.

37. Ibid., 48.

38. Ibid., 49.

39. Ibid., 166.

An Exercise in Upbuilding
Edith Wyschogrod

1. Søren Kierkegaard, *Concluding Unscientific Postscript*, trans. David Swenson and Walter Lowrie (Princeton, N.J.: Princeton University Press, 1941), 276.

2. Søren Kierkegaard, *Eighteen Upbuilding Discourses*, trans. Edward V. Hong and Walter Lowrie (Princeton, N.J.: Princeton University Press, 1990), 504.

3. "Hospitality, Justice and Responsibility: A Dialogue with Jacques Derrida," in *Questioning Ethics: Contemporary Debates in Philosophy*, ed. Richard Kearney and Mark Dooley (London: Routledge, 1999), 66.

4. Emmanuel Levinas, "Reality and Its Shadow," in *Collected Philosophical Papers*, trans. Alphonso Lingis (Dordrecht: Martinus Nijhoff, 1987), 13.

5. Milan Kundera, "What Is a Novelist?" in *The Curtain: An Essay in Seven Parts* (New York: HarperCollins, 2007), 89.

6. Ibid., 95.

7. Hans-Georg Gadamer, "Letter to Dallmayr," in *Dialogue and Deconstruction: The Gadamer–Derrida Encounter,* eds. Diane P. Michelfelder and Richard E. Palmer (Albany: State University of New York Press, 1989), 96.

8. Paul Ricoeur, "Universality and the Power of Difference," in Richard Kearney, *Debates in Continental Philosophy: Conversations with Contemporary Thinkers* (New York: Fordham University Press, 2004), 220.

9. Paul Ricoeur, *Oneself as Another*, trans. Kathleen Blamey (Chicago: University of Chicago Press), 3.

10. Edith Wyschogrod, "Fact, Fiction, *Ficciones*: Truth in the Study of Religion," *Crossover Queries: Dwelling with Negatives, Embodying Philosophy's Others* (New York: Fordham University Press, 2006), 356.

11. Emmanuel Levinas, "Ethics of the Infinite," in *Questioning Ethics*, 80.

12. Hans-Georg Gadamer, "*Destruktion* and Deconstruction," in *Dialogue and Deconstruction,* 106.

13. Edith Wyschogrod and John D. Caputo, "Postmodernism and the Desire for God: An E-mail Exchange," in *Crossover Queries*, 307.

14. Hans-Georg Gadamer, "Text Matters," in *Debates in Continental Philosophy,* 177.

15. Jacques Derrida, "*Sauf le nom*," trans. John P. Leavey, in *On the Name* (Stanford, Calif.: Stanford University Press, 1995), 68.

16. Wyschogrod, "Intending Transcendence, Desiring God," in *Crossover Queries*, 26–27.

17. Edith Wyschogrod, "Crucifixion and Alterity," in *Thinking through the Death of God: A Critical Companion to Thomas J. J. Altizer*, ed. Lissa McCullough and Brian Schroeder (Albany: State University of New York Press, 2004), 101.

18. Alain Badiou, *Saint Paul: The Foundation of Universalism,* trans. Ray Brassier (Stanford, Calif.: Stanford University Press, 2003), 47.

19. Ibid., 45.

20. Alain Badiou, *Theoretical Writings* (London: Continuum Press, 2004), 98.

21. Ibid., 99.

22. Jared Woodard, "Faith, Hope and Love: The Inducement of the Subject in Badiou" in *Journal of Philosophy and Scripture* 3, no. 1 (2005), www.philosophyandscripture.org/Issue3–1/Woodard/Woodard.html, PDF p. 29.

23. Ibid.

24. Jacques Derrida, "Sauf le nom," 58.

25. See Oona Ajzenstat, *Driven Back to the Text: The Premodern Sources of Levinas's Postmodernism* (Pittsburgh: Duquesne University Press, 2001), 149.

26. Wyschogrod, "From Neo-Platonism to Souls *in Silico*: Quests for Immortality," in *Crossover Queries*, 198.

27. Charles Sanders Peirce, "A Neglected Argument for the Reality of God," in *The Essential Peirce: Selected Philosophical Writings*, ed. the Peirce Edition Project (Bloomington: Indiana University Press, 1998), 2: 434–50; Peter Ochs, *Peirce: Pragmatism and the Logic of Scripture* (Cambridge: Cambridge University Press, 1998), 228.

28. Jean-Paul Sartre, *Being and Nothingness*, trans. Hazel Barnes (New York: Washington Square Press, 1956), 101f.

29. Ochs, 316–17.

30. See Wyschogrod, introduction to *Crossover Queries*, 4.

31. Wyschogrod, *An Ethics of Remembering: History, Heterology, and the Nameless Others* (Chicago: University of Chicago Press, 1998), 167.

32. Ibid., 62.

33. Edith Wyschogrod and Carl Raschke, "Heterological History: A Conversation," in *Crossover Queries*, 320.

Contributors

Thomas J. J. Altizer is Professor Emeritus of Religious Studies at the State University of New York at Stony Brook. He is the author of *The Self-embodiment of God* (University Press of America, 1987) and fifteen other books, most recently *Living the Death of God: A Theological Memoir* (State University of New York Press, 2006).

Bettina Bergo is associate professor in the Department of Philosophy at the Université de Montréal. She is author of *Levinas Between Ethics and Politics: For the Beauty That Adorns the Earth* (Duquesne University Press, 2001) and the translator of numerous books by Levinas and other titles in Continental philosophy of religion. Most recently she has co-edited and cotranslated *Judeities: Questions for Jacques Derrida* (Fordham University Press, 2007) and *Nietzsche and the Shadow of God* (Northwestern University Press, forthcoming).

Eric Boynton is Associate Professor of Philosophy and Religious Studies at Allegheny College. His interests include the intersection of the philosophies of art and religion, as well as the question of evil. He has published articles on the Continental philosophy of religion and aesthetics, served as guest editor for an issue on evil for the journal *Janus Head*, and co-edited *The Enigma of Gift and Sacrifice* (Fordham University Press, 2002).

John D. Caputo, Watson Professor of Religion and Humanities, Syracuse University, is a hybrid philosopher/theologian whose past books have argued that hermeneutics goes all the way down (*Radical Hermeneutics: Repetition, Deconstruction, and the Hermeneutic Project*; Indiana University Press, 1987), that Derrida is a thinker to be reckoned with by theology (*The Prayers and Tears of Jacques Derrida: Religion without Religion*; Indiana University Press, 1997), and that theology is best served by getting over its love affair with power and authority and embracing what Caputo calls, following St. Paul, *The Weakness of God* (Indiana University Press, 2006). He has also addressed wider-than-academic audiences in *On Religion* (Routledge, 2001) and *What Would Jesus Deconstruct?: The Good News of Postmodernism for the Church* (Baker Academic, 2007).

Robert Gibbs is Professor of Philosophy and Director of the Jackman Humanities Institute at the University of Toronto. He is the author of *Correlations in Rosenzweig and Levinas* (Princeton University Press, 1992), and *Why Ethics: Signs of Responsibilities* (Princeton University Press, 2000), as well as co-editor with Elliot R. Wolfson of *Suffering Religion* (Routledge, 2002) and co-author with Steven Kepnes and Peter Ochs of *Reasoning After Revelation* (Westview,1998). He has published widely on Continental philosophy and modern Jewish philosophy and is currently engaged in a major project on law and ethics.

Amy Hollywood is Elizabeth H. Monrad Professor of Christian Studies at Harvard Divinity School. She is a historian of Christian thought specializing in mysticism, with strong interests in feminist theory, queer theory, psychoanalysis, and Continental philosophy. She has published *The Soul as Virgin Wife: Mechthild of Magdeburg, Marguerite Porete, and Meister Eckhart* (University of Notre Dame Press, 1995) and *Sensible Ecstasy: Mysticism, Sexual Difference, and the Demands of History* (University of Chicago Press, 2002).

Martin Kavka is Associate Professor in the Department of Religion at Florida State University. He is the author of *Jewish Messianism and the History of Philosophy* (Cambridge University Press, 2004), which was awarded the Jordan Schnitzer Book Award, recognizing the best book in Jewish philosophy/thought published between 2004 and 2008, by the Association for Jewish Studies. He is also the co-editor of *Tradition in the Public Square: A David Novak Reader* (Eerdmans, 2008).

Werner H. Kelber is the Isla Carroll and Percy E. Turner Professor Emeritus of Biblical Studies at Rice University. His work on early Christian history and literature has focused on canonical and extra-canonical texts, oral tradition in early Judaism and Christianity, Gospel narrativity, biblical hermeneutics, the historical Jesus, orality-literacy studies, memory, rhetoric, text criticism, and the media history of the Bible. His major work, *The Oral and the Written Gospel: The Hermeneutics of Speaking and Writing in the Synoptic Tradition* (Fortress Press, 1983; French trans. Editions du Cerf, 1990; reprint Indiana University Press, 1997), examines points and processes of transition from oral performance to scribality in the early Christian tradition.

Peter Ochs is Edgar M. Bronfman Professor of Modern Judaic Studies at the University of Virginia and co-founder of the Societies of Textual Reasoning and of Scriptural Reasoning. His publications include *Peirce, Pragmatism, and the Logic of Scripture* (Cambridge University Press, 1998), and *Reasoning After Revelation: Dialogues in Postmodern Jewish Philosophy* (with Stephen Kepnes and Robert Gibbs; Westview Press, 1998). He is also the editor of David Weiss Halivni's *Breaking the Tablets: Jewish Theology After the Shoah* (Rowman and Littlefield, 2007), and the co-editor of *Reviewing the Covenant: Eugene Borowitz and the Postmodern Revival of Jewish Theology* (State University of New York Press, 2000), *Textual Reasonings: Jewish Philosophy and Text Study at the End of the Twentieth Century* (Eerdmans, 2003), and *The Jewish-Christian Schism Revisited* (Eerdmans, 2003). With Stanley Hauerwas, he co-edits the Radical Traditions series, published by Eerdmans Publishing Company and SCM Press.

Adriaan T. Peperzak is Arthur J. Schmitt Chair of Philosophy at Loyola University, Chicago. He has composed five books on Hegel and three on Levinas. His latest books include *Philosophy Between Faith and Theology: Addresses to Catholic Intellectuals* (University of Notre Dame Press, 2005) and *Thinking: From Solitude to Dialogue and Contemplation* (Fordham University Press, 2006).

Mark C. Taylor is Chair of the Department of Religion and Co-Director of the Institute for Religion, Culture, and Public Life at Columbia University. A leading figure in debates about postmodernism, Taylor has written on topics ranging from philosophy, religion, literature, art, and architecture to education, media, science, technology, and economics. His latest work includes *The Moment of Complexity: Emerging Network Culture* (University of Chicago Press, 2001), *Confidence Games: Money and Markets in a World without Redemption* (University of Chicago Press, 2004),

Mystic Bones (University of Chicago Press, 2007), and *After God* (University of Chicago Press, 2007).

Graham Ward is the head of the School of Arts, Histories and Cultures at the University of Manchester and also Professor of Contextual Theology and Ethics. Among his published works are *Barth, Derrida, and the Language of Theology* (Cambridge University Press, 1995), *Cities of God* (Blackwell, 2000), *True Religion* (Blackwell, 2003), and *Christ and Culture* (Blackwell, 2005). He has also edited a number of volumes, including *The Postmodern God: A Theological Reader* (Blackwell, 1997), *The Certeau Reader* (Blackwell, 2001), *Religion and Political Thought* (with Michael Hoelzl; Continuum, 2006), and *The New Visibility of Religion: Studies in Religion and Cultural Hermeneutics* (with Michael Hoelzl; Continuum, 2008).

Merold Westphal is Distinguished Professor of Philosophy at Fordham University. He has served as President of the Hegel Society of America and of the Søren Kierkegaard Society and as Executive Co-Director of the Society for Phenomenology and Existential Philosophy (SPEP). He is the author of nine books, including most recently *Overcoming Onto-Theology: Toward a Postmodern Christian Faith* (Fordham University Press, 2001), *Transcendence and Self-Transcendence: On God and the Soul* (Indiana University Press, 2004), and *Levinas and Kierkegaard in Dialogue* (Indiana University Press, 2008).

Elliot R. Wolfson is the Abraham Lieberman Professor of Hebrew and Judaic Studies at New York University. His main area of scholarly research is the history of Jewish mysticism, and he has brought to bear on that field training in philosophy, literary criticism, feminist theory, postmodern hermeneutics, and the phenomenology of religion. His publications include *Through a Speculum That Shines: Vision and Imagination in Medieval Jewish Mysticism* (Princeton University Press, 1994), *Along the Path: Studies in Kabbalistic Myth, Symbolism, and Hermeneutics* (State University of New York Press, 1995), *Circle in the Square: Studies in the Use of Gender in Kabbalistic Symbolism* (State University of New York Press, 1995), *Abraham Abulafia—Kabbalist and Prophet: Hermeneutics, Theosophy, and Theurgy* (Cherub Press, 2000), *Language, Eros, Being: Kabbalistic Hermeneutics and Poetic Imagination* (Fordham University Press, 2005), *Venturing Beyond: Law and Morality in Kabbalistic Mysticism* (Oxford University Press, 2006), *Alef, Mem, Tau: Kabbalistic Musings on Time, Truth, and Death* (University of California Press, 2006), and *Open*

Secret: Post-Messianic Messianism and the Mystical Revision of Menahem Mendel Schneerson (Columbia University Press, 2009).

Edith Wyschogrod, J. Newton Rayzor Professor of Philosophy and Religious Thought emerita at Rice University, has written extensively on the meanings of God, being and language, the ethics of the other, and the philosophy of history. Her recent works include *Crossover Queries: Dwelling with Negatives, Embodying Philosophy's Others* (Fordham University Press, 2006), *An Ethics of Remembering: History, Heterology, and the Nameless Others* (University of Chicago Press, 1998), *Saints and Postmodernism: Revisioning Moral Philosophy* (University of Chicago Press, 1990), *Spirit in Ashes: Hegel, Heidegger, and Man-Made Mass Death* (Yale University Press, 1985). She has been instrumental in introducing the thought of French philosopher Emmanuel Levinas to the English-speaking world and is a past president of the American Academy of Religion.

Index

modernism, 99, 229f., 233, 236
Moses, 56, 104, 120f., 191, 248, 252
mysticism, 10, 11, 53ff., 86, 117, 121,
  133, 139, 146, 214, 246, 252f.

naming, 67, 71, 78, 81, 162, 247, 255
  and God, 99, 106, 247
Nancy, Jean-Luc, 73, 213ff.
narrative, 65f., 73, 88f., 164, 178, 182,
  190, 198, 214, 223–30, 233, 237,
  244, 246
  historical, 216, 258
  sacred, 206
  saintly, 48–53, 227f., 255
  of trauma, 196
Nazi, 55
neighbor, 11, 60, 75f., 92, 266
Neoplatonism, 9, 34, 55, 119
New Testament, 35, 49, 68, 222
  Letter to the Hebrews, 65
Nietzsche, Friedrich, 18f., 33, 35f., 38,
  41–45, 47, 114ff., 175, 206, 213,
  245, 248
  Birth of Tragedy, 202
  Thus Spoke Zarathustra, 86
nihilism, 10, 18, 31f., 41, 43, 45, 78, 116,
  245, 258
Nozick, Robert, 214

Oedipus myth, 12, 157f.
Other, 13, 18, 24–28, 51–54, 59f., 64,
  75ff., 162, 176, 179, 181, 192f.,
  210, 224, 232, 244, 247, 249
  exile before, 73f.
  face of, 100
  as guest, 71
  saintly, 52
  suffering, 219–28, 234, 242, 255
  voice of, 220, 229–31, 235ff.

Parmenides, 84
parousia, 213f.
Pascal, Blaise, 165, 235
Passion narratives, 180–201, 256
  artistic responses to, 180, 182, 257
  in Jewish memory, 181, 201, 257
  in Gospel of John, 188ff.
  in Gospel of Luke, 186ff.

  in Gospel of Mark, 182f.
  in Gospel of Matthew, 184ff.
passivity, 5, 51, 52, 55, 59f., 106
patriarchy, 12, 156f.
Paul, 34, 37ff., 41–44, 92, 215, 243, 249
Peirce, Charles S., 224, 235, 255f.
Penrose, Roger, 9
phenomenology, 5, 12, 53, 224
  and Descartes, 99
  of eros, 76
  and Husserl, 165
  and Kristeva, 224
  and Levinas, 73, 77
  of time, 136
philosophy, 50–53, 82f., 86–89, 97, 103
  call to, 99, 101
piety, 54ff., 256
pilgrim, 64–70, 75, 247
Plato, 51, 84, 86, 88, 116, 173
Plotinus, 2, 9, 34, 252
Pontius Pilate, 183–88, 257
postmodernism, 12, 16, 58, 72, 162, 165,
  176, 219, 222f., 230, 234, 236
practice, 51f., 54, 59, 80
praxis, 53
prayer, 6, 58, 78, 82, 133, 181, 199, 227
  contemplative, 132
  Jewish, 106f.
  liturgical, 132
prophecy, 119ff., 139, 197, 248
prophetic revolution, 35f., 40
proximity, 13, 25, 91f., 210, 226f., 231,
  234–37, 255
psychoanalysis, 12, 83, 150, 175, 178, 251
  as "Jewish science," 153
  and patriarchy, 155
Purim, 127

Qumran, 38, 195
Qur'an, 222

redemption, 39, 43, 66, 74, 124ff., 181f.,
  203f., 213
refugees, 49, 60–63, 69–72, 78
relation, 10, 14, 26, 101, 207ff., 235
religion, 53, 84
remembering, 51, 164, 180, 182, 199,
  201, 205

Vattimo, Gianni, 73, 78
violence, 64, 183, 196, 199, 205, 208, 210, 245
virtuality, 155
visual culture, 8
vulnerability, 5, 58, 60, 102, 108, 112, 177

wandering, 65f., 68, 74, 112
war, 18
White, Hayden, 8, 164f., 207, 230
Wiesel, Elie, 6, 50
witness, 1, 37, 121, 143, 178, 203, 204, 215
  of the dead, 17, 212, 216
  false, 197, 199f.

of the Infinite, 101f., 112
and the Word of God, 58, 65, 292
Wittgenstein, Ludwig, 75
Wyschogrod, Edith, works of
  "Doing Before Hearing: On the Primacy of Torah," 5
  An Ethics of Remembering, 8, 12ff., 24, 46, 67, 69, 72, 161, 164, 167, 172, 176, 179, 206, 218f., 223, 229f, 257
  Saints and Postmodernism, 7, 10, 13, 16, 32, 220, 237
  Spirit in Ashes, 6, 16, 33, 232
  "The Warring Logic of Genocide," 21

Yerushalmi, Yosef, 12, 150–58, 251

Perspectives in Continental Philosophy Series

John D. Caputo, series editor

John D. Caputo, ed., *Deconstruction in a Nutshell: A Conversation with Jacques Derrida.*

Michael Strawser, *Both/And: Reading Kierkegaard—From Irony to Edification.*

Michael D. Barber, *Ethical Hermeneutics: Rationality in Enrique Dussel's Philosophy of Liberation.*

James H. Olthuis, ed., *Knowing* Other-*wise: Philosophy at the Threshold of Spirituality.*

James Swindal, *Reflection Revisited: Jürgen Habermas's Discursive Theory of Truth.*

Richard Kearney, *Poetics of Imagining: Modern and Postmodern.* Second edition.

Thomas W. Busch, *Circulating Being: From Embodiment to Incorporation—Essays on Late Existentialism.*

Edith Wyschogrod, *Emmanuel Levinas: The Problem of Ethical Metaphysics.* Second edition.

Francis J. Ambrosio, ed., *The Question of Christian Philosophy Today.*

Jeffrey Bloechl, ed., *The Face of the Other and the Trace of God: Essays on the Philosophy of Emmanuel Levinas.*

Ilse N. Bulhof and Laurens ten Kate, eds., *Flight of the Gods: Philosophical Perspectives on Negative Theology.*

Trish Glazebrook, *Heidegger's Philosophy of Science.*

Kevin Hart, *The Trespass of the Sign: Deconstruction, Theology, and Philosophy.*

Mark C. Taylor, *Journeys to Selfhood: Hegel and Kierkegaard.* Second edition.

Dominique Janicaud, Jean-François Courtine, Jean-Louis Chrétien, Michel Henry, Jean-Luc Marion, and Paul Ricœur, *Phenomenology and the "Theological Turn": The French Debate.*

Karl Jaspers, *The Question of German Guilt*. Introduction by Joseph W. Koterski, S.J.

Jean-Luc Marion, *The Idol and Distance: Five Studies*. Translated with an introduction by Thomas A. Carlson.

Jeffrey Dudiak, *The Intrigue of Ethics: A Reading of the Idea of Discourse in the Thought of Emmanuel Levinas*.

Robyn Horner, *Rethinking God as Gift: Marion, Derrida, and the Limits of Phenomenology*.

Mark Dooley, *The Politics of Exodus: Søren Keirkegaard's Ethics of Responsibility*.

Merold Westphal, *Overcoming Onto-Theology: Toward a Postmodern Christian Faith*.

Edith Wyschogrod, Jean-Joseph Goux, and Eric Boynton, eds., *The Enigma of Gift and Sacrifice*.

Stanislas Breton, *The Word and the Cross*. Translated with an introduction by Jacquelyn Porter.

Jean-Luc Marion, *Prolegomena to Charity*. Translated by Stephen E. Lewis.

Peter H. Spader, *Scheler's Ethical Personalism: Its Logic, Development, and Promise*.

Jean-Louis Chrétien, *The Unforgettable and the Unhoped For*. Translated by Jeffrey Bloechl.

Don Cupitt, *Is Nothing Sacred? The Non-Realist Philosophy of Religion: Selected Essays*.

Jean-Luc Marion, *In Excess: Studies of Saturated Phenomena*. Translated by Robyn Horner and Vincent Berraud.

Phillip Goodchild, *Rethinking Philosophy of Religion: Approaches from Continental Philosophy*.

William J. Richardson, S.J., *Heidegger: Through Phenomenology to Thought*.

Jeffrey Andrew Barash, *Martin Heidegger and the Problem of Historical Meaning*.

Jean-Louis Chrétien, *Hand to Hand: Listening to the Work of Art*. Translated by Stephen E. Lewis.

Jean-Louis Chrétien, *The Call and the Response*. Translated with an introduction by Anne Davenport.

D. C. Schindler, *Han Urs von Balthasar and the Dramatic Structure of Truth: A Philosophical Investigation*.

Julian Wolfreys, ed., *Thinking Difference: Critics in Conversation*.

Allen Scult, *Being Jewish/Reading Heidegger: An Ontological Encounter*.

Richard Kearney, *Debates in Continental Philosophy: Conversations with Contemporary Thinkers*.

Jennifer Anna Gosetti-Ferencei, *Heidegger, Hölderlin, and the Subject of Poetic Language: Towards a New Poetics of Dasein*.

Jolita Pons, *Stealing a Gift: Kirkegaard's Pseudonyms and the Bible*.

Jean-Yves Lacoste, *Experience and the Absolute: Disputed Questions on the Humanity of Man*. Translated by Mark Raftery-Skehan.

Charles P. Bigger, *Between Chora and the Good: Metaphor's Metaphysical Neighborhood*.

Dominique Janicaud, *Phenomenology "Wide Open": After the French Debate*. Translated by Charles N. Cabral.

Ian Leask and Eoin Cassidy, eds., *Givenness and God: Questions of Jean-Luc Marion*.

Jacques Derrida, *Sovereignties in Question: The Poetics of Paul Celan*. Edited by Thomas Dutoit and Outi Pasanen.

William Desmond, *Is There a Sabbath for Thought? Between Religion and Philosophy*.

Bruce Ellis Benson and Norman Wirzba, eds., *The Phenomoenology of Prayer*.

S. Clark Buckner and Matthew Statler, eds., *Styles of Piety: Practicing Philosophy after the Death of God*.

Kevin Hart and Barbara Wall, eds., *The Experience of God: A Postmodern Response*.

John Panteleimon Manoussakis, *After God: Richard Kearney and the Religious Turn in Continental Philosophy*.

John Martis, *Philippe Lacoue-Labarthe: Representation and the Loss of the Subject*.

Jean-Luc Nancy, *The Ground of the Image*.

Edith Wyschogrod, *Crossover Queries: Dwelling with Negatives, Embodying Philosophy's Others*.

Gerald Bruns, *On the Anarchy of Poetry and Philosophy: A Guide for the Unruly*.

Brian Treanor, *Aspects of Alterity: Levinas, Marcel, and the Contemporary Debate*.

Simon Morgan Wortham, *Counter-Institutions: Jacques Derrida and the Question of the University*.

Leonard Lawlor, *The Implications of Immanence: Toward a New Concept of Life*.

Clayton Crockett, *Interstices of the Sublime: Theology and Psychoanalytic Theory*.

Bettina Bergo, Joseph Cohen, and Raphael Zagury-Orly, eds., *Judeities: Questions for Jacques Derrida*. Translated by Bettina Bergo and Michael B. Smith.

Jean-Luc Marion, *On the Ego and on God: Further Cartesian Questions*. Translated by Christina M. Gschwandtner.

Jean-Luc Nancy, *Philosophical Chronicles*. Translated by Franson Manjali.

Jean-Luc Nancy, *Dis-Enclosure: The Deconstruction of Christianity*. Translated by Bettina Bergo, Gabriel Malenfant, and Michael B. Smith.

Andrea Hurst, *Derrida Vis-à-vis Lacan: Interweaving Deconstruction and Psychoanalysis*.

Jean-Luc Nancy, *Noli me tangere: On the Raising of the Body*. Translated by Sarah Clift, Pascale-Anne Brault, and Michael Naas.

Jacques Derrida, *The Animal That Therefore I Am*. Edited by Marie-Louise Mallet, translated by David Wills.

Jean-Luc Marion, *The Visible and the Revealed*. Translated by Christina M. Gschwandtner and others.

Michel Henry, *Material Phenomenology*. Translated by Scott Davidson.

Jean-Luc Nancy, *Corpus*. Translated by Richard A. Rand.

Joshua Kates, *Fielding Derrida*.

Michael Naas, *Derrida From Now On*.

Shannon Sullivan and Dennis J. Schmidt, eds., *Difficulties of Ethical Life*.

Catherine Malabou, *What Should We Do with Our Brain?* Translated by Sebastian Rand, Introduction by Marc Jeannerod.

Claude Romano, *Event and World.* Translated by Shane Mackinlay.

Vanessa Lemm, *Nietzsche's Animal Philosophy: Culture, Politics, and the Animality of the Human Being.*

B. Keith Putt, ed., *Gazing Through a Prism Darkly: Reflections on Merold Westphal's Hermeneutical Epistemology.*